Water Resources Development and Management

Challenges to Inclusive Growth

WATER RESOURCES DEVELOPMENT AND MANAGEMENT

Challenges to Inclusive Growth

Editor
MANISH DEV

Published on behalf of
THE INDIAN ECONOMIC ASSOCIATION

REGAL PUBLICATIONS
New Delhi - 110 027

WATER RESOURCES DEVELOPMENT AND MANAGEMENT
Challenges to Inclusive Growth

ISBN 978-81-8484-246-3

Typeset by
RAHUL COMPOSERS
New Highway Apartments, Lakshmi Niwas
760, Pocket-D, Lok Nayak Puram, New Delhi - 110 041

Printed in India at
MAYUR ENTERPRISES
WZ Plot No. 3, Gujjar Market, Tihar Village, New Delhi - 110 018

Published by
REGAL PUBLICATIONS
F-159, Rajouri Garden, New Delhi - 110 027 • Phone : 45546396
E-mail : regalbookspub@yahoo.com

Contents

Preface

Water is one of most important natural resources that are needed for the survival and growth of not only the human beings, but also of the entire animal kingdom and flora and fauna. Although the water is available in abundance on earth as 71 per cent of earth space is covered with water but out of this only a fraction of it (2.7%) is suitable for human consumption. Continuously increasing pressure of population rise and development activities have raised the demand of water. As a result, the water resources—both the surface water and ground water have been over-exploited causing the severe water crisis in some areas. Rapidly expanding urban areas severely damaged the rivers and nearby lakes and ponds by discharging sewage and other waters into them. Industrial as well as agricultural development also exploited the water resources and polluted many of them through excessive discharge of untreated waste water into the rivers or lakes. Shortage and unsuitability of water have questioned the sustainability of water resources. Keeping in view the importance of water for sustainable development of the country and for making the growth process more inclusive, the Indian Economic Association has chosen "Sustainable Growth and Transformation—(A) Water, and (B) Energy" as one of the themes of 94th Annual Conference held at Bharati Vidyapeeth deemed University, Pune on 22-29 December, 2011.

The present book is edited version of 25 papers presented in the technical session chaired by Prof. Mihir Shah, Member, Planning Commission. I am highly thankful to Prof. Sukhadeo Thorat, President and Dr. Montek Singh Ahluwalia, Conference President for the selection of this theme and allowing me to bring this book. I extend my sincere thanks and gratitude to the contributors of the research papers. I am also thankful to Regal Publication for bringing the book within a short span of time.

MANISH DEV

List of Contributors

Ajay Kumar Rao, Assistant Teacher, Middle School, Barauriya, Nautan, Dist. West Champaran (Bihar).

Amlendu Kumar, Department of Agricultural Economics, Bhagalpur, TCA, Dholi, (RAU), Muzaffarpur (Bihar).

Asha Singh, Professor and Head, Department of Economics, Magadh Mahila College, Patna (Bihar).

Asha Tank, Assistant Teacher, Girls' Primary School, Limdachowk, At Mangrol, Dist. Junagadh (Gujarat).

Babilata Shroff, Department of Economics, Rayagada Auto. College, Rayagada (Orissa).

Basant Kumar Jha, Director, Agro Economic Research Centre, T.M. Bhagalpur University, Bhagalpur (Bihar).

Bhavna Chhabra, Assistant Professor, Institute of Business Management and Research, Gurgaon (Haryana).

C. Mythili, Ph.D. Research Scholar, Department of Economics, Bharathiar University, Coimbatore (T.N.).

Dhiren Vandra, College of Rural Studies, Shardagram, Mangrol (Gujarat).

Elango J. Parimalam, Ph.D., Research Scholar, R.K.M. Vivekananda College, Chennai (T.N.).

Giribabu, M., Assistant Professor, Department of Economics, Nagaland University, Lumani (Nagaland).

Gyanindra Dash, Faculty of Economics, Kendrapara Autonomous College, Kendrapara (Orissa).

Inderjeet Singh, Professor, Economics Department, Punjabi University, Patiala (Punjab).

Jaywant R. Bhadane, Assistant Professor, Department of Economics, K.R.A.College, Deola, Nashik (Maharashtra).

K. Govindarajalu, Professor, Department of Economics, Bharathiar University, Coimbatore (T.N.).

K. Madhu Babu, Assistant Professor, Department of Economics, Acharya Nagarjuna University, Guntur (A.P.).

K. Pazhani, Principal, T.D.M.N.S. College, T. Kallikulam (T.N.).

Kishore Babu, K., Research Scholar, Department of Economics, Acharya Nagarjuna University, Guntur (A.P.).

Lakshmi Chatterjee, Research Scholar, Department of Economics, M.G. Kashi Vidyapeeth, Varanasi (U.P.).

Manindra Kumar Singh, Department of Economics, M.A.M. College, Naugachia (Bihar).

Manish Dev, General Manager, Trident Flight Handlers, Indira Gandhi International Airport, Terminal C-I, New Delhi.

Manoj Shankar Gupta, Department of Commerce, R.K.D. College, (Magadh University), Patna (Bihar).

Mritunjay Pd. Singh, Assistant Professor-*cum*-Jr. Scientist, P.O. Jamunia, Naugachia (Bihar).

Mun Mun Saran, Assistant Professor, Department of Economics, P.K. Roy Memorial College, Dhanwad (Jharkhand).

Purushottam Sahu, Gopalpur College, Gopalpur-on-sea (Orissa).

R.P. Mahto, Head, Department of Economics, SRPS College, Jaitpur, Distt. Muzaffarpur (Bihar).

Rabindra K. Choudhary, Reader in Economics, M.J.K. College, Bettiah, Distt. West Champaran (Bihar).

Ramna, Assistant Professor, Government P.G. College, Mandi (H.P.).

Ranjan Kumar Sinha, Research Officer, Agro Economic Research Centre, T.M. Bhagalpur University, Bhagalpur (Bihar).

Roli Misra, Department of Commerce, D.B.S. College, Kanpur (U.P.).

S. Thirunavukkarasu, Professor and Head, Department of Economics, R.K.M. Vivekananda College, Chennai (T.N.).

S.S. Kalamkar, Gokhale Institute of Politics and Economics (Deemed University), Pune (Maharashtra).

Shambhu Deo Mishra, Research Associate, Agro Economic Research Centre, T.M. Bhagalpur University, Bhagalpur (Bihar).

Subodh Kumar Sinha, Department of Economics, S.N. Sinha College, Muzaffarpur (Bihar).

Sudheer, B., Research Scholar, Department of Economics, Acharya Nagarjuna University, Guntur (A.P.).

Suvranshu Pan, Assistant Professor in Economics, Kashipur M.M. Mahavidyalaya, Purulia (W.B.).

U.P. Sinha, Professor of Economics, T.M.B.U., Bhagalpur (Bihar).

V. Mohanasundaram, Associate Professor, Department of Economics, PSG College of Arts and Science, Coimbatore (T.N.).

Vinod Kumar Srivastava, Faculty Member, Department of Economics and Rural Development, Dr. Ram Manohar Lohia Avadh University, Faizabad (U.P.).

Introduction

Uninterrupted and a balanced supply of fresh, potable and unpolluted water to all sectors of the economy and all sections of the society is a necessary condition of sustainable and inclusive growth. Sustainable and inclusive growth of an economy like India largely depends upon the availability of water for irrigation purposes, drinking and industrial production. "At the end of the twentieth century, the world faces a number of challenges affecting the availability, accessibility, use and sustainability of its fresh water resources. These could have serious implications for the present and future generations of humanity as also for natural ecosystems. India, which was 16 per cent of the world's population, has roughly four per cent of world's water resources and 2.45 per cent of world's land area. The distribution of water resources in the country is highly uneven over space and time. Over 80 to 90 per cent of the runoff in Indian rivers occurs in four months of the year and there are regions of harmful abundance and acute scarcity. Vast populations live in latter areas. The country has to grope with several critical issues in dealing with water resource development and management..." (GOI, 1999, p. i).

Although the average annual rainfall in India is around 1170 mm, which can be said to be satisfactory, however, the erratic mansoon precipitation and its imbalanced distribution, results into floods in many areas with simultaneously droughts in other areas. Since irrigated area in India is about 42 per cent of net sown area, 58 per cent crops in the country are heavily dependent on the rain water. Even in irrigated areas the delay in mansoon seriously jeopardizes the prospects of not only the kharif crops but also rabi crops. The new techniques of agricultural production during the era of 'Green

Revolution' are water intensive so the exploitation of ground water in irrigated areas has increased by a rapid pace. It resulted into the continuous downfall of water tables in many parts of the country. As a result, many developmental blocks in Punjab, Haryana, Uttar Pradesh and Tamil Nadu turned into 'dark' category and the areas become water stressed. Rapidly increasing population, growing urbanization and expansion of industrial activities made the situation worse in many parts of the country. Scarcity and misuse of fresh water pose a serious threat to sustainable development and protection of environment. Human health and welfare, food security, industrial development and the ecosystems on which they depend, are all at risk, unless water resources are managed more efficiently in the present decade and beyond then they have been in the past.

It has been estimated that there is nearly 1.5 billion cubic kilometers of water associated with the earth. Of this volume 97.3 per cent is contaminated salt water in oceans, and 2.7 per cent is fresh water. The freshwater is partitioned between glacial and land ice (2.065%), groundwater (0.575%), lakes (0.017%), atmospheric water (0.0001%) and rivers (0.001%).

So far as India is concerned, Central Water Commission estimates the potentially utilizable volume of surface water in India at 690 BCM. This is the same as shown in the 1976 report of the National Agriculture Commission and in subsequent reports. The average annual precipitation received in India is about 4000 km^3, out of which 7003 km is immediately lost to atmosphere, 2150 km^3 soaks into the ground through recharging process and 1150 km^3 flows as surface runoff. The total water resources in the country have been estimated as 1953 km^3. Nearly 62 per cent or about 1202 km^3 of the total water resources is available in the Ganga-Brahmaputra-Meghna basin. The remaining 23 basins in the country have 751 km^3 of the total water resources. The annual water availability in terms of utilizable water resources in the country is 1122 km^3. As per international criterion, India with per capita availability of 1000 cubic meter per year is a water stressed country.

Groundwater, as a resource, is progressively moving out of the shadows of surface water hydrology, although it is part of the systemic water cycle that we all are aware of. The nature of the resource and the relative ease (and often, convenience) of decentralized access has meant that groundwater is the backbone of India's agriculture and drinking water security. It is a common-pool resource used by millions of farmers across the country. It remains the only drinking water source in most of India's rural households. Many industrial units in the country depend upon groundwater. With an estimated 30 million groundwater structures, India is fast hurtling towards a serious crisis of groundwater overuse and groundwater quality deterioration. The report of the Expert Group on Groundwater Management and Ownership (Planning Commission, 2007), states that, in 2004, 28% of India's blocks were showing alarmingly high levels of groundwater use. A recent assessment by NASA showed that during 2002 to 2008, India lost about 109 km^3 of water leading to a decline in water table to the extent of 0.33 meters per annum (Tiwari *et al.*, 2009). In addition to depletion, many parts of India report severe water quality problems, causing drinking water vulnerability. At the national level, therefore, the Mid-Term Appraisal of the 11th Plan notes that nearly 60 per cent of all districts in India have problems related to either the quantitative availability or quality of groundwater or both. This is a serious situation warranting immediate attention.

Growth process and expansion of economic activities inevitably lead to increasing demands for water for diverse purposes: domestic, industrial, agricultural, hydropower, thermal-power, navigation and recreation, etc. Agricultural sector is the major consumer of fresh water followed by industrial sector, while the gross irrigation potential is estimated to have increased from 19.5 million hectare at the time of independence to about 139.9 million hectare by the end of the Eleventh Five Year Plan. Further, development of a substantial order is necessary if the food and fiber needs of our growing population are to be met with. The drinking water needs of the people and livestock have also to be met. Domestic and industrial water needs have largely concentrated in or near urban areas. However, the demand for water in rural areas is likely to increase sharply as the development programmes improves economic conditions of rural inhabitants. Demand for water for hydro and thermal power generation and for other industrial purposes is also increasing at faster pace. As a result, water, which is already a scarce resource, will become scarcer in future. This underscores the need for the par atmost efficiency in water utilization and public awareness of the importance of conservation. Another area of concern is the quality of water which is deteriorating because of high inflow of untreated wastewater and sewage into the rivers and residual impact of fertilizers and pesticides in agriculture. Improvements in existing strategies, innovation of new techniques resting on a strong science and technology base are needed to eliminate the pollution of surface water and ground water resources, to improve quality.

The present book contains 25 chapters presented in the technical session on 'Sustainable Growth and Transformation—Water' chaired by Prof. Mihir Shah, Member, Planning Commission, at 94th Annual Conference of Indian Economic Association held at Bharathi Vidyapeeth, Pune on 27-29 December, 2011.

The chapter entitled—'*Water Resources Management in India*' by *S.S. Kalamkar* highlights the issue of availability and utilization of water in relation to increasing population, growing urbanization, and rapid industrialization coupled with the agricultural development. According to him the country is likely to face the challenges on the front of mismatch between demand and supply of water, in the form of (i) Improving and safeguarding existing drinking water supplies; (ii) managing water demand, which is escalating at alarming pace, across competing sectors; (iii) determining environmental requirements and prevention of water pollution. It is the irony of the situation that 83 per cent fresh water in the country is being used for irrigation purposes, which is essential for the agricultural development. The solution, according to Kalamkar lies in participatory Irrigation Management.

Inderjeet Singh and *Bhavna Chhabra*, analysed the demand side of the water resources through a case study undertaken in Punjab, in their chapter entitled, '*Spatial and Temporal Dynamics of Water Resources in India*'. The authors state that the share of agriculture in the use of fresh water is about 80 per cent at present along with the 6.06 per cent for domestic uses, 5.21 per cent for industrial purposes. Prediction shows that in future, percentage share of water use for agriculture sector will come down to about 68.39 per cent, while the industrial purposes, share will increase to 6.86 per cent and for domestic purposes to 9.41 per cent. The ever growing demand and the shortage of surface water availability, development and over exploitation of groundwater resources and deteriorating quality of water resources is a matter of serious concerns and requires urgent attention of the policy planners.

Manish Dev in his chapter, "*Water Resources in India : Need of Judicious Utilisation*" emphasis on the conservation of traditional water bodies along with the construction of check dams on small rivers and rainfed Nallahs. The author's analysis based on the demand and supply of water resources. As supply side measures, the author suggests that development of groundwater resources through suitable means; Augmentation of the groundwater resources through artificial recharge; and rainwater harvesting are of paramount importance. Demand side measures include prevention of excessive exploitation of water, use of water resources more judiciously.

The chapter—'*Water Resources Development in India: Critical Issues and Strategic Options*' by *Lakshmi Chatterjee* presents a road map for the reforms in the utilization and supply of water. The paper highlights integration for sustainable management of the water resources for meeting the demands of the present without compromising the needs of the future generations.

Ranjan Kumar Sinha, Basant Kumar Jha and *Shambhu Deo Mishra* discussed the impact of watershed development projects in rainfed areas in their chapter entitled, '*Impact Evaluation of Revised National Watershed Development Projects for Rainfed Areas in Bihar?*' They assessed the impact of watershed development project by using the change in cost per hectare, creation of employment opportunities, rate of return on investment, changes in productivity, cropping intensity, etc. The chapter—'*Water Crisis in India*' by *S. Thirunavukkarasu* and *Elango J. Parimalam* deals with the problem of water crisis in India with special reference to Tamil Nadu. The authors are of the view that the rapid expansion of irrigation and drainage infrastructure has been at the cost of groundwater depletion, water logging and salinity levels. Simultaneously the rising population, rapid urbanization and industrial development also contributed in the worsening of water crisis. *Amlendu Kumar, Mritunjay Prasad Singh* and *Manindra Kumar Singh* analysed the cost structure of man-made water resources—mainly the private tube-wells and pumping sets in their chapter—'*Dynamics of Groundwater Market : A Study of Villages of Rohtas district of Bihar.*' The authors conclude that expansion of private tube-wells and pumping sets increased the dependence of small and marginal farmers on large farmers as the new facilities have been created by large farmers.

Vinod Kumar Srivastava's chapter—'*Transforming Indian Agriculture through Water Resource Management*' present a holistic view of development of small, medium and large irrigation projects. He is of the view that while larger investment outlays are necessary, the emphasis and focus must be not on the magnitude of investment expenditure, but on the composition of improvements that increase the product potential of land and water resources already under use. *K. Madhu Babu* discussed the usefulness of tank irrigation in his chapter—'*Sustainable Growth through Tank Irrigation : A Case Study of North Coastal Andhra Pradesh*'. Tanks in coastal Andhra Pradesh are in use since time immemorial not only for irrigation purposes but also for domestic uses. However, the tank irrigation suffers from two drawbacks : (i) the quantum of rainfall, that decides the nature of water supply, and (ii) Inadequate maintenance of tanks reduced the catchment and storage capacity thereby a decrease in irrigation capacity of these tanks.

The chapter—'*Water Scarcity : Issues and Challenges*' by *Gyanindra Dash* examines the shortage of water for various purposes. *Sudheer, B.* and *Kishore Babu, K.* discussed the irrigation prospects and potential in Krishna district of Andhra Pradesh in their chapter—'*An Analysis of Irrigation Facilities in Krishna District*'. The main source of supply of water in this district is canal which has intermittent supply schedule thereby adversely affecting the crop productivity. The paper entitled—'*Realising Sustainable Growth Using Water Resources in India*' by *Suvranshu Pan* emphasizes on the management approach for maintainable development. An essential support to the water resources management system is the institutional framework for management, consisting of organisation, rules and codes governing the use of control of water resources. *Giribabu, M.*, chapter—'*Water Resources and Sustainable Development in India : Some Emerging Issues*' focuses on the sustainability of water resources which are in severe stress due to erratic rainfall, groundwater constraints in the form of depleting quantum, environmental threats in the form of ever increasing pollution of water resources, decreasing quality of water and water consumption-related hazards soil erosion and water runoff, crisis of fresh and wholesome water, etc. The author emphasis that '*Every drop extracted must be justified, every drop must be counted, every drop used must be recycled and reused whenever possible*'.

U.P. Sinha discusses the interface between water resources and sustainable development through three diagrammatic models in his chapter—'*Water Resources and Sustainable Development in New Millennium*'. The escalation of water crisis is due essentially to the unsustainable use and management of water resources and to the destruction of ecosystems such as forests, wetlands and soil that capture, filter, store and releases water, through our evaluation of water resources sustainability, we must not only increase the public awareness about the challenges the world facing in relation to water, but also we must change the way the water issue is perceived from being a driver of conflict to being a catalyst for collaboration. *K. Pazhani* analysis the water policy in the chapter entitled, '*Regional Water Policy: An Outline for South India*'. The author recommends a region-wise separate water policy based on the need and availability of water for various purposes. The region specific water policy should be framed with the (i) Information System; (ii) Infrastructure, (iii) Flood and Drought Management, (iv) Allocation of Funds; (v) Resettlement and Rehabilitation, (vi) Diversion of Rivers, and (vii) Participatory management. The chapter—'*Drinking Water Management through Community Participation: An Insight into the SWAJAL Project in Uttarakhand*' by *Roli Misra* is an attempt to look into the problem of drinking water in hilly region, where the SWAJAL Project has some success to mitigate the drinking water crisis through public participation. *Babilata Shroff* and *Purushottam Sahu* suggested a strategy of management of water resources by which the objective of inclusive growth can be realized in their chapter—'*Management of Water Resources: A Strategy for Inclusive Growth*'. The strategy is based on the experiences of Bolangir district of Odisha. '*Sea Water Intrusion and Sweet Water Management in Coastal Aquifer of Saurashtra (Gujarat)*', a chapter by *Dhiren Vandra* and *Asha Tank*, carefully examines the problem of salinity of ground water in coastal Saurashtra because of an increase in lateral ingress of sea water in the coastal aquifer.

Ramna recommended the watershed Management in the chapter—'*Watershed Management: A Step Towards Sustainable Growth in Himachal Pradesh*'. According to author the potential of groundwater exploitation in Himachal Pradesh is limited because of large hilly tract, hence the conservation and development of watershed is the only way to enhance crop productivity. '*Water Resources in India*', a chapter by *Jaywant R. Bhadane* discusses the availability of water resources in various parts of the country and their usages that have caused the shortage of water in many areas. *K. Govindarajalu* and *C. Mythili* examines the economic considerations for Groundwater Management and Protection in their chapter—'*Economic Instruments for Sustainable Groundwater Management*'. According to authors while the economic instruments to manage surface water and ground water are almost the same, they have their own peculiarities.

V. Mohanasundaram very carefully examines various issues of Groundwater Management at Micro-level in his chapter entitled, '*Economic, Institutional and Rights Issues in Groundwater Management at Micro-level*'. The chapter is based on a micro study of Coimbatore district of Tamilnadu. The study identifies three major issues namely, (i) No market exists in the village for groundwater, (ii) Earlier the village Panchayat, took the initiative in the strengthening of village ponds and tanks on the behest of rich and big farmers and maintenance of such rainwater storage points. Now it has been given up. So the hope of getting groundwater recharged by rainwater harvesting looks bleak; and (iii) As many farmers given up agriculture, the traditional institutions are found becoming very weak to resolve the village level issues pertaining to storage of rainwater and renovation of percolation ponds.

Mun Mun Sharan and *Subodh Kumar Sinha's* chapter entitled—'*Managing the Water Resources in India*' discussed the importance of water in relation to its availability and use. The author sees the significance of rainwater harvesting and linking of Himalayan Rivers. The chapter entitled, '*Economics of Safe Drinking Water and the Problems of Rural Health (A Case Study of Bihar)*' by *Rabindra K. Choudhary, R.P. Mahto* and *Ajay Kumar Rao* deals with the health-related issues of drinking water through a case study of Bihar. It is a well known fact that a large segment of population in rural areas is suffering from water born diseases, which are directly responsible for poor health of the people. The message is clear that supply of clean, safe, and wholesome water can reduce the incidence of water born diseases and result into a sound health of the rural population. '*Management of River Water*' a chapter by *Manoj Shankar Gupta* and *Asha Singh* deals with the management of river which are lifeline for many regions of the country. There are serious riparian conflicts among countries/states on the sharing of river water. The issue of management of river water is related to the sharing of water, flood control and construction of Dams, rehabilitation of displaced persons and other environmental concerns related to distribution of water.

Sustainable use and management of water resource—surface water as well as groundwater—is of paramount importance because of scarcity of water in relation to its demand which is scaling to new heights. Principle of 'Khet ka Pani Khet Main', 'Haar ka Paani Haar main', and 'Gaon ka Pani Gaon main', is a time tested in India since ancient times. It can be applied to control and save the rain water through the construction of check dams on small rivers and other flowing water bodies. It will increase the recharging of groundwater and soil moisture which will reduce the need of irrigation and also help to increase the farm productivity in rainfed areas. Sustainable use and management of groundwater resources is a difficult task because majority of extraction of groundwater is done by privately owned devices, such as, wells, tube-wells, hand pumps, etc. In this situation groundwater resources assessment is of critical importance. Groundwater resources assessment should be an iterative process involving evaluation and refinement by incorporating new techniques and giving due consideration to climate change. Research and development support in the form of project-based studies (Regional and local scale) should be dovetailed with the National assessment for refinement of parameters used in resources estimation, e.g. estimation of base flow, recharge from streams, inflow-outflow across assessment boundary on pilot basis in select areas another area of critical importance is Aquifer Mapping which should be done at the scale of 1:50000. Such mapping can taken up at appropriate scales (higher or lower) as per specific requirements. Comprehensive plan for participatory groundwater management based on the understanding and outcome of aquifer mapping shall be given top priority Institutional strengthening at Central and State level be given due consideration while planning the sustainable use of groundwater resources.

As a long-term strategy, non-conventional methods for utilization of water such as through inter-basin transfer, artificial recharge of groundwater, desalination of brackish or sea water and recycling of waste water as well as traditional water conservation practices like rainwater harvesting, including roof-top rainwater harvesting need to be practiced to further increase the utilizable water resources. Promotion of frontier research and development in a focused manner, for these techniques is necessary.

Erstwhile rulers of India developed some unique model of water conservation to provide water for their subjects. In the Charkhari state of Bundelkhand the king constructed interlinked seven ponds/ tanks under which the rainwater of Charkhari town and other surrounding areas is collected and utilized during the whole of the year. Such type of ponds/tanks had been constructed in other cities of the Bundelkhand. Lakes of Udaipur and Ajmer are other examples of rainwater conservation. Planners of modern cities have done opposite to it. Almost all the ponds/tanks of cities either have been encroached by illegal construction or were covered by dumping of wastes. This caused heavy water logging in cities during rains. Feasibility study of Charkhari model is of utmost importance.

In view of the vital importance of water for human and animal life and vegetation for maintaining ecological balance and for economic and developmental activities of all kinds, and considering its increasing scarcity, the planning and management of this resource and its optimal, economic and equitable use has become a matter of the utmost urgency. Concerns of the community need to be taken into account for water resources development and management.

References

Government of India (2007); Report of the Expert Group on Groundwater Management and Ownership, Planning Commission, New Delhi, p. 61.

Government of India (2010); Mid-term Appraisal, 11th Plan, Planning Commission, New Delhi.

Government of India (2012); Report of Working Group on Sustainable Groundwater Management, Planning Commission, New Delhi.

Tiwari, V.M.; Wahr, J.M. and Swenson, S. (2009); Dwindling Groundwater Resources in Northern Indian Region, From Satellite Gravity Observations, Geoph. Res. Hett. No. 36, L18401, Doc.10.1029/2009/GL039401.

Chapter 1

Water Resources Management in India

S.S. KALAMKAR

INTRODUCTION

Water resources of a country constitute one of its vital assets. India with 2.4 percent of the world's total area has 16 percent of the world's population; but has only 4 percent of the total available fresh water (Planning Commission, GOI, 2008). It has the largest irrigated area in the world, accounting for 22 per cent of global irrigated area. Increasing population, growing urbanization, and rapid industrialization combined with the need for raising agricultural production generates competing claims for water. India is currently facing a daunting set of water-related challenges. Urban and industrial demand for water is going up rapidly, without commensurate augmentation of supply. There is a growing perception of a sense of an impending water crisis in the country. The Standing Sub-Committee Report (CWC, 2000) estimated that the total demand for water by all sectors would surpass the total utilizable water resources by the year 2050, posing a big challenge to the country. The water challenges for the country and particularly for its states,[1] are manifold: (a) improving and safeguarding existining drinking water supplies, (b) managing water demand across competing sectors, and (c) determining environmental requirements and prevention of pollutions (Raju, 2010). This clearly indicates the need for water resource development, conservation, and optimum use.

Irrigation constitutes the main use of water and is thus the focal issue in water resources development. About 83 per cent of the total fresh water available in the country is used for irrigation. Irrigation sector has been fundamental to India's economic development and poverty alleviation. In agriculture, irrigation water is always considered to be an engine of agricultural growth. Irrigation expansion has been one of the three input-related driving factors (the other two being seeds of modern HYVs and fertilizer) in the Green Revolution process. Irrigation development increases the cropping intensity, alters the cropping pattern in favour of high value crops, encourages the adoption of technological inputs (HYV seeds, fertilisers, pesticides, etc.) as well as machineries, all of which one way or the other help to augment the crop output. Besides providing direct benefits to the farming community, it also indirectly benefits the non-farming community substantially (Narayanamoorthy and Kalamkar, 2011). While benefiting the landless agricultural labourers in terms of increased employment opportunities and wage rate, irrigation helps to reduce the rural poverty in a sustained manner (Narayanamoorthy, 2001; Saleth, *et al.*, 2003; Hussain and Hanjra, 2003; Bhattarai and Narayanamoorthy, 2003; Shah and Singh, 2004). Increased production of foodgrains and other commodities that takes place mainly because of irrigation development also makes dent in the prices of agricultural commodities, which indirectly benefits millions of non-agricultural rural and urban consumers.

In view of the importance of irrigation development in agriculture and other sectors, the policy makers in India have been giving increased thrust for the development of irrigation since the independence. The investment in irrigation sector (irrigation and flood control) has increased manifold over the years, from Rs. 455.07 crore in the First Plan (1951-56) to a level of Rs. 101699.4 crore at the end of the Tenth plan (2002-07) (MOWR, 2006). That is, altogether about Rs. 2597.30 billion (in current prices) have been spent exclusively for the development of irrigation by the public sector alone till the end of 2006-07.[2] As a result of massive investment, the area under irrigation has increased from 22.56 million hectares (mha) in 1950-51 to over 87 mha in 2007-08. The coverage of irrigation to cropped area increased from 17.11 percent in 1950-51 to over 44.5 percent in 2007-08. This massive irrigation development has also increased the cropping intensity from about 111 percent to over 139 percent during corresponding period at the all India level (GOI, 2011).

Irrigation development in India has undoubtedly brought many benefits, but is has also been characterised by many problems, weakness, and failures. There are problems in relation to canal irrigation, groundwater irrigation, tank irrigation, and rainfed agriculture (Raju, 2010). Despite significant achievements in development of irrigated area, the overall performance of irrigation sector has not been very appreciable in India. While the water use efficiency is very low (ranging from 30-40 percent under surface method of irrigation) in India as compared to other countries (Rosegrant, 1997), the financial performance of the state managed irrigation sector has been deteriorating over the years. The percent of recovery rate (ratio of irrigation revenue to operation and maintenance cost) of irrigation and multipurpose river valley projects, which are completely managed by the state agency, has declined from 36.4 percent in the 1976-77 to as low as 5.7 percent in 1999-2000.[3] Though there are many reasons for the dreadful performance of the irrigation sector, significant increase in operation and maintenance (O&M) expenditures of the irrigation sector and unrevised irrigation water rates charged from farmers are often cited as the main reasons for the poor financial performance of the publicly funded irrigation sector (GOI, 1992; Gulati, *et al.*, 1994; Vaidyanathan, 1999). Many argue that the poor water use efficiency, which exists across different regions in India, is the result of low water price fixed for different crops (see, Vaidyanathan, 1999; World Bank, 2005). Poor participation of farmers in irrigation management related activities is also cited as one of the major reasons for the deteriorating performance of irrigation sector in India. Researchers working on irrigation related issues in different countries suggest that the poor performance of irrigation sector can be improved substantially by extensively involving the users (farmers) in the management activities of the irrigation sector (Brewar, *et al.*, 1999). The Command Area Development Programme (CADA) started in 1974 envisaged the participation of farmer organisations as a necessary step to run the micro system. The Committee on Pricing of Irrigation Water (1992) also recommended farmers participation in the management of irrigation systems. In-spite of the growing realisation of the urgent need for farmers' participation in the management of irrigation, the progress has been slow so far (GOI, 2006). By far the most serious challenges are those of management of the existing infrastructure and of the water resource itself.

Over the past few years several high-level commissions have been appointed to deal with water management issues and also new national/state policies have been promulgated.[4] However, not much of it has been implemented effectively. This divide between the problem and practice has led to extensive loss of credibility of the state apparatus for water development and management. Problem is balancing between service providers and users of all kind. Participatory Irrigation Management (PIM) is emerging as an important tool for ensuring better equity in distribution of water, which in turn also results in better operation and maintenance (O&M), better on farm management, and increased productivity. With this background, an attempt has been made in this paper to study the water resources availability, its requirement and irrigation water management system in India with special focus on participatory irrigation management.

WATER RESOURCE AVAILABILITY

The water resource potential of the country has been assessed from time to time by different agencies (MOWR, 2006). The different estimates are shown in Table 1. It may be seen that since 1954, the estimates have stabilized and are within the proximity of the currently accepted estimate of 1869 billion cubic metre (bcm) which includes replenishable groundwater which gets charged on annual basis. Within the limitations of physiographic conditions, socio-political environment, legal and constitutional constraints, and the technology available at hand, the utilizable water resources of the country have been assessed at 1123 bcm, of which 690 bcm is from surface water and 433 bcm from groundwater sources (CWC, 1993). Harnessing of 690 bcm of utilizable surface water is possible only if matching storages are built. Trans-basin transfer of water, if taken up to the full extent as proposed under the National Perspective Plan, would further increase the utilizable quantity by approximately 220 bcm. As per Mid-term Appraisal report of XI Plan, current water use is 634 bcm (Planning Commission, 2011). Standing Sub-Committee of Ministry of Water Resources (MoWR) estimates total water demand rising to 1093 bcm in 2025, thus reaffirming a comfortable scenario.

TABLE 1
Estimates of Water Resources in India

Agency	*Estimate in bcm*	*Deviation from 1869 bcm*
First Irrigation Commission (1902-2003)	1443	-23%
Dr. A.N. Khosla (1949)	1673	-10%
Central Water and Power Commission (1954-66)	1881	+0.6%
National Commission on Agriculture	1850	-1%
Central Water Commission (1988)	1880	+0.6%
Central Water Commission (1993)	1869	—

Source : Planning Commission, GOI, 2007.

The water budget India has a highly seasonal pattern of rainfall, with 50 percent of precipitation falling in just 15 days and over 90 per cent of river flows occurring in just four months. India receives annual precipitation of around 4000 km^3. The total average annual flow per year for the Indian rivers is estimated as 1953 km^3. The total annual replenishable groundwater resources are assessed as 432 km^3. The annual utilizable surface water and groundwater resources of India are estimated at 690 km^3 and 396 km^3 per year, respectively (Kumar, *et al.*, 2005). Due to spatial and temporal variability in precipitation the country faces the problem of flood and drought syndrome. Table 2 presents the estimates of India water budget, i.e. annual flow of water available for human use after allowing for evapo-transpiration and minimum required ecological flow. More recent calculations based on higher estimates of the amount of water lost to the atmosphere by evapo-transpiration are much less comforting. Narasimhan (2008) has recalculated India's water budget, using an evapo-transpiration rate of 65 per cent which compares with worldwide figures ranging from 60 per cent to 90 per cent instead of the 40 per cent rate assumed in the official estimates. The result is sobering. After allowing the same 48.8 per cent for ecological flows, his estimate of water utilizable for human use comes to only 654 bcm, which is very close to the current actual water use estimate of 634 bcm (Planning Commission, 2011).

As a consequence of the increasing demand on finite water resources to meet the varied demands of the burgeoning population,

TABLE 2
India's Water Budget (BCM), 2009

Particulars	*Analysis based on Estimates of Ministry of Water Resources*	*Estimates Based on Worldwide Comparison*
Annual rainfall	3,840	3,840
Evapo-transpiration	3,840–(1,869 + 432) = 1,539 (40 per cent)	2,500 (65 per cent) Worldwide Comparison
Surface run-off	1,869 (48.7 per cent)	Not used in estimate
Groundwater recharge	432 (11.3 per cent)	Not used in estimate
Available water	2,301 (60 per cent)	1,340 (35 per cent)
Utilizable water	1,123 (48.8 per cent of 2,301) Gupta and Deshpande (2004)	654 (48.8 per cent of 1,340)
Current water use	634	634
Remarks	Current use (634) well below 1,123	Current use (634) close to 654

Source : Narasimhan, T.N. and V.K. Gaur (2009): A Framework for India's Water Policy, National Institute for Advanced Studies, Bangalore, as quoted in Planning Commission, 2011.

its availability is declining each passing day. While the total water resource availability in the country remains constant, the per capita availability of water has been steadily declining since 1951 due to population growth (Table 3). The twin indicators of water scarcity are per capita availability and storage. The per capita availability of water at national level has been reduced from about 5177 cubic meters in 1951 to the estimated level of 1,820 cubic meters in 2001 with variation in water availability in different river basins. Given the projected increase in population by the year 2025, the per capita availability is likely to drop to below 1,000 cubic metres, which could be labeled as a situation of water scarcity[5] (GOI, 2006). While on an average we may be nearing the water-stressed condition, on an individual river basin-wise situation, nine out of our 20 river basins with 200 million populations are already facing a water-scarcity condition. The facts indicate that India is expected to become 'water stressed' by 2025 and 'water scarce' by 2050. The National Commission for Integrated Water Resource Development

(NCIWRD) has estimated that against a total annual availability of 1953 BCM (inclusive of 432 BCM of ground water and 1521 BCM of surface water) only 1123 BCM (433 BCM ground water and 690 BCM surface water), i .e., only 55.6 per cent can be put to use. The high-level of pollution further restricts the utilizable water thus posing a serious threat to its availability and use.

TABLE 3
Population Growth and Per Capita Water Availability in India

Year	*Population (Million)*	*Per Capita Water Availability (Cubic Metres)*
1951	361	5177
1955	395	4732
1991	846	2209
2001	1027	1820
2025	1394	1341
2050	1640	1140

Source : www.indiatstat.com.

India annually receives about 350 million hectare meter (mhm) rain water, but almost half of it finds its way back to the sea. Even after constructing 4525 large and small dams, the per capita storage in the country is 213 m^3 as against 6103 m3 in Russia, 4733 m^3 in Australia, 1964 m^3 in the United States (US), and 1111 m^3 of China. It may touch 400 m^3 in India only after the completion of all the ongoing and proposed dams. A total storage capacity of 212.78 Billion Cum (BCM) has been created in the country through major and medium projects. The projects under construction will contribute to an additional 76.26 BCM, while the contribution expected from projects under consideration is 107.54 BCM. The total availability of water in the 76 major reservoirs was 109.77 BCM at the end of the monsoon of 2005 (GOI, 2006). The irrigation potential of the country has been estimated to be about 140 mh without inter-basin sharing of water and 175 mh with inter-basin sharing. The Central Ground Water Board (CGWB) has estimated that it is possible to increase the groundwater availability by about 36 BCM, by taking up rainwater harvesting and artificial recharge over an area of 45 mha through

TABLE 4

Zone-wise Ground Water Resources Availability, Utilization and Stage of Development (bcm/year)

Sl. No.	*State/Union Territories*	*Net Ground Water Availability*	*Projected Demand for Domestic and Industrial Uses up to 2025*			*Projected Demand for Domestic and Industrial Uses upto 2025*	*Ground Water Availability for Future Irrigation*	*Stage of Groundwater Development (%)*
			Irrigation	*Domestic and Industrial Use*	*Total*			
(1)	*(2)*	*(3)*	*(4)*	*(5)*	*(6)*	*(7)*	*(8)*	*(9)*
1.	North	105.45	86.55	5.19	91.71	8.01	11.43	87
2.	South	75.71	42.34	4.01	46.34	6.43	30.58	61
3.	East	112.12	28.87	4.31	32.99	6.52	76.66	29
4.	West	105.93	54.77	4.79	59.58	8.21	43.62	56
	Total	399.20	212.53	18.29	230.62	29.16	162.28	56

Source : Central Ground Water Board, Annual Report, 2005-06, as quoted in Planning Commission, 2007.

surplus monsoon runoff. Thus, the groundwater availability may correspondingly increase. The zone-wise groundwater resources availability, utilization and stage of development is presented in Table 4. While the North Zone has already developed 87 per cent of its groundwater, the East Zone has over 70 per cent of its groundwater unexploited for irrigation purposes. Considering that 70 per cent of the groundwater in the East Zone is unexploited, and the region has high poverty intensity, larger allocations and technical support should be provided by the Centre to this zone for judiciously developing and utilizing water resources towards increased, sustained and inclusive agricultural growth.

The ultimate irrigation potential for the country has been estimated at about 140 m ha (59 m ha through major and medium irrigation projects, 17 m ha through minor irrigation schemes and 64 mha through groundwater development). So far, the irrigation potential of nearly 100 m ha has already been created, but only about 86 m ha is being utilized, thus leaving a gap of 14 mha between created and utilized potential. This huge gap of 14 mha between irrigation potential created and utilized reduces the irrigation intensity to only 135 per cent which should have been raised to 175 per cent or more. Besides low water use efficiency, there is high inequity in water use and irrigation development, let alone the fast receding aquifers and blocks after blocks turning "dark" and "grey" in certain parts of the country. Over exploitation of ground water is leading to falling water levels in many areas especially, the hard rock areas. Over 29 per cent of the blocks in the country are in the category of over exploited areas of groundwater use. Nearly 60 percent of the blocks in Punjab and 40 percent of the blocks in Haryana have turned "dark" and over exploited–the heartland of the green revolution. While there is over-exploitation in some parts of the country, under-exploitation of ground resources especially in the east and northeast is a matter of concern.

WATER REQUIREMENT

The allocation of water to agriculture is facing a losing battle with the industrial, domestic, power and other sectors. At the same time, there is the compulsion of enhancing agricultural production in an eco-friendly sustainable manner with limited land and water resources. It is projected that the agriculture sector in India has been and is likely to remain the major user of water but share of water allocate to irrigation is likely to decrease by 10 to 15 percent in the next two decades (Singh, 2004). The requirement of water for various sectors has been assessed by the National Commission on Integrated Water Resources Development (NCIWRD) in the year 2000. This requirement is based on the assumption that the irrigation efficiency will increase to 60 percent from the present level of 35-40 percent. The Standing Committee of MoWR also assesses it periodically. The recent estimates (GOI, 2006) on water demand are made by : (a) Standing Sub-Committee of the Ministry of Water Resources (MoWR), and (b) the National Commission for Integrated Water Resources Development (NCIWRD); their estimates (See Table 5) are made till the year 2050. Both of them have triggered warning bells on the intensity of the problem. The Union Ministry of Water Resources has estimated the countries water requirements to be around 1093 BCM for the year 2025 and 1447 BCM for the year 2050. With projected population growth of 1.4 billion by 2050, the total available water resources would barely match the total water requirement of the country. The estimates by MoWR indicates that, by year 2050,

TABLE 5
Water Requirement for Various Sectors

Sector	*Water Demand in km³ (or bcm)*					
	Standing Sub-Committee of Mo WR			*NCIWRD*		
	2010	*2025*	*2050*	*2010*	*2025*	*2050*
Irrigation	688 (84.62)	910 (83.26)	1072 (74.08)	557 (74.08)	611 (78.45)	807 (72.48)
Drinking water	56 (6.89)	73 (6.68)	102 (7.05)	43 (7.05)	62 (6.06)	111 (7.35)
Industry	12 (1.48)	23 (2.10)	63 (4.35)	37 (4.35)	67 (5.21)	81 (7.95)
Energy	5 (0.62)	15 (1.37)	130 (8.98)	19 (8.98)	33 (2.68)	70 (3.91)
Others	52 (6.40)	72 (6.59)	80 (5.53)	54 (5.53)	70 (7.61)	111 (8.30)
Total	813	1093	1447	710	843	1180

Note : Figures in parenthesis are percentage to the total.
Source : Planning Commission, GOI, 2007.

India needs to increase by 5 times more water supplies to industries, and 16 times more for energy production, while its drinking water demand will double, and irrigation demand will raise by 50 percent. The XI Plan recognized the special challenges of water resources management facing India and the likelihood that these would only intensify over time due to rising population, expected growth in agricultural and industrial demand, the danger of pollution of water bodies and, over the longer-term, the effect of climate stress on water availability in many parts of the country. To address the water-related issues and thereby launch a massive awareness programme all over the country, the Government of India has declared year 2007 as 'Water Year'[6] (ADB, 2009). The XI Plan aims to give thrust to irrigation expansion. Accounting for the 7 mha through the trend scenario, the additional 10 mha irrigated area under *Bharat Nirman* by the year 2009 and the stipulated additional 14 mha to be brought under pressurized irrigation, by the end of the XI Plan, the country would have an additional 27 mha under irrigation.

MANAGEMENT OF WATER RESOURCES : IRRIGATION WATER MANAGEMENT

Water Resources management is a very important issue with regard to the conservation and the protection of water. Water demand management is meant to manage the available water resources wisely and to deliver the necessary amount for sustainable development (Bhat, 2009). The tightening competition among multiple users of water, between agriculture and other sectors, recently exacerbated by consecutive years of drought, brought to light some weaknesses of current state water policies, and their associated regulatory and institutional arrangements. Increasing conflicts among users and the unsustainable use of water in many areas result from limited coordination among various water resource (surface and groundwater) development initiatives, and the absence of policies defining water entitlements, pricing, and inter-sectoral allocation rules; and if these policies exist, the inconsistencies among some of them. The state Irrigation Departments are placed in the difficult position of resolving these conflicts because of their role as both "regulator" and the largest "user" (World Bank, 2004).

To improve agricultural production, it is essential to increase the efficiency of each of the components of the irrigation system and crop production to prevent wasteful and ecologically damaging use of water. One of the major problems in the irigation system is the loss of water while it is being transported from the reserviours to the fileds. This can be as 50 percent and, in many command areas, it has led a serious problems of waterlogging and secondary salination. The price of water in canal commands is abysmally low and this fact also contributes to its low use effiecncy. Another basic flaw is that the irrigation system is supply-driven rather than demand-dricen (Singh, 2004). Over the years, many reformers have been attempted in answer to the problems and weaknesswes in irrigation water management. These combine, in varying degrees, policy changes, institutional reformers, administrative and procedural changes, new laws, and attitudinal changes. The real concern was about the gap between the creation and utilisation of irrigation potential. In order to address this problem, the Centrally sponsored Command Area Development (CAD) Programme was launched in 1974-75 with the main objectives of improving the utilization of created irrigation potential and optimizing agriculture production and productivity from irrigated agriculture through a multi-disciplinary team under an Area Development Authority. Initially, 60 major and medium irrigation projects were taken up under the CAD Programme, covering a Culturable Command Area (CCA) of about 15.00 million hectare. From 1974-75 till now 314 projects with a CCA of 28.95 Million ha. have been included under the programme. After inclusion of new projects, deletion of completed projects and clubbing of some projects, there are now 136 projects under implementation. The programme was restructured and renamed as Command Area Development & Water Management (CADWM) Programme w.e.f. April 2004. The scheme is now being implemented as a State sector scheme during the XI Five Year Plan (2008-09 to 2011-12).

There have been several evaluation of CADP and, by and large, the findings are that while CADP has undoubtedly improved the utilisation of the created irrigation potential, it has failed to achieve some of the larger objectives behind the undertaking of the programme. The main emphasis has been on physical works such as the construction of field channels, on-farm development works, and land levelling. CADP has not brought about significant improvements in water-use efficiency or in agricultural production (Raju, 2010). Several studies have also indicated that the weakest aspect of CADP is the failure to involve the farmers in the programme. The general 'top-down' approach of the state water resources departments continues (NCIWRP, 1999). If the 'utilisation gap' problems led to the CADP, the failure of major and medium projects to provide satisfactory irrigation services to the farmers led to the idea of Participatory Irrigation Management (PIM). The dysfunctionality of the system and a growing feeling even within the government that it could not really run these huge, far-fling irrigation networks efficiently and render proper service, combined with the dissatisfaction of the farmers, led to the idea of transferring parts of the system to the farmers themselves for management.

PARTICIPATORY IRRIGATION MANAGEMENT (PIM)

Since 1985, Ministry of Water Resources (MoWR) has been inspiring farmers' participation in water distribution and management of tertiary system in the projects covered under the Command Area Development Programme (CADP). Government of India accepted the concept of PIM as a policy and included the same in the National Water Policy adopted in 1987, which read as *"Efforts should be made to involve farmers progressively in various aspects of management of irrigation systems, particularly in water distribution and collection of water rates. Assistance of voluntary agencies should be enlisted in educating the farmers in efficient water-use and water management"*. In April 1987, the Ministry of Water Resources issued guidelines for farmers' participation in water management. The guidelines covered all aspects like, objectives of PIM, area of operation of farmers' associations in different irrigation schemes, duties and responsibilities of the farmers, training and monitoring. With the help of NGOs, it also pioneered many action research programmes on formation of WUAs. Various objectives of PIM as enunciated by MoWR are as follows:

1. To create a sense of ownership of water resources and the irrigation system among the users, so as to promote economy in water use and preservation of the system.
2. To improve service deliveries through better operation and maintenance.
3. To achieve optimum utilization of available resources through sophisticated deliveries, precisely as per crop needs.
4. To achieve equity in water distribution.
5. To increase production per unit of water, where water is

scarce and to increase production per unit of land where water is adequate.

6. To make best use of natural precipitation and ground water in conjunction with flow of irrigation for increasing irrigation and cropping intensity.
7. To facilitate the users to have a choice of crops, cropping sequence, timing of water supply, period of supply and also frequency of supply, depending on soils, climate and other infrastructure facilities available in the commands such as roads, markets, cold storages, etc., so as to maximize the incomes and returns.
8. To encourage collective and community responsibility on the farmers to collect water charges and payment to irrigation agency.
9. To creat healthy atmsphere between the Irrigation Agency personnel and the users.

ROLE OF WATER USERS' ASSOCIATION (WUA) IN IRRIGATION MANAGEMENT

Involving farmers in water management activities is not a new idea as far as India is concerned. In the name of *kudimaramath*, the users (farmers) were involved in tank repairs, management works, distilling of tanks, removal of weeds, distribution of water and collecting revenue even during the 17th and 18th century, much before the British rule (Reddy, 1996, Maloney and Raju, 1994). Unfortunately, due to various reasons, the users' participation in water management has declined drastically over the years. Now, partly because of pressure from donor agencies such as the World Bank and others, the users' participation in irrigation water has become a widespread strategy in all countries in Asia including India at least from the mid-eighties (Vermillion, 1992 and 1997; Easter, 2000).

The ultimate aim of the decentralized water management with predominant users' participation is to improve the overall performance of irrigation sector. In India, much emphasis was given for users' participation only after the announcement of the first National Water Policy: 1987, where gradual involvement of farmers in system management was advocated. The second National Water Policy of India: 2002 also reiterates the importance of farmers' participation in irrigation management activities (MOWR, 2002). It emphasises that "management of the water resources for diverse uses should incorporate a participatory approach; by involving not only the various governmental agencies but also the users and other stakeholders, in an effective and decisive manner, in various aspects of planning, design, development and management of the water resources schemes. Necessary legal and institutional changes should be made at various levels for the purpose, duly ensuring appropriate role for women. Water Users' Associations (WUAs) and the local bodies such as municipalities and *gram panchayats* should particularly be involved in the operation, maintenance and management of water infrastructures/facilities at appropriate levels progressively, with a view to eventually transfer the management of such facilities to the users' groups/local bodies".

Why has the government decided to involve farmers in water management activities? Apart from aid agency pressures, there could be two main reasons for this. First, despite the introduction of Command Area Development Programme (CADP) during 1974-75 (Fifth Five-Year Plan) for increasing the water use efficiency, it could not make any big change in the existing water use efficiency as of today (Brewer, *et al.*, 1999).[7] Second, the financial performance of irrigation sector of India has deteriorated over the years and the present collection of revenue from irrigation sector is not even enough to manage the operation and maintenance cost of irrigation sector (GOI, 1992; CWC, 2004). Under these circumstances, the experiences of the countries where farmers were allowed to involve in system management showed very encouraging results in both water management and financial recovery (for details please see, Narayanamoorthy and Kalamkar, 2006 and 2011). This has helped the policy-makers to encourage farmers' participation in system management in a big way. In so far as the results are concerned, it has been clearly established that users-managed systems outperformed the systems which are managed by the irrigation agency all over the world including India (Easter, 2000; Vermillion, 1997). The most often found positive impacts of users-managed systems are: (a) reduction in the cost of irrigation to farmers and government; (b) enhanced financial self-reliance of irrigation schemes; (c) expansion of irrigation; (d) reduction in the amount of water delivered per hectare; and (e) significant increase in cropping intensity and yield of crops.

Undeniably, the transfer of irrigation system from government agency to farmers' (users') group has also made some negative impacts in certain places as well. The often cited negative impacts are increased costs to farmers, failing financial viability of lift schemes and deteriorating infrastructure (Vermillion, 1997). Though majority studies show positive impacts due to users managed systems, most of the studies have not applied proper methodology for assessing the performance. It is rightly pointed out by Vermillion (1997) "... much of the so-called evidence about impacts is based upon qualitative reports, without before-and-after or with-and-without comparisons, without independent measurements with quantitative data, without systematic sampling of farmers, and a failure to distinguish possible alternative causes of the observed 'impacts' of transfer" (p. 29). Though the transfer of system management has increased area under irrigation and productivity gains, the coverage of area by water users' association is very meagre when compared to the total irrigated area so far. Vaidyanathan committee on pricing of irrigation water observes that "the area covered by these initiatives is very small, less than 1 percent of area irrigated at present. The general consensus among knowledgeable people is that they have been fitful and have not really made much of an impact. For the most part the outlet and canal committees are there only in name; they are not consulted on substantive issues; nor are department officers required to follow their advice. There is also considerable reluctance, if not oppositions, from the operational staff of irrigation departments to involving users in management; and even users themselves tend to be apathetic to the idea" (GOI, 1992). The number of WUAs and area covered by them is presented in Table 6. It can be seen from the table that 56,934 users' associations has been created and 13.54 mha area was covered (*www.mowr.gov.in*).

Water users' associations are functioning mostly at the tertiary level, which cannot accomplish their duties in improving supply and management of irrigation as the supply of water is controlled by the irrigation agency. Users' organisations that exist in small irrigation systems namely tank, etc., could perform their duty relatively better than WUAs that are established in large irrigation network, namely, canal. There are two reasons for this. First, the control of government agency is very meagre under small irrigation systems like tanks. Second, users' group can clearly understand the demand and supply position of water and make decisions accordingly.

As regards WUAs in larger irrigation systems, the overall results are not encouraging so far. Turnover of irrigation systems has been

TABLE 6
State-wise Number of WUAs and Area Covered

Sl. No.	*Name of the State*	*WUAs Formed*		*Area Covered*		*Area (ha)/ WUA*
		No.	*Share (%)*	*(' 000 ha)*	*Share (%)*	
1.	Andhra Pradesh	10800	18.97	4169	40.75	386.0
2.	Arunachal Pradesh	39	0.07	9.02	0.09	231.3
3.	Assam	720	1.26	47.04	0.46	65.3
4.	Bihar	67	0.12	182.36	1.78	2721.8
5.	Chhattisgarh	1324	2.33	1244.56	12.17	940.0
6.	Goa	57	0.10	7.01	0.07	123.0
7.	Gujarat	576	1.01	96.68	0.95	167.8
8.	Haryana	2800	4.92	200	1.96	71.4
9.	Himachal Pradesh	876	1.54	35	0.34	40.0
10.	J & K	39	0.07	2.758	0.03	70.7
11.	Karnataka	2557	4.49	1318.93	12.89	515.8
12.	Kerala	4163	7.31	174.89	1.71	42.0
13.	Madhya Pradesh	1687	2.96	1691.88	16.54	1002.9
14.	Maharashtra	1539	2.70	667.0	6.52	433.4
15.	Manipur	73	0.13	49.27	0.48	674.9
16.	Meghalaya	123	0.22	16.45	0.16	133.7
17.	Mizoram	110	0.19	14.00	0.14	127.3
18.	Nagaland	23	0.04	3.15	0.03	137.0
19.	Orissa	16196	28.45	1537.92	15.03	95.0
20.	Punjab	957	1.68	116.95	1.14	122.2
21.	Rajasthan	506	0.89	619.65	6.06	1224.6
22.	Tamil Nadu	1457	2.56	1176.21	11.50	807.3
23.	Uttar Pradesh	245	0.43	121.21	1.18	494.7
24.	West Bengal	10000	17.56	37	0.36	3.7
	Total	56934	100	13537.94	100	179.7

Source : www.mowr.gov.in (Status of PIM in India—Policy Initiatives Taken and Emerging Issues, http://wrmin.nic.in/writereaddata/mainlinkFile/File421.pdf, accessed on August 21, 2011).

slow in most of the large irrigation projects in different parts of the world including India. There are reports that staffs who are managing irrigation systems see WUAs as potential threat to their jobs (Vermillion, 1997; Easter, 2000). Therefore, the wholehearted involvement in establishing and supporting WUAs by the agency staff may not be very high. Moreover, unlike other South Asian countries, irrigation systems are very large in India which is practically not possible to manage efficiently by WUAs without adequate support from the irrigation agency. In order to encourage the farmers' attachment with WUAs, it is essential to demonstrate the benefits of WUAs in delivering water supply at required quantity and time. Importantly, WUAs should be able to reduce the cost of water over time in order to show the advantages of WUAs to the farmers (Vermillion, 1997).

WUAs have to be legally established in order to increase their responsibility and decisions related to water management.[8] It is always difficult for WUAs to provide better water supply and other services to their members without legal standing (Easter, 2000). With an improved service, WUAs can convince the farmers to pay the charges for the water that they use. As the committee on Pricing of Irrigation Water (GOI, 1992) rightly observes that "An essential pre-condition is to convince users that they will benefit from such group activity by getting more water, more assured supplies according to a pre-specified schedule (or according to the needs of the crops), greater flexibility in the use of water, or some combinations of these. Improvement in any of these dimensions will almost certainly increase productivity and therefore induce farmers to take the idea of users' groups more seriously". Continued support from government agencies is essential even after transforming the systems management to users' group in order to sustain the participation of farmers. Importantly farmers at any level should not be allowed to think that the transfer of irrigation management is adopted in order to reduce the financial burden of the government.

STATUS OF ENACTMENT OF LEGISLATION FOR PIM

The equitable and optimal use of water from canal irrigation has been a matter of continuing concern. The traditional approach of pursuing these objectives through the field-level functionaries of irrigation department had its limitations. The participation of actual beneficiaries through PIM and the maintenance of village-level distribution channels through WUAs have been found useful. There is broad consensus that this has been a step in the right direction. The experience across States has been uneven. As a result of various conferences/seminars organised by the Ministry, there has been an increased consciousness in States about the need for actively involving farmers in management of irrigation system. Accordingly States of Andhra Pradesh, Assam, Chhattisgarh, Goa, Gujarat, Karnataka, Kerala, Madhya Pradesh, Maharashtra, Orissa, Rajasthan, Sikkim, Tamil Nadu and Uttar Pradesh have enacted exclusive legislation for involvement of farmers in irrigation management. Government of Bihar has issued a notification '*The Bihar Irrigation, Flood Management and Drainage Rules, 2003*', in exercise of the powers conferred by The Bihar Irrigation Act, 1997.

PANI PANCHAYAT (WATER COUNCIL)

In order to mitigate the drought situation and to reduce poverty level in rural areas, there are several new water institutions established in different regions in India with the support of NGOs and other voluntary organisations especially since early 1980 onwards. One of the new water institutions emerged during the seventies in the rainfed areas of Maharashtra State is Pani Panchayat (water council).[9] This institution is not promoted by the State agencies, but established by a Trust (*Gram Gourav Prathishthan*) with the voluntary support from users' group. Deshpande and Reddy (1990) studied the overall functioning as well as the impact of Pani Panchayat on different parameters. This study shows that the establishment of Pani Panchayat has increased the irrigated area and also changed the cropping pattern from low value crops to high value crops in this area and the yield rate was also improved substantially (Deshpande and Reddy, 1990). However, owing to breakdown of Pani Panchayat Institution and other technical reasons, presently most of the Pani Panchayat Institutions are not performing well. Recent studies by Thakur and Pattnaik (2002) and Keremane, *et al.*, (2006) have highlighted the reasons for the decline of Pani Panchayat Institutions in a detailed manner.

STRATEGIC OPTIONS

Tenth Plan was declared as a Water Plan for focused attention on the integrated development of water resources in the country

(Planning Commission, GOI, 2007). The strategic options suggested by the researcher are as follows:

- Water is a finite resource and it has to be shared between the various sectors and sub-sectors optimally. There is a need to increase investments in conservation of water, improved techniques to ensure its timely supply, and improve its efficient use.
- India needs to shift its focus from 'water resources development' to 'water resources management' by restructuring and strengthening existing institutions for better service delivery and resource sustainability. Planning for big water resources projects should be interdisciplinary with all environmental, ecological and human concerns internalized and thereby assessing the impacts by a concrete statute.
- The philosophy of development of the water sector needs a sea-change to move away from government owned and operated systems to participation of beneficiaries in construction, operation and maintenance. Some state governments have already made changes in existing Irrigation Acts or introduced new Acts to facilitate and motivate such participation. Others should follow suit with the central government acting as a catalyst.
- State governments also need to be persuaded to enact other suggested legislation for ground water regulation, dam safety and flood plain zoning. The central government should also take the initiative for drawing up guidelines and initiating policy changes for private sector participation in the irrigation sector.
- This needs to be pursued more vigorously with genuine empowerment of WUAs. The objective should be to cover the entire command of all major and medium projects with WUAs.
- The pricing structure for water needs a serious review to reflect the scarcity value of water. Water charges must ensure that the revenues earned by state governments cover the operation and maintenance (O&M) costs of irrigation and water supply systems.

- Stress has to undoubtedly continue on developing water resources but more emphasis now has to be laid on sustainable management of water resources for optimal production along with the completion of on-going projects and their development. Efforts need to be concentrated on the quick completion of ongoing projects, especially the old ones, and proper maintenance of the created infrastructure. The assistance programmes of the central government need to be restructured to encourage this.
- Over exploitation of ground water is leading to falling water levels in many areas especially, the hard rock areas. The systematic approach to the management of ground water requires a sustainable legal framework.
- For optimal utilisation of the water resources and to ensure sustainable development, the highest standards of scientific activity have to be taken up in the sector. With this objective, research and development (R&D) efforts have to be speeded up through sponsored research as well as through invited research proposals.
- As like in Maharashtra, Water Resources Regulatory Authority (WRRA), be constituted by each state some states, having powers to fix the rates for use of water for agriculture, industrial, drinking and other purposes and several related matters.
- Reuse and recycling of wastewater management for irrigation without a detrimental effect on crops and the soil is another aspect that needs to be tackled in a systematic manner, in addition to the management of poor quality of groundwater, which is fairly widespread in the country.
- The allocation of water to agriculture is facing a losing battle with the industrial, domestic, power and other sectors. At the same time, there is the compulsion of enhancing agricultural production in an eco-friendly sustainable manner with limited land and water resources. There is, therefore, an urgent need of the speedy transfer of resource-efficient technology to increase the productivity of water at field and the regional level.

CONCLUSION

Water resources of a country constitute one of its vital assets.

India with 2.4 percent of the world's total area has 16 percent of the world's population; but has only 4 percent of the total available fresh water. India is currently facing a daunting set of water-related challenges. Increasing population, growing urbanization, and rapid industrialization combined with the need for raising agricultural production generates competing claims for water. There is a growing perception of a sense of an impending water crisis in the country. The facts indicate that India is expected to become 'water stressed' by 2025 and 'water scarce' by 2050. Irrigation constitutes the main use of water and is thus the focal issue in water resources development. In view of the importance of irrigation development in agriculture and other sectors, the policy-makers in India have been giving increased thrust for the development of irrigation since the independence. As a result of massive investment, the area under irrigation has increased significantly during last five decades. Despite significant achievements in development of irrigated area, the overall performance of irrigation sector has not been very appreciable in India. Though there are many reasons for the dreadful performance of the irrigation sector, poor participation of farmers in irrigation management-related activities is also cited as one of the major reasons for the deteriorating performance of irrigation sector in India. PIM is emerging as an important tool for ensuring better equity in distribution of water, which in turn also results in better operation and maintenance (O&M), better on farm management, and increased productivity. The participation of actual beneficiaries through PIM and the maintenance of village-level distribution channels through WUAs have been found useful. There is broad consensus that this has been a step in the right direction. The experience across States has been uneven. Most of the States have enacted exclusive legislation for involvement of farmers in irrigation management. The allocation of water to agriculture is facing a losing battle with the industrial, domestic, power and other sectors. At the same time, there is the compulsion of enhancing agricultural production in an eco-friendly sustainable manner with limited land and water resources. There is, therefore, an urgent need of the speedy transfer of resource-efficient technology to increase the productivity of water at field and the regional level.

Notes and References

1. As per List-II—State list, Seventh Schedule of the Indian Constitution, water is a State subject. Therefore, water resources projects for irrigation

and flood control are formulated, designed, executed, owned and operated by the State Governments. However, this is subject to the provisions of entry of List I—Union List, wherein Union Government has been given powers to regulate and develop inter-State rivers and river valleys to the extent such regulation and development under the control of Union is declared by Parliament by Law to be expedient in public interest. Further Economic and Social Planning has been included in List III—Concurrent List, Item 20. The National Water Resources Council was set-up in March 1983 to frame policy and coordinate action at the central level. (MOWR, 2006).

2. In addition to this, about Rs. 2,31,800 crore have been allocated for the irrigation development during the Eleventh Plan Period (2007-12), which is currently underway (Planning Commission, GOI, 2011). If we include this, the total investment in irrigation sector would go up to Rs. 2454.42 billion. However, the share in total plan expenditure has decreased from around 23 percent in the First Plan to about 6.7 percent in the Tenth Plan.
3. Detailed analysis about the deteriorating financial performance of India's irrigation sector can be seen from GOI (1992); Gulati, *et al.*, (1994); Saleth, (1996); Deshpande and Narayanamoorthy, (2001); CWC, (2004).
4. At the national level, a number of national commissions have been constituted by the central government to review specific water policy issues as well as plan for a long-term development of the water sector. Among them, the notable ones are the Committee on Pricing Irrigation Water 1992 (for rationalization of water rates, volumetric water allocation, and system modification), Committee on Private Sector Participation in Major and Medium Irrigation Projects 1995 (documenting the rationale, feasibility, and actual state level initiatives for involving the private corporate sector, especially in the construction and modernization of irrigation schemes) and the National Commission of Integrated Water Resources Development Plan, 1997 (developing a national master plan for the water sector by synthesizing and updating similar plans prepared earlier by the CWC as well as investigating the economic, technical, and institutional issues in the water sector from a national perspective (ADB, 2009).
5. A per capita availability of less than 1700 cubic metres (m^3) is termed as a *water-stressed condition* while if per capita availability falls below 1000 m^3, it is termed as a *water scarcity condition.*
6. Some of the important activities planned during this year are: (a) National Congress on Groundwater; (b) Farmers Participatory Action Research Programme in 5000 villages to promote 'more crop and income per drop' of water; (c) Training of Water Masters in each Pani Panchayat and institution of an Award for the best Pani Panchayat; (d) Wider dissemination of know-how to the user level through electronic and print media; (e) Organisation of workshops/seminars on water-related technical and management issues; and (f) Participation in festivals, fairs, training programmer, mass awareness programmes, etc. (*www.adb.org*).

7. The Command Area Development Programme (CADP) was introduced during the fifth plan period with an objective to increase overall efficiency of water use in the canal command areas by bridging the gap between potential created and utilised. As of 2001-02, about Rs. 6838 crore has been spent under this account. However, the gap between potential created and utilised has not declined after the introduction of CADP, but rather widened substantially.
8. How to form users' group and what kind of powers should be given to farmers in order to increase the participation of farmers in irrigation management have been clearly explained in Vaidyanathan Committee report on pricing of irrigation water (GOI, 1992).
9. In Maharashtra, WUAs are operating not only in canal command areas but also in the areas where lift irrigation is used for cultivation. Unlike the formal WUAs established in canal command areas, the Pani Panchayat Institution is formed with certain novel principles which were not imposed by any external agents but emerged out of the discussions with the farmers keeping in view the water availability and potential for rainfed cultivation (Deshpande and Reddy, 1990; Thakur and Pattnaik, 2002; Keremane, *et al.*, 2006).

References

ADB (2009), Water Resources Development in India: Critical Issues and Strategic Options, *Asian Development Bank*, February 2009. *Available at http://www.adb.org/Documents/Assessments/Water/IND/Water-Assessment.pdf, Accessed on August 18, 2011).*

Bhat, Sairam (2009), *Water Resource Management in India: Few Reflections* (available at *http://www.nlsenlaw.org/resources/essay7.pdf*), Accessed on August 18, 2011.

Bhattarai, M. and Narayanamoorthy, A. (2003), "Impact of Irrigation on Rural Poverty: An Aggregate Panel-data Analysis for India", *Water Policy*, Vol. 5, Nos. 5-6, pp. 443-58.

Brewer, R.; Kolavalli, S.; Kalro, A.H.; Naik, G.; Ramnarayan, S.; Raju, K.V. and Sakthivadivel, R. (1999), *Irrigation Management Transfer in India: Policies, Processes and Performance*, Oxford and IBH Publishing Co. Pvt. Ltd., New Delhi.

CWC (1993, 2000 and 2004), *Water and Related Statistics*, Central Water Commission, Ministry of Water Resources, Government of India, New Delhi.

——, (2000), *Assessment of Availability and Requirement of Water for Diverse Uses in India*, Standing Sub-Committee Report, Central Water Commission, Government of India, New Delhi.

Deshpande, R.S. and Narayanamoorthy, A. (2001), "Issues before the Second Irrigation Commission of Maharashtra", *Economic and Political Weekly*, Vol. 36, No. 12, pp. 1034-43.

Deshpande, R.S. and Reddy, V. Ratna (1990), "Social Dynamics and Farmers' Society: A Case Study of Pani Panchayat", *Indian Journal of Agricultural Economics*, Vol. 45, No. 3, pp. 355-61.

Easter, K.W. (2000), "Asia's Irrigation Management in Transition: A Paradigm Shift Faces High Transaction Costs", *Review of Agricultural Economics*, Vol. 22, No. 2, pp. 370-88.

GOI (1972), *Report of the Second Irrigation Commission*, Ministry of Irrigation and Power, Government of India, New Delhi.

———, (1992), *Report of the Committee on Pricing of Irrigation Water*, Planning Commission, Government of India, New Delhi.

———, (2002), *Tenth Five Year Plan: 2002-07*, Vol. II, Planning Commission, Government of India, New Delhi.

———, (2006), *Report of Sub-Committee on more Crop and Income per drop of Water Advisory Council on Artificial Recharge of Ground Water*, Ministry of Water Resources, Government of India, October 2006.

———, (2011), *Agricultural Statistics at a Glance, 2010,* Directorate of Economics and Statistics, Ministry of Agriculture, Government of India, New Delhi.

Gulati, Ashok; Svendsen, Mark; Choudhury, Nandini Roy (1994), "Major and Medium Irrigation Schemes: Towards Better Financial Performance", *Economic and Political Weekly*, Vol. 29, No. 26, pp. A72-A79.

Gupta, S.K. and Deshpande, R.D. (2004), "Water for India in 2050 : First Order Assessment of Available Options", *Current Science*, Vol. 86.

Hussain, I. and Hanjra, M.A. (2003), "Does Irrigation Water Matter for Rural Poverty Alleviation: Evidence from South and South-East Asia", *Water Policy*, Vol. 5, Nos. 5-6, pp. 429-42.

Keremane, G.P.; Mckay, Jennifer and Narayanamoorthy, A. (2006), "The Decline of Innovative Local Self-Governance Institutions for Water Management: the Case of Pani Panchayats", *International Journal of Rural Management*, Vol. 2, No. 1, pp. 107-122.

Kumar, Rakesh; Singh, R.D. and Sharma, K.D. (2005), "Water Resources of India", *Current Science*, Vol. 89, No. 5, 10 September 2005, 794-811.

Maloney, C.T. and Raju, K.V. (1994), *Managing Irrigation Together: Practice and Policy in India,* Sage Publication, New Delhi.

MOWR (1987 and 2002), *National Water Policy*, Ministry of Water Resources, Government of India, New Delhi, September.

———, (1999), *Report of the Working Group on Water Availability for Use*, National Commission for Water Resources Development Plan, Ministry of Water Resources, Government of India, New Delhi.

———, (2006), *Report of the Working Group on Water Resources for the XI Five Year Plan (2007-12)*, Ministry of Water Resources, Government of India, New Delhi, December.

Narasimhan, T.N. (2008), "A Note on India's Water Budget and Evapotraspiration", *Journal of Earth System Science*, Vol. 117.

——— and V.K. Gaur (2009), *A Framework for India's Water Policy*, National Institute for Advanced Studies, Bangalore.

Narayanamoorthy, A. (2001), "Irrigation and Rural Poverty Nexus: A State-wise Analysis", *Indian Journal of Agricultural Economics*, Vol. 56, No. 1, January-March, pp. 40-56.

——–, (2002), "Indian Irrigation: Five Decades of Development", *Water Resources Journal*, No. 212, June, pp. 1-29.

——– and Kalamkar, S.S. (2006), *Evaluation of Participatory Management in Maharashtra,* Agro-Economic Research Center (AERC) Report, Gokhale Institute of Politics and Economics (Deemed University), Pune, December.

Narayanamoorthy, A. (2011), *Participatory Irrigation Management: Evolution and Impact*, Gyan Publishing House, New Delhi, 2011 (ISBN 97888121210942).

NCIWRDP (1999), *Report of the National Commission for Integrated Water Resources Development Plan*, National Commission for Integrated Water Resources Development Plan, Ministry of Water Resources, Government of India, New Delhi.

Planning Commission (2007), *Report of the Working Group on Natural Resources Management Eleventh Five Year Plan (2007-12), Volume I : Synthesis*, Planning Commission, Government of India, February 2007.

——–, (2008), *Agriculture, Rural Development, Industry, Services, and Physical Infrastructure,* Vol. III, Eleventh Five Year Plan, 2007-12, Planning Commission, Government of India, New Delhi.

——–, (2011), *Mid-Term Appraisal Eleventh Five Year Plan, 2007-12*, Planning Commission, Government of India, New Delhi.

Raju, K.V (2010), "Sustainable Water Use in India: A Way Forward", in *Agriculture, Food Security, and Rural Development,* Asian Development Bank, Oxford University Press.

Reddy, M.A. (1996), "Kudimaramat" in B.C. Barah (ed.), *Traditional Water Harvesting Systems: An Ecological Economic Survey,* New Age International Publications, New Delhi, pp. 101-19.

Rosegrant, W. Mark (1997), *Water Resources in the Twenty-first Century: Challenges and Implications for Action,* Food and Agriculture, and the Environment Discussion Paper 20, International Food Policy Research Institute, Washington, D.C., U.S.A.

Saleth, R.M. (1996), *Water Institutions in India: Economics, Law and Policy*, Commonwealth Publishers, New Delhi.

Saleth, R.M.; Samad, M.; Molden, D. and Hussain, I. (2003), "Water, Poverty and Gender: A Review of Issues and Policies", *Water Policy,* Vol. 5, No. 5-6, pp. 385-98.

Shah, T. and Singh, O.P. (2004), "Irrigation Development and Rural Poverty in Gujarat, India: A Disaggregated Analysis", *Water International,* Vol. 29, No. 2, pp. 167-77.

Singh, Anil Kumar (2004), "Emerging Trends and Issues in Water Management for Agricultural Production", in M.S. Swaminthan, Pedro Medrano, Daniel J. Gustafson and Pravesh Sharma (Eds.) *National Food Security Summit, 2004—Selected Papers,* World Food Programme, New Delhi.

Thakur, Manish K. and Pattnaik, Binay K. (2002), "How Effective are 'Pani Panchayats'?: A Field View from Maharashtra", *Sociological Bulletin*, Vol. 51, No. 2, pp. 243-68.

Vaidyanathan, A. (1999), *Water Resources Management: Institutions and Irrigation Development in India*, Oxford University Press, New Delhi.

Vermillion, Douglas, L. (1997), *Impacts of Irrigation Management Transfer: A Review of the Evidence*, Research Report 11, International Irrigation Management Institute, Colombo, Sri Lanka..

World Bank (2004), "Water Resources Sector Strategy", Strategic Directions for World Bank Engagement, Washington, DC.

World Bank (2005), *India's Water Economy: Bracing for a Turbulent Future*, Report No. 34750-IN, Agriculture and Rural Development Unit, South Asia Region, The World Bank, Washington, D.C., USA.

Chapter 2

Spatial and Temporal Dynamics of Water Resources in India

INDERJEET SINGH AND BHAVNA CHHABRA

INTRODUCTION

The modern economists emphasize the catalytic role that technological changes play in the growth of an economy. The technological changes bring about an increase in per capita income, either by reducing the amount of inputs per unit of output or by yielding more output for a given amount of input (Mathur, 1953). Technological change in an economy, therefore, refers to changes in the input-output relations of production activities. Consequently, as the economy moves from lower to higher stages of development, there occurs a shift from simpler to more modern and complicated techniques of production on the one hand and ecological fallouts on the other (Leontief, 1963). International evidence is indicative of the fact that urbanization and agriculture revolution has raised alarming signs for the ecology also.

Worldwide the ground water quantity and the quality has been the first victim of agricultural revolution (World Bank, 1990). Next are the health and the existence of species. From the ecological perspective, heavy and indiscriminate use of chemicals and pesticides has contaminated the surface and ground water, damaged fisheries, destroyed freshwater ecosystems, entered the food chain in a subtle way and the very human existence of mankind is facing an extreme danger (Dung and Dung, 1999; Dung *et al.*, 1999; Huan *et al.*, 2000; Kishi and Hirschborn, 1995; and Tardiff, 1992). Punjab has been the leader of Green Revolution in India. The model of intensive agriculture is presently being questioned about its sustainability from the point of view of its adverse impact on ecology, in general, and on the water resources, in particular. Falling water table and groundwater overdraft has become a serious problem. In this context, the paper is an attempt to analyze the emerging water crisis in India by using the Punjab experience as a case study.

COVERAGE

Basically, the paper is targeted to analyze the demand side of the system. Indian water resource scenario, taking Punjab as a case study, has been analyzed. Secondary data from different published and unpublished sources has been used. Technique of data mining has been used. Past trends, current status and future scenario of the system has been analyzed. For analysis, tabular technique along with growth rates has been used.

ANALYSIS

Water is important resource and its spatial and temporal dynamics is very complex. Before starting the analysis, to put our work in a proper perspective, let us put some stylized facts about water resources. Some stylized facts about the world are: (a) eighty percent of the human body is made up of water; (b) water is a crucial element of our food and materials; (b) seventy percent of the earth's surface is covered with water, only three percent, is fresh; (c) only one percent of the water is available for human consumption; and (d) much of this water contains chemicals making it inappropriate for human consumption. Further, the facts about India are: (a) India has 2 percent of world's land, 4 percent of freshwater, 16 percent of population, and 10 percent of its cattle; (b) geographical area is 329 Mha of which 47 percent is cultivated and 23 percent is forested, 7 percent is under non-agricultural use, 23 percent is waste.; and (c) per capita availability of land 50 years ago was 0.9 ha., could be only 0.14 ha. in 2050. It shows that the water resources are precious.

WATER USE : CHANGING TRENDS OF THE FUTURE

Sector-wise water usage, its present and future scenario and the growth rate of the same is given in Table 1. Due to irrigation,

TABLE 1
Sector-wise Water Requirement, Present and Future Scenario

Uses	*Year 2010*		*Year 2050*		*Growth Rate (Percent)*
	Water Requirement (in km³)	*Percent*	*Water Requirement (in km³)*	*Percent*	
Irrigation	557	78.45	807	68.39	44.88
Domestic	43	6.06	111	9.41	158.14
Industries	37	5.21	81	6.86	118.92
Others	31	4.37	105	8.90	238.71
Power	19	2.68	70	5.93	268.42
Inland Navigation	7	0.99	15	1.27	114.29
Environment: Ecology	5	0.70	20	1.69	300.00
Evaporation Losses	42	5.92	76	6.44	80.95
Total	710	100.00	1180	100.00	66.20

Source : National Institute of Hydrology (www.nih.ernet.in), Roorkee, India.

agriculture sector is the main consumer of water. Presently 78.45 percent of the water use is for irrigation purposes. It is 6.06 percent for domestic, 5.21 percent for domestic use and rest for other uses and evaporation losses. Predictions show that in future, percentage of water use by agriculture sector will come down from the present 78.45 percent to about 68.39 percent while the usage share by domestic households, industries and others will increase. Industrial usage share of water will increase from 5.21 to 6.86 percent and domestic household use will increase from 6.06 to 9.41 percent. In other uses category, the increase will be from 4.37 percent to 8.90 percent. Thus, the future scenario is indicative of the fact that water use in others sectors, followed by industrial sector and domestic sector, in order, will grow and use share of agricultural sector will shrink. In growth terms, the total water requirement of the country will grow by 66.20 percent in 2050 as compared to 2010. Major chunk of this growth (238.71 percent) will be because of other uses. It will be followed by domestic (158.14 percent), industrial (118.92 percent) and agriculture (44.88 percent) sector in order. Thus, because of improvement in production technologies and decreased share of agriculture in future transformation of agriculture, the water requirement for irrigation will grow less as compared to the household and industrial sector.

Total annual requirement of fresh water for the country from various sectors including irrigation, domestic, industrial, hydropower and other uses is estimated to grow from 710 km^3 in year 2010 to 1,180 km^3 by the 2050. Disaggregate analysis by source (Table 2) is indicative of the fact that at aggregate level the water requirement, by

TABLE 2

Source and Sector-wise Water Usage, Present and Future Scenario

Uses	*Year 2010*		*Year 2050*		*Growth Rate (Percent)*
	Water Requirement (in km^3)	*Percent*	*Water Requirement (in km^3)*	*Percent*	
Surface Water					
Irrigation	339	47.75	463	39.24	36.58
Domestic	24	3.38	65	5.51	170.83
Industries	26	3.66	57	4.83	119.23
Power	15	2.11	56	4.75	273.33
Inland Navigation	7	0.99	15	1.27	114.29
Environment: Ecology	5	0.70	20	1.69	300.00
Evaporation Losses	42	5.92	76	6.44	80.95
Total	458	64.51	752	63.73	64.19
Ground Water					
Irrigation	218	30.70	344	29.15	57.80
Domestic	19	2.68	46	3.90	142.11
Industries	11	1.55	24	2.03	118.18
Power	4	0.56	14	1.19	250.00
Total	252	35.49	428	36.27	69.84
Grand Total	710	100.00	1,180	100.00	66.20

Source : National Institute of Hydrology (www.nih.ernet.in), Roorkee, India.

year 2050 as compared to 2010, will grow by 69.84 percent for ground water as compared to 64.19 percent for surface water. In terms of percentage share the irrigation requirement of water is going to be almost the same (29.15 percent) for groundwater. Table shows that over a period of time agriculture sector will shift from surface water to ground water. Groundwater represents one of the most important water sources in India and accounts for over 400 km^3 of the annual utilizable resource in the country.

Due to the highly variable nature of the climate, groundwater has become a popular alternative for irrigation and domestic water use across India. Reliance on groundwater resources is particularly strong where dry season surface water levels are low or where wet season flows are too disruptive to be easily tapped. In addition to being accessible, groundwater quality is generally excellent in most areas and presents a relatively safe source of drinking water for Indians in rural and urban centers. The presence and availability of groundwater varies greatly with changes in topography, subsurface geology and the prevailing climate in the region. In some areas, groundwater exists in deep aquifers while in others the water is stored near the surface. The location of the aquifer also affects its recharge rate and its susceptibility to pollution and overuse.

Sector-wise industrial use of water is given in Table 3. Presently, the total water requirement for the industries is around 37.263 km^3 for the year 2010 which is likely to touch the level of 61.124 km^3 and 80.525 km^3 in the years 2025 and 2050 respectively. Table shows that in year 2010, the 'textile and jute' industry forms 51.04 percent of the total water requirement of the industry. It is followed by 'iron and steel' (15.67 percent) and 'food processing' (14.94 percent) industry. A look on the future scenario shows that water requirement of these top three water consumer industries is going to decrease because of improved technologies and demand considerations. But the share of 'paper and pulp' industry in total water consumption which is 7.78 percent in 2010 will touch the percentage mark of 16.67 and 23.48 percent in years 2025 and 2050 respectively. Hence, this is high time to plan for the promotion of water saving industries or water saving techniques. As the economy is planning to achieve the higher growth path, water requirement is also likely to shoot up and strain the already strained future requirement of water.

TABLE 3

Subsector-wise Industrial Water Usage, Present and Future Scenario

Category of Industry	*Water Requirement km³*					
	Year 2010		*Year 2025*		*Year 2050*	
	Value (km³)	*Percent*	*Value (km³)*	*Percent*	*Value (km³)*	*Percent*
(1)	*(2)*	*(3)*	*(4)*	*(5)*	*(6)*	*(7)*
Integrated Iron and Steel	5.838	15.67	5.739	9.39	10.941	13.59
Smelters	0.024	0.06	0.032	0.05	0.043	0.05
Petrochem and Refinery	0.031	0.08	0.036	0.06	0.049	0.06
Chemicals—Caustic Soda	0.010	0.03	0.010	0.02	0.012	0.02
Textile and Jute	19.019	51.04	36.518	59.74	35.193	43.70
Cement	1.205	3.23	1.383	2.26	1.873	2.33
Fertilizer	0.631	1.69	1.026	1.68	1.193	1.48
Leather Products	0.088	0.24	0.090	0.15	0.143	0.18
Rubber	0.004	0.01	0.006	0.01	0.006	0.01
Food Processing	5.568	14.94	8.043	13.16	8.319	10.33
Inorganic Chemicals	1.600	4.29	3.346	5.47	3.008	3.74
Sugar	0.071	0.19	0.334	0.55	0.318	0.40
Pharmaceuticals	0.184	0.49	0.243	0.40	0.343	0.43
Distillery	0.067	0.18	0.098	0.16	0.117	0.15
Pesticides	0.002	0.01	0.004	0.01	0.006	0.01
Paper and Pulp	2.898	7.78	10.189	16.67	18.905	23.48
General Engineering	0.024	0.06	0.028	0.05	0.056	0.07
Total	37.263	100.00	61.124	100.00	80.525	100.00

Source : www.nih.ernet.in.

TABLE 4

State-wise Net Water Requirement in 2010 and 2050

States/UTs	Net water requirement (km^3)						Growth Rate (Percent)
	Year 2010			Year 2050			
	Low	High	Average	Low	High	Average	
(1)	(2)	(3)	(4)	(5)	(6)	(7)	(8)
Andhra Pradesh	45.70	46.90	46.30	70.60	85.60	78.10	84.88
Arunachal Pradesh	0.90	0.90	0.90	11.40	11.70	11.55	1200.00
Assam	12.10	12.50	12.30	28.50	38.50	33.50	213.01
Bihar	32.80	33.30	33.05	58.70	81.00	69.85	145.08
Goa	0.40	0.40	0.40	0.60	0.70	0.65	75.00
Gujarat	25.80	26.40	26.10	39.00	44.30	41.65	69.73
Haryana	22.30	22.60	22.45	24.40	24.60	24.50	9.58
Himachal Pradesh	4.80	4.90	4.85	5.40	5.50	5.45	13.40
Jammu & Kashmir	4.50	4.50	4.50	9.10	12.00	10.55	166.67
Karnataka	25.30	26.00	25.65	36.30	46.40	41.35	80.90
Kerala	7.60	7.80	7.70	19.40	23.80	21.60	209.09
Madhya Pradesh	35.60	36.70	36.15	64.60	89.90	77.25	148.69
Maharashtra	39.10	40.60	39.85	65.50	78.90	72.20	97.99
Manipur	1.00	1.00	1.00	1.80	4.00	2.90	300.00

Meghalaya	0.70	0.80	0.75	1.50	1.70	1.60	126.67
Mizoram	0.20	0.20	0.20	0.80	0.90	0.85	350.00
Nagaland	0.80	0.80	0.80	5.60	5.70	5.65	612.50
Orissa	16.90	17.30	17.10	32.50	38.60	35.55	125.73
Punjab	36.80	36.90	36.85	37.40	37.60	37.50	2.04
Rajasthan	37.80	39.90	38.85	44.40	45.80	45.10	17.89
Sikkim	0.30	0.30	0.30	0.50	0.60	0.55	100.00
Tamil Nadu	30.60	31.00	30.80	40.00	47.50	43.75	54.22
Tripura	1.10	1.10	1.10	5.90	6.20	6.05	463.64
Uttar Pradesh	84.90	86.20	85.55	112.30	133.10	122.70	55.58
West Bengal	26.70	27.40	27.05	40.70	51.60	46.15	90.76
UTs	1.10	1.10	1.10	2.30	2.60	2.45	136.36
Total States	496.00	508.00	502.00	759.00	919.00	839.00	83.07

Source : www.nih.ernet.in.

State-wise present and future scenario of water requirements is given in Table 4. In addition to temporal dimension, net requirement of water has wide spatial variations. Table is indicative of the fact that there is wide variation in the water requirement in year 2050 as compared to the present one. In the states, with already at a higher consumption level, the growth of future water requirement will be relatively low, e.g., Punjab and Haryana. On the other hand, in some states of north-eastern region, the net water requirement will grow by more than three hundred percent. This differential behaviour of water requirement needs to be explored at a higher level of disaggregation.

WATER BUDGET OF INDIA

The average annual precipitation received in India is 4,000 km^3, out of which 700 km^3 is immediately lost to the atmosphere, 2,150 km^3 soaks into the ground and 1,150 km^3 flows as surface runoff. The total water resources in the country have been estimated as 1,953 km^3. Nearly 62 percent or 1,202 km^3 of the total water resources is available in the Ganga-Brahmaputra-Meghna basin. The remaining 23 basins have 751 km^3 of the total water resources. The annual water availability in terms of utilizable water resources in India is 1,122 km^3. Besides this, the quantity of 123 km^3 to 169 km^3 additional return flow will also be available from increased use from irrigation, domestic and industrial purposes by the year 2050. The per capita availability of utilizable water (Table 5), which was about 3,000 m^3 in the year 1951, has been reduced to 1,100 m^3 in 1998 and is expected to be 687 m^3 by the year 2050. Quantum of total water resources available is almost constant; on an average its growth rate is hovering around zero growth rates. On the other hand, the population growth is going to be massive in the future. As compared to year 2010, population will grow by 15.21 percent by 2025 and the corresponding growth of water resources will be rather negative (-0.02 percent). Likewise, the population growth will be 18.60 percent if we compare year 2050 with 2025 and the corresponding water resources will grow by just 0.10 percent. So, the future scenario shows that there is going to be a heavy pressure on water resources because of fast growing population. The per capita availability of water (m^3/person/year) is going to shrink very fast. In the next fifteen years, it will shrink by 13.22 percent and in the following twenty-five years it will shrink by 15.60 percent. If we take the long-term, i.e., 1951 to 2051, table

TABLE 5

Indian Per Capita Annual Water Availability (cu.m/capita/year)

Year	Total Water Resources		Population		Average Water Resources	
	Value (m^3/year)	Percentage Growth over Previous Period (%)	Value (10^6)	Percentage Growth over Previous Period (%)	Value (m^3/person/year)	Percentage Growth over Previous Period (%)
(1)	(2)	(3)	(4)	(5)	(6)	(7)
1951	1085888	—	361	—	3008	—
1991	1085803	-0.01	846	134.43	1283	-57.35
2010	1085266	-0.05	1157	36.71	938	-26.89
2025	1085062	-0.02	1333	15.21	814	-13.22
2050	1086147	0.10	1581	18.60	687	-15.60

Source : www.nih.ernet.in.

underscores an important fact that per capita water resource availability is shrinking at the rate of 0.77 percent per annum; which is alarming by all norms. This shrinkage in quantum will affect the quality also. As per international criterion for classification less than 1700 (cu.m/capita/year) is considered as water stressed. Presently, in India, the water availability is 1000 (cu.m/capita/year). This indicates that a large part of India will become water stressed by 2025.

The development of ground water in different areas of the country has not been uniform. Highly intensive development of ground water in certain areas in the country has resulted in over exploitation leading to decline in the levels of ground water and sea water intrusion in coastal areas. There is a continuous growth in dark and over-exploited areas in the country. As per the latest assessment of ground water resources carried out jointly by the Central Ground Water Board (CGWB) and the States, the assessment units are categorized as 'Over exploited'/'Critical' and 'Semi-critical' based on the stage of ground water development and the long-term water level declining trend during the past decade (1995-2004). Out of 5723 assessment units (Blocks/Mandals/Talukas) in the country, 839 units in various States have been categorized as 'Over-exploited', i.e., the annual ground water extraction exceeds the annual replenishable resource. In addition 226 units, 11 'Critical', i.e., the stage of ground water development is above 90 per cent and within 100 per cent of annual replenishable resource. There are 550 semi-critical units; where the stage of ground water development is between 70 per cent and 100 per cent.

Uncertainty and inconvenience is associated with surface water sources like canals, ponds and lakes, etc. Ease in use and availability of electricity, diesel and technologies will work as a catalytic agent to push the irrigation system in favour of tube-wells and that too the electric tube-wells. Growth of industrial requirement for water is going to be the same for both surface and ground water sources. Domestic water usage of surface water will grow faster than the ground water. In the coming four decades, country is going to face a situation where the biggest user, the agriculture will move on the path of ruthless mining of groundwater. There will be overdraft of groundwater, i.e., more withdrawal than the recharge. In this regard, Punjab agriculture is a best case to be mentioned, where the irrigation use of ground water has generated a crisis like situation.

CASE STUDY : THE PUNJAB MODEL OF AGRICULTURE

The Green Revolution in the state has been a chemical centered agriculture system. Agriculture in Punjab has undergone a significant structural change since the advent of Green Revolution in the mid-sixties. The traditional agriculture has progressively given way to modern and commercial agriculture. To meet the ever-growing demand of the country, food grain production has been increased by increasing productivity through intensive use of water and inputs like fertilizer, insecticides and pesticides. The adoption of this strategy has raised many development-related problems on economic, social and environmental fronts. Punjab is predominantly an agrarian State having 85 percent of its geographical area under cultivation with an average cropping intensity of 189 percent. Water is the only natural resource available and the state is devoid of any other mineral or natural resources. Punjab's agriculture being highly intensive is dependent on heavy requirement of water.

Availability and deficit of surface water is given in Table 6. Agriculture in Punjab is primarily an artificial irrigation-based, i.e., using surface as well as ground water resources. Intensive agriculture, based on wheat-rice rotation, has led to a serious imbalance in use and availability of ground resources. The total water supply of 3.13 m ham falls short by 1.27 m ham of the total water demand of 4.40 m ham. The deficit is met by over-exploitation of groundwater reserves through tube-wells and wells. As a result, groundwater has become a major source of irrigation in the State. To relieve stress on ground water, a greater emphasis is needed on efficient conveyance and distribution system for optimal utilization of available surface water.

TABLE 6

Status of Water Resources in Punjab

Detail	*m ham*
Annual canal water at head-works	14.54
Annual canal water at outlets	1.45
Annual ground water available	1.68
Total annual available water resources	3.13
Annual water demand	4.40
Annual water deficit	1.27.

Source : A.K. Jain and Raj Kumar (2007).

Punjab needs to be given greater share in its river waters to decrease stress on ground water resources and power consumption.

Water use by source of irrigation is presented in Table 7. An analysis of net area irrigated in Punjab by source of irrigation is indicative of the fact that only 28 percent of the total area is irrigated by surface water or canals and rest 72 percent area is irrigated by tube-wells and wells. The historical dependence on canals and other sources of surface water has gradually beem reduced in favour of groundwater. In Punjab, there are only two major sources of irrigation; the govt. canals and tube-wells and wells. On the eve of Green Revolution, there was an even dependence on both the sources of irrigation. The net area irrigated by canals came down from 44.53 in the year 1970-71 to 42.28 percent in 1980-81. It slightly rose to 42.47 percent in the year 1990-91. It has settled around 27 to 28 percent in the last few years. On the other hand, because of easy

TABLE 7

Net Area Irrigated in Punjab by Source ('000 Hectare)

Year	*Govt. Canals*	*Private Canals*	*Tube-wells*	*Others*	*Total*
1970-71	1286 (44.53)	6 (0.21)	1591 (55.09)	5 (0.17)	2888 (100)
1980-81	1430 (42.28)	—	1939 (57.33)	13 (0.38)	3382 (100)
1990-91	1660 (42.47)	9 (0.23)	2233 (57.12)	7 (0.18)	3909 (100)
2000-01	1002 (24.92)	—	3017 (75.03)	2 (0.05)	4021 (100)
2002-03	1148 (28.45)	—	2880 (71.38)	7 (0.17)	4035 (100)
2003-04	1129 (28.03)	—	2889 (71.72)	10 (0.25)	4028 (100)
2004-05	1101 (27.29)	7 (0.17)	2919 (72.34)	8 (0.20)	4035 (100)
2005-06	1134 (27.93)	4 (0.10)	2914 (71.77)	8 (0.20)	4060 (100)
2006-07	1148 (28.19)	—	2878 (70.68)	46 (1.13)	4072 (100)

Note : Figures in parentheses denote the percentages.
Source : Statistical Abstract, Govt. of Punjab, various issues.

availability of cheap or free electricity, the dependence on groundwater has drastically increased especially during the decade of 1990s. Presently, more than 70.68 per cent of the net area irrigated in Punjab is dependent on tube-wells and wells, i.e., the groundwater. The availability of surface water resources is unable to meet the demand for agriculture and as such there is an increasing pressure on underground water resources. The ground water is being over exploited to meet increasing demand for diverse purposes i.e., intensive irrigation, drinking, industry and power generation.

Another important fact underscored by growth of number of tube-wells (Table 8) is that in Punjab there are two types of tube-wells: diesel operated and electric operated. The total number of tube-wells that was 1.92 lakh in 1970-71; rose to 6 lakhs in 1980-81; to 8 lakhs in 1990-91; to 9.3 lakh in 2000-01 and finally touched the level of 12.76 lakh in the year 2008-09. So over a span of past four decades, the number of tube wells has grown by more than 6 times. Further break-

TABLE 8
Number of Tube-wells in Punjab (Lakhs)

Year	*Diesel Operated*		*Electricity Operated*		*Total*
	No.	*Percent*	*No.*	*Percent*	*No.*
1970-71	1.01	52.60	0.91	47.40	1.92
1980-81	3.20	53.33	2.80	46.67	6.00
1990-91	2.00	25.00	6.00	75.00	8.00
1998-99	1.70	88.54	7.45	81.42	1.92
1999-2000	1.70	18.38	7.55	81.62	9.25
2000-01	1.70	18.18	7.65	81.82	9.35
2001-02	1.75	18.42	7.75	81.58	9.50
2002-03	2.91	25.30	8.59	74.70	11.50
2003-04	2.88	25.17	8.56	74.83	11.44
2004-05	2.88	24.66	8.80	75.34	11.68
2005-06	2.88	24.14	9.05	75.86	11.93
2006-07	2.80	22.73	9.52	77.27	12.32
2007-08	2.75	22.07	9.71	77.93	12.46
2008-09	2.80	21.94	9.96	78.06	12.76

Source : Statistical Abstract, Govt. of Punjab, 2009.

up of number of tube-wells into diesel and electric operated is indicative of the fact that with minor variations, the number of diesel operated tube-wells has remained fairly stable but the number of electric operated tube-wells has increased nearly by 10 times in the 30 years and much of this increase can be attributed to the current decade. The share of electric operated tube-wells has crossed the mark of 80 percent. The end of decade of 1990 has been characterized by concession to the farmers in the form of free electricity. The free electricity along with convenience of use has led to ever before pressure on groundwater. Widespread rural electrification coupled with a flat-fee electricity subsidy that has led to a dramatic increase in the number of wells, groundwater-based irrigation now far surpasses surface water use.

Ground water draft and fluctuations in water table are given in Table 9. In the absence of any systematic policy to regulate the demand for water, the unconstrained mining of this resource has resulted in over exploitation of groundwater. As per the table, the present groundwater development is 145 percent as on March 2004. Out of 137 blocks of the state, 103 blocks are "over exploited", 5 blocks are "critical", 4 blocks are "semi-critical" and 25 blocks are in "safe category". A look on the temporal dimension of categorization of blocks shows that in year 1984 only 44.92 percent were the "over-exploited" blocks and about 49 percent blocks were semi-critical or safe. But in the year 1992, 52 percent of the blocks went into the category of "over exploitation" and share of semi-critical and safe went down to 40 percent. Presently as per the 2004 statistics, the number of "over exploited" blocks has gone to 75.18 percent and the number of "semi-critical" and "safe" blocks has shrunk to 21 percent. Thus, over exploitation of groundwater and reduced share of canal water is drastically depleting the only resource of the Punjab economy.

Thus the Punjab model of agriculture has deteriorated the ecology of the region, in general, and the water resources in particular. The repercussions have started to show up in the form of depleted ground water, wide spread salinity, deteriorating water quality and specific kind of disease patterns in human beings. Clearly, over the years, a number of issues and challenges have emerged in the development and management of the water resources.

TABLE 9

Categorization of Blocks on the Basis of Groundwater Draft in Punjab

Category of Block	*Year*											
	1984		*1986*		*1989*		*1992*		*1999*		*2004*	
	No.	*%*	*No.*	*%*	*No.*	*%*	*No.*	*%*	*No.*	*%*	*No.*	*%*
(1)	*(2)*	*(3)*	*(4)*	*(5)*	*(6)*	*(7)*	*(8)*	*(9)*	*(10)*	*(11)*	*(12)*	*(13)*
Dark (Over-exploited)	53	44.92	55	46.61	62	52.54	63	53.39	73	52.90	103	75.18
Dark/Critical	07	05.93	09	07.63	07	05.93	07	05.93	11	07.97	05	03.65
Grey/Semi-critical	22	18.64	18	15.25	20	16.95	15	12.71	16	11.59	04	02.92
White/Safe	36	30.51	36	30.51	29	24.58	33	27.97	38	27.54	25	18.25
Total	118		118		118		118		138		137	

Source : Central Ground Water Board, Punjab.

CONCLUSION

The ever growing demand and the shortage of surface water availability, development and over-exploitation of ground water resources and deteriorating water quality of water resources is a matter of serious concern and calls for judicious and scientific resource management and conservation. All these concerns need to be addressed on the basis of common policies and strategies with a vision of a new considered approach by adopting emerging research in science and technology.

REFERENCES

Dung, N.H. and Dung, T.T.T. (1999), "Economic and Health Consequences of Pesticide Use in Paddy Production in the Mekong Delta, Vietnam", EEPSEA Research Report Series (*www.eepsea.org*).

Dung, N.H., Thien, T.C. and Others (1999), "Impact of Agro-Chemical Use on Productivity and Health in Vietnam". EEPSEA Research Report Series, Available at: *http://www.eepsa.org*.

Huan, N.H. and Le Van Thiet (2000), "Results of Survey for Confidence, Attitude and Practice in Safe and Effective Use of Pesticides", In, *Agro-Chemicals Report,* Vol. II, No. I, January-March 2002.

Jain, A.K. and Kumar, Raj (2007), "Water Management Issues, Punjab-North West India", Website: ttp://akicb.ifas.ufl.edu/upload/proceedings/jainak_water_management.pd

Kishi, M., N. and Hirschhorn, Qjajadisastra, M. and others (1995), "Relationship of Pesticide Spraying to Signs and Symptoms in Indonesian Farmers", *Scandinavian Journal of Work & Environmental Health*, 21:124-33.

Leontief, W.W. (1963), *Studies in the Structure of American Economy*, Oxford University Press, New York.

Mathur, P.N. (1953), "An Efficient Path of Technological Transformation of an Economy", in Barna, T. (ed.), *Structural Dependence and Economic Development*, Macmillan.

Pimental, D., H. and Acquay M. Biltoneṅ (1992), "Environmental and Economic Costs of Pesticide Use", *Bioscience*, Vol. 42, pp. 750-60.

Singh, Karam (2007), *Punjab, The Dance of Water Table*, The Punjab Farmers' Commission, Govt. of Punjab, p. 13.

Singh, Karam and Jain, K.K. (2002), *Dynamics of Structural Shifts in Cost and Returns in Farm Economy in Punjab,* Report for ACCP, Agro Economic Research Centre, PAU, Ludhiana, March.

Tardiff, R.G. (1992), *The e-pesticide Manual: A World Compendium*, 13th Edition, Alton, Hampshire.

WHO (1990), *Public Health Impact of Pesticides Used in Agriculture*, World Health Organization: New York, USA.

Chapter 3

Water Resources in India

Need of Judicious Utilization

MANISH DEV

Rahiman paani rakhiye, bin paani sab soon.
paani gaye naa ubarai, moti manush choon.

The above couplet of poet *Rahim* emphasizes the importance of water for human kind. Water is the most precious resources that have been provided by nature. The water is available in two forms—the Ground water and the Surface water. The availability and exploitability of ground water is limited while the surface water is available in abundance. However, the quality of surface water is so poor that is not safe for the consumption by human and the animal. Although, the ground water has also many impurities but the same is safer than surface water. 97.5 per cent of the water on the Earth is salt water, and only 2.5 per cent is fresh water of which 68.7 per cent is in the form of Glaciers, 30.1 per cent is in the form of Ground water and the remaining 0.8 per cent is Permafrost. Out of the available surface water 67.4 per cent is in lakes, 12.2 per cent is in the form of soil moisture, 9.5 per cent is in atmosphere, 8.5 per cent is under wetlands, 1.6 per cent is flowing through rivers and the remaining 0.8 per cent is in plants and animals (Shiklomenov and Rodda, 2003). Thus, only a fraction of total water is available for consumption. Fresh water has a global volume of 35.2 million cubic kilometers.

Fresh water is a renewable resource, yet the world's supply of clean, fresh water is steadily decreasing because of rise in the population, a wave of industrialization and increasing urbanization. Water demand already exceeds supply in many parts of the world and as the world population continues to rise, so too does the water demand. Awareness of the global importance of preserving water for ecosystem services has only recently emerged as, during the 20th century, more than half the world's wetlands have been lost along with their valuable environmental services. Biodiversity-rich fresh water ecosystems are currently declining faster than marine or land ecosystems. (Hoekstra, A.Y., 2006).

The framework for allocating water resources to water users (where such a framework exists) is known as water rights. Surface water is water in a river, lake or fresh water wetland. Surface water is naturally replenished by precipitation and naturally lost through discharge to the oceans, evaporation, evapotranspiration and sub-surface seepage. It is estimated that 69 per cent of worldwide water use is for irrigation, with 15-35 per cent of irrigation withdrawals being unsustainable. An assessment of water management in agriculture was conducted in 2007 by the International Water Management Institute in on Lanka to see if the world had sufficient water to provide food for its growing population. (Molden, D., 2007). It assessed the current availability of water for agriculture on a global scale and mapped out locations suffering from water scarcity. It found that a fifth of the world's people, more than 1.2 billion, live in areas of physical water scarcity, where there is not enough water to meet all demands. A further 1.6 billion people live in areas experiencing economic water scarcity where the lack of investment in water or insufficient human capacity makes it impossible for authorities to satisfy the demand for water. (Charters, C. and Verma, S., 2010), It is estimated that 22 per cent of worldwide water is used for industrial purposes It is estimated that 8 per cent of worldwide water is used for household purposes. (WBCDS, 2009)

So far as the availability of water in India is concerned the situation is deteriorating steadily, as some parts of the country are facing the water shortage. Serious conflicts have arisen between farmers and the other users of water. The latest one was in the state of Maharashtra where three innocent farmers were died in indiscriminate police firing. These farmers were protesting at Mavai, near Pune, against the diversion of water from Pavna dam to the

Pimpri Chinchwad municipal corporation. River water disputes between Karnataka and Tamilnadu, Maharashtra and Andhra Pradesh, Panjab and Haryana are of the same nature. In fact, the protests over power and steel plants could get louder if they are bound up with inter-State disputes over water use, as is probable in Karnataka. The setting up of steel and cement plants in the Krishna basin area in northern Karnataka could impact water availability to downstream farmers in Andhra Pradesh, a concern expressed by the State's Irrigation officials. When the Global Investors' Meet was staged in Karnataka in 2010, there was little or no emphasis on water conservation, though the envisaged projects would draw large quantities of water from the Alamatti dam. The problem lies in the mismatch in demand and supply of the water.

In view of the above general observation the present paper entitled "*Water Resources in India: Need of Judicious Utilization*" analyses the nature of water uses and the strategy for the conservation, protection and development of water resources sustainably. The paper is divided into four sections, namely, I. Availability of Water Resources in India, II. Ground Water Development: Utility to Scarcity, III. Policy Framework for the Conservation and Protection of Water Resources, and IV. Concluding Observations.

AVAILABILITY OF WATER RESOURCES IN INDIA

The water resource potential of India has been assessed from time to time by different agencies (Table 1). It may be seen that since

TABLE 1

Estimates of Water Resources in India

Agency	*Estimate*	*Deviation*
	In bcm	*From 1869 bcm*
First Irrigation Commission (1902-03)	1443	–23%
Dr. A.N. Khosla (1949)	1673	–10%
Central Water and Power Commission (1954-66)	1881	+0.6%
National Commission on Agriculture	1850	–1%
Central Water Commission (1988)	1880	+0.6%
Central Water Commission (1993)	1869	—

Source : GOI (2008): Eleventh Five Year Plan: 2007-12, Planning Commission, Vol. II, p. 44.

1954, the estimates have stabilized and are within the proximity of the currently accepted estimate of 1869 billion cubic meters (bcm) which includes replenishable groundwater which gets charged on annual basis.

Within the limitations of physiographic conditions, socio-political environment, legal and constitutional constraints, and the technology available at hand, the utilizable water resources of the country have been assessed at 1123 bcm, of which 690 bcm is from surface water and 433 bcm from groundwater sources (CWC, 1993). As per the latest assessment, the annual replenishable ground water resource of country has been estimated as 433 billion cubic meter (bcm), out of which 399 bcm is considered to be available for development for various uses. The irrigation sector remains the major consumer of ground water, accounting for 92 per cent of its annual withdrawal. The development of ground water in the country is highly uneven and shows considerable variations from place to place. Though the overall stage of ground water development is about 58 per cent, the average stage of ground water development in North Western Plain States (Panjab, Haryana and Western U.P.) is much higher (98%) as compared to the Eastern Plain States (Eastern U.P., Bihar, Jharkhand, West Bengal) (43%) and Central Plain States (Rajasthan, M.P., Chhattisgarh) (42%).

Harnessing of 690 bcm of utilizable surface water is possible only if matching storages are built. Trans-basin transfer of water, if taken up to the full extent as proposed under the National Perspective Plan, would further increase the utilizable quantity by approximately 220 bcm. The irrigation potential of the country has been estimated to be 139.9 MH without inter-basin sharing of water and 175 MH with inter-basin sharing.

While the total water resource availability in the country remains constant, the per capita availability of water has steadily declined from 6000 cubic meters in 1947 to 1829 cubic meters in 2001. The per capita availability of water might further be deteriorated to 1600 cubic meters in 2017 if adequate steps have not been taken to conserve and protect steadily declining water resources. (Chauhan, 2003). The twin indicators of water scarcity are per capita availability and storage. A per capita availability of less than 1700 cubic meters is considered as a water-stressed condition while if per capita availability falls below 1000 m^3, it is termed as a water scarcity condition. While on an average India may be nearing the water-stressed condition, on an individual river basin-wise situation, nine out of India's 20 river basins with 200 million populations are already facing a water-scarcity condition. Even after constructing 4525 large and small dams, the per capita storage in the country is 213 m^3 as against 6103 m^3 in Russia, 4733 m^3 in Australia, 1964 m^3 in the United States (US), and 1111 m^3 in China. It may touch 400 m^3 in India only after the completion of all the ongoing and proposed dams. (GOI, 2008):

GROUNDWATER DEVELOPMENT: UTILITY TO SCARCITY

Rainfall is the major source of ground water recharge in India, which is supplemented by other sources such as recharge from canals, irrigated fields and surface water bodies. A major part of the ground water withdrawal takes place from the upper unconfined aquifers, which are also the active recharge zones and holds the replenishable ground water resource. The replenishable ground water resource in the active recharge zone in the country has been assessed by Central Ground Water Board jointly with the concerned State Government authorities. The assessment was carried out with Block/Mandal/ Taluka/Watershed as the unit and as per norms recommended by the Ground Water Estimation Committee (GEC)-1997. As per the latest assessment, the annual replenishable ground water resource in this zone has been estimated as 432 billion cubic meter (bcm), out of which 399 bcm is considered to be available for development for various uses after keeping 34 bcm for natural discharge during non-monsoon period for maintaining flows in springs, rivers and streams (Central Ground Water Board, 2006).

Ground Water Estimation Committee has developed certain norms upon which the stage of ground water development has been assessed. (Table 2). As per the assessment, out of the total of 5723 assessment units in the country, 14.7 per cent assessment units (i.e., 839 development Blocks) have found excessive exploitation of water. These units have been categorized as 'Over-exploited'. Ground water development was found to be to the extent of 90 to 100 percent of the utilizable resources in 226 assessment units (3.9 per cent), which have been categorized as 'Critical'. 550 assessment units with stage of ground water development in the range of 70 to 100 per cent and long-term decline of water levels either during pre- or post-monsoon period have been categorized as 'Semi-Critical' and 4078 assessment units with the stage of ground water development below 70 per cent

TABLE 2
Assessment of Units (Blocks) on the Level of Ground Water Development in India

Sl. No.	*GEC Norms*	*No. of Units*	*Percentage to total*	*Category*
1.	Ground water development is more than 100% of the utilizable resources	839	14.66	Over exploited
2.	Ground water development to the extent of 90 to 100% of the utilizable resources	226	3.9	Critical
3.	Ground water development to the extent of 70 to 100% of the utilizable resources and long-term decline of water levels either during pre- or post-mansoon period.	550	9.61	Semi critical
4.	Ground water development below 70% of the utilizable resources	4078	71.26	Safe
5.	Unit excluded from the assessment due to salinity of ground water	30	0.52	Salinity
	Total	5723	100.00	

Source : Ground Water Estimation Committee.

have been categorized as 'Safe'. 30 assessment units had been excluded from the assessment due to the salinity of ground water in the aquifers in the replenishable zone.

The rapid urbanization and agricultural development has led to over-exploitation of groundwater in certain parts of the country. In 15 per cent of the blocks the annual extraction of groundwater exceeds annual recharge and in 4 per cent of the blocks it is more than 90 per cent of recharge. As the groundwater recedes wells have to be deepened and more energy has to be used to pump water. Thus in rural and industrial areas, there is a positive correlation between the level groundwater development and the consumption of energy.

SURFACE WATER

So far as the availability of surface water is concerned, the utilizable surface water resources In India are about 690 bcm (GOI, 2008). Harnessing of 690 bcm of utilizable surface water is possible only if matching storages are built. Trans-basin transfer of water, if taken up to the full extent as proposed under the National Perspective Plan, would further increase the utilizable quantity by approximately 220 bcm. The irrigation potential of the country has been estimated to be 139.9 MH without inter-basin sharing of water and 175 MH with inter-basin sharing.

POLICY FRAMEWORK FOR THE CONSERVATION AND PROTECTION OF WATER RESOURCES

Management of ground water resources and sharing of fresh surface water in Indian context is an extremely complex proposition as it deals with the interactions between the human society and the physical environment on the one hand while the politics of vote bank through water resources on the other. The highly uneven distribution of ground water availability and its utilization indicates that no single management strategy can be adopted for the country as a whole. So is the case with the sharing of river and reservoir water. Simultaneously, each situation demands a solution which takes into account the geomorphic set-up, climatic, hydrologic and hydro-geological settings, water availability, water utilization pattern for various sectors and the socio-economic set-up of the region.

Any strategy for scientific management of ground water resources involves a combination of :

(A) *Supply side measures* aimed at (i) increasing extraction of ground water depending on its availability, and (ii) Conserving rain water to the maximum extent through the principle of:

> "*khet kaa paani khet mein,*
> *haar kaa paani haar mein* ,
> *gaon kaa paani gaon mein*"

(B) *Demand side measures* aimed at controlling, protecting and conserving available resources. Various options falling under these categories are described in detail in the following sections.

SUPPLY SIDE MEASURES

These measures are aimed at increasing the ground water availability, taking the environmental, social and economic factors into consideration. These are also known as 'structural measures', which involves scientific development and augmentation of ground water resource. These may be classified into the following :

- Development of additional ground water resources through suitable means
- Augmentation of the ground water resources through artificial recharge
- Rain water harvesting

For an effective supply-side management, it is imperative to have full knowledge of the hydrologic and hydrogeological controls that govern the yields of aquifers and behavior of ground water levels under abstraction stress. Interaction of surface and ground water and changes in flow and recharge rates are also important considerations in this regard.

Supply side management of water resources rests with the following twin pillars:

Preventing Over-exploitation of Water

As has been said earlier, ground water development in India is extremely erratic. In some parts of country it reached at dangerous level. All the regulatory provisions have failed so far. The following measures should be adopted:

1. Every person who extracts groundwater should take all precautions to prevent waste of water.
2. Effective schemes and measures should be formulated and implemented to conserve groundwater by effective measures for replenishing and recharging the same.
3. Any use of groundwater, surface water or land and forest resources or activity in relation to these resources, which is likely to have significant negative impacts on local sources of groundwater must be subjected to an environmental and social impact assessment.
4. The protection, conservation, management and regulation of groundwater should be undertaken in such a way that it is integrated with the protection, conservation, management and regulation of surface water.
5. The appropriate authority should endeavour to ensure that conjunctive use of surface and groundwater sources is undertaken for all uses of groundwater.
6. The state at all levels is the public trustee of groundwater.

The appropriate authority must ensure that water is protected, used, developed, conserved, managed and controlled in a sustainable and equitable manner, for the benefit of all persons and the environment, and in accordance with their respective constitutional mandate

7. Although, the water is essential the survival of the human and animal kingdom and all-round development of the country, the same should not be utilized in injudicious manner. Use of water for commercial purposes, be it agriculture or industry, it should be priced in such a manner that actual economic and social costs are realized from the user. Practice of supplying the water at highly subsidized rates resulted into the wastage of water and caused much harm to the community in the form of water scarcity.

AUGMENTING UTILIZABLE WATER

Another area of concern is augmenting utilizable water .Usable water availability can be increased by tapping water that otherwise would have run-off to the sea. Water storage above ground through dams and diversion through weirs are the conventional means. However, water can also be stored underground by enhancing percolation through artificial recharge. Rain water harvesting in many small ponds through construction of bunds can also add to water availability it will help in checking the continuous decline in groundwater levels. Artificial recharge of groundwater can be done through construction of check dams Local storage is cost effective. There is significant potential for increasing the overall utilizable water through rainwater harvesting, construction of check dams, watershed management, and restoration of traditional water bodies as well as creation of new ones. In areas where groundwater is under severe stress, artificial recharging would need to be undertaken Inter-linking of rivers was another brilliant idea that could be utilized for equitable distribution of water in vast country like India where large differentials exists in the availability and consumption of water. A large part of geographical area is submerged every year causing loss of lives and property, while some parts of the country faces severe drought that too result in hardship of the people. The problem of abundance and shortage has a deep rooted solution in inter-linking of rivers.

DEMAND SIDE MEASURES

Apart from scientific development of available resources, proper ground water resources management requires to focus attention on the judicious utilization of the resources for ensuring their long-term sustainability. Ownership of ground water, need-based allocation pricing of resources, involvement of stake holders in various aspects of planning, execution and monitoring of projects and effective implementation of regulatory measures wherever necessary are the important considerations with regard to demand side ground water management. Delivering the valedictory address at the concluding day of the 93rd annual conference of the Indian Economic Association (IEA) on the Panjab University campus on 29th Dec. 2010, Dr. Ahluwalia said if the situation of growing water scarcity continued at present pace, the government might think of taking steps to introduce statutory regulation of water, citing example of Maharashtra where Water Regulation Authority has been set-up to ensure judicious use of water. According to him, "The water crisis is even more serious than the energy problem".

The issues of sustainable use of groundwater and the question of ownership of the groundwater has been addressed by an expert group on 'Groundwater Management and Ownership' under the chairmanship of Kirit S. Parikh, member planning commission. The group has noted that the experiences at national and international levels have shown that a command and control mechanism has not yielded good results in protecting the groundwater resources from over exploitation. The group recommended that: (GOI: 2007)

1. The ownership of the groundwater below the land will continue to remain with the owner of the land as per the Easement Act 1882 as long as the exploitation of groundwater is not causing depletion in the ground water levels so the similar rights of the adjoining landowners and public at large are not encroached upon.
2. Centre's intervention would be required when the groundwater level falls below the replenishable level. In such events, the affected area will be declared as an area under threat and any exploitation will be regulated.
3. The Central Ground Water Authority, under the provisions of Environment Act 1986, is empowered to make such declarations and it would be the responsibility

of the State Government to ensure that the exploitation in the area is regulated.

4. The regulation/reduction/restriction on the groundwater usage can be made effective by the State Government only with the co-operation of user groups and community participation involving PRIs.
5. The user groups will be responsible for regulating the ground water usage among various sectors that is irrigation, drinking, and industrial.
6. Effective monitoring mechanism should be developed with active collaboration of the State/Central Ground Water Board (CGWB).

CONCLUSION

Water, is the most invaluable gift of the nature to mankind for his survival and development .However injudicious consumption of water made this commodity scarce not only in India but in whole of the world. Since, the availability of fresh water is limited so it is of paramount importance that water resources are managed efficiently. The Twelfth Plan approach paper lays special emphasis on water management, yet there is no evidence of serious forethought on how the conflicts that emerged out of sharing of water resources can be sorted out. Just as a Bill on giving farmers a better deal in land acquisition awaits Parliament approval, an institutional framework must be created for water distribution that addresses the interests of all stakeholders—farmers, the urban population and industry. The model Bill on groundwater—the Groundwater (Protection, Conservation, Management and Regulation) Bill, 2011—gives us some leads. It accords top priority to livelihood needs, generally estimated at 70-150 liters per capita per day, and spells out the need to use water for livestock, fishing, irrigation, and power generation, industrial and recreational uses. Agriculture and industry can improve their water efficiency. Irrigation accounts for over three-fourths of all water used; there is scope to reduce water usage in crops such as rice and sugarcane, in particular by using better varieties. With appropriate water tariffs, industries will be persuaded to adopt water recycling and conservation practices. Likewise, municipal bodies can reassess water pricing for residential consumers to reduce wastage, while, however, ensuring that every person's needs are met. Conflicts over land and water may become disturbingly common if we do not develop the institutional framework and long-term policies to ensure their equitable distribution.

References

Central Water Commission (1993): "Water and Related Statistics, New Delhi: Statistical Directorate, Central Water Commission.

Charters, C. and Verma, S. (2010): Out of Water from Abundance to Scarcity and How to Solve The World Water Problems, FT Press (USA).

Chauhan, Shyam Sunder Singh (2003): "Water Resources Management", *Yojna*, Publication Division, Ministry of Information and Broadcasting, GOI, New Delhi, June.

GOI (2007): Report of Expert group on "Ground Water Management and Ownership Management", Planning Commission, New Delhi.

———, (2008): Eleventh Five Year Plan: 2007-12, Planning Commission,Vol. II, p. 44.

———, (2008): Eleventh Five Year Plan: 2007-12, Planning Commission, Vol. II, p. 51.

Hoekstra, A.Y. (2006): The Global Dimension of Water Governance: Nine Reasons for Global Arrangements in Order to Cope with Local Problems. *Value of Water Research Report Series,* No. 20, UNESCO.

Molden, D. (2007): (Ed.). *Water for Food, Water for Life: A Comprehensive Assessment of Water Management in Agriculture.* Earthscan/IWMI, 2007.

Shiklomenov and Rodda, (ed.) (2003): World Water Resources at the beginning of the 21st century/Scientific Leader and Editor, I.A. Shiklomanov, John, C. Rodda, Cambridge [England], New York : Cambridge University Press, 2003, xiv, 435 p. ill., maps ; 28 cm.

Chapter 4

Water Resources Development in India

Critical Issues and Strategic Options

LAKSHMI CHATTERJEE

INTRODUCTION

The abundant water resources in India are sufficient for the water supply in whole of India only if proper and efficient water supply management is adopted. The water infrastructure in India includes tapping of the available water sources by the water board and department in India, proper water treatment and purification, water storage facilities with regular cleaning of the water storage tanks, usage of water, crisis in water supply, water pollution, problems due to scarcity of water. Indian water policy for water conservation and water harvesting, etc.

The water sources in India include the vast oceans surrounding the Indian peninsula–Indian Ocean, Bay of Bengal and Arabian Sea, the inland rivers–both the Himalayan rivers and the rivers in the south, ground water and rain water available in plenty through the abundant monsoons in India. The problem area here is the water resources management, where India fails. The management of water resources and sources in India is the responsibility of the Ministry of Water Resources of India. It looks after the water management services in India, the issues and problems related to the water supply in India arrangement of abundant water supply facilities, methods all over India formulating the water supply policies and strategies for an equated supply and division of water resources of India.

Water is an important resource available for humans and fresh water is much more important given its limited availability and erratic distribution over space and time. The availability of fresh water per capita has come down in India from about 5,177 cubic meter per head in 1951 to 1,820 cubic meter per head in 2001 and it is expected to further go down to 1,140 by 2050 AD *(Sankarnarayan, 2005)*. The total water availability in India is 2,301 bcm, of which surface water accounts for 1,869 bcm and ground water accounts for 432 bcm. However, only 690 bcm of the surface water can be utilized through storage structures and ground water can be utilized only to the extent of its annual recharge.

OF all the planet's renewable resources, water has a unique place. It is essential for sustaining all forms of life, food production, economic development, and for general well being. It is impossible to substitute for most of its uses, difficult to de-pollute, expensive to transport, and it is truly a unique gift to mankind from nature. Water is also one of the most manageable of the natural resources as it is capable of diversion, transport, storage, and recycling. All these properties impart to water its great utility for human beings. The surface water and groundwater resources of the country play a major role in agriculture, hydropower generation, livestock production, industrial activities, forestry, fisheries, navigation, recreational activities, etc. According to National Water Policy, 2002 in the planning and operation of systems, water allocation priorities should be broadly as: (i) Drinking Water, (ii) Irrigation, (iii) Hydropower, (iv) Ecology, (v) Agro-Industries and Non-Agricultural Industries, and (vi) Navigation.

India receives annual precipitation of about 4000 km^3, including snowfall. Out of this, monsoon rainfall is of the order of 3000 km^3. India is gifted with a river system comprising more than 20 major rivers with several tributaries. Many of these rivers are perennial and some of these are seasonal. The rivers like Ganges, Brahmaputra and Indus originate from the Himalayas and carry water throughout the year. The snow and ice melt of the Himalayas and the base flow contribute the flows during the lean season.

Apart from the water available in the various rivers of the country, the groundwater is also an important source of water for drinking, irrigation, industrial uses, etc. It accounts for about 80 per cent of domestic water requirement and more than 45 per cent of the total irrigation in the country. As per the international norms, if per-capita water availability is less than 1700 m^3 per year then the country is categorized as water stressed and if it is less than 1000 m^3 per capita per year then the country is classified as water scarce. In India per capita surface water availability in the years 1991 and 2001 were 2309 and 1902 m^3 and these are projected to reduce to 1401 and 1191 m^3 by the years 2025 and 2050 respectively. Hence, there is a need for proper planning, development and management of the greatest assets of the country, viz. water and land resources for raising the standards of living of the millions of people, particularly in the rural areas.

Water supply and sanitation is a State subject in India and State/ Urban Local Bodies (ULBs) are vested with constitutional right for planning, designing, implementing, and operation and maintenance of water and sanitation projects. The Union Ministry provides technical assistance to States/ULBs in project formulation. National Water Policies provide guidelines on priority of allocation, methods of management, resource management and institutional issues, emerging approaches and trends. The National Water Policy, 2002 assigned overriding priority to drinking water in planning and operation of water resources.

STATUS OF WATER

The India Infrastructure Report (2004) mentions that in terms of water supply service India appears on par with the Asia-Pacific and South Asian countries.

Country	*Access to Water Supply (as %)*	*GDP per capita (US $)*
Philippines	87	3805
Sri Lanka	83	3279
China	75	3617
India	89	2248
Pakistan	88	1834
Bangladesh	97	1483

The service levels and quality are very poor, for example, the average water supply is just 2-4 hours a day. Moreover, in terms of absolute figures, only 36.86 million of the 53.69 urban households have tap water supply, of which 26.67 have in their premises, 8.08 million have outside their premises and 2.09 million have within 100 metres *(Sankarnarayan, 2005)*. Large metropolitan cities, in particular, are becoming critical areas due to increasing water demand for domestic consumption, which often competes with other uses of fresh water. Apart from the challenges of water availability, major attention needs to be paid to their management in the urban context i.e., achieving maximum gains within the constraints through efficient use of all resources *(Saleth and Dinar, 1997)*.

WATER RESOURCES OF INDIA

Although India occupies only 3.29 million km² geographical areas, which forms 2.4 per cent of the world's land area, it supports over 15 per cent of the world's population. The population of India as on 1 March 2001 stood at 1,027,015,247 persons. Thus, India supports about 1/6th of world population, 1/50th of world's land and 1/25th of world's water resources. India also has a livestock population of 500 million, which is about 20 per cent of the world's total livestock population. More than half of these are cattle, forming the backbone of Indian agriculture. The total utilizable water resources of the country are assessed as 1086 km³. The details of surface and groundwater water resources of India is given below in Table 1 and Table 2.

TABLE 1

Basin-wise Average Flow and Utilizable Water (in km³/year)

Sl. No.	*River basin*	*Average annual flow*	*Utilizable flow*
1.	Indus	73.31	46
2.	Ganga–Brahmaputra–Meghna Basin		
	(a) Ganga	525.02	250
	(b) Brahmaputra sub-basin	629.05	24
	(c) Meghna (Barak) sub-basin	48.36	
3.	Subarnarekha	12.37	6.81
4.	Brahmni–Baitarani	28.48	18.3
5.	Mahanadi	66.88	49.99
6.	Godavari	110.54	76.3

7.	Krishna	69.81	5
8.	Pennar	6.32	6.86
9.	Cauvery	21.36	19
10.	Tapi	14.88	14.5
11.	Narmada	45.64	34.5
12.	Mahi	11.02	3.1
13.	Sabarmati	3.81	1.93
14.	West-flowing rivers of Kachchh and Saurashtra including Luni	15.1	14.98
15.	West flowing rivers south of Tapi	200.94	36.21
16.	East-flowing rivers between Mahanadi and Godavari	17.08	
17.	East-flowing rivers between Godavari and Krishna	1.81	13.11
18.	East-flowing rivers between Krishna and Pennar	3.63	
19.	East-flowing rivers between Pennar and Cauvery	9.98	16.73
20.	East-flowing rivers south of Cauvery	6.48	
21.	Area of North Ladakh not draining into Indus	0	NA
22.	Rivers draining into Bangladesh	8.57	NA
23.	Rivers draining into Myanmar	22.43	NA
24.	Drainage areas of Andman, Nicobar and Lakshadweep Islands	0	NA
	Total (rounded)	1953	690

Source : Integrated water resources development—A plan for action, Report of The National Commission for Integrated Water Resources Development, Ministry of Water Resources, New Delhi, 1999.

Groundwater Resources

TABLE 2

Groundwater Resources of India (in km³/year)

1.	Total replenishable groundwater resource	432
2.	Provision for domestic, industrial and other uses	71
3.	Available groundwater resource for irrigation	361
4.	Utilizable groundwater resource for irrigation (90% of the sl. no. 3)	325
5.	Total utilizable groundwater resource (Sum of sl. nos 2 and 4)	396

TOTAL WATER REQUIREMENTS

Total annual requirement of water for various sectors has been estimated and its break up is given Table 3. With the increasing population as well as all round development in the country, the utilization of water has also been increasing at a fast pace. In 1951, the actual utilization of surface water was about 20 per cent and 10 per cent in the case of groundwater. The utilizable water in river basins is highly uneven. For example in the Brahmaputra basin, which contributes 629 billion m^3 of surface water of the country's total flow, only 24 billion m^3 is utilizable.

WATER SUPPLY IN INDIA

Continuous water supply is the requirement of every industry in India. India being a primarily agriculture based society requires huge amount of water sources for regular irrigation of the farms as the monsoons are not a reliable water source considering the vast geographical as well as climatic variation in India.

Also safe drinking water supply is another area where the government needs to emphasize more as groundwater is not an everlasting water resource: The water quality is tested at regular intervals and only if the water quality standards fulfil certain quality parameters, the water is certified to be safe for drinking.

NEED FOR REFORMS

In spite of the enormous challenge, water resource management in India, in general, in urban areas, in particular, is focused on the supply expansion, whereas a good scope exists for demand management and improving use efficiency, which means taking a balanced approach to water management *(Maheshwari and Pillai, 2001).* In reality, Indian cities are not fully geared-up for reforms as (i) they are highly top-driven and follow the old guiding principle of water development and supply expansion, (ii) they use irrational water pricing methods and inefficient tariff structures, (iii) they persist with ill-adequate organizations and systems and are yet to formulate their agenda in implementable terms. Service delivery organizations have to reform organizational design to be effective *(Rangachari, 2003).* This calls for wider range of reforms in urban water sector and a shift in focus.

TABLE 3

Annual Water Requirement for Different Uses (in km^3)

Use	*Year*									
	1997-98	*2010*			*2025*			*2050*		
		Low	*High*	%	*Low*	*High*	%	*Low*	*High*	%
(1)	*(2)*	*(3)*	*(4)*	*(5)*	*(6)*	*(7)*	*(8)*	*(9)*	*(10)*	*(11)*
Surface water										
Irrigation	318	330	339	48	325	366	43	375	463	39
Domestic	17	23	24	3	30	36	5	48	65	6
Industries	21	26	26	4	47	47	6	57	57	5
Power	7	14	15	2	25	26	3	50	56	5
Inland navigation		7	7	1	10	10	1	15	15	1
Environment-Ecology	5	5	1	10	10	1	20	20	2	
Evaporation losses	36	42	42	6	50	50	6	76	76	6
Total	399	447	458	65	497	545	65	641	752	64
Groundwater										
Irrigation	206	213	218	31	236	245	29	253	344	29
Domestic	13	19	19	2	25	26	3	42	46	4

(Contd.)

Table 3 (*Contd.*)

(1)	*(2)*	*(3)*	*(4)*	*(5)*	*(6)*	*(7)*	*(8)*	*(9)*	*(10)*	*(11)*
Industries	9	11	11	1	20	20	2	24	24	2
Power	2	4	4	1	6	7	1	13	14	1
Total	230	247	252	35	287	298	35	332	428	36
Grand total	629	694	710	100	784	843	100	973	1180	100
Total water use										
Irrigation	524	543	557	78	561	611	72	628	807	68
Domestic	30	42	43	6	55	62	7	90	111	9
Industries	30	37	37	5	67	67	8	81	81	7
Power	9	18	19	3	31	33	4	63	70	6
Inland navigation	0	7	7	1	10	10	1	15	15	1
Environment-Ecology	0	5	5	1	10	10	1	20	20	2
Evaporation losses	36	42	42	6	50	50	6	76	76	7
Total	629	694	710	100	784	843	100	973	1180	100

Source : Integrated water resources development—A plan for action, Report of The National Commission for Integrated Water Resources Development, Ministry of Water Resources, New Delhi, 1999.

From	*Towards*
Water resource development	Water resource management
Supply-oriented approach	Demand-driven approach
Disjoint water management	Conjunctive water management
Use maximization and extraction	Use efficiency and conservation
Treating water as social good	Treating water as economic and social good
Public sector management	Public-private partnerships
Public sector monopoly	Private sector participation
Top-down approach	Participatory approach
Centralised operations	Decentralised operations
Government responsibility	Stakeholder engagement

Source : World Bank (1999).

WATER CONSERVATION

Water conservation implies improving the availability of water through augmentation by means of storage of water in surface reservoirs, tanks, soil and groundwater zone. It emphasizes the need to modify the space and time availability of water to meet the demands. This concept also highlights the need for judicious use of water. There is a great potential for better conservation and management of water resources in its various uses. On the demand side, a variety of economic, administrative and community-based measures can help conserve water. Also, it is necessary to control the growth of population since large population is putting massive stress on all natural resources.

The Indian government provided the masses with adequate water supply but the management of the water supply systems wasn't undertaken efficiently this has resulted in deteriorating condition of the water supply network. Thus, majority is forced to pump out ground water to fulfil the water requirements that has in turn created a huge drop in the ground water levels. Thus, an effective strategy for water conservation is the need of the hour. The steps taken in this regard include water treatment plants, water pollution control so as to keep the water resources safe for other usage, careful scrutiny of water supply division and projects. The water supply department by adopting timely conservation methods can help solve the water shortage problem in India and deal with the ongoing water crisis in India.

RAIN WATER HARVESTING

Rain water harvesting can also provide a solution to the water crisis in India. Certain areas in India receive plenty rainfall and thus creating huge rain water harvesting water tanks can help is accumulation of natural water and then after some treatment can be utilized as a drinking water substitute.

Rain water harvesting is the process to capture and store rainfall for its efficient utilization and conservation to control its runoff, evaporation and seepage. Some of the benefits of rainwater harvesting are:

- It increases water availability.
- It checks the declining water table.
- It is environmentally friendly.
- It improves the quality of groundwater through dilution, mainly of fluoride, nitrate, and salinity.
- It prevents soil erosion and flooding, especially in the urban areas.

Since agriculture accounts for about 69 per cent of all water withdrawn, the greatest potential for conservation lies in increasing irrigation efficiencies. Just a 10 per cent improvement in irrigation efficiency could conserve enough water to double the amount available for drinking. In India, sprinkler irrigation is being adopted in Haryana, Rajasthan, Uttar Pradesh, Karnataka, Gujarat and Maharashtra. The use of sprinkler irrigation saves about 56 per cent of water for the winter crops of bajra and jowar, while for cotton, the saving is about 30 per cent as compared to the traditional gravity irrigation. An important supplement to conservation is to minimize the wastage of water. In urban water supply, for example, almost 30 per cent of the water is wasted due to leakages, carelessness, etc. while most metro cities face deficit in supply of water. It is, therefore, imperative to prevent wastage. In industries also, there is a scope for economy in the use of water. Prices of water for all uses should be fixed, keeping in mind its economic value, control of wastage, and the ability of users to pay. As water is becoming scarcer, pricing will be an important factor in avoiding wastage and ensuring optimal use.

WATER PURIFICATION INDUSTRY

Large-scale water treatment is being undertaken so as to utilize the existing water resources to an optimum level. Water purification has become an industry in itself. The water purification industry in India deals in improving water quality standards of drinking water, management and treatment of ground water, bottling of mineral water available in various parts of the country and providing this bottled water throughout India as a safe drinking water solution. The major water treatment plants owners and water treatment companies in India products in the bottled water industry include Kinley, Bisleri, Aquafina, and Kingfisher, etc.

WATER RESERVOIR DAMS AND PROJECTS

As a solution to the water crisis in India, the government took up building of huge dams and water reservoirs that provided multiple solutions. The dams build on various rivers provided safety against the floods that used to frequent these rivers, effective use of natural water resource, providing irrigation facilities to the surrounding field and farms and also in the production of hydroelectricity.

The major dams and water reservoir in India include :

- Nagarjuna Sagar Dam, Andhra Pradesh
- Sardar Sarover Project build on river Narmada, Gujarat
- Bhakra Nangal Dam build on river Sutlej, Himachal Pradesh
- Gobind Sagar and Maharana Pratap Sagar Dam, Himachal Pradesh
- Krishna Raja Sagara Dam on Cauvery River, Karnataka
- Tunga Bhadra Dam
- Neyyar Dam, Kerala
- Narmada Dam project, Madhya Pradesh
- Hirakund Dam build on Mahanadi River, Orissa
- Farakka Barrage.

WATER DEMAND REDUCTION AND MANAGEMENT MEASURES

The demand or water use reduction measures conserve the existing limited water supply through the practices which require less water and reduce wastage and misuse of water. These measures are directed towards making the existing inadequate supply, whatever it may be, serve water users as effectively as possible and a balance between supply and demand is achieved. Thus, the fundamental nature of these measures is their effectiveness in accomplishing a temporary allocation of the limited supply in a manner which serves the users to bridge the gap between supply and demand. The various techniques used for the purpose are based either on giving economic incentives or penalties or involve rationing, legal sanctions and various other types of social or political pressures. These may be based on strategies that include legal restrictions, economic incentives and issuance of public appeals.

Legal Restrictions on Water Use

One of the active strategies could include provisions of legal restrictions on use of water, mainly during the period of scarcity. In India a national water policy 2002 has been adopted, which includes policy directions for development and management of water resources. Also, provision of legal restrictions on proper utilization of groundwater resources has been advocated at various fora in the country. In fact, Gujarat has already enacted such legislation and other states may also follow the suit. However, provision of legal restrictions should be carefully thought of and need mobilization of qualified water specialists to explore effective solutions. The legal strategies so adopted should be such which can be implemented with minimum probability of being rendered ineffective by injunctions and law suits.

Land Use Planning and Cropping Pattern

Another strategy that could be adopted refers to planning of land use especially in new land developments. Areas where water supply priorities are low can be planted with drought-resistant varieties of trees. For this purpose, these variety of trees need to be developed. Another strategy that could be suggested can be in the agricultural sector.

The selection of cropping pattern as per availability of water will reduce adverse impacts of drought on potential water consuming crops.

Demand Management for Urban Areas and Industries

Demand management for urban areas and industries is another strategy which could be adopted to reduce demands in urban water supply or households and industries. However, before taking such measures it is necessary to study the actual savings the measures will result in based on practical data. Such information will help in planning curtailment of household demand during drought periods. Similarly, another strategy is to go for demand reduction approaches in the industry during periods of scarcity. Apart from ensuring leakage control, water technology to ensure efficient use of cooling and process water and necessary pollution control mechanisms. A sound water budgeting in industry can reduce the water demand to a considerable extent. The water conservation and reuse strategies should be planned at the time of setting up of a new industry to build in the conservation and reuse requirements from the beginning. Studies are required to develop production functions relating industrial policies to (i) availability of resource inputs like water, energy, etc., (ii) technology of production, (iii) waste water discharge constraint, etc. for devising measures of reducing water demands in the industry.

People Participation and Capacity Building

For making the people of various sections of the society aware about the different issues of water resources management, a participatory approach may be adopted. Mass communication programmes may be launched using the modern communication means for educating the people about water conservation and efficient utilization of water. Capacity building should be perceived as the process whereby a community equips itself to become an active and well-informed partner in decision-making. The process of capacity building must be aimed at both increasing access to water resources and changing the power relationships between the stakeholders. Capacity building is not only limited to officials and technicians but must also include the general awareness of the local population regarding their responsibilities in sustainable management of the water resources. Policy decisions in any water resources project should be directed to improve knowledge, attitude and practices about the linkages between health and hygiene, provide higher water supply service levels and to improve environment through safe disposal of human waste. Sustainable management of water requires decentralized decisions by giving authority, responsibility and financial support to communities to manage their natural resources and thereby protect the environment.

WATER MANAGEMENT POLICIES OF GOI

The Government of India (GOI) has formed various water management systems and authorities in India. These include Central Water Commission, Central Ground Water Board, National Water Development Agency, National Projects Construction Corporation Ltd., etc. for efficient water resources management. The Policies thus formulated include Irrigation Management Policy, National Policy Guidelines to allocate water resources like rivers flowing through multiple states, National Commission for Integrated Water Resources Development Plan, Water Information Bill, River Basin Organization Policy, and many more. Various water reservoir projects were also taken up by the Ministry of Water Resources like construction and management of dams on various rivers.

NATIONAL WATER POLICY: 1987 AND 2002

The National Water Policy adopted by the Indian National Water Resources Council recognizes that water is a scarce and precious resource and thereby outlines the broad principles that govern the management of the country's water resources.

The broad goals of the policy are:

(1) Establish a well-developed information system for water related data at national/state level to ensure appropriate resource planning.

(2) Effective water resources planning by encouraging non-conventional methods of water use such as in inter-basin water transfers, artificial recharge of aquifers and desalinization of brackish water, as well as traditional water conservation practices like rain water harvesting and incorporating quantity and quality aspects as well as environmental considerations.

(3) Develop and manage water resources by reorienting existing institutions and creating new ones wherever necessary.

(4) Establishing water allocation priorities as: first, drinking water, second, irrigation, third, hydropower, fourth, ecology, fifth, industries, sixth, navigation and then other uses.

(5) Preserving quality of environment and ecological balance implementing and operating a water resource project.

(6) Groundwater development.
(7) Fixing water charges in such a way that they cover at least the maintenance and operation costs of providing the service initially, and a part of the capital costs subsequently.
(8) Ensuring treatment of effluents before discharging into natural streams.
(9) Promoting water conservation consciousness through education, regulation, incentives and disincentives.

The first National Water Policy was adopted in September, 1987. However, very little has been achieved in the fulfilment of the objectives laid down in the first policy. Hence, there was a need to revise the National Water Policy of 1987 and a new policy was thus adopted in 2002 with a few more provisions (GOI, 1987; 2002).

The National Water Policy-2002 stresses participatory approach in water resources management. It has been recognized that participation of beneficiaries will help greatly for the optimal upkeep of irrigation system and utilization of irrigation water. Since water is provided very cheaply or even free of charge by public water utilities, users do not feel the urge to use water as a resource economically. The new policy however fails to deal with this aspect and does not provide any guidance for pricing of water for various uses.

11th Five Year Plan Focus

The 11th Five Year Plan (2007-12) lays down provisions for efficient management of water resources in the country. These are as follows (GOI, 2006):

(i) With efficient management of resources three major projects, namely, Mahi, Bisalpur and Ratanpura distributory, four medium projects, Panachana, Chaapi, Chauli, Bethali and 139 minor irrigation projects are likely to be completed by the end of Tenth Five Year Plan, which would create additional irrigation potential of 299.16 thousand hectare;
(ii) The *Jal Abhiyan Programme* was launched in December 2005 for mass awareness among the stakeholders about scarcity of water, method for recharging of ground water, management of surface and ground water for efficient utilization, which covered about 20,000 villages, developed

1 lakh water harvesting structures and revamped canal system;

(iii) Focus on water harvesting structures and improving water use efficiency through better maintenance of irrigation system and promoting efficiency through drip/sprinklers;

(iv) State Water Policy is under consideration with main objective of utilizing all available water resources, (surface and groundwater), in a judicious, equitable and economic manner;

(v) *Water Users' Associations* are being formed for maintenance, distribution and revenue collection;

(vi) *Rural infrastructure*: The *Bharat Nirman Programme* launched in 2005 identifies seven major areas where infrastructure gaps need to be addressed. The programme currently extends into initial two years of the 11th Plan. Bharat Nirman is a time-bound business plan for action in rural infrastructure over the four year period (2005-09). Under Bharat Nirman, action is proposed in the areas of irrigation (to create 10 million hectares of additional irrigation capacity), rural roads, rural housing, rural water supply, rural electrification and rural telecommunication connectivity.

The main objectives of the XI Plan, as pointed out in the MoWR working group report (GOI, 2006) are: (a) Creation of additional potential of around 16 mha; (b) Reducing gap between Potential created and its utilization; (c) Mitigation of flood damages; and (d) Promotion of mass awareness on water-related issues. In order to achieve these objectives, the group recommends a few strategies viz., completion of ongoing irrigation projects and extension, renovation and modernisation of old schemes; improvement in the efficiency of irrigation system; Command Area Development and Water Management; Participatory Irrigation Management; sustainable groundwater development and management; research and development activities on priority areas; establishment of River Basin Organizations; information, education and communication for mass awareness. The plan emphasizes the creation of irrigation potentials and thereby highlights the need to close the gap between irrigation potential created and irrigation potential utilized so as to ensure effective 'development' and 'management'.

Some of the other important suggestions of the Working Group (GOI, 2006) are:

(1) Creation of more storage is absolutely essential for future requirements. The State Governments could be provided with incentives for creation of additional storage, if necessary. Extension, restoration and modernisation projects should be given due priority where the eroded potential can be restored with moderate expenditure.

(2) A separate plan fund may be provided as irrigation maintenance fund.

(3) There is need to reorient the approach from groundwater development to management and a comprehensive act for regulation of groundwater development on sustainable basis. Artificial recharge to ground water and rain water harvesting should be implemented in identified areas through participatory approach.

(4) Incentives may be provided for activities of WUAs. The WUAs should include women members from land owning house holds in the command area, irrespective of their ownership of land.

(5) State Governments may institute Water Regulatory Authorities for fixing water rates.

(6) While undertaking construction of dams, adequate flood cushion may be provided in reservoirs. If required, the Central Government may provide necessary support for the same.

(7) Projects on interlinking of rivers should be expedited.

(8) Training and capacity building scheme for State/Central Government officials may be made comprehensively.

WATER RESOURCES MANAGEMENT IN INDIA

In view of the existing status of water resources and increasing demands of water for meeting the requirements of the rapidly growing population of the country as well as the problems that are likely to arise in future, a holistic, well planned long-term strategy is needed for sustainable water resources management in India. The water resources management practices may be based on increasing the water supply and managing the water demand under the stressed water availability conditions. Data monitoring, processing, storage, retrieval and dissemination constitute the very important aspects of the water resources management. These data may be utilized not only for management but also for the planning and design of the water resources structures. In addition to these, now a days decision support systems are being developed for providing the necessary inputs to the decision-makers for water resources management. Also, knowledge sharing, people's participation, mass communication and capacity building are essential for effective water resources management.

Given the central need is to introduce comprehensive measures to handle urban water resources issues in India, the following needs and options shall be explored in terms of the intervention areas like—

Policy, Legislative and Regulatory Framework

The constitutional provisions and water legislation in India do not provide appropriate framework for tackling water issues across jurisdictions, between sectors as well as individuals. The current set-up has following short-comings: (a) water has been delegated as state subject but water resource issues cross these boundaries, (b) surface water rights are ill-defined, unsecure and non-transferable leaving little scope for their utilization, whereas ground water rights are purely private causing environmental damages, and (c) environmental laws have not been comprehensively operationalised and regulatory standards are either not enforced or do not exist.

Institutional Arrangements and Mechanisms

The current institutional arrangements for water resource management do not enable comprehensive water allocation, planning and management. The main problems are (World Bank, 1999):

(i) Inadequacies in necessary institutions for comprehensive water allocation, planning and management at city, basin and state levels, which are frequently absent
(ii) Lack of coordination between the institutions; duplication of responsibility and accountability gaps.
(iii) Inadequate fostering of grass-root institutions.
(iv) Lack of involvement of civil society-local community, NGOs, private sector and academia.

ECONOMIC AND FINANCIAL INCENTIVES AND MECHANISMS

The current incentive structure of water resource management leaves little scope for efficient use of water and its allocation between the sectors and users in an economically efficient manner. *Bagchi (2003)* clearly notes that cost recovery of water supply in major cities is far less from satisfactory. Inappropriate pricing, lack of well designed tariffs and absence of metering all lead to wastage of water and make the water services delivery to the risks of poor maintenance due to inadequate recovery of financial costs.

Information, Technology and Database Systems

There is a great scope for improvement on these fronts, given the large gaps in these areas of water systems. The water losses at plants, during conveyance and distribution are very high to the tune of almost 30-50 per cent in many urban water systems. Database management and technology upgradation are not undertaken periodically and any type of audit is not prevalent. Metering, billing and pipeline flow inspection are not well executed and management structures are largely absent.

WATER SERVICES GOVERNANCE

However, apart from improving water allocation and management efficiency of water sector through reform process, it is also to undertake the reforms in the service delivery, wherein the potential is also very high due to the much closer interface with public. The major areas of reform in service delivery include:

Governance and Management

Urban water governance is highly skewed towards bureaucratic or departmental functioning without much involvement of all stakeholders. Even in the current design, the institutional arrangements are weak and the management organization lacks incentives for giving better outputs. Most of the water supply functions are catered by the public health engineering, municipal water works and public works departments with little coordination among them. The organizational structures do not encourage efficiency and outputs, but reward positions based on the tenure and past experience. It is therefore geared towards serving the needs of public/departmental services rather than catering to the needs of the customers/citizens. Moreover, decentralized governance principles are yet to be followed i.e., citizen group empowerment, local level access and community/public involvement.

Organizational Design and Focus

The organizational design is hierarchical, which is mostly the case of large public organizations, and not suited to a customer-focused service delivery. The departments within the organization confine to the functions but their integration is a real challenge to the senior management. The technical staff members (engineers) are promoted based on their tenure but not outcomes; the service staff is assigned jurisdictions but its accountability is often poor. The focus of the organization has also to shift from that driven by supply expansion and bureaucratic style of functioning to that driven by customers' demand and service-oriented functioning, which requires appropriate organizational design *(Rangachari, 2003).*

Information/Database Management and Deployment of Technology

Most of the water supply entities lack good management information systems (MIS) of their organization. The data generation methods and recoring are poor, data formats are not well designed, record maintenance and retrieval is done in a haphazard manner. The result is poor capacity of the organization to understand its own business and run it in an efficient manner. Not only that there is potential for automation of operations but also restructuring the organization and management structures. For this to be effective and to enhance the capacity to monitor water resources—both quantity and quality-deployment of new technologies is very necessary.

Economic Incentives and Accounting Systems

The current structure of water tariffs do not provide any economic incentives in terms of recovering costs—both operation and maintenance and depreciation of capital—in the urban areas; rather, they provide incentives for over consumption and inefficient use while not reflecting the scarce conditions of water availability. Further, most of the water supply organizations face financial constraints as their business is not completely run on the revenues, especially when it comes to the capital works this is a major constraint. It is therefore imperative that they become more proactive and borrow finances from private sector to provide adequate returns. Water accounting needs to be separated from general pool and it should be based on the double entry or fund-based accounting systems.

CONCLUSION

The paper presents availability and demands of water resources in India as well as describes the various issues and strategies for developing a holistic approach for sustainable development and management of the water resources of the country. It also highlights integration for sustainable management of the water resources for meeting the demands of the present, without compromising the needs of the future generations.

References

Bagchi, Soumen (2003), 'Pricing and Cost Recovery of Urban Services: Issues in the Context of Decentralized Urban Governance in India', *International Journal of Regulation and Governance,* 3(2): 103-34.

Maheshwari, G.C. and Pillai, B.R.K. (2001), 'The Water Crisis in India: Need for a Balanced Management Approach', *International Journal of Regulation and Governance,* I(2): 159-79.

Rangachari, C.S. (2003), 'Organisational Design for Service Delivery', *CGG Working Papers: Volume 2*, pp. 38-64, Centre for Good Governance, Hyderabad.

Saleth, R.M. and Dinar, A. (1997), 'Satisfying Urban Thirst: Water Supply Augmentation and Pricing Policy in Hyderabad City, India', *World Bank Technical Paper No. 395*, The World Bank, Washington DC.

Sankarnarayan, K. (2005), 'Urban Water Supply—Challenges Ahead', Presentation made in the XII World Water Congress of the International Water Resources Association held on November 25-26, 2005.

The World Bank (1999), *Initiating and Sustaining Water Sector Reforms: A Synthesis*, Published by Allied Publishers Limited, New Delhi for The World Bank, Washington DC.

Inter-basin Transfer of Water in India—Prospects and Problems Water Management Forum (2003), The Institution of Engineers (India), New Delhi.

National Water Policy (2002), Ministry of Water Resources, New Delhi.

Padma, T.V., India Unveils New Moonsoon Forecast Model, *Sources*: Sci. Dev. Net, http://www.clivar.org/recent/moonsoo_force2.htm.

Groundwater Resources of India (1995), Central Groundwater Board, New Delhi.

Chapter 5

Impact Evaluation of Revised National Watershed Development Projects for Rainfed Areas (NWDPRA) in Bihar

RANJAN KUMAR SINHA, BASANT KUMAR JHA AND SHAMBHU DEO MISHRA

India has looked to watershed development as a way to realize its hopes for agricultural development in rainfed and semi-arid areas. These areas were bypassed by the Green Revolution and have experienced little or no growth in agricultural production for several decades. By capturing scarce water resources and improving the management of soil and vegetation, watershed development has the potential to create conditions conducive to higher agricultural productivity, while conserving natural resources. Virtually three main government ministries are in-charge of watershed development programme i.e., Ministry of Agriculture, Ministry of Rural Development, and Ministry of Environment & Forest. The Ministry of Agriculture (MoA) has worked in watershed development since 1960s. In 2000, watershed development project has been thoroughly restructured. The revised programme undertaken by the MoA is popularly known as NWDPRA envisaged as WARSA JAN

SAHBHAGITA. This paper is based an evaluative study on NWDPRA in Bihar conducted in four districts viz., Nawada (I), Kaimur (II), Aurangabad (III), and; Rohtas (IV) comprising a total sample of 320 village households. The impact of the project has been assessed on land use, irrigation, area and production of the crop, cost of cultivation, disposal of produce, income, livestock holdings, quality of life and overall impact. The analysis finds that the IRR of the project is up to 202 per cent, which clearly reveals that the project is beneficial but the problem of sustainability continues. The beneficiaries were found passive recipients rather than active contributors. To make the programme success some emerging issues have been raised and thereof recommendations are given, which need due attention.

BACKGROUND

The Green Revolution that transformed agriculture elsewhere in India had little impact on rainfed agriculture where agricultural productivity is low, natural resources are degraded, and the people are poor. It is one of the reasons of poverty. A vast majority of the rural poor depend on these degraded natural resources for their livelihood. These areas are characterized by a large human and cattle population, which are continuously putting heavy pressure on the already fragil natural resource-base for food, fodder and fuel. A scientific natural resource management approach was needed to improve the vegetative cover and groundwater potential of these areas, while at the same time involving the rural poor in planning, implementing and managing the resource-base. Accordingly, following the recommendation of the Hanumantha Rao Committee, at watershed approach was adopted from 1995. The Ministry of Agriculture (MoA), Ministry of Rural Development (MoRD) and Ministry of Environment and Forest (MoEF) along with their respective departments in the state are the three main government ministries in-charge of watershed development programmes in the country. Each programme focuses on different aspects and activities within the ministry's development criteria.

The Ministry of Agriculture has worked in watershed development since 1960s. The largest project in terms of scope and extent is the National Watershed Development Project for Rainfed Areas (NWDPRA) being implemented by Ministry of Agriculture. The broad objectives of the NWDPRA are as follows:

- Conservation, development and sustainable management of natural resources including their use.
- Enhancement of agricultural productivity and production in a sustainable manner.
- Restoration of ecological balance in the degraded and fragile rainfed eco-systems by greening these areas through appropriate mix of trees, shrubs and grasses.
- Reduction in regional disparity between irrigated and rainfed areas.
- Creation of sustained employment opportunities for the rural community including the landless.

REVIEW OF LITERATURE

The literature on watershed development is growing rapidly but most of it is confined to qualitative descriptions of success stories. The few quantitative studies available tend to be based on a small number of heavily supervised projects, with no information about long term effects. At the same time the vast majority of projects were never evaluated, and there were good reasons to suspect that most of them had little impact (Kern & Singh, 1992). Watershed projects have become wide-spread in rainfed areas in recent years, with a current annual budget that exceeds US $ 500 million (Farrington, Turton & James, 1999). A study (Sastry *et. al.*; 2002) in Kupan area of Chittor district of Andhra Pradesh revealed that many water harvesting structures such as check dam cascades, percolation tanks and farms/ sunken ponds were constructed to augment water resources in addition to canopy development. Thus, groundwater recharge has increased tremendously. Non-land-based activities were supported in watershed programme village with some support had a set back after withdrawal of watershed programme. However, there are some activities that have been continuing even today (Reddy *et. al.*, 2002). Sastry *et. al.* (2003) found that the sustainability of agriculture is possible by harvesting rain water and improving the groundwater. A study conducted by Policy and Development Initiatives (2001) indicated that the employment benefit is the most favourable impact of the watershed programme. Benefits accrued from the watershed development strengthened the livelihood of the village community. In addition to this, the watershed programme intervention created a spirit of collectivization of resources among the villagers (Mishra, 2007). A watershed changed whole eco-system and socio-economic scenario in a village of Hassan district of Karnataka (Kakade *et. al*, 2001). There is no separation of the terms watershed development and livelihood intervention because the watersheds as the bio-physical environment are the basis of livelihoods for all villagers (felix.gnetem@ideamail.ch). A study in Kanpur Dehat district of Uttar Pradesh found that implementation of watershed development project has resulted in area expansion, increase in livestock population and improvement in crop productivity (Babu *et. al.*; 2004). Ameja & Khara (2005) concluded that watershed development can be the most effective approach in not only mitigating the effects environmental crisis but also in increasing the employment opportunities.

But it is important to examine the weaknesses so that the programme achieves its objectives and the nation gets full value of time, money and priority (Seth, 2000). Development is understood in terms of how the whole village or area can best support itself with the resources it already has (ifpri.org, 2001). Mishra & Mishra (2009) found that watershed management suffers from major constraints like lack of funds, insufficient manpower, poor co-ordination, low mobility, etc. Mishra (2009) said that its inclusive development strategy has broadened the scope of the watershed development programme as an intervention to improve the living standard of the tribal households of Koraput district in Orissa. But Planning Commission's Working Group of Natural Resource Management (NRM)-2007 noted that in spite of spending about US $ 4500 million for watershed development in the rainfed region, the results are invisible and treated areas have reverted to their original status, thus development processes require a through examination. Hence, a situation specific assessment needs to be done at the regular intervals.

OBJECTIVE AND METHODOLOGY

The basic objective of the paper is to assess the impact of the programme and prescribe suitable policy implications. The paper is based on an empirical study conducted by the Agro-Economic Research Centre for Bihar and Jharkhand, T.M. Bhagalpur University, Bhagalpur (Bihar). The primary data was collected from various units through canvassing structured schedules viz., village schedule and household's schedule. The village schedule was administered in micro-watersheds village and the household schedule amongst the beneficiaries and non-beneficiaries of the programme comprising a total sample of 320 village households. The sample was drawn on the basis of a multistage stratified sampling method. In the first stage four districts were selected on the basis of larger physical and financial achievements under the projects/schemes. These districts are Nawada (WS-I), Kaimur (WS-II), Aurangabad (WS-III), and Rohtas (WS-IV). In the second stage one micro-watershed from each of the selected districts was selected on the basis of the same criteria. Thereafter lists of beneficiaries and non-beneficiaries from each of the selected watershed areas/villages were prepared and classified in 5 categories of households viz., landless, marginal (1 ha.), small (1-2 ha.), medium (2-4 ha.) and large (4 ha. and above). A total of 40 households each from beneficiary and non-beneficiary groups in each selected watershed areas were randomly selected without replacement. Thus, 80 households formed the size of sample in each district, which taken together accounted for 320 households in total. The reference periods are 2001-02 (before) and 2006-07 (after) respectively.

IMPACT OF THE PROGRAMME

In Bihar, the work activities commenced in 2002-03 and completed in 2006-07. Land and water resource development activities constitute the primary areas of intervention. The expenditure (Table 1) on management constitutes about 18.38 per cent whereas

TABLE 1

Allocation of Funds in Different Components of the Project (2002-07)

Sl. No. Particulars	*Rs. (In Lakh)*	*% of Exp.*
A. Management Component	246.36	18.38
B. Development Component		
I. Natural Resource Management		
a. Arable Land		
(i) Soil and moisture conservation activities	97.472	7.27
(ii) Contour bunding/field building executed	—	—
(iii) Agronomic conservation practices	46.272	3.45
(iv) Others	30.67	2.29
b. Non-Arable		
(i) Run-off management structures/ Check Dams	40.00	2.98

(ii) Water harvesting structures/SDD	87.40	6.53
(iii) Dry land horticulture	88.528	6.60
(iv) Conservation and development of biomass	63.885	4.77
(v) Others	32.212	2.40
c. Drainage Lines		
(i) Upper reaches	49.372	3.68
(ii) Middle reaches	51.575	3.85
(iii) Lower reaches	108.722	8.12
Total	696.108	51.94
II. Farm Production system for land owning families		
a. Establishment of nurseries and production of seedlings	44.95	3.35
b. Testing and demonstration of new technologies/demonstration	90.95	6.78
c. Diversification of production system	60.787	4.54
d. Adoption of proven technologies (organic farming, use of bio-fertilizers, integrated pest management, on-farm management, development of micro-irrigation system, etc.)	53.547	4.00
e. Livestock management	25.67	1.91
f. Others	—	—
Total	275.904	20.58
III. Livelihood Support system for landless families		
a. Household production system	24.758	1.85
b. Bio-mass-based rural industry activities	25.083	1.87
c. Dairy, sericulture, goat breeding, beekeeping, mushroom cultivation, commercial poultry, etc.	27.731	2.07
d. Livestock management	23.558	1.76
e. Others	20.778	1.55
Total	121.908	9.10
Sub-total – B	1093.92	81.62
Grand total (A+B)	1340.28	100.00

Source : Directorate of Soil Conservation, Bihar, Patna.

81.62 per cent incurred on development components, which includes resource management (51.64%), farm production system for land owning families (20.58%) and livelihood support system for landless families (9.10%).

Land Use

In WS-I, the area under private wasteland decreased by 16.67 per cent indicating development of waste lands by way of plantation, etc. the benefits from which would also be available to the non-landholders. Similarly in WS-II, the area under Government wasteland and private wasteland decreased by 15.00 per cent and 22.00 per cent respectively, which reveals that community as well as private plantations have also been made in the area. In WS-III and IV, decrease in Government and private wasteland by 21.92 per cent and 21.43 per cent and 31.44 per cent respectively have been found, clearly indicating increase in community and private plantations (Table 2).

Irrigation Development

The change in irrigational status of agricultural land in 2006-07 over 2001-02 of the watershed indicated marginal increase in irrigated area in all the selected watersheds and almost in all the crop seasons, which may be due to increase in number of water harvesting structures (tanks, check dams, ponds, etc.). The increase was mainly found on big farms, which showed that perceived benefits are concentrated on large farms. Of course, it is not a new concern. In fact, it needs group owned water harvesting structures in real sense rather jointly owned by own relatives/neighbours or raiyets. The approach to sharing the benefits of water harvesting structure among the resource poor farmers is to develop well, which has been found important sources of irrigation (Table 3).

AREA AND PRODUCTION OF THE CROP

The land development and creation of new water harvesting structures in all the watershed areas have not much effectively brought some additional areas under the important crops both in kharif and rabi. The data indicate that there is increase in the area under paddy crops from 0.64 per cent to 4.37 per cent, maize 0.65 per cent to 3.37 per cent, pulses 0.99 per cent to 2.08 per cent and oilseeds up to 1.85 per cent. Of course, there is increase in area of important crops but it is not much appreciable. It is worth to mention here that

TABLE 2

Information Regarding Land of the Villages under Selected Watersheds

Nature of land	*Watershed – I (Nawada Dist.)*			*Watershed – II (Kaimur Dist.)*			*Watershed – III (Aurangabad Dist.)*			*Watershed – IV (Rohtas Dist.)*		
	Area in ha.		*% change in area*	*Area in ha.*		*% change in area*	*Area in ha.*		*% change in area*	*Area in ha.*		*% change in area*
	2001-02	*2006-07*		*2001-02*	*2006-07*		*2001-02*	*2006-07*		*2001-02*	*2006-07*	
(1)	*(2)*	*(3)*	*(4)*	*(5)*	*(6)*	*(7)*	*(8)*	*(9)*	*(10)*	*(11)*	*(12)*	*(13)*
Govt. wasteland	20	20	0.00	10.00	8.50	-15.00	–	–	–	12.79	10.05	-21.43
Private wasteland	06	05	-16.67	2.25	1.75	-22.22	64.04	50.00	-21.92	10.21	7.00	-31.44
Forest land	100	100	00.00	73.10	74.95	2.23	–	–	–	24.50	26.50	8.16
Agricultural land	417	417	00.00	432.50	432.65	0.035	442.96	443.25	0.065	493.00	494.79	0.36
Others if any	17	18	5.00	3.15	3.15	–	–	–	–	03.50	3.50	00.00
Total	560	560	00.00	521.00	521.00	00.00	507.00	493.25	-2.71	544.00	541.84	-0.39

Source : Field Survey.

TABLE 3

Information Regarding Gross Irrigated Area by Sources of the Villages under Selected Watersheds

Sl. No. Type of sources	Watershed – I (Nawada Dist.)			Watershed – II (Kaimur Dist.)			Watershed – III (Aurangabad Dist.)			Watershed – IV (Rohtas Dist.)		
	Area in ha.		% change in area	Area in ha.		% change in area	Area in ha.		% change in area	Area in ha.		% change in area
	2001-02	2006-07		2001-02	2006-07		2001-02	2006-07		2001-02	2006-07	
(1)	(2)	(3)	(4)	(5)	(6)	(7)	(8)	(9)	(10)	(11)	(12)	(13)
A. Irrigated land (Govt.)												
Tank	103.20	103.20	0.00	42.50	42.65	0.35	49.60	49.95	0.71	40.10	42.00	4.74
Tube-well	—	—	—	—	—	—	—	—	—	—	—	—
Well	12.80	13.05	1.95	8.15	9.05	11.04	21.70	23.05	6.22	28.70	30.10	4.88
Others	74.96	76.15	1.59	26.00	29.22	12.38	67.30	67.65	0.52	45.38	47.60	4.89
Total	190.96	192.40	0.75	76.65	80.92	5.57	138.60	140.65	1.48	114.18	119.70	4.83
B. Irrigated land (Pvt.)												
Tank	30.12	30.40	1.00	67.15	70.50	4.99	72.40	78.40	8.29	88.25	88.47	0.25
Tube-well	28.40	24.70	(-)13.03	—	—	—	—	—	—	—	—	—
Well	7.15	10.50	46.85	18.20	20.07	10.27	32.15	38.09	18.48	23.70	25.45	1.75
Others	33.08	35.70	7.92	103.09	100.50	(-) 02.51	86.87	74.87	(-) 13.81	121.44	123.15	1.41
Total	98.75	101.30	2.58	188.44	191.07	1.39	191.42	191.36	(-) 0.03	233.39	237.07	1.58

Source : Field Survey.

TABLE 4

Information Regarding Important Crop Cultivated Area (in ha.) of the Sample Farmers under Selected Watersheds

Sl. No. Name of the Crop	Watershed – I (Nawada Dist.)			Watershed – II (Kaimur Dist.)			Watershed – III (Aurangabad Dist.)			Watershed – IV (Rohtas Dist.)		
	Cultivated Area in ha.		% change in area	Cultivated Area in ha.		% change in area	Cultivated Area in ha.		% change in area	Cultivated Area in ha.		% change in area
	2001-02	2006-07		2001-02	2006-07		2001-02	2006-07		2001-02	2006-07	
(1)	(2)	(3)	(4)	(5)	(6)	(7)	(8)	(9)	(10)	(11)	(12)	(13)
Beneficiary												
1. Paddy	78.25	78.75	0.64	68.55	71.55	4.37	85.00	86.55	1.82	87.00	89.17	2.49
2. Wheat	22.00	22.17	0.77	15.10	15.28	1.19	17.00	18.10	6.47	17.40	17.83	2.47
3. Maize	13.78	13.88	0.72	08.00	08.27	3.37	12.20	12.28	0.65	10.22	10.52	2.93
4. Pulses	09.12	09.22	1.10	10.05	10.15	0.99	12.00	12.25	2.08	11.25	11.38	1.15
5. Oilseeds	05.00	05.00	–	06.10	06.10	–	07.00	07.10	1.42	8.10	08.25	1.85
All	128.15	129.02	0.68	107.80	111.35	3.55	133.20	136.28	3.08	133.97	137.15	2.37

(Contd.)

TABLE 4 (*Contd.*)

(1)	(2)	(3)	(4)	(5)	(6)	(7)	(8)	(9)	(10)	(11)	(12)	(13)
Non-Beneficiary												
1. Paddy	62.78	62.80	0.03	55.25	56.28	1.86	70.82	70.99	0.24	71.82	72.48	0.92
2. Wheat	11.30	11.30	—	12.00	12.20	1.67	14.00	14.16	1.14	14.64	14.75	0.75
3. Maize	07.00	07.15	2.14	05.10	05.20	1.96	05.54	05.70	2.89	06.72	06.78	0.89
4. Pulses	09.25	09.25	—	02.65	02.72	2.64	03.19	03.21	0.62	04.10	04.14	0.98
5. Oilseeds	01.00	01.00	—	01.75	01.75	—	02.10	02.12	0.95	02.00	02.04	2.00
All	91.33	91.50	0.19	76.75	78.15	1.82	95.65	96.18	0.55	99.28	100.19	0.92

almost similar increase has been indicated by the non-beneficiary respondents.

In regard to production, it increased from 1.11 per cent to 4.87 per cent in case of paddy, 1.25 per cent to 6.97 per cent in case of wheat, 2.28 per cent to 6.61 per cent in case of maize, 1.24 per cent to 3.97 per cent in case of pulses and oilseeds witnessed negative growth. The findings indicate that the production increase is higher in rabi season for wheat, pulses and oilseeds across all the watersheds and this indicates the overall effectiveness of the watershed activities. Similar change was also indicated in case of non-beneficiary respondents, which revealed that benefits were not centered on the beneficiaries rather shared with non-beneficiaries also (Table 5).

COST OF CULTIVATION

It is generally presumed that if the facilities are extended to farmers, the cost of the production of the crops will come down provided the prices of the inputs are constant. But things are different. Neither the cost fallen nor is the prices of any inputs constant. Among the beneficiary farmers, it rose at the overall level to 8.16 per cent in WS-I, 5.54 per cent in WS-II, 4.38 per cent in WS-III and 13.08 per cent in WS-IV. Among the non-beneficiary farmers, it increased to 8.53 per cent in WS-I, 12.36 per cent in WS-II, 12.39 per cent in WS-III and 5.16 per cent in WS-IV. The reason for increase in cost of cultivation is mainly due to increase in prices of the inputs like fertilizer, irrigation, seeds, etc. The watershed development programme could not slash to the cost of production. The reason is obvious lesser the impact of the programme (Table 6).

DISPOSAL OF PRODUCE

The disposal for all the crops level in WS-I is lower among the beneficiary households. However, it is a bit higher among the non-beneficiary households. The reason behind low disposal may be lower production. Among the beneficiary households, the percentage of disposal is comparatively higher across all the three watersheds viz., 34.47 per cent in WS-II, 18.82 per cent in WS-III and 19.86 per cent in WS-IV. It is by 0.39 per cent in WS-I, 6.46 per cent in WS-II, 17.15 in WS-III and 21.93 per cent in WS-IV among the non-beneficiary households. It revealed that the volume of disposal has increased, which may be due to distribution of benefits amongst the households or villagers (Table 6).

TABLE 5

Information Regarding Cost of Cultivation (in Rs./ha.) of the Sample Farmers under Selected Watersheds

Sl. No.	Name of the Crop	Watershed – I (Nawada Dist.)			Watershed – II (Kaimur Dist.)			Watershed – III (Aurangabad Dist.)			Watershed – IV (Rohtas Dist.)		
		Cost of Cultivation (in Rs.)		% change in cost of cultivation	Cost of Cultivation (in Rs.)		% change in cost of cultivation	Cost of Cultivation (in Rs.)		% change in cost of cultivation	Cost of Cultivation (in Rs.)		% change in cost of cultivation
		2001-02	2006-07		2001-02	2006-07		2001-02	2006-07		2001-02	2006-07	
(1)		(2)	(3)	(4)	(5)	(6)	(7)	(8)	(9)	(10)	(11)	(12)	(13)
Beneficiary													
1.	Paddy	5100.00	5361.90	5.14	5255.70	5489.06	4.44	4972.80	5175.00	4.07	4412.75	4818.00	9.18
2.	Wheat	5042.50	5362.74	6.35	4717.15	5011.25	6.23	4221.10	4671.00	10.66	4417.20	4690.10	6.18
3.	Maize	6080.00	6325.00	4.03	5390.50	5915.19	9.73	4912.75	5070.60	3.21	4885.15	5117.19	4.75
4.	Pulses	2187.00	2212.00	1.14	2288.00	2436.00	6.47	2611.10	2942.92	12.71	2913.27	3115.22	6.93
5.	Oilseeds	2538.00	2749.00	8.31	2942.00	3011.50	2.36	2217.18	2419.27	9.11	2692.50	3351.15	24.46
	All	4823.30	5217.00	8.16	5392.25	5691.15	5.54	4725.00	4932.17	4.38	5120.70	5790.60	13.08

Non-Beneficiary													
1.	Paddy	5030.12	5568.70	10.71	4639.15	5218.65	12.49	4372.50	4979.00	13.87	4072.00	4491.80	10.31
2.	Wheat	4972.30	5125.90	3.09	4731.85	5029.25	6.29	4215.70	4594.40	8.98	4218.42	4362.00	3.40
3.	Maize	4798.50	4952.17	3.20	3992.10	4101.70	0.03	4213.10	4431.70	5.19	4010.00	4292.00	7.03
4.	Pulses	2412.15	2672.75	10.68	2591.20	2881.00	11.18	2892.81	2911.50	0.65	3217.45	4012.50	24.71
5.	Oilseeds	2319.40	2517.15	8.53	2615.60	2939.00	12.36	3481.00	3912.25	12.39	3790.14	3985.75	5.16
	All	4615.00	5420.00	17.44	5020.00	5715.00	13.84	3990.00	4828.00	21.00	4919.00	5420.00	10.18

TABLE 6

Information Regarding Disposal of Yield (in Qnt.) of the Sample Farmers under Selected Watersheds

Sl. No.	Name of the Crop	Watershed – I (Nawada Dist.)			Watershed – II (Kaimur Dist.)			Watershed – III (Aurangabad Dist.)			Watershed – IV (Rohtas Dist.)		
		Disposal of Yield (in qnt.)		% change in disposal of yield	Disposal of Yield (in qnt.)		% change in disposal of yield	Disposal of Yield (in qnt.)		% change in disposal of yield	Disposal of Yield (in qnt.)		% change in disposal of yield
		2001-02	2006-07		2001-02	2006-07		2001-02	2006-07		2001-02	2006-07	
	(1)	(2)	(3)	(4)	(5)	(6)	(7)	(8)	(9)	(10)	(11)	(12)	(13)
Beneficiary													
1.	Cereals	552.87	465.75	(-)15.61	230.23	321.52	39.65	482.78	582.66	20.68	689.08	833.63	20.97
2.	Pulses	21.00	21.60	2.86	41.46	46.17	11.36	56.38	60.64	7.55	58.73	64.56	9.93
3.	Oilseeds	13.75	08.40	(-)38.91	15.50	18.48	19.23	17.15	17.68	3.09	22.72	25.34	11.53
	All	587.62	495.75	(-)15.63	287.19	386.17	34.47	556.31	660.98	18.82	770.53	923.53	19.86
Non-Beneficiary													
1.	Cereals	404.67	397.14	(-)1.86	385.20	410.39	6.54	508.39	598.82	17.79	373.87	460.09	23.06
2.	Pulses	37.00	46.00	24.32	12.54	14.14	12.76	16.46	17.08	3.77	20.61	22.07	7.08
3.	Oilseeds	03.25	03.50	7.69	06.13	05.44	(-)11.26	06.28	06.27	(-)0.16	06.00	06.14	2.33
	All	444.92	446.64	0.39	403.87	429.97	6.46	531.13	622.17	17.15	400.48	488.30	21.93

Source : Primary Data.

TABLE 7

Information Regarding Average Annual Income (in Rs.) of the Sample Farmers under Selected Watersheds

Sl. No.	Name of the Occupation	*Watershed – I (Nawada Dist.)*			*Watershed – II (Kaimur Dist.)*			*Watershed – III (Aurangabad Dist.)*			*Watershed – IV (Rohtas Dist.)*		
		Annual Income (in Rs.)		*% change in annual income*	*Annual Income (in Rs.)*		*% change in annual income*	*Annual Income (in Rs.)*		*% change in annual income*	*Annual Income (in Rs.)*		*% change in annual income*
		2001-02	2006-07		2001-02	2006-07		2001-02	2006-07		2001-02	2006-07	
	(1)	(2)	(3)	(4)	(5)	(6)	(7)	(8)	(9)	(10)	(11)	(12)	(13)
Beneficiary													
1.	Agriculture	25500	27350	7.25	39000	45500	16.67	24948	32417	29.94	40124	44965	12.07
2.	Service	—	—	—	—	—	—	—	—	—	322	615	91.00
3.	Business	5045	5110	1.29	12800	16254	26.98	1342	1467	9.31	1290	1248	(-)3.26
4.	Others	6000	4200	(-)30.00	—	—	—	4932	5219	5.82	2512	2419	3.70
	Total	36545	36660	0.31	51800	61754	19.22	31222	39103	25.24	44248	49247	11.30
Non-Beneficiary													
1.	Agriculture	20185	22765	12.78	28912	32310	11.75	41742	44387	6.34	36671	44931	22.52
2.	Service	317	412	29.97	404	92	(-)77.23	1309	687	(-)17.52	—	—	—
3.	Business	221	303	41.18	1205	985	(-)18.26	442	389	(-)3.68	605	540	10.74
4.	Others	765	942	23.14	540	320	(-)40.74	1217	392	(-)67.79	342	865	+152.92
	Total	21288	24422	14.72	32061	33707	5.13	44710	45855	2.56	37618	46336	23.18

Income

The total average income of beneficiary group has increased in all the sample watersheds but it recorded higher in WS-III, 25.24 per cent followed by WS-II, 19.22 per cent, WS-IV, 11.30 per cent and WS-I, 0.31 per cent. Almost similar is the case of non-beneficiary group. It increased by 23.18 per cent in WS-IV followed by 14.72 per cent in WS-I, 5.13 per cent in WS-II, and 2.56 per cent in WS-III (Table 7).

Livestock Holdings

The data suggest in all watersheds milk and meat generating animals/birds are kept by a large number of families to supplement their food items and cash resources, while cows and buffaloes are kept for sourcing domestic milk consumption of children and of course for generating income. In all the selected watersheds the total number of livestock increased. It increased as much as 73.00 per cent in WS-I, 30.74 per cent in WS-IV, 21.32 per cent in WS-III and 10.78 per cent in WS-II. It reveals that the project has facilitated in keeping larger number of livestock. But in absence of clear and agreed livestock holding and grazing practices there can not be favourable long-term impact on conservation of common land resources.

Quality of Life

The perceptions of beneficiary farmers indicate that positive changes have taken place in recharging of groundwater level and qualitative aspects of livelihoods by about 15.00 to 20.00 per cent across the watersheds. Irrigation, afforestation and availability of irrigation have changed positively to the tune of 17.50 per cent, absorption of women in various activities (7.50 to 15.00%), production (10.00 to 15.00%), cropping intensity (7.50 to 10.00%), etc. Non-beneficiary farmers also indicated positive change of the programme on improvement in groundwater conditions (7.50 to 15.00%), qualitative aspect of livelihood (5.00 to 12.50%), production (2.50 to 7.50%), availability of irrigation (5.00 to 15.00%). The analysis reveals that there is a general improvement in quality of life but in overall sense, the impact of the programme in these watersheds has been somewhat lower.

Overall Impact

In fact, there is no single indicator of successful watershed development, so the most feasible approach is to compare the performance of a variety of indicators, which also reflect the diversity of project objectives. It is noteworthy that the cost per hectare is helpful in assessing their cost effectiveness. It is calculated at Rs. 8213/ ha. in WS-I, Rs. 8144/ha. in WS-II, Rs. 7103/ha. in WS-IV and Rs. 6561/ha. in WS-III. The programme has significant positive impact on creation of employment opportunities. It has been created about 7142 mandays in WS-I to the highest of 8915 of mandays in WS-III. The internal rate of return calculated on the basis of the additional income over and above the pre-project income from agriculture, micro-enterprises, wages, etc. within the village, varies from 187.00 per cent to 202.00 per cent (average of 4th and 5th year) across the sample watersheds. The cost and benefit ratio also varies from 1:1.87 to 1:2.02. The average employment generation per hectare works out to 12.75 mandays in WS-I, 14.80 mandays in WS-IV, 16.31 mandays in WS-II and 17.58 mandays in WS-III. The quantitative impact on productivity of the crops indicates that except pulses (-2.55%) in WS-III, the productivity of major crops have noticed positive change but in case of cereals, pulses (-)2.55% to 10.44%, oilseeds from 0.59% to 6.78% and vegetables and others from 0.19% to 2.40% across the watersheds. The cropping intensity has fallen by 4.72 per cent in WS-III whereas that of increased to 2.55 per cent in WS-II and 2.00 per cent in WS-I. No change has been found in WS-IV. As regards the income benefit it has increased from 8.22 per cent to 13.28 per cent per hectare per annum. Similarly, annual per hectare family income has also increased from 5.45 per cent to 10.49 per cent across the sample watersheds. However, its equity depends on the magnitude of the households of the area. Positive change has also been found in case of level of groundwater and coverage of green/biomass in the villages.

EMERGING ISSUES AND RECOMMENDATIONS

Based on our findings from four sample watershed areas in Bihar, we have identified some issues that need attention of the policy makers as well as the project functionaries. The emerging issues and recommendations are presented as below:

1. People's participation in watershed activities is poor except in case of wage earners/subsidy beneficiaries. Most of the farmers expressed that improved, certified and guaranteed seeds in addition to enlarging water potential and providing market would usher agriculture in rainfed agro-eco-regions. In fact, people's participation is expected only

when provisions of direct benefits to the farmers are made. So watershed activities should be taken up in such a way (PRA and action research) that majority of villagers could be encouraged/incentivized to participate.

2. We have found in our sample watersheds that although rain fed and water scarce areas have been chosen for the programme, the land areas developed are essentially private croplands. The community land development activities do not get much attention. As the target of PIA is to develop a total area of 500 ha, with no minimum expenditure or area earmarked for community land. PIAs usually opt for the easier course of developing only the flatter terrain of cropland areas, where quick participation of land owning households is also possible. In such a situation land beneficiaries are deprived of any direct benefits. In order to avoid such problem and conflict between the beneficiaries and non-beneficiaries, development of community land resources and introduction of income generating activities for the landless and other weaker sections should be considered.
3. There should be a Detailed Project Report (DPR) of the selected micro watershed area in the initial year of project and get it known to all by displaying the list of activities to be undertaken during the project period. It should be prepared by a team of technical experts on the basis of felt needs of local people.
4. The effectiveness of community organization and sustaining watershed activities largely depend on the training and awareness of the members of WA, WC & WDT. The roles and responsibilities of these groups are defined but not in practice, which need to be activated by regular reviewing and monitoring of the programme
5. There is need to diversify the role of WDT to get associated in the post-project area activities for a minimum of 3-4 years after the project is completed to help various user groups. It requires re-validation of WDT as a professional body to render its services in the area.
6. Last but not the least, we have found that high breed she-goats are given to SHG members under livelihood support

system to landless families, which could not survive after a month or so in local conditions, as reported. Hence, the husbandry ability of the beneficiary members as well as suitability of the area must be considered before extending the assistance under the programme.

References

Agriculture Statistics at a Glance (2008), Ministry of Agriculture, Government of India, New Delhi, 11th Plan Document, Planning Commission, New Delhi, Vol. II, *Economic Survey* (Bihar) 2008-09, Government of Bihar.

Arneja, C.S. and Khara, Sandeepika (2005), Watershed Development Approach for Sustainable Agricultural Development, *Kurukshetra*, July issue.

Babu, Govind; Singh, R.K. and Singh, Babu (2004), Socio-Economic Impact of Watershed Development in Kanpur, *Agricultural Economics Research Review*, October.

Farrington, J., Turton, C. and James, A.J. eds. (1999), Participatory Watershed Development: Challenges for the Twenty-first Century, New Delhi, Oxford University Press.

IFPRI (2001), Communicating Development Research.

Kakade, B.K.; Neelam G.S., Petare, K.J. and Doreswamy, C.; "Rejuvenation of Rivulets: Farm Pond based Watershed Development" searched in google on '*Studies of Watershed Development in India.*'

Kerr, J. and Sanghi, N.K. (1992), Indigenous Soil and Water Conservation in India's Semi-arid tropics, Sustainable Agriculture Programme, Gatekeeper Series Programme Paper No. 34, London International Institute for Environment and Development.

Mishra, C. (2007), Community Participation in Watershed Development: A Case Study of Tribal Villages of Jharkhand, Kurukshetra, September Issue.

Mishra, Chittaranjan (2009), Watershed plus as a Sustainable Strategy of Livelihood: A Study of Karapat District of Orissa, January issue.

Mishra, K.C. and R.C. Mishra (2009), "Watershed Development: Key to Agricultural Development in Rural India," *Kurukshetra*, January issue.

Planning Commission (2007), Report of the Working Group on Natural Resources Management: Eleventh Five Year Plan (2007-12), Planning Commission, GoI, New Delhi.

Policy and Development Initiatives (2001), Assessment of Watershed Development Programme in Gujarat, Submitted to Planning Commission in October.

Sastry, G. Reddy; YVR, Om Prakash and Singh, H.P. (2002) Watershed Programmes in India, Agricultural Situation in India, LIX, No. 8, 487-92.

———, (2002), Impact of Watershed Development Programme on Bio-physical and economic factors in India, *Journal of Soil and Water Conservation in India* Vol. 1, No. 4, 296-303.

Sastry, G; Reddy, YVR; Om Prakash (2003), Final Report on "Impact of Watershed Management Practices on Sustainability of Land Productivity and Socio-Economic Status," CRIDA, Hyderabad, 1-170.

Seth, S.L. (2000), Watershed Management in India, *Kurukshetra*, July issue.
Sinha, R.K., Mishra, S.D. and Marandi, R.K. (2009), Study Report on Impact Evaluation of NWDPRA in Bihar, Study No. 27, Agro-Economic Research Centre for Bihar & Jharkhand, T.M. Bhagalpur University, Bhagalpur, Bihar.

Chapter 6

Water Crisis in India

S. THIRUNAVUKKARASU AND ELANGO J. PARIMALAM

INTRODUCTION

Water is an essential component of life and the supply is depleting but the demand for water is ever expending. This poses water crisis and its economic effect is going to be very severe. The first attack of water crisis would be not only economics but also psychological, social, technological, etc. The efficacy of such crisis would add to scarcity and will check the both ends of common man. The cost on water is likely to widens the gap not only in the household budget but also in the state and national budget. In this paper, an attempt is made to analyze the impact of water crisis on the following aspects:

1. Water crisis in India
    a. Supply of Water in India
    b. Demand for water in India
2. Water crisis in Tamil Nadu
    a. Surface water in Tamil Nadu
    b. Ground water in Tamil Nadu
    c. Sectoral water demand in Tamil Nadu

WATER CRISIS IN INDIA

A region where renewable fresh water availability is below 1700 cubic meters/capita/annum is a 'water stress' region, and one where availability falls below 1000 cubic meters/capita/annum experiences chronic 'water scarcity'. The annual per capita availability of renewable freshwater in the country has fallen from around 5,277 cubic meters in 1955 to 2,464 cubic meters in 1990. Given the projected increase in population by the year 2025, the per capita availability is likely to drop to below 1,000 cubic meters. The actual utilizable water is around 1122 cubic meter per year. The situation is still aggravating with the increase in population. Optimal utilization of natural resources will result in sustainability. But due to the pro-environmental behavior of self-interested individuals, who are de-motivated by similar personalities, go beyond optimal level. The ultimate result is as Garret Hardin rightly pointed out exhibits a situation which is nothing but the "Tragedy of Common". India witnesses a crucial situation, the fixed supply of water resources is stressed and depleting while demand for it from different sectors growing rapidly. The per capita availability of water gone down drastically

While the estimated global population in 2010 was 6908.7 million, at present, a little more than one out of every six persons in the world is from India. India the world's largest democracy, the seventh largest country with a landmass of 3.29 million square kilometers and a population of 1,21,01,93,422 supports 1/25th of world's water resources.

It is observed that economic development and many of the poverty eradication programs in India relied on irrigated agricultural sector. The rapid expansion of irrigation and drainage infrastructure has been one of India's major achievements. However, this achievement has been at the cost of ground water depletion, water logging and salinity levels affecting large areas. As a result of increase in population, urbanization, rising income and industrial growth the demand for water goes on increasing. Thus, uses of water include agricultural, industrial, household, recreational and environmental activities. Virtually all of these human uses require fresh water. Fresh water is a renewable resource, yet the world's supply of clean, fresh water is steadily decreasing. Water demand already exceeds supply in many parts of the world and as the world population continues to rise, so too does the water demand.

SUPPLY OF WATER IN INDIA

Average annual precipitation in India is nearly 4000 cubic km. and the average flow in the river system is estimated to be 1869 cubic km. Because of concentration of rains only in the three monsoon months, the utilizable quantum of water is about 690 cubic km. However, conditions vary widely from region to region. Whereas, some regions are drought affected, others are frequently flooded. In India also, with the rapid increase in the population, the demand for irrigation, human and industrial consumption of water has increased considerably, thereby causing depletion of water resources.

TABLE 1

Water Availability—Basin-wise

Name the River Basin	*Average Annual Availability (cubic Km/year)*
Indus (up to Border)	73.31
Ganga	525.02
Brahmaputra, Barrak and others	585.6
Godavari	110.54
Krishna	78.12
Cauvery	21.36
Pennar	6.32
East Flowing Rivers Between Mahanadi & Pennar	22.52
East Flowing Rivers Between Pennar and Kanyakumari	16.56
Mahanadi	66.88
Brahmani & Baitami	28.48
Subernarekha	12.37
Sabarmati	38.1
Mahi	11.2
West Flowing Rivers of Kutch, Sabarmati including Luni	15.1
Narmanda	45.64
Tapti	14.88
West Flowing Rivers from Tapi to Tadri	87.41
West Flowing Rivers from Tadri to Kanyakumari	113.53
Area of Inland drainage in Rajasthan and desert	Negligible
Minor River Basins Draining into Bangladesh & Burma	31
Total	1869.35

Source : Ministry of Water Resources, 2006.

DEMAND FOR WATER IN INDIA

1. Irrigation

Water supply for irrigation is the most important requirement and it's about 83 percent in the year 1997-98 and the projection for 2025 and 2050 exhibits it will be 72 percent and 68 percent respectively. That is the demand which stood at 524 km^3 in 1997-98 is projected as 561 km^3 if low demand scenario 611 km^3 if high demand scenario in 2025 and 628 km^3 if low demand scenario, 817 km^3 if high demand scenario in 2050.

2. Domestic Use

Table 2 shows that in the year 1997-98 about 17 km^3 of the surface water and 13 km^3 of the ground water are being used by community water supply in urban and rural areas for domestic use whereas as per the projection it will be 48 km^3 for low demand scenario, 42 km^3 for high demand scenario and 65 km^3 for low demand scenario, 46 km^3 for high demand scenario of surface water and groundwater respectively. That is the total domestic use of water increases from 30 km^3 to 90 km^3 for low demand scenario and 111 km^3 for high demand scenario.

3. Industrial Water Requirement

In 1997-98, 21 km^3 of surface water and 9 km^3 of ground water used for Industrial use, the projection shows that in 2050 the requirement will be 57 km^3 of surface water and 24 km^3 of ground water amounting to 81 km^3.

The reason for the shift in water requirement may be when development takes place the significance of secondary and tertiary sector will go on increase as it is seen from Table 2 industrial use of water which is 4.76 percent will increase to 5 percent in 2025 and 7 percent in 2050. In absolute terms it amounts to 81 km^3.

The inclusion of evaporation loses, environment ecology, requirement of water for power and inland navigation the total requirement in the year 1997-98 was 629 km^3 and the projected increase for the year 2025 if low demand scenario 784 km^3 and if high demand scenario 843. Similarly, the projected requirement of water for the year 2050 is 973 if low demand scenario and 1180 if high demand scenario.

TABLE 2
Water Requirements for Different Uses in India

Uses	*Year*									
		2010			*2025*			*2050*		
	1997-98	*Low*	*High*	*%*	*Low*	*High*	*%*	*Low*	*High*	*%*
(1)	*(2)*	*(3)*	*(4)*	*(5)*	*(6)*	*(7)*	*(8)*	*(9)*	*(10)*	*(11)*
Surface of Water										
Irrigation	318	330	339	28	325	366	43	375	463	39
Domestic	17	23	24	3	30	36	5	48	65	6
Industries	21	26	26	4	47	47	6	57	57	5
Power	7	14	15	2	25	26	3	50	56	5
Inland Navigation	—	7	7	1	10	10	1	15	15	1
Environment-Ecology	—	5	5	1	1	10	1	20	20	2
Evaporation Losses	36	42	42	6	6	50	6	76	76	6
Total	399	447	458	65	497	545	65	641	752	64
Ground Water										
Irrigation	206	213	218	31	236	245	29	253	344	29
Domestic and Municipal	13	19	19	2	25	26	3	42	46	4

(Contd.)

TABLE 2 (*Contd.*)

(1)	*(2)*	*(3)*	*(4)*	*(5)*	*(6)*	*(7)*	*(8)*	*(9)*	*(10)*	*(11)*
Industries	9	11	11	1	20	20	2	24	24	2
Power	2	4	4	1	6	7	1	13	14	1
Total	230	247	252	35	287	298	35	332	428	36
Grand Total	629	694	710	100	784	843	100	973	1180	100
Total Water Use										
Irrigation	524	543	557	78	561	611	72	628	817	68
Domestic	30	42	43	6	55	62	7	90	111	9
Industries	30	37	37	5	67	67	8	81	81	7
Power	9	18	19	3	31	33	4	63	70	6
Inland Navigation	0	7	7	1	10	10	1	15	15	1
Environment Ecology	0	5	5	1	10	10	1	20	20	2
Evaporation Loses	36	42	42	6	50	50	6	76	76	7
Total	629	694	710	100	784	843	100	973	1180	100

Sources : Central Water Commission, 2007.

WATER CRISIS IN TAMIL NADU

Tamil Nadu accounts for 4 per cent of the land area and 5.96 percent of the population, but only 3 per cent of the water resources of the country. The average rainfall is 943 mm against the average rainfall of 1170 mm of the Country. It varies from 1200 mm near coastal area to 550 mm in inland area. In Tamil Nadu, more than 90 percent of the available surface water and 45 percent of the ground water were drawn and utilized as far as in 1970 itself. But the demand of water is continuously on the rise with the growth of population, Industry and Agriculture whereas the availability of water remains almost constant.

The estimated population of Tamil Nadu increased from 6.24 crore to 7.21 crore in the last decade. The percentage of total population of Tamil Nadu was 6.07 percent in 2001 and it came down to 5.96 percent in 2011 whereas the density of population increased from 480/km^2 in 2001 to 555/km^2 in 2011.

RAINFALL

The State gets relatively more rainfall during north-east monsoon, especially, in the coastal regions. The normal rainfall in south-west and north-east monsoon is around 322 mm and 470 mm which is lower than the National normal rainfall of 1250 mm.

TABLE 3

Surface and Ground Water in Tamil Nadu

Sl. No.	*Basins*	*Minor River Basins*	*Surface Water*	*Ground Water*
(1)	*(2)*	*(3)*	*(4)*	*(5)*
1.	Chennai	Araniyar	849	1119
	Kosaithalaiyar			
	Cooum			
	Adyar			
2.	Palar	Palar	1772	3416
3.	Varahanadhi	Ongur	545	1237
	Varahanadhi			
4.	Ponnaiyar	Malattar	820	1499

(Contd.)

TABLE 3 (*Contd.*)

(1)	(2)	(3)	(4)	(5)
	Ponnaiyar			
	Gadilam			
5.	Vellar(n)	Vellar(n)	1027	1021
6.	Cauvery	Cauvery	7067	10573
7.	Agniyar	Agniyar	447	555
	Ambuliyar			
	Vellar(s)			
8.	PAP	Parambikulam Basin Complex	866	899
9.	Pambar	Koluvanar	551	879
	Pambar			
	Manimuthar			
10.	Kottakaraiar	Kottakariar	218	398
11.	Vaigai	Vaigai	1272	760
12.	Gundar	Uttarakosaamangai	451	866
	Gundar			
	Vembar			
13.	Vaippar	Vaippar	310	669
14.	Kallar	Kallar	203	37
	Korampallamar			
15.	Tambaraparani	Tambaraparni	1706	827
16.	Nambiyar	Nambiyar	194	276
	Karimaniar			
	Hanumanadhi			
17.	Valliar	Palayaru	421	241
	Valliar			
	Kodaiyar			
	Others	6145		
	Total	24864	25291	

Source : Tamil Nadu Development Report, 2005.

Similarly, the per capita water availability of the State is 800 cubic meters which is lower than the National average of 2300 cubic meters.

SURFACE WATER RESOURCES OF TAMIL NADU

The total surface water potential of the state is 36 km^3 or 24,864 M cum. There are 17 major river basins in the State with 61 reservoirs and about 41,948 tanks. Of the annual water potential of 46,540 million cubic metres (MCM), surface flow account for about half. Most of the surface water has already been tapped, primarily for irrigation which is the largest user. There are about 24 lakh hectares are irrigated by surface water through major, medium and minor schemes. The utilisation of surface water for irrigation is about 90 percent.

GROUND WATER RESOURCES OF TAMIL NADU

The utilisable groundwater recharge is 22,423 MCM The current level of utilisation expressed as net groundwater draft of 13.558 MCM is about 60 percent of the available recharge, while 8875 MCM (40 percent) is the balance available for use. Over the last five years, the percentage of safe blocks has declined from 35.6 per cent to 25.2 percent while the semi-critical blocks have gone up by a similar percentage. Over-exploitation has already occurred in more than a third of the blocks (35.8 percent) while eight blocks (2 percent) have turned saline. The water level data reveals that the depth of the wells range from an average of 0.93 metres in Pudukottai district to 43.43 metres in Erode. According to the Central Groundwater Board, there has been a general decline in groundwater level in 2003 due to the complete desaturation of shallow aquifers. There has been a considerable failure of irrigation wells in Coimbatore District.

WATER RESOURCES

Though the Table 4 exhibits surplus in Net Annual Groundwater availability, there is wide variation among the regions in water availability. There are areas with excessive water and areas with scarcity of water. Moreover, the availability of water is not evenly distributed throughout the year. Due to limited conservative mechanism huge amount of water become run-off which flows into the sea.

The annual water potential of the State including surface and ground water is assessed as 46,540 MCM (1643 TMC) while the

TABLE 4
Ground Water Resources

Unit: BCM/year

	Annual Replenishable Ground Water Resources				*Total*	*Natural Discharge during non monsoon season*	*Net Annual Ground Water Availability*	*Annual Ground Water Draft*		
	Monsoon Season		*Non-Monsoon Season*							
	Recharge from rainfall	*Recharge from other sources*	*Recharge from rainfall*	*Recharge from other sources*				*Irrigation*	*Domestic and Industrial use*	*Total*
(1)	*(2)*	*(3)*	*(4)*	*(5)*	*(6)*	*(7)*	*(8)*	*(9)*	*(10)*	*(11)*
Tamil Nadu	4.91	11.96	4.53	1.67	23.7	2.31	20.76	16.77	0.88	17.65
All India	248.01	69.59	4.85	73.18	433.03	33.77	399.25	212.50	18.10	230.59

Source : Central Ground Water Board, Hydrology Project, Ministry of Water Resources.

estimated demand is 54,395 MCM (1921 TMC) in 2001 which is likely to go up to 57,725 MCM in 2050.

Table 5 shows that, the domestic use is projected to go up from 4 percent to 5 percent due to increase in population and urbanization. The domestic requirement would increase by 55.72 percent. Agriculture use will remain stagnant or may even decrease due to progressive urbanization. The share of industry may not change much, but in absolute terms the increase will be about 27.7 percent. Provision of 1600 MCM in 2050 would be made for minimum flow in rivers for ecological purpose, which is a new category for water resources.

TABLE 6

Sectoral Water Demand in Tamil Nadu (2001, 2050)

Sector	*2001*	*%*	*2050*	*%*	*% increase*
Domestic	2222	4.08	3460	6.00	5572
Irrigation	49978	91.88	49978	86.58	0.00
Industries	1555	2.86	1985	3.44	27.65
Power	118	0.22	180	0.31	52.5
Livestock	519	0.96	519	0.90	0.00
Aquaculture	2		2		0.00
Recreation	1		1		0.00
Minimum Flows	—		1600	2.77	N.A
Total	54395	100.00	57725	100.00	6.12

Source : Institute of Water Studies, 1998.

Thus, increasing population and urbanization poses more responsibility on the state to provide infrastructural facility including water. The growing scarcity and competition for water stand as major threats to future. The public along with the government have to come forward the preserve precious natural resource for themselves and for the future generation. Here in this context demonstration effect plays an important role in conservation of resources. As we say charity begins at home, so the conservation of water should be. If we save water today and spend water consciously, it will surely motivate others to do so. Saving water will be the first step to overcome the water crisis, which should start from the individual level.

References

Compendium for Environmental Statistics, India, 2008-09.

Economic Appraisal 2003-04, 2004-05, Evaluation and Applied Research Department, Government of Tamil Nadu.

Environmental Planning Framework for Water Resources Management in Tamil Nadu, Final Draft, 2001, Public Works Department. Government of Tamil Nadu.John Briscoe; Malik, R.P.S. (2006), "Indias Water Economy Bracing for a Turbulent Future", Oxford University Press; New Delhi.

Pangare, Vasudha (2005), "Global Perspectives on Integrated Water Resources Management", Academic Foundation.

———, (2005), "Springs of Life India Water Resources", Academic Foundation, Delhi.

Prasad, K. (2003), "Water Resources and Sustainable Development (Challenges of 21st Century)", Shipra Publication, Delhi.

Rao, Nageswara M. (2006), "Water Resources Management Realities and Challenges", New Century Book House P. Ltd., Chennai, 2006.

Ramaswamy Iyar, L. (2007), "Towards Water Wisdom Limits Justice Harmony", Sage Publication Inc, London.

Thapliyal, B.K. (2008), "Democratisation of Water", Serials Publications, New Delhi.

Vaidyanathan (2006), "India's Water Resources Contemporary Issues on Irrigation", Oxford University Press; London.

Vohra, B.B. (1990), Managing India's Water Resources, Intach, New Delhi.

———, (2011), Economic Survey, 2010-11, Government of India, Ministry of Finance, Feb.

———, (2005), Tamil Nadu Development Report, Planning Commission, Government of India.

Chapter 7

Dynamics of Ground Water Market

A Study of Villages of Rohtas District of Bihar

AMLENDU KUMAR, MRITUNJAY PD. SINGH
AND MANINDRA KUMAR SINGH

BACKGROUND

The state of Bihar has been divided into three agro-ecological sub-zones by Planning Commission and ICAR. They are North-West Gangetic plain, North-East Gangatic plain and South Bihar plain. Bihar is spread over 9.40 million ha. of land and south Bihar plain constitute about 44 thousand ha. of the total geographical area of the state. The districts of Aurangabad, Banka, Babhua, Bhagalpur, Bhojpur, Buxar, Gaya, Jamui, Jehanabad, Lakhisarai, Munger, Nalanda, Nawada, Patna, Rohtas and Shekhpura fall under south Bihar plain. The main characteristics of this zone are that it is highly irrigated (more than 75 per cent of GCA) has larger concentration of population (38 per cent of state population) having 1065 population density, has highest rate of literacy (55.01 per cent), and has 42 per cent of poverty. The agriculture in the zone is predominated by small farms with fragmented land holdings (more than 85 per cent). More than 65 per cent of land resources in the subzone are used for crop production of which food grain crops account for about 88 per cent of the gross cropped area. Rice and wheat crops only constitute nearly 70 per cent of the total cropped area. Only 9 per cent area occupied by commercial crops.

According to the latest information south Bihar plain zone is a highly irrigated zone (more than 76 per cent). Except Jamui district, the level of irrigation in almost all districts of this zone is intensively irrigated as they have higher level of irrigation. Lakhisarai and Munger have very high level of irrigation (90 per cent), Rohtas (91 per cent), Jehanabad (86 per cent), Bhagalpur (81 per cent), Buxar (80 per cent). Among various resources of irrigation it is the tubewell (39 per cent) followed by Canal (37 per cent) which dominate the irrigation network in the zone. It has been observed that among different sources of irrigation, tubewells have shown expansion (diesel tubewells) whereas canals have shown shrinkage in their share. The irrigation by electric tubewell is almost constant or on decline. There is around 654 thousand hectares of the gross irrigated in the zone and the intensity of irrigation has not increase since last so many years.

GROUND WATER MARKET : THE GENESIS

The major expansion of irrigated area has occurred on all fronts. The major and medium surface schemes have increased more than three-fold from 1951 to 2007 while ground water irrigation, largely through private investment, has expanded seven-fold. Today groundwater irrigation has major share percentage in net irrigated area followed by canal, tank and others. Thus, in the country one of the most striking features of irrigation development during the last four decades is the rapid growth in the use of ground water because it is cheap and easy. It is available when one desires it. It can give that quantity of water, which is required by the field. Hence, the strategy in revolutionizing irrigation should consist in using ground water resources on a massive scale.

In the state of Bihar poor irrigation facilities and dependence on monsoons are the main problem in agricultural production. Groundwater irrigation through tubewells (Electric and diesel) is the most common source of irrigation because of having more benefits of ample availability of water resources at a reasonable cost and during short time period. During the year 1975, Dr. Chaudhary in his study gave advice to large landholders to install tubewells with higher water discharge capacity. As per Meinzen Dick, 1994 informal markets of irrigation water extracted by the private tubewells provide an important means of increasing access to ground water resources for the non-tubewell owners. As per Jagdish Prasad in 1993 the complete failure of state tubewells in the villages has paved the way for development of the groundwater market which does not seem to be competitive because of large variations in water charges and the presence of various discriminations, particularly to small and marginal farmers in the supply of water to them. In the state of Bihar in general and sampled sub-zone in particular there is plentiful reserve of ground water (2,86,540 lakh m^3) about 8.4 per cent of the water resources.

In this study area mainly two types of tubewells (Electric operated and diesel operated) are common. But the larger percentage of diesel operated tubewells are working due to poor electricity facilities. Per unit area of water application is less but cost is more than the electric operated tubewells. In the sampled area due to poor maintenance of canal irrigation system, the number of tubewells is increasing day by day and water in this way markets have developed. As per D.R. Singh and R.P. Singh the marginal and small farmers sell less water and buy more water in comparison to other categories of farmers.

In 1970, during the early green revolution period, tubewells emerged as the most important source of irrigation in the state due to their low cost of installation. It covers very high per cent of the net irrigated area but is still potential to increase the area under tubewell irrigation. Since last one and half decades the cheaper shallow tubewells including bamboo boring have entered into the groundwater market and the monopoly of deep tubewells have faced competition in the groundwater market.

It has already been mentioned that the south Bihar is considered as agriculturally well developed region endowed with assured irrigation system through private diesel-operated tubewells. In this area most of the non-tubewell owners are forced to purchase water from the tubewell owners during the rabi seasons and kharif when rainfall scanty. In this region, Rohtas is one of the highly irrigated districts (91 per cent) where Paddy and Wheat are intensively cultivated. Keeping in view the importance of groundwater for increasing the agricultural production, the present study made evaluation at the time of conducting a study on "Agricultural Input Subsidies in India: Quantum of Subsidies to SC/ST Farmers in Bihar".

In this study an effort has been made to examine the costs which are involved in groundwater through tubewell.

METHODOLOGY

The study was based on the primary data obtained from two randomly selected villages in Sasaram block of the Rohtas district (Bihar). A sample of 80 farmers comprising 12 from marginal, 24 from small, 28 from medium and 16 from large farm categories were selected for indepth study through stratified random sampling technique. The sample size was based on probability proportion to size among different categories of farms. The survey method was used to collect the required information from the sampled respondents relating to the agricultural year, 2000-01.

FEATURES OF THE SELECTED DISTRICT

The district of Rohtas being one of the agriculturally developed districts has a total geographical area of 7,33,000 ha. Out of it around 54.71 per cent is net cultivated area. The area cultivated more than once is around 29.33 per cent of the net cultivated area. Around 64 per cent were marginal farmers, 17 per cent were small farmers, 11.50 per cent were medium farmers and 7.50 were large farmers in the district. In the district 51.25 per cent of the GCA is under paddy with productivity of 1550 kg/ha. The area under wheat is about 16 per cent of the GCA. The cropping intensity of the district is about 151 per cent which is higher than that of state average (141). The complete picture of agriculture may be summarized here as the net sown area is 4,05,533 ha. Gross corpped area is 6,27,489 ha. Net irrigated area is 2,46,147 ha and gross irrigated area is 3,32,161 ha. As per 2001 census the total population of the district is 24,48,762. Out of its total population 7,46,460 were total workers and out of the total worker 2,92,479 were agricultural workers. Around 62.36 per cent of the population was literate. Thus, the district is basically an agricultural district where a large proportion of the population still depends on agriculture for their livelihood.

CHARACTERISTICS OF THE SAMPLE HOUSEHOLDS

The data regarding average size of landholding of marginal, small, medium and large farms were collected from the respondents with irrigated area. The collected data have been presented in Table 1.

TABLE 1
Characteristics of the Sampled Households

Sl. No.	*Farm size*	*Number of respondents*	*Total operating area (ha.)*	*Average size of landholding (ha)*	*Average irrigated area (ha.)*
1.	Marginal farm (below 1 ha.)	12 (15.00)	7.44 (3.00)	0.62 —	0.57 (91.93
2.	Small farm (1-2 ha.)	24 (30.00)	37.68 (15.19)	1.57 —	1.42 (90.44)
3.	Medium farm (2.01-4.0 ha.)	28 (35.00)	91.84 (37.03)	3.28 —	3.15 (96.04)
4.	Large farm (Above 4.01 ha.)	16 (20.00)	111.04 (44.78)	6.94 —	6.15 (88.62)
	Total	80 (100.00)	248 (100.00)	3.1 —	2.84 (91.61)

Note : Figures in paranthesis indicate percentage to total.

It may be observed from Table 1 that that the total operating area of the sampled respondents was 248.0 ha. in which large farms constitute 44.78 per cent followed by medium farms 37.03 per cent, small farms 15-19 per cent and marginal farms only 3.0 per cent of the total operating area. The average size of land holding of marginal, small, medium and large farms was 0.62 ha., 1.57 ha., 3.28 ha. and 6.94 ha. respectively. However, the average size of landholding of all categories was 3.10 ha. The table further reveals that out of total operated area about 9.74 per cent area was irrigated. This indicates that this region is more important from the point of view of irrigation. The tubewells are important source of irrigation after canal irrigation. Mostly small and marginal farmers donot own the wells and pump sets and even when they own, their ownership is not profitable. Irrigation works are being carried there within three days and thereafter machines become useful for the rest of the year. Money was locked up and creates financial loss to the owner. In this situation these farmers are not interested to install tubewell and in general they buy water and irrigate the small chunk of field. Hence, this condition creates a water market in the area. However, in case of canal irrigation there is no water market because the beneficiaries use to pay water rate or tax. The payment is determined neither on the basis of volume of water nor on the basis of hours of supply. This situation does not create a market. Water market exists when there is a private seller of water and there are private buyers of water. The seller has water-extracting machine and he uses it to irrigate his own fields. When this is done his equipment remains idle and here arises an objective condition to sell water.

COST OF IRRIGATION THROUGH TUBEWELLS OF THE SAMPLED FARMS

The cost of irrigation water was estimated under two sub-headings, i.e.

(i) Installation cost, and
(ii) Working cost.

Under the installation cost different components have been identified and with the discussion it is estimated as follows:

Installation Cost

The table reveals that on an average installation cost per tubewell was worked out to be Rs. 28893.75. Among different components of installation cost, cost of pumpset was higher 5.62 per cent followed by drilling cost 17.50 per cent, shed construction 13.63 per cent, pit digging and wall pipe construction 11.71 per cent and cost of irrigation pipe 6.54 per cent.

TABLE 2

Installation Cost of Tubewells in the Study Area (Average of five informants)

Different Components	*Average cost (In Rs.)*
Digging of pit and wall pipe construction	3381.28(11.71)
Construction of shed	3939.04(13.63)
Cost of pumpset	14626.08(50.62)
Irrigation pipe	1891.68(6.54)
Drilling cost	5055.67(17.50)
Total Cost	28893.75(100.00)

Note : Parentheses indicate the percentage of total.

Working Cost for Irrigation Water

The Table 3 shows the estimated working cost of irrigation

TABLE 3
Cost of Irrigation Water as per Average of Five Informants

Different items	*Average*
Average number of working hours per year	746
Average fixed expenses per year (Rs.)	6389
Cost of irrigation water per hour in term of fixed expenses (Rs./ha.)	8.56
Average variable expenses per year (Rs.)	21,337
Cost of irrigation water per hour in terms of variable cost (Rs./hr.)	28.60
Cost of irrigation water per hour (Rs./hr.)	37.16

water. On an average per hour estimated cost of irrigation water was worked out to be Rs. 37.16. Out of it Rs. 8.56 was fixed expenses per hour and Rs. 28.60 was variable expenses per hour. The table further indicates that the average working hours of a tubewell in the area was estimated to be 746 hours. The average fixed expenses per year was estimated to be Rs. 6389 and average variable expenses per year to be Rs. 21,337.

FACTOR AFFECTING THE SALE AND PURCHASE OF IRRIGATION WATER

During the course of field survey it was observed that the non-owners of tubewells mostly purchase the irrigation water in the study area. It was also observed that the sale of water depends on the factors like surplus water to the owners, location of buyer's and nearer to tubewell, profit motives of sellers and prevailing social relation in the areas. Another factor, which affects the purchasing of irrigation water, was the non-availability of canal irrigation for majority of farmers. It was reported that the small and fragmented agricultural land also compel the farmers for purchase of irrigation water. It was observed that in a village there are a very limited number of tubewells are installed. The owners installed their tubewells generally for their own use when the surplus irrigation water from their use is left over during the reason they use to sell it to other farmers for irrigation on payment basis. A number of tubewell owners do not sell the irrigational water on account of their social compulsion. The owners and buyers generally belong to large and medium size groups of farmers whereas small and marginal farmers largely use to buy the irrigation water in the study area. The small categories of farmers generally use to hire out the irrigation water.

CONCLUSION

From the discussion it may be concluded that the tubewell owners are generally from large, medium and small categories. The large and medium categories generally use to install their tubewells for their own purpose and up to some extent for selling purpose. However, the small categories generally install for selling purpose. The diesel operated tubewells are the most important device of irrigation which is generally used in marketing of irrigation water. The findings of the study also indicate that the marginal and small farmers do participate in water make at a large scale. Hence, there is a difference between general market and water market. A general market refers to a place where buyers meet the sellers for the purchase of goods. But in marketing of irrigation water place is replaced by a close physical proximity where both the buyers of water and the sellers of water mostly use to live.

POLICY IMPLICATIONS

On the basis of the finding of the study the following policy implications have emerged:

- In the study area marginal, small and landless of farmers cultivate land on share basis and participate in water market on a large scale. Thus, there is a need to provide assured and cheaper irrigation to them by the state government.
- Mostly landless, marginal and small farmers depend on large farmers for irrigation of their crop. If financial support is given to them for installation of tubewells, it would reduce their dependence. Thus, there is a need to invite financial institutions for extending financial assistance.
- For reducing the costs of irrigation there is a need to improve electric facilities with regular supply and fair price of diesel in the area through the government departments of irrigation and electricity.

- For securing livelihood to lower farm size groups public canal system should be strengthened by major irrigation projects.
- Sound law and order can reduce the social problems. Hence the regional police officers should take proper care in this regard.

References

Choudhary, S.K. (1975), "An Economic Analysis of Some Important Source of Irrigation of Muzaffarpur", Unpublished thesis, R.A.U. Pusa (Bihar).

Prasad, J. (1993), A Case Study of Private Groundwater market in Bihar, *The Bihar Journal of Agricultural Marketing,* Vol. 2: 209.

Singh, D.R. and R.P. Singh (2003), Groundwater Markets and the Issues of Equity and Reliability to Water Access: A Case of Western Uttar Pradesh, *Indian Journal of Agricultural Economics*, 58 (1): 115-27.

Jha, U.M. (1984), *Irrigation and Agricultural Development*, Deep & Deep Publication, New Delhi.

Shah, Tushaar and K. Vengama Raju (1987), "Working of Groundwater Markets in Andhra Pradesh and Gujarat: Result of two Village Studies", *Economic and Political Weekly,* Vol. 22, No. 13, March 26.

Shankar, Kripa (1992), Water Market of Eastern U.P.", *Economic and Political Weekly,* Vol. 27, No. 18, May 2.

Singh, *et al.* (2007), Ground Water Marketing in Nalanda District of Bihar", *Agricultural Economic Research Review,* Vol. July-December, pp. 333-44.

Chapter 8

Transforming Indian Agriculture through Water Resource Management

VINOD KUMAR SRIVASTAVA

INTRODUCTION

Sustainable development and efficient management of water is an increasingly complex challenge in India. Increasing population, growing urbanization, and rapid industrialization combined with the need for raising agricultural production generates competing claims for water, but lack of its resources and proper management create water crisis in Indian agrarian sector. An Attempt has been made in this paper to present an overview about "*Transforming Indian Agriculture Through Water Resource Management*". The paper is divided into Five Sections. Section first covers a brief introduction about the theme, Section second has been devoted to examine the sources of irrigation and availability of water in Indian economy, Section third deals with water resource management and use of irrigation, Section four has been devoted to examine about Eleventh Five Year Plan strategy for major, medium and minor irrigation facilities in Indian economy. The Paper conclude with Section five which gives some suggestions about policy recommendation and further way for improvements for better transformation of Indian agriculture through proper management of water resources.

There is a growing perception of a sense of an impending water crisis in the country. Some manifestations of this crisis are: there is hardly any city which receives a 24-hour supply of drinking water. Many rural habitations which had been covered under the drinking water programme are now being reported as having slipped back with target date for completion continuously pushed back. There are pockets where arsenic, citrate, and fluoride in drinking water are posing a serious health hazard. In many parts, the ground water level declines due to osier-exploitation imposing an increasing financial burden on farmers who need to deepen their wells and replace their pump sets and on state Governments whose subsidy burden for electricity supplies rises, many major and medium irrigation (MMI) projects seem to remain under execution forever as they slip from one plan to the other with enormous cost and time overruns. Owing to lack of maintenance, the capacity of the older systems seems to be going down, the gross irrigated area does not seem to be rising in a manner that it should be given the investment in irrigation. The difference between potential created and area actually irrigated remains large. Unless we bridge the gap, significant increase in agricultural production will be difficult to realize. Floods are a recurring problem in many parts of the country degradation of catchment areas and loss of flood plains to urban development and agriculture have accentuated the intensity of floods. Water quality in our rivers and lakes is far from satisfactory. Water in most parts of rivers is not fit for bathing, let alone drinking. Untreated or partially treated sewage from towns and cities is being dumped into the rivers. Untreated or inadequately treated Industrial effluents pollute water bodies end also contaminate ground water, at the same time water conflicts are increasing. Apart from the traditional conflicts about water rights loser riparian in a river, conflicts about quality of water, people's right for rainwater harvesting in a watershed against down-stream users, industrial use of groundwater and its impact on water levels and between urban and rural users have emerged. Along with HYV seeds and fertilisers, water forms another important input of the package of new technology. An important source of water is rainfall. The average rainfall is about 88 cm, one of the highest in the world. But it is mostly confined to a few monsoon months in the year, and there are great variations in its incidence from year to year. Moreover, rainfall in a large part of the country is low and uncertain in its distribution. Even where it high the available soil moisture in the winter and summer months is not adequate to support multiple-cropping. These vagaries of weather frequently give rise to drought and scarcity. Therefore, there is an increased need for providing assured supplies of water through irrigation systems.

The problems posed by the irrigation development programme in the country can be classified into three groups i.e. problems relating to the creation of new capacity, delay in the completion of major irrigation projects and rising costs with inadequacy of finance and organization. A number of major multi-purpose river valley projects that were expected to give a boost to the irrigation potential in the economy were started during the second and the Third Plans, i.e. almost 40-45 years ago. Quite a few of these projects have as yet to be completed. Delay in the completion of these projects has been caused by a number of factors, some of which are: a lack of thorough investigation before the start of projects, changes in the size and nature of projects after starting work on them, a lack of organisation to monitor the progress on the work, lack of proper interlinking of rivers and difficulties of getting adequate and timely requirements of water supply in canals.

The recent response of the government has been to set up the Accelerated Irrigation Benefit Programme. It will assist the states to accelerate the completion of unfinished medium and major irrigation projects and also to undertake reforms by revising user charges and setting up of water users associations. India with 2.4 per cent of the world's total area has 16 per cent of the world's population; but has only 4 per cent of the total available fresh water. This clearly indicates the need for water resource development, conservation and optimum use. Fortunately, at a macro-level India is not short of water. The

TABLE 1

Irrigation Potential in India

(*In million hectares*)

	1950-51	*2006-07*
Minor Irrigation	12.9	39.50
Major Irrigation	9.1	62.25
Total	22.0	101.75

Source : Publication Division, Ministry of Information & Broadcasting, Government of India.

problems that seem to loom large over the sector are manageable and the challenges facing it are not insurmountable. Growth of irrigation in the Indian sub-continent, to this day, is an unparalleled human achievement. An additional irrigation potential of 80 million hectares has been created during the nearly five decades of planning as would be seen from Table 1.

SOURCES OF IRRIGATION AND AVAILABILITY OF WATER IN INDIAN ECONOMY

Depending on the availability of surface or ground water, types of relief, soils and the moisture requirement of crops, various types of irrigation are practiced in India, more important among these are canals, wells and tanks. Wells provide the most widely distributed source of irrigation in India. It make use of the underground water. Well irrigation, therefore, is possible even in low rainfall areas provided sufficient quantity of ground water is available. Well irrigation is also within the reach of small farmers. It accounts for about 40 per cent of the total irrigated area in the country. Canals are the other important source of irrigation. India has one of the world's largest canal systems stretching over more than one lakh km. and serving more than 20 million hectares. Canals are of two types (a) Foundation canals, and (b) Perennial canals. Canals taken out from rivers without any regulating system are called Foundation canals. Perennial canals too are taken-off from perennial rivers or reservoirs with a weir system to regulate the flow of water, which is maintained throughout the year. Tank irrigation is the most feasible and practiced method of irrigation in States like Tamil Nadu, Karnataka, Orissa, etc. Tank irrigation Involves a high rate of evaporation and occupation of fertile land particularly as the depth of most of the tanks is shallow and the water spreads over a large area. Therefore, wherever canal irrigation has been introduced, tanks have been reclaimed for cultivation. The proportion of tank irrigation to the total irrigation capacity, therefore, has fallen over the years.

Sources of irrigation can be classified into two broad groups, viz. (a) minor irrigation, and (b) medium and major irrigation. Major irrigation works involve a huge investment and take a long period for completion. Micro Irrigation is globally believed to be one of the most efficient methods of irrigation as it enables application of water to the root zone of crops using a network of pipes using emitters. This approach increases crop productivity with less water usage saves

TABLE 2
Estimates of Water Resources in India

(In billion cubic metre)

Agency	*Estimate in bcm*	*Deviation from 1869 bcm*
First Irrigation Commission (1902-03)	1443	-23%
Dr. A.N. Khosla (1949)	1673	-10%
Central Water and Power Commission (1954-66)	1881	+0.6%
National Commission on Agriculture	1850	-1%
Central Water Commission (1988)	1880	+0.6%
Central Water Commission (1869)	—	

Source : Eleventh Five Year Plan (2007-12) Vol. III, Planning Commission, Government of India, 2008, p. 44.

electricity and enhances fertiliser use efficiency. It promotes precision farming, doing away with problems such as water logging, minimising pest infection in crops and maintains water levels. Due to the universality of its application, it can also be used to irrigate India's vast tracts of wasteland and make them productive, as well as in arid zones, hilly areas and saline land. Studies show that the more advanced drip systems achieve 85 per cent efficiency of water use and sprinkler systems around 60 per cent. The water resource potential of the country has been assessed from time to time by different agencies. The different estimates are shown in Table 2. It may be seen that since 1954, the estimates have stabilized and are within the proximity of the currently accepted estimate of 1869 billion cubic metre (bcm) which includes replenishable groundwater which gets charged on annual basis.

Within the limitations of physiographic conditions, socio-political environment, legal and constitutional constraints, and the technology available at hand, the utilizable water resources of the country have been assessed at 1123 bcm, of which 690 bcm is from surface water and 433 bcm from groundwater sources (CWC, 1993). Harnessing of 690 bcm of utilizable surface water is possible only if matching storages are built. Trans-basin transfer of water, if taken up to the full extent as proposed under the National Perspective Plan, would further increase the utilizable quantity by approximately 220 bcm. The irrigation potential of the country has been estimated to be

139.9 MH without inter-basin sharing of water and 175 MH with inter-basin sharing. While the total water resource available in the country remains constant, the per capita availability of water has been steadily declining since 1951 due to population growth. The twin indicators of water scarcity are per capita availability and storage. A per capita availability of less than 1700 cubic Metres (m) is termed as a water-stressed condition while if per capita availability falls below 1000 m', it is termed as a water-scarcity condition. While on an average we may be nearing the water stressed condition, on an individual river basin-wise situation, nine out of our 20 river basins with 200 million populations are already facing a water-scarcity condition. Even after constructing 4525 large and small dams, the per capita storage in the country is 213 m' as against 6103 m' in Russia, 4733 m' in Australia, 1964 m' in the United States (US), and 1111 m' of China. It may touch 400 m' in India only after the completion of all the ongoing and proposed dams. The demand for irrigation water in India is very large. However, the limits to storage and transfer of water restrict the potential for irrigation, the potential created, and the potential utilized to end of the Tenth Plan are given in Table 3

TABLE 3

Ultimate Irrigation Potential (UIP), Potential Created and Potential Utilised (In M.H.)

Sector	*Ultimate Irrigation Potential*	*Potential Created*		*Potential Utilized*	
		Till end of Ninth Plan	*Anticipated in Tenth Plan*	*Till end of Ninth Plan*	*Anticipated in Tenth Plan*
MMI	58.47	37.05	5.3	31.01	3.41
MI					
Surface water	17.38	13.6	0.71	11.44	0.56
Ground water	64.05	43.3	2.81	38.55	2.26
Sub-Total	81.43	56.9	3.52	49.99	2.82
Total	139.9	93.958.82	81.00	6.23	

Source : Eleventh Five Year Plan (2007-12), Vol. III, Planning Commission, Government of India, 2008, p. 45.

The assessment of UIP needs to be periodically reviewed to account for revision in scope, technological advancement, inter-basin transfer of water, induced recharging of groundwater, etc. The creation of irrigation potential depends upon the efficiency of the system for delivering the water and its optimal use at the application level. With the modern techniques of integrating micro irrigation with canal irrigation as has been done in the case of Narmada Canal Project, Rajasthan, and the UIP can further be increased. Similarly in the case of groundwater, innovative methods of recharging the groundwater and also storing water in flood plains along the river banks may enhance the UIP from groundwater to more than 64 MH (Million Hectare). The requirement of water for various sectors has been assessed by the National Commission on Integrated Water Resources Development (NCIWRD) in the year 2000. This requirement is based on the assumption that the irrigation efficiency will increase to 60 per cent from the present level of 35-40 per cent. The Standing Committee of MoWR (Ministry of Water Resources) also assesses it periodically. These are shown in Table 4.

TABLE 4
Water Requirement for Various Sectors

Sector	*Water Demand in Km (or bcm)*					
	Standing Sub Committee of MoWR			*NCIWRD*		
	2010	*2025*	*2050*	*2010*	*2025*	*2050*
Irrigation	688	910	1072	557	611	807
Drinking Water	56	73	102	43	62	111
Industry	12	23	63	37	67	81
Energy	5	15	130	19	33	70
Others	52	72	80	54	70	111
Total	813	1093	1447	710	843	1180

Source : Eleventh Five Year Plan (2007-12), Vol. III, Planning Commission, Government of India, 2008, p. 46.

WATER RESOURCES MANAGEMENT AND USE : IRRIGATION

The question of a trade-off between competing claims on water becomes most important in the from of ecological requirement. The

National Water Policy (NWP) places ecology in the fourth place in the order of priorities for water use management. Yet, there is a general agreement amongst all that any water diversion needs to take care of river ecosystem downstream. The problem is of quantifying the Environment Flow Releases (EFR) that is the flow required for maintaining ecosystem. Usable water will be reduced to that extent. During 2004-05, the Ministry of Environment and Forests (MoEF) appointed a committee headed by Member, Central Water Commission (CWC), to develop guidelines for determining the EFR. The committee submitted its report in 2005. Depending on what the final accepted recommendation is, the minimum flow required for maintaining the river regime and environment will be decided and considered in water resources development and proper management. Irrigation has two roles:

- Protective aspect, i.e. to make up the deficiency in soils during the cropping season so as to ensure proper and sustained growth of the crops with appropriate management of water resources.
- Additional land use aspect, i.e. to enable second or third crop being raised on the lands which could otherwise not be cultivated efficiently, more particularly during the post or pre-monsoon period.

Thus, irrigation, on the one hand, is an insurance against the vagaries of nature and, on the other helps raises the productivity of land. Development of irrigation has conferred immense benefits to the Indian rural economy. These benefits can be classified in two categories: direct benefits are—promoting the greater utilization of land; enlarging the average size of the farm; generating demand for additional farm labour; bringing a shift in crop pattern in favour of new and improved varieties of crops; increasing additional productive investment in farm business; bringing favorable input-output ratio and widening the scope for increase in land revenue and other local receipts. Indirect benefits are—expansion of secondary and tertiary activities in the area affected by it resulting in greater work opportunities leading to a reduction in migration of rural poor to the urban areas; more employment to both family and hired labour; higher value of output per industrial unit—and higher turnover of business establishments in the project areas. The annual plans, 1979-80 and the Sixth Plan witnessed new starts and then the focus was shifted towards completion of irrigation projects. By the end of the Eighth plan (1996-97), central assistance was provided under AIBP (Accelerated Irrigation Benefit Programme) to help the State, Governments in early completion of the projects. Although plan expenditure on irrigation has increased from Rs. 441.8 crore in the First Plan to Rs. 95743.42 crore (outlay) in the Tenth Plan, the share in total plan expenditure has decreased from 23 per cent in the First Plan to 6.3 per cent in the Tenth Plan. Even after achieving the UIP of 139.89 MH and considering the average irrigation intensity of 140 per cent, the ultimate irrigated area in the country would be only 70 per cent of the net sown area. The increasing difference between irrigation potential created and utilized is ascribed to a number of reasons. Irrigation systems are designed for extensive irrigation for a 75 per cent confidence level. Thus, water availability in some basins would be less the designed amount.

The problems relating to the existing irrigation projects can be divided into two parts, i.e. the problem of underutilisation, and the problem of drainage, congestion, water logging, maldistribution and wastage of water, etc. The problem of underutilisation of the irrigation potential has been a serious problem confronting us since the First Plan itself. More than 10 per cent of the total irrigation potential remains unutilised. Underutilisation has been there on account of causes like:

- Lack of coordination between the departments of agriculture and irrigation at the project formulation stage.
- Failure to carry out adequate, oil surveys and assess suitability of the land and soil for irrigation.
- Failure to minimise conveyance losses and associated problems of water logging and soil salinity.
- Structural inadequacies with the main system and consequent inability to deliver the right quantity of water at the right time to the irrigation outlets.
- Absence of field distribution system, water control structures and farm drainage facilities.
- Failure to formulate appropriate cropping patterns based on water availability and soil characteristics.
- Failure to get land shaped and leveled.
- Absence of infrastructural facilities like roads, marketing, credit, etc.
- Lack of farmer organisations and proper extension services.

Another important development has been the significant shift in the government's approach in the form of emphasis on participatory irrigation management for distribution of water by beneficiaries themselves and taking up the maintenance and operation up to a portion of irrigation system. The government has activated the second phase of the National Water Management Project. Irrigation has also raised the problems relating to drainage, congestion, water logging, maldistribution and wastage of water, etc. Canals and road construction interfere with natural drainage. Rivers are the most effective natural drainage system, and any unplanned, interference with them is bound to have it repercussions on the natural drainage land, therefore, on the incidence of floods in a country with the rainfall concentrated in short periods. Lack of Coordination between Irrigation and Agricultural Development so changes in the cropping pattern and practices alter the demand for water both in the volume and the time of its supply. The irrigation authority takes action to adjust the supply to changes in demand after a considerable time lag. Consequently, proper use of irrigation facilities has bean quite a delayed process.Financial returns from the existing irrigation facilities have been very low, in this way proper water resource management is required. For example, a recent study of the Chambal irrigation project revealed that the revenue from irrigation fell short of even the working expenses by 73 percent. This has been largely due to the fact that the existing pricing formula for irrigation water has no relation to the cost structure. The Vaidyanathan Committee which recently went into the whole issue of costing and pricing of irrigation water has highlighted the need to reverse the flow of low return from the irrigation sector. The committee has made specific recommendations as to how the water rate structure can be modified, implemented and the irrigation systems made self-sustainable.

ELEVENTH FIVE YEAR PLAN STRATEGY FOR MAJOR, MEDIUM AND MINOR IRRIGATION

The Government of India launched Bharat Nirman Programme in 2005-06. The irrigation component of the programme envisages creation of an additional 6.2 MH of irrigation potential. This target will be achieved through major, medium and minor projects for surface water and ERM schemes. It has also been decided to provide assistance under AIBP to the projects providing irrigation facilities to drought-prone tribal areas as well as to States which are having irrigation development of their potential below national average. It has been observed that utilization of the created irrigation potential through AIBP is not up to the expected level. One of the reasons for non-utilization or low utilization of created irrigation potential is non-completion of CAD work in the area where irrigation facilities have been created. The CAD Programme should be integrated with the project implementation and upon completion of the project the water should reach to the farm gate instead of creating the irrigation potential which is not immediately utilized. It is; ho pertinent to mention that the cost of land development works should also be integrated with the project cost which may be funded under AIBP. The inclusion of CAD component with the cost of the project may affect the benefit-cost ratio of the project.

For quite sometime many State Governments have been raising the issue of declaring some irrigation projects as National Projects. The criteria for the selection of these projects, their mode of implementation and pattern of funding, etc. are yet to be finalized. However, it is obvious that the projects which are on international borders and the projects benefiting two or more States should figure as National Projects. During the end of the Tenth Plan, the Planning Commission insisted on monitoring of the project funded under AIBP through remote sensing. Accordingly, a pilot scheme for monitoring Teesta and Upper Krishna Projects through remote sensing has been taken loses to actual. Accordingly the MoWR has assigned the job of monitoring of 53 projects covering the area of 5 MH for remote sensing monitoring. The following steps could be taken for major, medium, and minor irrigation sector for the Eleventh Five Year Plan:

- Funds would be earmarked by the Planning Commission in the State plans so that the ongoing schemes under AIBP can be completed in time and cost over-run is avoided.
- Foremost priority should be given for completion of the ongoing projects. Ongoing projects which have already achieved 90 per cent or more of the ultimate potential should be considered as completed.
- Inter-sector priority should be decided considering various aspects such as externally aided projects, inter-state projects, projects benefiting drought prone or tribal areas, etc. as per the guidelines prepared by National

Commission for Integrated Water Resources Development Plan.

- High priority should be accorded to the pre-Seventh and Seventh Plan projects for funding under IBP to complete these projects during the eleventh plan.
- Schemes should be given out on fixed cost time certain contract basis with incentive and penalty clause.
- The CAD works and project execution should be in one package to ensure the availability of water upon completion of the project.
- To improve efficiency, irrigation projects should be benchmarked for performance evaluation by an independent expert group so that optimum use of water is realized. The AIBP assistance in the form of grants should be made according to the performance parameters.
- A separate budget head upto 15 per cent of Plan fund may be provided as Irrigation Maintenance Fund (IMF) and full amount of irrigation revenue as collected should be credited to thc IMF.
- System maintenance and revenue realization should be handed over to beneficiaries groups or Water Users' Associations (WUAs).
- The existing regional and State-level institutions such as Water and Land Management Institutes should be strengthened and brought into mainstream activities for irrigation management improvement.
- Dam safety measures should be taken up systematically for Disaster Prevention and Management. 5 per cent of plan fund may be allocated for undertaking dam safety activities to ensure that dams in distress get special and timely attention.
- The performance evaluation of completed projects needs to be continued for benchmarking and improvement in irrigation efficiency.
- Introduce the concept of National Projects.
- Review the requirements and process of environmental clearance.
- Renovation and restoration of old tanks as well as old diversion channels in hilly regions may be given high priority.

- Micro-irrigation system in water deficit areas should be promoted.
- Groundwater development in areas having untapped and unutilized potential, particularly in the Eastern Region should be promoted through a time-bound programme.
- A comprehensive strategy as recommendation by the expert group for regulation of ground water development and use on sustainable basis should be implemented.

CONCLUSION

While larger investment outlays are necessary, the emphasis and focus must be not on the magnitude of investment expenditure, but on the composition of improvements that increase the product potential of land and water resources already under use. This requires; Reduction of allocations for different ongoing projects and prioritisation of individual projects after careful critical review of the quality of preparatory work, designs and cost estimates and stage of construction. A significant increase in allocations for improvement and modernisation of existing systems to reduce waste and achieve letter control over water distribution and increased allocation for integrated watershed development for rain-fed areas. The focus must not be only on the magnitude of investments allocated to these activities but on their efficient implementation. This calls for:

- Close scrutiny of cost estimates of large projects to minimise over-design and internal consistency between different components, strict monitoring to ensure that allocations are used as approved and time schedules are adhered to.
- *Rationalise*: All soil and water conservation programmes into a single unified watershed programme under a single agency at the ground level.
- Restructure the organisation for implementation of programmes to ensure that the panchayats have a central role in planning and implementation with government agencies providing technical advice and support.
- Review the performance of the research system and take measures to reorient their work to generate technologies and practices for sustained increases in productivity especially for rain-fed areas and for methods by which costs of irrigated agriculture can be reduced, and adverse

environmental consequences contained, by proper control over timing and quantum of water and fertiliser application.

- Ensure that the institutional and policy reforms create an environment that enables and induces users of land and water to make more prudent and efficient use of these resources.
- Transfer the responsibility for deciding and enforcing rules of water allocation and maintenance and repair and levy and collection of water charges to autonomous and financially self-reliant user-controlled organisations with government officials providing technical expertise and support.
- Increase the price of canal water, electricity and fertilisers to cover costs of providing them at reasonable levels of efficiency and ensure proper assessment and prompt collection of dues from users.

The measures suggested for the Eleventh Plan address the whole range of issues concerning water management and irrigation. The long gestation period in building irrigation infrastructure and thin spread of resources are the main reasons for delay in completion of a number of ongoing projects. During the Eleventh Plan a total of 477 projects including 166 major, 222 minimum and 89 ERM projects are likely to spill over. The spill over cost of these projects during the Eleventh Plan is estimated to be about Rs. 1,33,746 crore. There is a need for reducing the gestation period and making available the benefits of irrigation to the users by way of integrating CAD programme with the projects. The projects should be implemented on a construction scheduled not more than four to five years the land acquisition and R&R works should be taken simultaneously with the project formulation. Irrigation efficiency in the systems needs to be upgraded from the present level of 35 per cent to about 60 per cent in case of surface water system and from about 65 per cent to 75 per cent in ground water system. The efforts of the other departments such as Rural Development and Agriculture, etc. should be converged and an integrated approach for water resources development and conservation should be adopted. The various schemes of MoRD for rain water harvesting, watershed development. There is a need for Public-Private Partnership (PPP) in development of water resource projects as this issue has already been addressed by NWP 2002. The modern scientific development of water resources conservation, transfer and application to the field is needed to be applied in the irrigation command. In flood management, the recurrence interval of the floods should be the guiding factor for taking up flood control measures. The flood control measures should not be taken in isolation but it should be based on Master Plan approach in an integrated manner. The sustainability of ground water is one of the core areas which require attention for meeting irrigation water requirements. Use of ground water should be limited and linked with the quantum of water being recharged. The issue of monitoring ground water levels through scientific methods such as Piezo meters, etc. should be left to the group of beneficiaries with proper technical support from the Central Government and the State Governments. If we get success to do all these above mentioned approaches of water collection and better storage, then we shall properly meet out our water requirements regarding agricultural use and will also be able to remove the water crisis in Indian agrarian economy.

References

A.M. Khusro, Economics of Land Reform and Farm Size in India, p. XIV.

Acharya, G. (2000), "Approaches to Valuing the Hidden Hydrological Services of Wetland Ecosystems". *Ecological Economics*, Vol. 35, No. 1, pp. 63-74.

Acharya, G. and Barbier, E.B. (2000), "Valuing Groundwater Recharge through Agricultural Production in the Hadejia-Nguru Wetlands in Northern Nigeria". *Agricultural Economics*, Vo. 22, No. 3, 247-59.

Agarwal, Anil and Narain, Sunita (1989), Towards Green Villages: A Strategy for Environmentally Sound and Participatory Rural Development, Centre for Science and Environment: New Delhi.

Agarwal, Anil and Narain, Sunita (1995), In the Belly of the River. *Tribal Conflicts over Development in the Narmada Valley*. Oxford University Press: Delhi.

Apoorva Oza (2007), "Irrigation: Achievements and Challenges", *Indian Infrastructure Report*, New Delhi.

Bardhan, E. and Udry, C. (1995), *Development Microeconomics*. New Delhi: Oxford University Press.

Bystorm, O., Anderson, H. and Gren, L.M. (2000), "Economic Criteria for Using Wetlands as Hydrogen Sinks under Uncertainty". *Ecological Economics*, Vol. 35, No. 1, pp. 35-45.

Chopra, K. and Dasgupta, P. (2003), The Nature of Household Dependence on Common Pool Resources: An Econometric Study for India. New Delhi: Institute of Economic Growth [Working Paper Series No. E/232/2003].

Coelli, T.J., Parelman, S. (1999), A Comparison of Parametric and Non-parametric Distance Functions: with Application to European Railways. *Euro J. Operat Res*, 117, 326-39.

Coggins, J.S., Swinton, J.R. (1996), The Price of Pollution: A Dual Approach to Valuing SO_2 Allowances. *J. Environ Econ Manag*, Vol. 30, No. 1, pp. 58-72.

Dandekar, V.M. (1966), Transforming Traditional Agriculture: A Critique of Prof. Schultz, *Economic and Political Weekly*, 20 August.

Dhavan, B.D. (1988), "Indian Irrigation: An Assessment", *Economic and Political Weekly*, May 7, p. 965.

Dziegielewska, D.A.P, Mendelsohn, R. (2005), Valuing Air Quality in Poland. *Environ Resour Econ*, Vol. 30, pp. 131-63.

Eleventh Five Year Plan (2007-12), Vol. III, Planning Commission, Government of India-2008, p. 46.

Eleventh Five Year Plan (2007-12), Vol. III, Planning Commission, Government of India, 2008, p. 46.

Ellis, G. and Fisher, A. (1987), "Valuing the Environment as an Input". *Journal of Environmental Management*, Vol. 25, pp. 149-56.

Ghosh, Alak (1962), Indian Economy : Its Nature & Problems, Calcutta: The World Press Pvt. Ltd.

Hanneman, W.M. (2001), 'Contingent Valuation and Economics' in U. Sarkar (edited), *Environmental Economics*, Readers in Economics, New Delhi, Oxford University Press.

India, 2010 Publications Division, Ministry of Information & Broadcasting, Government of India.

Kolavalli, Shashi and Ken, John (1997), 'The Ideology and Politics of Community Participation: Tank Irrigation Development in Colonial and Contemporary Tamil Nadu in R.D. Grillo and R.L. Stirrat (eds.) Discourses of Development: Anthropological Perspectives. Berg Publishers: New York.

Kolavalli, Shashi and Ken, John (2002), 'Mainstreaming Participatory Watershed Development' in *Economic and Political Weekly*, Vol. 37, No. 3, pp. 225-42.

Kumar, S., Gupta, S. (2004), Resource use Efficiency of US Electricity Generating Plants during the SO_2 Trading Regime: A Distance. *Function Approach*. Working Paper 17, National Institute of Public Finance and Policy, New Delhi.

OIKOS and IIRR (2000), *Social and Institutional Issues in Watershed Management in India*. OIKOS, India and International Institute of Rural Reconstruction, Philippines.

Raj Krishna's and Dharm Narain's Studies quoted in C.H. Hanumantha Rao (e.d.), *Agriculture, Food Security, Poverty and Environment* (New Delhi, 2005).

Rajora, Rajesh (1998), *Integrated Watershed Management*. Rawat Publications: Jaipur.

Rao, C.H. Hanumantha (2000), 'Watershed Development in India: Recent Experience and Emerging Issues' in *Economic and Political Weekly*, Vol. 35, No. 45, pp. 3943-47.

Rao, C.H. Hanumantha (2005), *Agriculture, Food Security, Poverty and Environment*, New Delhi.

Rao, C.H. Hanumantha, "Agriculture: Policy and Performance". In Bimal Jalan (E.D.) *The Indian Economy: Problems and Prospects* (New Delhi, 1992).

Shultz, T.W. (1953), Economic Organization of Agriculture, McGraw Hill Book Co., New York.

Chapter 9

Sustainable Growth through Tank Irrigation

A Case Study of North Coastal Andhra Pradesh

K. MADHU BABU

INTRODUCTION

In recent years the concept "Equity" has become mantra of development strategy. The development economists argue that equity is necessary for sustainable development because "equity" represented by the equal opportunities for all members of the society makes them socially active, politically influential and economically productive (World Bank, 2006). As a result, the equal opportunities exert potentially beneficial effects on poverty reduction. If we interpret this equity concept to irrigation poverty particularly focusing on the poor farmers, who are not having sufficient access to and deprived of adequate irrigational facilities, it is certain that this strategy reduces irrigation poverty in rural areas in general and the marginalized farmers in particular.

THE RESEARCH PROBLEM

Poverty will decline only when agriculture sector is the full participant in economic growth, especially that of small and marginal farmers. Poverty reduction is driven ultimately by raising farm incomes spent on locally produced goods and services that lead to more village level employment opportunities. A high growth rate, even more than 4 per cent in agricultural sector is essential with in expected economic growth rate of 8 per cent without its poverty reduction will be a futile exercise growth rate in agriculture can be boosted with existing appropriate irrigation technologies and methods, which are ecologically favorite, investment-saving and farmer-friendly, i.e. tank irrigation systems.

Tanks in India and in our states were known for their antiquity and created essentially as a multiple use structures for irrigation, livestock and human uses. Tanks were considered not a mere bodies of stored water but they were treated as a method of conservation on bio-diversity and also a technology for improving environmental quality. They have been performing different special functions in irrigated agriculture-water conservation, soil conservation, flood control and protection of ecology of surrounding area. Tanks represent for extraordinary engineering, managerial and social skills and an extensive system of rain water harvesting structures. However, after independence, the Government under successive planning had not given due attention or provided adequate financial support to keep these tanks in a good state. Most of the public investment in irrigation has gone to major and medium canal irrigation and development of ground water under minor irrigation (Siva Subrahmanyam, 2005, GOI, 1997). No doubt, the area under irrigation increased substantially but tank irrigation areas showed a steady decline in the past 50 years.

NEED FOR THE STUDY

In many area specific studies, it is observed that rural areas are characterized by extension of cultivation on marginal and sub-marginal lands, over grazing due to higher density of livestock and decline in the area under forests. A consequence of this is the degradation of rural environment, which in turn may lead to soil erosion, deterioration of tank irrigation and decline in crop yields. To suggest a policy for arresting this trend, there is a need for a detailed study on the nexus between environmental degradation, tank irrigation and agricultural yields. But the nexus between these three varies from region to region. So keeping in view the necessity of area specific on these aspects, North Coastal Districts of Andhra Pradesh are studied.

BACKGROUND OF THE SELECTED STUDY AREA

The north coastal districts namely Srikakulam, Vijayanagaram and Visakhapatnam represent a high percentage of forest and hilly zones include the Eastern Ghats and they frequently face the problems of forest degradation, encroachments and shifting cultivation mainly in tribal belt of the North Coastal Region to a greater extent. Similarly, frequent droughts in the region are the root cause of low yields and poverty of the region through the rainfall is high when compared to the rest of the state. This region is lagged behind the other districts in its performance of agricultural development, inspite of the fact that its proportion of irrigated area in cropped area is higher than the state average. This may be due to the reason that major source of irrigation in this region is tanks and they are getting deteriorated and providing poor quality of irrigation.

North Coastal Andhra (NCA) Pradesh region is also characterized by relatively higher proportion of small holdings higher density rate of deforestation, lower proportion of cropped area, higher proportion of agricultural workers in total workers, higher proportion of rural population, higher density of population and lower infrastructural facilities, when compared to state level figures. This causes mainly to the neglect of soil and water management in both plain and hilly areas because the farmers do not have a concern for the future and are conscious of their stake in the sustainable use of natural resources. Therefore, it is likely that this region may fall in the vicious circle of environmental degradation leading to deterioration in tank irrigation, leading to decline in crop yields, leading to increase in poverty, leading to environmental degradation. In order to suggest measures for achieving sustainable agricultural development in these regions, there is a need to study the linkages between environment, tank irrigation, crop yields and poverty.

OBJECTIVES OF THE STUDY:

1. to examine the impact of environmental degradation on tank irrigation,
2. to examine the impact of deterioration in tank irrigation on crop yields and poverty, and
3. to examine the impact of poverty on environment.

METHODOLOGY AND DATA

This study is a micro level study on tank irrigation at village level. The required statistical data was collected through primary and secondary sources. Secondary data is collected from seasonal crop report and statistical abstract of Andhra Pradesh published by Government of Andhra Pradesh. Out of three districts in North Coastal part of Andhra Pradesh, two districts, namely, Vijayanagaram and Srikakulam which represent a maximum cropped area cultivated under tank irrigation were selected. At the second stage, five villages from two mandals per district were selected. The total number of sample villages is ten. The sample of farmers was drawn from the lists of farmers provided by the irrigation department for various tanks in the selected villages. Fifteen farmers from different categories of farms were selected from each village randomly with probability proportional to the numbers in the three groups. The total sample comes to 150 farmers. The reference period for the collection of primary data was 2009-10.

TRENDS IN TANK IRRIGATION IN NORTH COASTAL ANDHRA PRADESH

Size of the tank plays an important role in storing the water and supplies it through sluices. The quality of irrigation certain improves under big tanks and channel fed tanks. Tank irrigation in NCA region not only declined in relative terms but in absolute terms also. An analysis of decline in tank irrigated area proves this fact. The trends in tank irrigation during the period under study are shown in Table 1.

As can be seen from the Table 1, the absolute decline of net area irrigated from all sources together was 41,790 hectares, which accounted for a decline of 10.26 percent in 2009-10. It is clear that there are fluctuations in the tank irrigated area from year to year but there has been a rapid decline on the whole. The steady decline in tank irrigation is not a healthy sign on the part of agricultural development and it is a recurring problem of the region for many decades. It is necessary to take steps to stabilize and improve the performance of the existing tanks that are eco-friendly, productive and low expensive of surface irrigation.

LAND USE PATTERN OF SAMPLE FARMERS

Land is the most important resources and means of employment and income of the farmers. Based on the empirical study conducted in

TABLE 1

Trends in Tank Irrigation in NCA (Net Area Irrigated from 1960-61 to 2009-10)

(in Hectares)

Period	*Canals*	*% Increase/ Decrease over the earlier period*	*Tanks*	*% Increase/ Decrease over the earlier period*	*Dug Wells*	*% Increase/ Decrease over the earlier period*	*Tube Wells*	*% Increase/ Decrease over the earlier period*	*Other Sources*	*% Increase/ Decrease over the earlier period*	*All Sources*	*% Increase/ Decrease over the earlier period*
(1)	*(2)*	*(3)*	*(4)*	*(5)*	*(6)*	*(7)*	*(8)*	*(9)*	*(10)*	*(11)*	*(12)*	*(13)*
1960-61	132769	—	240139	—	16898	—	1120	—	16258	—	407184	—
1970-71	113256	-14.70	260372	8.43	16493	-2.40	411	-63.30	32668	100.93	423128	3.92
1980-81	144086	27.22	243204	-6.59	4794	-70.93	1482	260.58	19105	-41.52	412881	-2.42
1990-91	186736	29.60	220532	-9.32	24944	420.32	5589	277.13	25566	33.82	464085	12.40
2000-01	177699	-4.84	199150	-9.70	22467	-9.93	19353	246.27	33918	32.67	452809	-2.43
2005-06	156936	-11.68	137382	-31.02	21265	-5.35	23709	22.51	26120	-22.99	365386	-19.31
1960-61 to 2005-06 Increase(+) Decrease (-)	24167	18.20	-102757	-42.79	4367	25.84	22589	2016.87	9862	60.66	-41790	-10.26

Source : Season and Crop Reports of A.P.

TABLE 2

Land Particulars of Sample Farmers during 2009-10

(Area in Hectares)

Size group of OPH	*No. of Sample HHs*	*Owned Land*	*Leased in*	*Leased Out*	*Permanent fallows*	*Operational holdings*
(1)	*(2)*	*(3)*	*(4)*	*(5)*	*(6)*	*(7)*
Small	80	72.56 (0.91)	3.18 (0.04)	3.24 (0.04)	1.21 (0.02)	71.29 (0.89)
Medium	50	94.53 (1.89)	26.10 (0.52)	—	—	120.64 (2.41)
Large	20	104.59 (5.23)	16.63 (0.83)	7.28 (0.36)	—	113.94 (5.70)
Overall	150	271.69 (1.81)	45.91 (0.31)	10.52 (0.07)	1.21 (0.01)	305.86 (2.04)

Note : Figures in Brackets indicate per holding data.

Source : Primary data from field survey.

the NCA under the some agro-climatic conditions, land particulars are presented in the Table 2.

The total sample holdings consist of owners, owner tenants and tenants were reported in all size-groups. Leasing-in land on payment of low fixed cash rent was a common practice in this region. But, the extent of land leased-in or leased-out is very limited because of un-assured irrigation and poor quality of the soils. In aggregate, the average size of operational holdings of the small farmers was 0.89 hectares and for all the households combined it was 2.04 hectares. The disturbing feature of these farms was that besides being small, they were fragmented and on an average each farm having five to six fragments. Owned and leased-in lands of the tenants were in the proportion of 0.86 and 0.14. So, magnitude of tenancy depends upon the workforce and the crops that are raised in that region associated with irrigation facilities.

IRRIGATION PARTICULARS OF SAMPLE FARMS

Irrigation particulars of sample farmers of study area is presented in Table 3.

TABLE 3

Irrigation Particulars during 2009-10

Size group of OPH	*Operated Area Irrigated by Various Sources*				
	Canals	*Tanks*	*Wells*	*Others Sources*	*Total Irrigated Area*
Small	—	54.07	1.09 (0.01)	—	55.16
	—	(0.01)	1.98	—	(0.69)
%	—	92.02		—	100
Medium	—	76.75	—	—	76.75
	—	(1.53)	—	—	(1.53)
%	—	100	—	—	100
Large	—	69.83	4.05	—	73.88
	—	(3.49)	(0.20)	—	(3.69)
%	—	94.52	5.48	—	100
Overall	—	200.64 (1.34)	5.14	—	205.78
	—	97.50	(0.03)	—	(1.37)
%	—		2.5	—	100

Notes : (1) Figures in Brackets indicate per holding data.
(2) Percentages relate to total area irrigated.

Source : Primary data from field survey.

Farmers in the tank command areas are predominantly small in size, 60 percent of them hold less than 1 hectare and 80 percent of them have less than 2 hectares. Among the source of irrigation, tanks account for 97.5 percent of the gross cropped area of the sample farmers and constitute the most important source. This shows the intensity of tank irrigation and alternative dependable sources are not available for paddy crops in the region. It is reported that the tank irrigation failed many times for the past five years and yields that obtained were marginal due to tank water deficits. Though irrigation expansion has been chosen as the prime engine in the strategy of agricultural development and poverty alleviation, irrigation requirements are growing with growing population and with crop diversification. It would adversely effect the living conditions of relatively poor farmers, who could not afford to go for well irrigation and who continue to depend on tanks.

CROP PATTERN AND INTENSITY OF CROPPING

Now it is interest to analyse cropping pattern and intensity of cropping for sample farmers in the study area. Cropping system is dependent on seasonal rainfall and availability of irrigation water. Irrigation through tanks is the common feature and the frequency of tank filling depends on the rainfall and thus adequate irrigation is uncertain. The small farmers in general attempt to become self-sufficient in the food needs of farm family by concentrating on the production of paddy. The crop pattern of sample farmers presented in Table 4.

The Table 4 shows that 61.25 per cent of the gross cropped area was under paddy and also an important irrigated crop in kharif. Pulses, Sugarcane, Groundnut, etc. were grown in kharif, though in limited extents under irrigated dry conditions. Horticulture crops which constitute 20.18 per cent of gross cropped area occupy the second important position in crop pattern. Pulses, which from around 10 percent of the GCA, are the major group among rabi crops mostly sown in rice follows. The overall intensity of cropping was 114 percent and no major variations found across the size groups with regard to intensity of cropping. This low intensity of cropping was due to erratic rainfall and inadequate tank source. In the absence of irrigation, the farmers can not utilize land and other available resources to the maximum extent possible. The farmers were still under subsistence level of farming in this region and habituated to

TABLE 4

Cropping Pattern of Sample Holdings during 2009-10

Size group of OPH	*Kharif Crops (irrigated)*							*Kharif (Un-irrigated)*		
	Paddy	*Vegetables*	*Ground-nut*	*Sugar-cane*	*Pulses*	*Other Crops*	*Total*	*Horticulture Crops*	*Ground-nut*	*Mesta*
(1)	*(2)*	*(3)*	*(4)*	*(5)*	*(6)*	*(7)*	*(8)*	*(9)*	*(10)*	*(11)*
Small	56.11	0.30	0.81	0.81	0.38	2.41	60.82	7.45	1.09	0.20
Ph	0.70	—	0.01	0.01	—	0.03	0.76	0.09	0.01	—
%	69.31	0.37	1.00	1.00	0.47	2.97	75.13	9.20	1.35	0.25
Medium	85.45	—	0.47	0.61	2.02	0.69	89.23	23.94	3.48	1.52
Ph	1.71	—	0.01	0.01	0.04	0.01	1.78	0.48	0.07	0.03
%	61.54	—	0.34	0.44	1.46	0.50	64.27	17.24	2051.00	1.09
Large	72.26	—	0.16			1.62	74.04	39.09	0.81	
Ph	3.61		0.01			0.08	3.70	1.95	0.04	
%	55.70		0.12			1.25	57.07	30.14	0.62	
Overall	213.82	0.30	1.44	1.42	2.41	4.71	224.09	70.48	5.38	1.72
Ph	1.43		0.01	0.01	0.02	0.03	1.49	0.47	0.04	0.01
%	61.17	0.09	0.41	0.41	0.69	1.35	64.11	20.16	1.54	0.49

(*Contd.*)

TABLE 4 (*Contd.*)

Size group of OPH	*Kharif (Un-irrigated)*			*Kharif Total*	*Rabi*			*Total Rabi*	*Gross Cropped Area (K+R)*	*Intensity of Cropping*
	Other Crops	*Pulses*	*Total*		*Pulses*	*Maize*	*Other Crops*			
(1)	*(12)*	*(13)*	*(14)*	*(15)*	*(16)*	*(17)*	*(18)*	*(19)*	*(20)*	*(21)*
Small	1.32	0.40	10.46	71.29	6.74	0.40	2.53	9.67	90.96	113.56
Ph	0.02	0.01	0.13	0.89	0.08	0.01	0.03	0.12	1.01	
%	1.62	0.50	12.92	88.05	8.32	0.50	3.12	11.95	100.00	
Medium	2.47	—	31.40	120.54	14.45	—	3.76	18.21	138.85	115.09
Ph	0.05	—	0.63	2.41	0.29	—	0.08	0.36	2.78	
%	1.78	—	22.62	86.38	10.41	—	2.71	13.12	100.00	
Large			39.90	113.94	12.55		3.24	15.78	129.72	113.85
Ph			2.00	5.70	0.63		0.16	0.79	6.49	
%			30.76	87.83	9.67		2.50	12.17	100.00	
Overall	3.78	0.40	81.77	305.86	33.73	0.40	9.53	43.26	349.53	144.14
Ph	0.03		0.55	2.04	0.22	0.00	0.06	0.29	2.33	
%	1.08	0.12	23.39	87.51	9.66	0.12	2.73	12.51	100.00	

Note : Ph: Per Sample Holding.

Source : Primary data from field survey.

continue the same pattern of cultivation. No shifts in crop pattern towards labour intensive and high value crops were observed with the adoption of modern agricultural technology.

YIELDS OF IMPORTANT CROPS

Yields of important crops grown by the sample cultivators are presented in Table 5. It is clearly evident from the data that the yields of various crops obtained on sample farms were lower than the sate averages.

TABLE 5
Yield per Hectare of Different Crops Grown on Sample Farms

Season/Crop	*Small*	*Medium*	*Large*	*Overall*
Kharif				
Paddy*	4094	4113	3880	4029
Groundnut	2000	828	1494	1001
Greengram	411	—	—	411
Blackgram	600	—	—	600
Sugarcane (Qtls.)	781	741	—	751
Rabi				
Greengram	165	141	247	181
Blackgram	196	165	247	209
Redgram	107	—	—	107
Maize	2000	—	—	2000
Ragi	1250	—	—	1250
Groundnut	—	1058	302	895
Gingelly	39	247	87	109
Sunflower	158	—	375	222
Cashew	214	468	124	251

Note : The yield per hectare of paddy as reported by sample households during Kharif 2009-10 was above the normal and unusual. This high yield level was a rare phenomena and could be possible owing to favourable monsoon and other weather conditions in the season.

Source : Primary data from field survey.

The above table reveals that, paddy is the dominant crop of the kharif season, which constitutes more than 60 percent of the area.

Horticulture crops and pulses to some extent were widely cultivated in the sample areas. Due to low fertility of soils, un-irrigated conditions and tank fed irrigation, groundnut, mesta, maize, ragi, etc. were cultivated along with tank fed paddy. Production and yield per hectare on these farms of NCA were stagnated due to decline in public investment in the agricultural sector and the rise in environmental resource degradation. As the family size is increasing, fulfilling the household food requirement necessitated the enhanced farm productivity in the diminishing size of their farms. More emphasis on development of assured irrigation and pro-small farmer technologies is needed.

IRRIGATION EFFICIENCY OF RAINFED TANK

Water is a prime natural resource and also scarce resource, which with judicious planning of conservation and utilization can provide long lasting benefits on a sustainable basis. The available water, therefore, must inevitably be harnessed for optimal use and must be released after generating maximum benefits with a minimum possible environmental effect. It is stated that the irrigation efficiency is about 40 per cent in the existing tank system in the study area. The data relating to efficiency aspects of tank irrigation collected from sample farmers are presented in Table 6(a).

As can be seen from the table, efficiency related aspects, the farmers were asked whether they got timely water availability and adequate supply of water they needed and other relevant factors. Since the size of the tanks are small and they cannot store excess water during the times of high rainfall and the uncertainty of water availability is fairly high as indicated by the tank contents in the previous few years. In an aggregate more than 86 percent of the sample farmers have reported against the timely availability of water and with regard to adequacy also. It is examined that the fluctuations in irrigation and yield levels of paddy and it is a common phenomenon under rainfed tanks in study area. It is further stated that there was no increase in area irrigated under tanks over the time and stagnation of irrigation under the source have been reported by 98.67 per cent of these households. There was no remarkable change in crop pattern under various tanks and majority of them have confirmed the view that irrigation through rainfed tanks makes agriculture a gamble with nature. Overall, it is expressed that the maintenance of irrigation structures to tanks are poor and neglected for decades and works to

TABLE 6(a)
Percent of Sample Farmers Respond to Irrigation Efficiency of Tanks

Size Group of OPH	*Timely water Availability*		*Adequate water Availability*		*Increase in Irrigation Area*		*Stagnation in Irrigation Area*	
	Yes	*No*	*Yes*	*No*	*Yes*	*No*	*Yes*	*No*
(1)	*(2)*	*(3)*	*(4)*	*(5)*	*(6)*	*(7)*	*(8)*	*(9)*
Small	7.5	92.5	8.75	91.25	15	85	100	—
Medium	8	92	12	88	—	100	100	
Large	30	70	35	65	—	100	90	10
Overall	10.67	89.33	13.33	86.67	8	92	98.67	1.33

(Contd.)

TABLE 6(a) (*Contd.*)

Size Group of OPH	*Change in crop pattern for the past 5 years*		*Maintenance of Irrigation structures*		*Year of repair to the Tank bund/field Channels*			
	Yes	*No*	*Better*	*Poor*	*2001 to 2005*	*2007*	*2008*	*2009*
(1)	*(10)*	*(11)*	*(12)*	*(13)*	*(14)*	*(15)*	*(16)*	*(17)*
Small	1.25	98.75	2.5	97.5	2.5	25	32.5	30
Medium	4	96	22	78		12	40	34
Large		100	30	70	10	25	30	20
Overall	2	98	12.67	87.33	2.66	20.67	34.67	30

Source : Primary data from field survey.

tank funds and some field channels were done only recently during the years 2005 to 2009.

ENVIRONMENTAL RELATED ASPECTS OF MINOR IRRIGATION TANKS

There is a wide spread evidence that in many villages currently facing severe environmental resource degradation, the resource users in the past were poorer compared to today and yet natural resource degradation was consciously prevented. Per capita availability of water resource is declining with rapidly growing population and economic development and urbanization. Initially priority has been in favour of surface irrigation infrastructural development, which is evident from the budget allocations in Five Year Plans. However, of late, with the inherent weaknesses in surface irrigation and environmental degradation, tank irrigation has declined over a period of three decades.

The reason attributed to decline in tank irrigation is the changes in rainfall pattern and reduced inflow to the tanks. The reduction in flow is largely due to encroachments in catchment areas which restricts run-off to the tanks. Whenever there was decline in rainfall, tank irrigated area also decreased, and irrigated area increased while rainfall is increased. But of late, run-off hydraulic pattern broke down, which impacts agriculture in tank command areas. Besides encroachments, several other reasons are very much responsible for degradation in tank irrigation which includes environment related. Percent of sample farmers of responded related aspects of tanks are presented in Table 6(b).

Interviews with farmers in the tank command that, about 73 per cent of them noticed soil erosion and 70 per cent face the problem of sitting up of feeder channels which affects the flow of water to the fields. There was no depletion of groundwater usage, because of luck of wells in the tank commands. These tanks were not used as per collated tanks unlike some other districts in the state. A majority of these farmers (73%) expressed the view that the activities like fishing, bathing and other human uses which were very active earlier in tank use were affected due to in sufficient water and reduction in storage capacity particularly during the years of low rainfall. The water in the tanks was available for a period of 4 months in a year from August to November. Almost all sample farmers expressed the presence of weeds and shrabs in the tank beds and on the bunds. In general, there

TABLE 6(b)
Percent of Sample Farmers Respond to Environment Related Aspects of Tanks

Size Group of OPH	*Soil Erosion*		*Silting up of Feeder Channels*		*Silting of Tank Beds*		*Fast Depletion of Ground Water*	
	Yes	*No*	*Yes*	*No*	*Yes*	*No*	*Yes*	*No*
(1)	*(2)*	*(3)*	*(4)*	*(5)*	*(6)*	*(7)*	*(8)*	*(9)*
Small	73.75	26.25	70.00	30.00	65.00	35.00	—	100.00
Medium	72.00	28.00	72.00	28.00	54.00	46.00	—	100.00
Large	70.00	30.00	65.00	35.00	65.00	35.00	—	100.00
Overall	72.67	27.33	70.00	30.00	61.33	38.67	—	100.00

(Contd.)

TABLE 6(b) (*Contd.*)

Size Group of OPH	*Farmers shift to Ground water usage*		*Duration of water in the tank in a normal year*		*Intensity of Weeds in Tank Beds*			
	Yes	*No*	*Better*	*Poor*	*2001 to 2005*	*2007*	*2008*	*2009*
(1)	*(10)*	*(11)*	*(12)*	*(13)*	*(14)*	*(15)*	*(16)*	*(17)*
Small	60.25	83.75	96.25	3.75	73.75	26.25	—	100.00
Medium	28.00	72.00	94.00	6.00	72.00	28.00	—	100.00
Large	10.00	90.00	95.00	5.00	70.00	30.00	—	100.00
Overall	19.33	80.67	95.33	4.67	72.67	27.33	—	100.00

Source : Primary data from field survey.

equity in distribution of water and an indicator of this is that crop pattern is more or less the same at all reaches of the system.

MANPOWER RESOURCES OF SAMPLE HOUSEHOLDS

Another important factor that contributes for the economic uplift of the farmers was man power resource utilization. The source of power for performing farm activities in the small farms was mainly from human labour. Predominance of intensive use of family labour was the general characteristic of these farms to minimize out of pocket expenses and ensure employment with in their own farm, whatever might be its worth. The main source of income of family depends on the proportion of the working population in agriculture and allied activities. Generally under uncertain source of irrigation, frequent crop failures, poverty, migration of labour in search of employment will be more and occupational diversification may be taken place. In order to examine these factors analysis was done taking the household characteristics in this part. In the event of droughts and low agricultural productivity, some of the workers move to other places in search of employment. This type of situation arises frequently in sample areas due to failure of tank irrigation and poor people are the ultimate sufferers without supplementary source of irrigation. The data pertaining to these points are given in Table 7.

It is a general practice of the workers in selected areas to temporarily migrate to towns or delta areas, when South-West Monsoon is delayed or in case of crop failure. The data indicate that this movement is fairly more in case of small farmer's category than the other two groups of farmers. On an aggregate 56 per cent reported in favour of the temporary migration in bad agricultural years. Overall 88.671 per cent of the sample farmers expressed the adverse effect of tank irrigation which damages the poorer sections that own small areas under tanks. Some of the important suggestions given by the sample farmers to stabilize and improve tank irrigation are diversification of canal water to tanks, whenever feasible (69.33%), removing of encroachments of tanks areas (7.0%) and desolation and timely repair of tanks (97.33%). All these problems and suggestions of farmers can be taken into account is viewing the better tank management to benefit all categories of farmers and to safeguard environmental resources in the villages in a big way.

TABLE 7

Percent of Sample Households Report Occupational Diversification and Out Migration in Adverse Seasonal Conditions

Size Group of OPH	*Shift over to other Activities in times of low Agricultural productivity*		*Impact of decline in tank management on poorer sections*		*Suggestions to stabilize and improve tank irrigation*		
	Yes	*No*	*Yes*	*No*	*Diversion of canal water to tanks*	*Removing Encroach-ments*	*Desolation of tanks and timely repair*
(1)	*(2)*	*(3)*	*(4)*	*(5)*	*(6)*	*(7)*	*(8)*
Small	70.00	30.00	96.25	3.75	80.00	60.15	97.50
Medium	44.00	56.00	82.00	18.00	56.00	80.00	98.00
Large	30.00	70.00	15.00	25.00	60.00	56.50	95.00
Overall	56.00	44.00	88.67	11.33	69.33	70.00	97.33

Source : Primary data from field survey.

POVERTY TRENDS IN STUDY AREA

The bulk of the poor continues to be in rural areas and with in rural areas, occupied in the agricultural sector. Together with the low rate of growth of food grain production in regions with high incidence of poverty, there has also been a low rate of growth of production of coarse cereals produced in dry areas and mostly consumed by poor people. Low rates of growth of production of pulses and oilseeds concentrated mainly in poorer dry areas should also be said to have adverse effects in relation to poverty. The rural poverty ratios of agricultural households are given in Table 8 for different regions of Andhra Pradesh as per the modified expert group in Andhra Pradesh.

The trend rate of decline in poverty ratio's is estimated for three categories namely cultivator, Agricultural labourers and the rural separately for the years 1983, 1987 and 1993. Despite an increase in rural population by 14 millions, the poverty ratio for the 'cultivators' group for Andhra Pradesh has declined from 28 percent in 1983 to 7 percent in 1993, whereas for NCA region from 41 percent to 15 percent during the same period.

It is further estimated that during 2005-06, the rural poverty ratios were 7 percent for Andhra Pradesh and 10.5 percent for NCA region (NSSO, 61st Round). It is sad commentary on the incidence of poverty that the ratio of poverty is high in NCA than the other regions of Andhra Pradesh for all the years that estimated. This region does not get much priority in irrigation development and stagnation both in irrigation and agricultural production is said to be the main reason for the backwardness and high incidence of poverty. Still majority of small and marginal farmers in this region are poor and in the clutches of a vicious circle of poverty arising out of low production with consequential low income. The rate of decline in poverty ratio of NCA may not be attributed for the better living conditions or raise in income levels of the poor, but it may be due to the general inflationary trend in the economy over the years. It would be far better for the state, if the backward regions are helped in their struggle to achieve higher levels of development in an environmentally sound way.

MAJOR FINDINGS OF THE PRESENT STUDY

I. A majority of sample farmers have reported that, over the years, the encroachment of tank foreshores and

TABLE 8

Rural Poverty Ratios Among Agricultural Households for Different Regions of A.P.

Region	*Cultivators*				*Agricultural Labourers*				*Rural*				
	1983	*1987*	*1993*	*Decline per annum*	*1983*	*1987*	*1993*	*Decline per annum*	*1983*	*1987*	*1993*	*Decline per annum*	*2005*
(1)	*(2)*	*(3)*	*(4)*	*(5)*	*(6)*	*(7)*	*(8)*	*(9)*	*(10)*	*(11)*	*(12)*	*(13)*	*(14)*
North Coastal Andhra	41	17	15	2.6	64	30	29	3.5	50	22	20	3.0	10.5
South Coastal Andhra	16	6	2	1.4	34	20	15	1.9	22	12	9	1.3	—
Rayalaseema	29	8	7	2.2	65	42	24	4.1	46	27	14	3.2	—
North Telangana	18	4	1	1:7	42	18	18	2.4	33	29	16	1.7	—
North Telangana	35	21	7	2.8	54	40	14	4.0	40	27	8	3.2	—
A.P. State	28	14	7	2.1	46	30	18	2.8	35	22	12	2.3	7.0

Note : Poverty ratios for the year 2005 are given for NCA ad A.P. are not available for other regions.

Source : Various rounds of NSSO.

unauthorized cultivation over the tank beds, feeding channels to tanks have reduced the incoming water. With this, the free catchments available to the tanks have reduced the incoming water.

II. Rural poverty was high in this region with predominance of tank irrigation has been stagnation.

III. Tank irrigation suffers from two drawbacks; being dependent on local rainfall, they cannot assume stable water supply and cause droughts or floods depending on vagaries of monsoon. Secondly, because of inadequate maintenance, their irrigation capacity has been on decline.

IV. There is a widespread evidence that in many sample villages currently facing severe environmental resource degradation, the resource users in the past were poorer compared to today and yet this degradation was consciously prevented.

V. In case of many tanks in the selected areas, where the catchment's area is being brought under cultivation thereby restricting free flow of water into tanks and leading to the drying up of the tanks during the periods of low rainfall. Continuous neglect of tank infrastructure in NCA has equity and sustainability implications.

VI. Thus the crop under tanks is mostly dependent on distribution of rain in monsoon period. Consequently the crop yields are unstable when the monsoons fail or distribution is erratic.

SUGGESTIONS AND CONCLUCION

As seen from the analysis, there is need to have renewed focus on traditional wisdom of tanks rehabilitating water bodies for rain water harvesting contrary to construction of large irrigation reservoirs. Tanks ensure equity, ground water sustainability, trap valuable sediment for recycling and thus play an important role in enhancing productivity and profitability from rain-fed agriculture. The links between drought, desertification and migration are complex, where climate fluctuations as well as mobility as overspread. Economic opportunities, decrease in rainfall, migrants education, the existence of social networks and access to transport and road networks, land degradation and environmental degeneration also witnessed high level of mobility. Finally, modernization of tanks is necessary to ensure equity, groundwater sustainability, trap valuable sediment for recycling and thus play an important role in enhancing productivity and profitability from rain-fed agriculture.

References

Climate Change (2001), *Synthesis Report*, Inter-Governmental Panel on Climate Change, Geneva, Switzerland.

Cline, William R. (2007), Climate Change and Agriculture : Impact Estimates by Country (Washington : Center for Global Development and Peterson Institute for International Economics).

Datta, K.L. (2008), An Estimation of Poverty Reduction Between 2004-05 and 2005-06, *Economic & Political Weekly*, November 22, pp. 61-67.

Government of India (2006), National Environment Policy, MOEF.

Massey, D.W. Axinn and Ghimire, D. (2007), "Environmental Change and Out-migration: Evidence from Nepal", Population Studies Centre Research Report 07 – 615 also Marrisey, J. (2009), "Environmental Change and Forced Migration: A State of the Art Review" Refugees Studies Centre, University of Oxford, Oxford.

Raju, K.V. (2000), Revitalization of Irrigation Tanks in Rajasthan : An Approach, *Economic & Political Weekly*, June 3-9, pp. 1930-36.

Various Issues of Statistical Abstract of Andhra Pradesh.

Chapter 10

Water Scarcity

Issues and Challenges

GYANINDRA DASH

One of the key focus areas of Bharat Nirman is drinking water. During Bharat Nirman period, 55,067 Uncovered and about 3.31 lakh slipped-back habitations are to be covered with provisions of drinking water facilities and 2.17 lakh quality-affected hesitations are to be addressed for water quality problem. Despite the increase in access to drinking water, the problem of supplying safe drinking water remains a big challenge. The large population is putting severe strain on the water sources, many of which get contaminated. There has been progress in the supply of safe drinking water but disparities remain between urban and rural areas.

By 2025, nearly 2 billion people will be living in countries or regions with absolute water shortage, where water resources per person falls below the recommended level of 500 cubic meters per year. The situation is getting worse due to population growth; urbanization and the increase in domestic and industrial water use. So circumstances compel to rely on unsafe sources of drinking water. Many countries do not have sufficient water to meet demand with the result that aquifer depletion due to over extraction is common. The scarcity of water is accompanied by deterioration in the quality of water due to pollution.

The world's Population however is quickly becoming urbanized as people migrate to the cities. In 1950, less than 3 per cent of the world's population lived in cities. This number grew to 47 per cent in the year 2000 (2.8 billion people) it is expected to grow to 60 per cent by the year 2025. Urbanization is occurring rapidly in many less developed countries between 2000 and 2030, the urban population in Africa and Asia is set to double. Asia's urban population will grow from 1.4 billion to 2.6 billion. Africa's urban population will surge to more than twice its size, from 294 million to 742 million. Latin America and the Caribbean will sea the urban population rise from 394 to 609 million. By 2030, 79 percent of world's urban dwellers will live in the developing world's towns and cities. Africa and Asia will account for almost seven in every 10 urban in habitants globally.

There is more than enough water available, in total, for everyone's basic needs. The U.N recommends that people need a minimum of 50 liters of water a day for drinking, washing, cooking and sanitation. The total domestic water demand in 1995 and 2025 under the three scenarios, which is shown in Table 1. Total domestic demand under CRI is 60 cubic km in developing countries including India.

TABLE 1

Domestic Water Consumption under Business-as-Usual Water Crisis, and Sustainable Water Use Scenarios, 1995 and 2025

Region/Country	*Domestic Water Demand (km³)*			
	1995 Baseline Estimates	*2025 Projections*		
		BAU	*CRI*	*SUS*
Asia	79.1	156.7	113.0	143.9
China	30.0	59.4	42.3	54.3
India	21.0	40.9	27.7	42.0
Southeast Asia	13.9	30.4	23.6	23.8
South Asia Excluding India	7.0	16.2	11.1	15.30
Latin America (LA)	18.2	30.7	24.7	22.8
Sub-Saharan Africa (SSA)	9.5	23.9	15.2	23.8
West Asia/North Africa (WANA)	7.1	13.1	9.9	11.2
Developed Countries	58.7	68.6	62.8	65.8
Developing Countries	110.6	221.0	159.7	198.7
World	169.3	289.6	222.5	264.5

Many countries, which have a fair estimate of their oil and mineral resources, hardly know their water resource potential. In our country the rainfall pattern is highly variable and most of the people depending up on agriculture and allied activities, the appraisal and planning of water resources has became an important component for its development. The Table 2 shows the global distribution of the fresh water.

TABLE 2
Global Distribution of Fresh Water

Sl. No.	*Water Source*	*Quantity of Water (in Cubic km)*
1.	Water in Ice form	24,000,000
2.	Water in Ponds, Lakes and reservoirs	2,80,000
3.	Water in streams and rivers	1200
4.	Water present in soil moisture	85,000
5.	Ground water	60,000,000
		Total = 84,366,200

IMPORTANCE OF WATER

Water is needed in almost every sphere of human activity. It is required for direct consumption for washing, cleaning, cooling water disposal and transportation. Water is essential for the irrigation, industries, livestock management, Thermal power generation, Domestic requirements, hydroelectric generation and various human activities.

TABLE 3
Sector-wise Consumption of Water in India

Sl. No.	*Sector*	*% of water compassion*
1.	Agriculture	76.0
2.	Power generation	6.2
3.	Industries	5.7
4.	Domestic sector	4.3
5.	Transport and other	7.8

Source : The India infrastructure Report, 1996.

Narattam Shah of the Bombay based center for monitoring Indian Economy stated Unbelievable as it may seem, till now we have no arrangements in this country to compile and publish on an annual basis, comprehensive data regarding various aspects of water which are important for policy analysis and programme formulation and for monitoring the efficiency use of our scarce water resources.

TABLE 4

Fresh Water Requirements of Various Sectors

Sl. No.	*Sector*	*1974*	*2000*	*2025*	*% Increase 2000-25*
1.	Agriculture	350	630	770	22
2.	Thermal Power generation	11	60	160	166
3.	Industries	5-5	30	120	300
4.	Domestic sector	8-8	26.6	39	44
5.	Livestock Management	4-7	7-4	11	36

Source : Astana and Asthana, 2003.

THREAT TO INDIA'S WATER RESOURCES

Water has became the biggest challenge of the 21st century. Global consumption of fresh water increased at a rate greater than twice the rate of population growth. Two out of every three people on earth will have to live in water stressed condition by the year 2025. About 25 per cent of the world's Population does not have access to safe drinking water and 40 per cent does not have sufficient water for adequate living and hygiene.

THE MAJOR THREATS TO INDIA'S WATER RESOURCES

Population Explosion

India with 16 per cent of world's population has only 2.5 per cent of the world's land resources and 4 per cent of the fresh water resources. Population growth is spurring a demographic change, as towns become cities and cities became metropolitan cities. The most important challenge is the availability of fresh water.

Industrial Farming

It has emerged as the worst depleted and polluted water as industrial farming increases water use by a factor of ten, it leads to ground water withdrawals beyond recharge capacity. Pollution by agro-chemicals has contaminated drinking water sources.

WATER EXPLOITATIONS BY MULTINATIONAL CORPORATIONS

A noted human rights activist of USA said in 1960, the global wealth held by corporate was just 16 percent. But it increased to 24 per cent in 1970 and 32 per cent in 1990.

WATER PRIVATIZATION

From this Eighth Plan onwards water has come to be treated as an economic good like any other commodity. In India's official planning commission documents, several measures to operate infrastructure projects including urban water supply and sanitation; on commercial lines either by private parties or through public-private partnership.

The International water management institutes, the world's premier water research group, estimate that India grain harvest could be reduced by up to one-fourth as result of aquifer depletion 70 Percent of the water consumed world wide, including both diverted from rivers and that pumped from underground, is used for irrigation while some 20 percent is used by industry and 10 percent for residential purposes. By projection for 2025 AD, almost, 92 per cent of the utilizable flow of water is likely to be consumed. Share of irrigation needs would be drawn from surface resources.

Measures

1. Fostering an awareness of water scarcity.
2. Region-wise plan should be formulated to study the water crisis.
3. Institutional capacity should be developed for water resources management.
4. Adequate research and training should be provided to the staff in meteorological, water resources departments including computer and Internet.
5. Water conservation measures from domestic level.
6. Protection of forests, soil and water resources.
7. New management approach should be needed for good governance.
8. Special funds should be provided for the extreme climate conditions.

CONCLUSION

The water available for use on the Earth is finite, and if we are not wise in its use, clean water will be a globally scarce commodity. No one solution will solve our water scarcity but we should use water judiciously. Fortunately for us and for the future of our country the challenge of managing water sustainably has been taken of in right earnest by all stakeholders.

REFERENCES

Environmental Studies, Santra.
Kurukshetra, March 2009.
Kurukshetra, May 2010.
Yojana, July 2010.

Chapter 11

Analysis of Irrigation Facilities in Krishna District

SUDHEER, B. AND KISHORE BABU, K.

I. INTRODUCTION

Only about 44 per cent of the cropped area in the country is reported as irrigated today. This is despite an estimated irrigation potential of about 140 mha. Although creation of irrigation potential has increased way above the 22.6 mha at pre-plan stage in 1951, there is an urgent need to expedite the harnessing of balance available irrigation potential through better water management practices. Andhra Pradesh is fortunate is having a rich irrigation potential. It has big rivers like the Godavari, Krishna, Pennar, Nagavali and Vamsadhra, etc. The State has also several smaller rivers whose waters are available for development of irrigation. Krishna district is predominantly an agricultural district and agriculture constitutes the mainstay for the living of the overwhelming majority of the people. In this regard, farmers are mostly dependent on canal irrigation for the supply of water is thus one of the causes responsible for the low productivity of agriculture. In the view of experts, irrigation offers the promise of dramatic improvements in agricultural performance. Adequate and dependable supplies of water should prevent crop failures and produce higher yields. Rural development programs should linkup to improve irrigation facilities in rural areas, which will be helpful to improve the production and yields per hectare.

Government should make sincere efforts to complete the irrigation projects in a legal manner without delay so that water could be made available to the needy farmers to achieve higher production.

This paper mainly focused on irrigation facilities along crop production in Krishna district; this study is mainly based on secondary source which available in reputed journals, magazines and statistical abstract of Krishna district in Andhra Pradesh. It is known fact that India has a very large population and different studies show that it will continue to rise at least till 2050 A.D. Since the land and water resource of any country is not going to change much over the years, the water resource planners have to make cautious decisions on optimizing the available resources for maximum benefit. In the next section, we look into the options available and the decisions that may be taken.

II. IRRIGATION IN INDIA

The Irrigation Projects of India are classified into three types according to their capacity of irrigation. They are : (i) Major Irrigation Projects, (ii) Medium Irrigation Projects and (iii) Minor Irrigation Projects. Irrigations in India carried are on in three different ways according to their sources, such as : (i) by canals, (ii) by wells, and (iii) by tanks. Out of the total area under irrigation, 40 per cent are irrigated by canals, 40 per cent by wells and 12 per cent by tanks. The rest 8 per cent of land are irrigated by other methods.

Irrigation by Canals

This is the most convenient method of irrigation. About half of the total area under irrigation by canals is situated in Punjab, Haryana, Uttar Pradesh and Andhra Pradesh. When there is excessive flow of water in the rivers in flood, the extra water flows in the canals rising from those rivers. Such canals are effective only during floods; hence those are known as the inundation canals. This type of canal is very few in number in the country, more in Punjab than elsewhere. There are many perennial canals in different regions of the country and the most famous of those are the Upper Bari Doab Canal and the Sirhind Canal in Punjab, the West Yamuna Canal and the Chakra Canal in Haryana. The Chakra Canal is the largest canal of the country. This canal serves the purpose of irrigation in the states of Punjab and Haryana. The Rajasthan Canal (The Indira Gandhi Canal) of Rajasthan is the longest canal of Asia. The north-western part of

Rajasthan is being irrigated by it. The other important canals are the Shard Canal, the Beta Canal, the Upper Ganga and the Lower Ganga Canals of Uttar Pradesh. Many canals have been dug out of the rivers Krishna, Godavari und Tungabhadra of Andhra Pradesh. The other important canals are the Son Canal of Bihar, the Damodar Canal of West Bengal, the Mahanadi and the Rushikulya Canals of Orissa, the Mettur and the Periyar Canals of Tamilnadu. The Krishnarajsagar, the Tungabhadra and the Ghataprava Canals of Karnataka.

Irrigation by Wells

The rain-water sinks down easily in the areas where the soil is soft and porous. So water is available at a lower depth when wells are dug and it helps irrigation. Primarily irrigation is carried on by wells in the western part of Uttar Pradesh, some parts of Bihar and in the blank cotton soil area of the Deccan. In addition to it, in the coastal strip of Tamilnadu and Andhra Pradesh, some parts of Rajasthan, Haryana and Gujarat irrigation is also carried on by wells.

Irrigation by Tanks

Tank irrigation is the most feasible and widely practiced method of irrigation all over the Peninsula, where most of the tanks are small in size and built by individuals or groups of farmers by raising bonds across seasonal streams. Besides, in rural areas of the Peninsula there are large number of small tanks for irrigation, but such tanks dry up during acute drought period and don't help in irrigation.

III. BENEFITS OF IRRIGATION

With the introduction of irrigation, there have been many advantages, as compared to the total dependence on rainfall. These may be enumerated as under:

Increase in Crop Yield

The production of almost all types of crops can be increased by providing the right amount of water at the right time, depending on its shape of growth. Such a controlled supply of water is possible only through irrigation.

Protection from Famine

The availability of irrigation facilities in any region ensures protection against failure of crops or famine due to drought. In regions without irrigation, farmers have to depend only on rains for growing crops and since the rains may not provide enough rainfall required for crop growing every year, the farmers are always faced with a risk.

Cultivation of Superior Crops

With assured supply of water for irrigation, farmers may think of cultivating superior variety of crops or even other crops which yield high return. Production of these crops in rain-fed areas is not possible because even with the slight unavailability of timely water, these crops would die and all the money invested would be wasted.

Elimination of Mixed Cropping

In rain-fed areas, farmers have a tendency to cultivate more than one type of crop in the same field such that even if one dies without the required amount of water, at least he would get the yield of the other. However, this reduces the overall production of the field. With assured water by irrigation, the farmer would go for only a single variety of crop in one field at anytime, which would increase the yield.

Economic Development

With assured irrigation, the farmers get higher returns by way of crop production throughout the year, the government in turn, benefits from the tax collected from the farmers in base of the irrigation facilities extended.

Hydro Power Generation

Usually, in canal system of irrigation, there are drops or differences in elevation of canal bed level at certain places. Although the drop may not be very high, this difference in elevation can be used successfully to generate electricity. Such small hydro electric generation projects, using ***bulb-turbines*** have been established in many canals, like Ganga canal, Sarada canal, Yamuna canal, etc.

Domestic and Industrial Water Supply

Some water from the irrigation canals may be utilized for domestic and industrial water supply for nearby areas. Compared to the irrigation water need, the water requirement for domestic and industrial uses is rather small and does not affect the total flow much. For example, the town of Siliguri in the Darjeeling district of West

Bengal, supplies its residents with the water from Teesta Mahananda link canal.

Table 1 reveals that the net area irrigated under various sources in Andhra Pradesh during 2005-06 to 2009-10. In this regard, net area irrigated through tanks have decreased year by year from 6.61 lakh hectares to 3.31 lakh hectares; constituted just 15.01 per cent in 2005-06 and negatively marked to respect totals is above -48.78 per cent in 2009-10 respectively. Net area irrigated through canals was 15.72 lakh hectares in 2005-06 whereas, this was 14.45 lakh hectares in 2009-10, which was slightly decreased. Nevertheless, net area irrigated through wells (tube and dug wells) showing fluctuating trends, though it increased from 19.86 lakh hectares in 2005-06 to 22.83 lakh hectares in 2009-10. But, very small number of holdings are irrigated by other sources i.e., just 1.72 lakh hectares in 2005-06 and slightly decreased to

TABLE 1

Net Area Irrigated by Different Sources in Andhra Pradesh

(In hectares)

Sl. No.	*Source of Irrigation*	*2005-06*	*2006-07*	*2007-08*	*2008-09*	*2009-10*
1.	Tanks	6.61 -15.06	6.02 (13.52)* (-8.97)˜	5.84 (12.59) * (-2.86) ˜	6.47 (13.43) * (10.74) ˜	3.31 (7.81) * (-48.78)˜
2.	Canals	15.72 -35.79	16.22 (36.44) * (3.21)˜	16.09 (34.55) * (-0.82)˜	16.69 (34.63) * (3.72)˜	14.45 (34.29) * (-13.41)˜
3.	Wells (dug wells and tube wells)	19.86 -45.22	20.73 (46.56) * (4.39)˜	22.87 (49.22) * (10.30)˜	23.23 (48.19) * (1.57)˜	22.83 (54.19) * (1.69)˜
4.	Other Sources	1.72 -3.92	1.54 (3.46) * (-10.37) ˜	1.62 (3.50) * (5.32)˜	17.98 (3.73) * (10.60)˜	1.53 (3.63) * (-14.75)˜
5.	Total	43.92 -99.99	44.52 -99.99 -1.37	46.44 -99.99 -4.29	48.2 -99.99 -3.79	42.14 -99.99 (-12.57)

Note : * Shows percentage to the respective totals.
˜ Implies simple growth rates.

Source : Compiled from Statistical Abstract of Andhra Pradesh, Directorate of Economics and Statistics, Government of Andhra Pradesh, Hyderabad, 2010, p. 174.

1.53 lakh hectares in 2009-10 in Andhra Pradesh. If we observed from the table, net irrigated through tanks is decreasing year by year and wells revealed that fluctuating trend. Net area irrigated through both canals and other sources also showed slightly decreased during 2005-06 to 2009-10 in Andhra Pradesh.

Table 2 shows that the Irrigation intensity is the ratio of Gross Irrigated Area to Net Irrigated Area. It is an important indicator to know the efficiency of irrigation. In this connection it is pertinent to study the trends of Gross Irrigated Area in the State during the period 1999-2000 to 2008-09. The total Gross Irrigated Area in the State during 1999-2000 which was 57.46 lakh hectares with fluctuating dwindled to 47.81 lakh hectares in 2003-04 thus recording a negative compound growth rate of 1.6 per cent during the entire period 1999-2000 to 2003-04. On the other hand, the Gross Irrigated Area in the State during 2004-05 which was 49.87 lakh hectares to as high as 67.41 lakh hectares in 2008-09 thus revealing a compound growth rate of 6.7 per cent during the period 2004-05 to 2008-09.

TABLE 2

Irrigation Intensity in Andhra Pradesh

Year	*Gross Irrigated Area (lakh hectares)*	*Net Irrigated Area (lakh hectares)*	*Irrigation Intensity*
1999-2000	57.46	43.84	1.31
2000-01	59.16	45.28	1.31
2001-02	55.49	42.38	1.31
2002-03	45.36	36.14	1.26
2003-04	47.81	38.81	1.32
2004-05	49.87	43.93	1.28
2005-06	59.96	44.52	1.36
2006-07	60.69	46.44	1.36
2007-08	62.85	46.44	1.35
2008-09	67.41	48.21	1.40
CAGR 1999-2000 to 2003-04	(-) 6.1	(-)5.8	
2004-05 to 2008-09	6.7	5.0	

Source : Vimala, P., Employment Generation through NREGs in Kerala, *Kurukshetra*, Vol. 50, No. 01, p. 19.

Table 3 shows that a particulars regarding area and production under food grains during 2004-05 to 2008-09 in Andhra Pradesh. During 2004-05, 62.66 lakh hectares of area covered under food grains which was increased 72.62 lakh hectares in 2009-10, while the production was marked with 133.94 lakh tones and reached to 204.21 lakh tones of production in the same period. If we observed their growth in respective of growth of area and production showing declining trend, and fluctuating trends respectively. By the end of the period, area covered under food grains was marked a growth rate was 0.74 per cent whereas production noted above 3.04 per cent in Andhra Pradesh. From the table it is observed that both area and production are not notably marked under food grains because of farmers are still utilizing the formal agricultural techniques in Andhra Pradesh in general and Krishna district in particular.

TABLE 3

Area and Production of Food Grains in Andhra Pradesh

Sl. No.	*Year*	*Area in Lakh Hectare*	*Production in Lakh Tones*
1	Average of preceding 5 year	69.8	160.17
2	2004-05	62.66	133.94
3	2005-06	71.68 (14.39)	169.5 (26.54)
4	2006-07	72.74 (1.47)	162.29 (-4.25)
5	2007-08	73.87 (1.55)	198.17 (22.10)
6	2008-09	74.42 (0.79)	204.21 (3.04)

Note : Parenthesis shows simple growth rates.

Source : Compiled from an Outline of Agricultural Situation in Andhra Pradesh, Directorate of Economics and Statistics, Government of Andhra Pradesh, Hyderabad, 2008-09, p. 20.

The Table 4 reveals the particulars regarding the irrigated area under various sources during 2004-05 and 2007-08 in Krishna district. During 2004-05, the total gross irrigated area was 3,39,313 hectares which had increased to 4,36,718 hectares by 2007-08 in Krishna district. In the case of irrigated area in Krishna district marking unique services to the farming community. In this regard, in Krishna district the irrigated area more than once was 37,841 hectares in 2004-05 which had greatly increased to 1,96,624 hectares in 2007-08.

TABLE 4

Irrigated Area Under Various Sources in Krishna District (2004-05 and 2007-08)

(Area in Hectares)

Item	*Krishna District*	
Source	*2004-05*	*2007-08*
Canal (Gross)	216481 (63.79)	314483 (72.01)
Tanks (Gross)	24825 (7.31)	18200 (4.16)
Lift irrigation (Gross)	14421 (4.25)	33627 (7.69)
Tube wells (Gross)	63822 (18.80)	51474 (11.78)
Other wells (Gross)	18295 (5.39)	11501 (2.63)
Other Sources (Gross)	1469 (0.43)	7433 (1.70)
Net Area Irrigated	301472 (88.89)	476180 (109.03)
Area irrigated more than once	37841 (11.15)	196624 (45.02)
Gross area Irrigated	339313 (99.97)	436718 (99.97)

Source : Compiled from Hand Book of Statistics, Compiled and Published by Chief Planning Officer, Krishna District, 2004-05 and 2007-08, p. 48.

These sources of irrigation of consist of canals, tanks, lift irrigation, tube wells, other wells and other sources. And, the net irrigated area which was 3,01,472 hectares in 2004-05 had increased to 4,76,180 hectares in 2007-08 in selected Krishna district. During 2004-05 to 2007-08, the irrigated area under canal source was 2,16,481 hectares and 3,14,483 hectares in Krishna district. Regarding, tank sources under irrigation facilities shows declining trend in gross cropped area in Krishna district. Lift irrigation in Krishna district is playing pivotal role by extending gross irrigated area which was 14,421 hectares in 2004-05 to 33,627 hectares by 2007-08.

Table 5 shows the area of principal crops under irrigation in Krishna district from 2004-05 to 2007-08. The district occupied the foremost place in the state for the cultivation of both food and commercial crops. The principal crops under canal, tanks, tube wells, and other sources of irrigation are paddy, chilies, turmeric, sugarcane, vegetables, groundnut, cotton and other crops.

TABLE 5

Area of Principal Crops under Irrigated in Krishna District (2004-05 and 2007-08)

(Area in hectares)

Item	*Krishna District*	
Crop	*2004-05*	*2007-08*
Paddy	262161 (78.62)	496324 (75.46)
Chilies	11030 (3.30)	10269 (1.56)
Turmeric	1806 (0.54)	1809 (0.27)
Sugarcane	39282 (11.78)	27837 (4.23)
Vegetables	5456 (1.63)	8896 (1.35)
Cotton	1124 (0.33)	34762 (5.28)
Groundnut	3970 (1.19)	7651 (1.16)
Other crops	8624 (2.58)	70155 (10.66)
Total	333453 (99.97)	657703 (99.97)

Source : Compiled from Hand Book of Statistics, Compiled and Published by Chief Planning Officer, Krishna District, 2004-05 and 2007-08, p. 48.

Of all the crops, paddy is very important crop in the district and has a vast position of irrigated areas extended to 2,62,162 hectares (78.62 per cent) in 2004-05, which was recorded as 4,96,324 hectares (75.46 per cent) in 2007-08 in Krishna district. In this district, sugarcane also has occupied prominent place with its area of 39,282

TABLE 6

Area, Production and Yield per Hectare of Major Crops in Krishna District, 2004-05 to 2007-08

Sl. No.	*Crop*	*Krishna District, 2004-05*			*Krishna District, 2007-08*		
		Area (in '000 hectares)	*Production (in '000 tones)*	*Yield (kgs.)*	*Area (in '000 hectares)*	*Production (in '000 tones)*	*Yield (kgs.)*
(1)	*(2)*	*(3)*	*(4)*	*(5)*	*(6)*	*(7)*	*(8)*
1.	Paddy	255.3	795	6777	262	905	3458
2.	Jowar	0.97	0	0	3	9	2719
3.	Maize	13.04	49	7682	36	288	3100
4.	Redgram	8.61	07	77	32	31	960
5.	Blackgram	32.48	2020	1496	68	46	669
6.	Greengram	20.93	12	1121	16	6	59
7.	Chilies	18.02	38	29	56	274	4900
8.	Sugarcane	39.3	4607	117240	2	151	76415
9.	Groundnut	9.67	16	79	5	12	2466
10.	Sesamun	1.08	0	471	10	3	364
11.	Castor	0	0	0	5	3	658
12.	Cotton (lint)	47.8	13	281	178	593	567
13.	Tobacco(V)	5.09	8	3395	4	7	1813

Source : Hand Book of Statistics, Compiled and Published by Chief Planning Officer, Krishna District, 2004-05 and 2007-08, p. 33.

hectares (11.78 per cent) under irrigation facilities in 2004-05, which had decreased to 27,837 hectares (4.23 per cent) in 2007-08.

Cotton is the commercial crop under irrigated area recorded as 34,762 hectares (5.28 per cent) in 2007-08, while it was just 1124 hectares (0.33 per cent) in 2004-05 in Krishna district. Similarly, 8624 hectares (2.58 per cent) of land under other crops were irrigated in 2004-05 which increased to 70,155 hectares (10.66 per cent) by 2007-08 in Krishna district. The irrigated area of vegetables greatly increased from 5456 hectares (1.63 per cent) in 2004-05 to 8,896 hectares (1.35 per cent) in 2007-08 in Krishna district.

From the table it can be observed that, Krishna district has the vast irrigated area under paddy with 75.46 per cent in 2007-08 and cotton in second place with 5.28 per cent in Krishna district in the same year. Sugarcane also occupies prominent place with 4.23 per cent in Krishna district.

The Krishna district is endowed with a rich variety of soils and have prominent place in agricultural sector. So, most of the people in this district are engaged in agriculture and allied activities. Many cereals, pulses and commercial crops are harvested in this district. Above table displays the list of major crops in the district with the area, production and yield per hectare for the years 2004-05 to 2007-08. During 2004-05 paddy occupied area is slightly increased from 255.33 thousand hectares to 355 thousand tones was produced with an yield of 6777 kgs per hectare and in the year 2007-08, the area of paddy has marked a production of 1299 thousand tones and recording yield of 7400 kgs per hectare in Krishna district.

With regard to maize in Krishna district, during 2004-05 to 2007-08, the crop occupied area was 13.04 thousand hectares to 17 thousand hectares. The production of the crop was also increased to 49 thousand tones to 125 thousand tones with a yield of 76,682 kgs to 13,859 per hectare respectively. Blackgram is also one of the major crops that will be harvested in the district. The crop occupied area is increased from 32.48 thousand hectares to 125 thousand hectares in 2004-05 to 2007-08, but its production decreased from 2020 thousand tones to 89 thousand tones in the same period. Its yield per hectare was 1496 kgs to 1259 kgs in 2004-05 to 2007-08 in Krishna district.

The commercial crops such as chilies, groundnut, sugarcane, cotton and tobacco are also harvested in the district. In 2004-05 chilies were grown over 18.24 thousand hectares and the production was 38 thousand tones while the yield was 29 kgs per hectare. In 2007-08, chilies were grown in 12 thousand hectares which produced 31 thousand tones and recorded 4072 kgs of yield per hectare in Krishna district. Groundnut was grown over 9.67 thousand hectares in Krishna district whereas 5 thousand hectares in the district in 2007-08. The production of this crop is 16 thousand hectares in Krishna district in 2004-05, while this was 20 thousand tones in Krishna district, its yield was 79 thousand kgs in Krishna district in 2004-05. Sugarcane was grown in 39.30 thousand hectares in Krishna district in 2004-05 but, this was decreased to 16 thousand hectares in 2007-08. Its yield was decreased from 1,17,240 kgs per hectare in 2004-05 to 79,075 kgs per hectare in Krishna district in 2007-08.

In the year 2004-05, cotton was grown over 47.85 thousand hectares in Krishna district. There is very least production with 13 thousand tones was recorded in this district. Its yield was recorded as very low i.e., 281 kgs in Krishna district. During 2007-08, cotton grown area was recorded as 178 thousand hectares in Krishna district and its production was recorded as 593 thousand tones in Krishna district.

IV. CONCLUSION

Krishna district is predominantly an agricultural district and agriculture constitutes the mainstay for the living of the overwhelming majority of the people. In this regard, farmers are mostly dependent on canal irrigation for the supply of water is thus one of the causes responsible for the low productivity of agriculture. In the view of experts, irrigation offers the promise of dramatic improvements in agricultural performance. Adequate and dependable supplies of water should prevent crop failures and produce higher yields. Rural development programs should linkup to improve irrigation facilities in rural areas, which will be helpful to improve the production and yields per hectare. Government should make sincere efforts to complete the irrigation projects in a legal manner without delay so that water could be made available to the needy farmers to achieve higher production. This paper mainly focused on irrigation facilities along crop production in Krishna district; this study is mainly based on secondary source which available in reputed journals, magazines and statistical abstract of Krishna district in Andhra Pradesh.

References

An Outline of Agricultural Situation in Andhra Pradesh, Directorate of Economics and Statistics, Government of Andhra Pradesh, Hyderabad, 2008-09, p. 20.

Hand Book of Statistics, Compiled and Published by Chief Planning Officer, Krishna District, 2004-05 and 2007-08, p. 33.

Panjiar, Umesh Narayana (2010), Efficient Water Management: Challenges and Initiatives, *Yojana*, July, Vol. 54, p. 5.

Statistical Abstract of Andhra Pradesh, Directorate of Economics and Statistics, Government of Andhra Pradesh, Hyderabad, 2010, p. 174.

Vimala. P., Employment Generation through NREGs in Kerala, *Kurukshetra*, Vol. 50, No. 1, p. 19.

Chapter 12

Realizing Sustainable Growth Using Water Resources in India

SUVRANSHU PAN

erosion and loss of land with long-term economic and ecological consequences.

With the exception of some river valleys or some areas such as the northern Italy, western Balkans and Turkey where water is in abundant supply, renewable resources have been intensively exploited and withdrawal of water is extensive not only in the south (Libya 100%, Malta 100%, Egypt 92%, Tunisia 70%, Morocco 40%, Algeria 32%) and in the east (Cyprus 42%, Israel 100%, Syria 47%), but also in the north (Spain 41%, Italy 30%). In the future, economic and social factors will make the demand for scarce resources more acute constraining existing supplies to the limit. Problems will be severely experienced among various economic sectors, and between urban and rural areas. The management of water resources will indeed become more complex and difficult. It is envisaged that considerable finance, expertise and innovative technologies would be required to tackle the daunting task.

This scenario reinforces the urgent need for Indian states to take concrete action now for development to be sustainable. The solution lies in an integrated approach towards the planning and management of water resources. The question is how to develop and implement an integrated water resource management approach that can cope with the deteriorating complex conditions in the coastal areas of country. In principle, integrated management has been accepted by various national governments and international organizations. However, integrated water resources management requires a more fundamental process of achieving society's overall objectives without sacrificing those of future generations.

Sustainable water resource management can therefore be regarded as the transformation of factor inputs, land, labour, capital and entrepreneurship, into coordination activities aimed at achieving society's objectives without putting at risk the legitimate aspirations of future generations (Hufschmidt and Tejwani, 1993). This view of sustainable water resources management emphasizes the fact that the main goal of the services provided by water resources must be to maintain if not to increase the value that society places on these services. Such values may incorporate environmental quality, human health, economic productivity and social fairness.

It is evident that the condition of physical resources—water, the soil and the biota in the land and water and coastal ecosystems—plays a critical role in upholding the social value of the services produced by the resources. For example, the pollution of groundwater aquifers by seepage or injection of organic or inorganic substances to the aquifer from urban, industrial and agricultural sources can cause a serious and extensive degradation of the resource. Water services are physically limited by economic constraints. Even if there was no environment deterioration and if the resource supply could be augmented by non-conventional means, reservoir storage, more efficient use, recycling and water treatment and reuse, economic constraints would limit the water available to provide sustainable services.

irrigation, enhancement of fishery and wildlife resources), for multiple-objectives (economic productivity, environmental quality, social equity, and before everything else human health); and through the use of multiple means such as physical structures, regulations, and economic incentives (Hufschmidt and Tejwani, 1993).

Recommended Management Approach for Sustainable Development

1. The managerial team should consist of competent and qualified managers, technicians and engineers responsible for a group of dedicated and reliable workers who operate and maintain the facility/system in efficient running order. Whenever large-scale projects are undertaken, sociologists and expert social scientists should support the technical and managerial team to advice on measures which will mitigate serious sociological impacts and reduce any social undesired interaction of the system with its surroundings.
2. A continuous and uninterrupted supply of wholesome and safe water shall be supplied fairly to all consumers in accordance with established health standards and supply regulations.
3. Maximization of efficiency is an ongoing process and should adjust to changing times.
4. Monitoring follows as an essential continuous process. Management should monitor performance and efficiency to minimize operating costs and provide the community with the most economic supply of freshwater.
5. A water development project has to operate in accordance with design specifications and it must recover all operating and running costs to be financially sustainable.
6. The sustainable development of water resources requires a strong commitment from politicians in support of managerial, technical and planning efforts to reach the desired goals.

Water Resources Management

Water resources management consists of three general systems: natural water system, human activity system and water resources management system. The natural water system consists of the hydrologic cycle with its components: precipitation, evaporation and evapotranspiration, surface water runoff, and groundwater flows including biota, soil, atmosphere and water. This system is the water and water-related natural resource endowment available for human uses and services. The human activity system is composed of many human activities that affect or are affected by the natural water resource system. These human activities comprise the demand side for water uses such as domestic water supply, irrigation, waste disposal, hydroelectric power, navigation, fisheries, and recreation and for the reduction of damages from flooding, water pollution, and drought.

The water resource management system consists of the activities and relationships in the public and private sectors concerned with harmonizing the supply and demand sides so as to achieve the objectives of the society. An essential support to the water resources management system is the institutional framework for management, consisting of organizations, rules and codes governing the use and control of water resources. Integration is the act of forming or blending these items into a whole, or incorporating more sub-systems into a larger overall system.

The case for adopting an integrated approach to water resources management has been put forward in a number of publications. In Hufschmidt and Kindler, 1991, the case is put as follows:

> "Although more research is definitely needed in some neglected technical areas, the highest priority in research should now be given to the integration of technical results with related non-technical factors. Without this integration, the existing technical achievements cannot be applied with less than the present high risk of failure. This is particularly true for developing countries of arid, semi-arid, and humid tropical zones where innovation has to be accommodated with many different long established but rapidly changing cultural, social and economic frameworks. There is a distinct need for more broadly based approaches to water resources management in these zones."

This situation is also true for the coastal areas within the Mediterranean region. Many things have been written about integrated methodologies and approaches, many of them emphasizing different aspects, but all with a common theme of adopting a systems approach to the issues. A systems approach means resolving the situation at hand by considering all aspects of a situation not just the part that seems to be a problem at the moment. The systems view is

Box I
Action Plan

Based on these, an action plan relevant to the coastal areas in the Mediterranean should seek to:

- establish unified national objectives and priorities for water resources management;
- adopt project formulation and evaluation criteria that involve cost benefit analysis, risk assessment and multi-objectives;
- establish an appropriate balance between new development and more efficient utilization of existing facilities;
- adopt approaches that acknowledge the independence of water uses and the role of pricing policies;
- provide for adequate (and reliable) funding for project operations and maintenance;
- plan for effective monitoring of projects; and
- provide practical training in water resource management, particularly on achieving integration throughout the entire management process (Danish Hydraulic Institute, 1994).

that the whole is more than just the summation of the parts and that if the separate parts are studied independently, critical interrelationships will be ignored or misunderstood. The parts of a system remain an indissoluble whole so that no part can be altered without affecting other parts. The sub-systems should work towards the goals of their higher system and not just pursue their own objectives (Box I).

Multipurpose Use of Water Resources

Maintaining a sustainable hydrological system is complicated due to a large number and variations of uses of the water resources which have complementary and conflicting effects on each other. This particularly refers to coastal areas where the fresh water resources management is further complicated due to the contacts and interaction with the sea. Therefore, water resources management has to be performed in an integrated way, which requires a balanced approach to various uses and services of water resources, and in coastal zones an appropriate approach to integrated management of salt and fresh water resources. The integrated approach enables strengthening of complementary effects and critical examination of conflicting uses. Apart from that, such an approach implements trade-offs between the conflicting uses in order to arrive at the most acceptable solution which contains not only the direct economic profit, but also other benefits which can not be directly measured from the economic point of view.

At that, the greatest difficulties are faced at adequate integration and valorization of environmental purposes, such as the maintenance and enhancement of biologically diverse ecosystems, fish and wildlife in fresh waters and the adjacent coastal sea water. Already at early stages of planning and assessment, environmental consequences of water development must be carefully examined. Environmental impact assessment studies of water developments on the hydrologic whole or continuum have to be made. These studies have to take into consideration, wherever appropriate, the ecological consequences of

Box II

Some Objectives of Human Interventions into the Water Resources Systems

- provision of water for domestic, commercial, municipal, industrial and other uses;
- public health, protection of recreational values, forests and crops;
- food production;
- provision of power for economic development and improved living standard;
- transportation of goods and passengers;
- flood damage prevention and reduction;
- protection of economic development, conservation storage, river regulation, protection of life, etc.;
- improvement of habitat for fish and wildlife, reduction of fish or wildlife losses associated with development;
- enhancement of sports opportunities;
- prevention of salt intrusion in the soil and groundwater; and
- conservation of the soil, sediment abatement, forest and grassland improvement, protection of water supply, and other.

water development on the coastal sea water resources (Box II). Typical environmental consequences of water development are:

1. Adverse impacts on fresh water and brackish water ecological systems, caused by pollution, erosion, and changes in stream-flow regimes;
2. Adverse impacts on sea water ecological system, caused by pollution, sedimentation and other impacts of fresh water;
3. Stream and reservoir sedimentation and eutrophication;
4. Coastal sea water eutrophication;
5. Soil salinization and waterlogging; and
6. Salinization of the coastal surface and underground water resources.

Environmental criteria can rarely be measured financially or numerically (non-commensurable), which complicates their valorization and comparison with other, measurable criteria. A good solution for these problems can be the use of a multiple-objective approach which represents a true synthesis of environmental consequences, social fairness and economic values. Unfortunately, the role of multi-objective analysis is particularly critical in addressing

TABLE 1

Elements of an Integrated Water Resources Management Plan

1. Domestic water supply	2. Water supply of tourist facilities
3. Industrial water supply	4. Irrigation
5. Drainage	6. Salinity control
7. Flood control	8. Pollution control
9. Aquatic ecosystem preservation	10. Recreational use of water
11. Navigation	12. Hydroelectric power
13. Sediment control	14. Watershed management, soil conservation, and erosion control
15. Insect control	16. Fish production
17. Sea water pollution control	18. Coastal sea water aquatic ecosystem preservation
19. Aquaculture	20. Recreational use of coastal sea water
21. Coastal erosion	22. Maintenance of interface between sea and fresh water
23. Desalinization	24. Treated wastewater reuse, and other sea and coastal waters related uses and services

non-structural elements for which the cost, benefits, and risks cannot be easily quantified in monetary terms as they can for more structured ones (Table 1).

III. WATER SUPPLY : INDIAN PERSPECTIVE

Inadequate coverage, intermittent supplies, low pressure, and poor quality are some of the most prominent features of water supply in the cities of India. With rapid increase in urban population and continuing expansion of city limits, the challenge of delivering water in Indian cities is growing rapidly.

Many large Indian cities have to source water from long distances ranging from 50 to 200 km due to exhaustion or pollution of nearby sources. This increases the cost of raw water and enhances the possibility of leakage during transmission. Even when water supply is adequate, poor maintenance and inadequate replacement lead to technical losses in the distribution network. Errors in metering, unbilled water consumption, and plain theft contribute to commercial losses. All this leads to high levels of non-revenue water. With no monitoring system in place and no incentive to reduce inefficiencies, the urban water scenario in India is one of poor service delivery, poor maintenance of physical systems, poor recovery of costs, and poor generation of revenues.

The high levels of commercial and physical losses in the distribution network are compounded by the unwillingness of local/ state governments to levy adequate user charges. Water utilities in India are typically able to recover only 30-35 per cent of the operations and maintenance (O&M) cost. In the Philippines and Cambodia, most water utilities recover the full O&M cost. Even in Bangladesh, water utilities recover about 64 per cent of their O&M cost (ADB, 2007). The brunt of the burden of poor quality of water delivery is borne by the poor. Lower-income households without access to public networks typically have to rely on market sources to access water at a higher price.

Intermittent water supplies force the poor to forgo work on days when water arrives, as they have to stand in line on those days to collect the same. Low pressure in the system encourages those consumers who can afford the cost to install booster pumps, thereby increasing energy consumption. Others make provision for storage of water by investing in storage tanks, which is difficult for low income households for want of money and space. The poor quality of water means that large amounts have to be spent subsequently by consumers on treatment of water-borne diseases, further adding to their financial burden. Box III makes a simple case for why cities should provide continuous water supply. Some excellent exceptions to this general state of affairs have emerged in recent years.

More recently, Nagpur has implemented a number of projects within an overall framework of integrated water management to achieve 24x7 water supply. The pilot project is in the demonstration zone of Dharampeth covering 10 per cent of the city's population. A private company was responsible for upgradation of the network, installation of meters, and putting in place a monitoring system and a customer service centre. The project initially ran into problems with

Box III

Why Cities Should Deliver Continuous Water Supply

In a continuously pressurised distribution system, contaminants surrounding the pipelines cannot penetrate even if there are breaks in the pipes and joints. Without continuous pressure, street run-off, drainage water, raw sewage from adjacent sewer lines and leaky septic tanks get sucked into the water mains. Providing continuous water supply in cities results in system efficiency and economic benefits to citizens. A distribution system which is operated under continuous supply conditions has longer life as it is subjected to fewer shocks (water hammer effect) and changes in pressure than one which is operated under intermittent supply conditions.

There is no need for households to invest in domestic storage, booster pumps, supplementary boreholes, domestic filters, and other treatment systems when water is in continuous supply. Also, there is no need to purchase water from private suppliers. Continuous water supply reduces unregulated recourse to groundwater and is, therefore, environment-friendly. The project essentially involves a performance-based contract with a private company for network upgradation and O&M of the system. It uses 10 to 15 per cent less bulk water and has attained efficiency through improvements in system design, revamp of the distribution network, and installing leakage.

Source:

ASCI (2010): *Report on Indian Urban Infrastructure and Services.*

the steep increase in water tariff, but a compromise solution was found. To scale up the project to cover the entire city of Nagpur, a contract has been awarded to the same private company. For the full city project, the private company is also contributing finances for capital investment.

In the cities of Karnataka and that of Nagpur, the significantly better supply situation is accompanied by considerable improvement in the revenue generated from water supply. Both are cases of partnership rather than privatisation. Both involved a number of governance reforms and tariff increases, and the private sector brought in efficiency gains. More generally, for PPPs to succeed, it is important to have tender documentation with well-structured? Requests for Proposals' and draft contracts ensuring a fair and balanced relationship with clear and realistic risk allocation. Only then will serious contenders from the private sector come forth. The legislative framework will also have to be streamlined to ensure that PPPs are effectively implemented over the long-run.

IV. POLICY PRESCRIPTIONS

Policy-makers will want to assess whether the cost curve can reflect either the difficulty of implementing a technical solution which along with other secondary impacts will inform their policy choices; they will want to understand the impact specific water policies may have on the adoption of measures; and will want to understand which types of policies may change the adoption economics. Accordingly, three refinements of the cost curve approach can help policymakers understand how to mobilize solutions.

(i) The measures on the cost curve can be *classified according to factors* influencing their ease of implementation, such as low institutional capacity, policy and cultural barriers, and the high number of stakeholders from whom action would be needed. Solutions that are in principle technically feasible may face one or more of such barriers, which—while not easily quantified in financial terms—are nevertheless very real for those charged with encouraging implementation. Policy-makers can use the cost curve to understand the financial trade-offs implied by different levels of commitment to tackle such implementation barriers.

In China and India we grouped the levers, independently of economic "sector", according to whether their adoption required few or many decision-makers, taking this as one illustration of "ease of implementation" from a public policy perspective. The result of such an exercise can help to quantify the costs of not pursuing certain sets of measures. The exercise exposed the reality that a solution made up only of those measures which required the action of a few central decision-makers would come at significantly greater cost than a solution incorporating all available measures, including those whose adoption would require changed behavior from millions of farmers and industrial or domestic water users. Avoiding these "more complex" levers and applying only the "less complex" levers would require an additional $17 billion a year in capital costs in India, while in China the full gap could not be filled at all using supply measures currently within reach—a high price for forestalling the institutional and organizational reforms needed to enable the least-cost solution. This is just one illustration. The real value of classifying levers in this way is as an aid to collaboration with the very policy makers who must make the difficult trade-offs on the path the water resource security, and who will have deeper and more nuanced views of what the barriers to implementation might be.

(ii) Policy-makers can construct *scenarios to assess the impact of policy decisions on water demand.* A policy-maker will want to know how a country's projected water supply demand gap would change when specific policy measures are enacted, or if greater-than expected economic growth were achieved. The cost curve can reflect a range of different policy and growth scenarios. For example, a number of studies suggest that reducing energy subsidies in India—which currently allow farmers to pump groundwater at very low cost—would reduce crop production, which would in turn lower irrigation water needs. An assumed 5 per cent decrease in irrigated crop production would reduce water demand by 8 per cent—both straightforward calculations—but our analyses show the actual cost to close the resulting gap would be reduced by 10 per cent. This is to be weighed against the reduced output in crops and the corresponding reduction in economic activity. An ethanol boom in Brazil would double the demand for water for agriculture in São Paulo state, and increase the size of the state's supply-demand gap from 2.6 to 6.7 billion m^3. As a consequence, the cost to close it would also double if relying upon the most efficient solution and increase even more if supply measures only are prioritized.

(iii) A "payback curve" can be developed to *quantify the economics of adoption for endusers.* The costs of measures to close a country's water supply-demand gap as seen by the end-user can be quite different from those perceived by government. The payback curve, a variation of the cost curve, can help (Exhibit VIII). It shows how long it will take for an investment to bear fruit, allowing comparison with the end user's expectations: a low-income farmer might need his money back in less than 3 years, whereas an industrial water user has more flexibility. Making financials more transparent can help policy-makers distinguish between those measures that need an extra push, and those that, on paper at least, are financially attractive to the end-user. In India and China, for example, almost 75 per cent of the gap could be closed with measures offering payback time of 3 years or less. São Paulo state, on the other hand, relies heavily on supply and efficiency measures that are not yet sufficiently attractive to adopters—86 percent have payback times above 5 years.

References

Abel, P.D., (1989), *Water Pollution Biology*, Ellis Harwood Ltd., UK.

Acher, W., Healy, R. (1990), *Natural Resources Policy-making in Developing Countries: Environmental, Economic Growth, and Income Distribution*, Duke University Press, London.

Bear, J. (1979), *Hydraulics of Groundwater*, McGraw-Hill, New York.

Biswas, A.K., Varis, O. and Tortajada, C. (2005), *Integrated Water Resource Management in South and South-East Asia*, Oxford University Press, New Delhi.

Bolloju, N., Khalifa, M., Turban, E. (2002), Integrating Knowledge Management into Enterprise Environment for the Next Generation Decision Support, *Decision Support Systems* , Vol. 33(2): 163-76.

Currie, J.C., A.T. Pepper (1993), *Water and the Environment*.

Dyck, S. (1990), *Integrated Planning and Management of Water Resources*, UNESCO, Paris.

FAO (1993), Egypt: *Expert Consultation on Seawater Intrusion into Coastal Aquifers of the Mediterranean Basin and the Near East*, Ministry of Public Works and Water Resources, Cairo, 10-13 October.

Gopalakrishnan, R., Jayaraman, M., Bala, G. and Ravindranath, N.H. (2011), "Climate Change and Indian Forest", *Current Science*, Vol. 101, No. 3, August.

Gosain, A.K., Rao, S. and Arora, A. (2011), "Climate Change Impact Assessment of Water Resources of India", *Current Science*, Vol. 101, No. 3, August.

Hufschmidt, H.H. and Tejwani, K.G. (1993), *Integrated Water Resources Management—Meeting the Sustainability Challenge*, UNESCO, Paris.

Jerman, M.K. (1987), *Water Resources and Water Management*, Elseveier, Paris.

Nature, Various Issues.

Pan, S. (2001), "Impact of Globalization on Indian Agriculture", *Conference Volume, No. 84*, p. 207, December, IEA, Vellore, Tamil Nadu.

———, (2006), "Emerging Agricultural Diversity", in Pal (ed.): *Economic Growth and Development: Emerging Issues*, pp. 99-109, Deep and Deep, New Delhi.

———, (2010), "Land Use in India in Climate Change Atmosphere", *Climate Change and Land Use in Developing Countries*, ISEE Conference, Oldenburg and Bremen, Germany.

———, (2011), *Foreign Direct Investment and Indian Economy*, Deep & Deep Publications Pvt. Ltd., New Delhi.

———, (2011), *Problems and Prospects of NREGS: A Case Study of Purulia District of West Bengal*, UGC-MRP.

——— and Sen, R.K. (2002), "Globalization of Trade In Food Items, FDI and Welfare in West Bengal during 1991-2001", Occasional Papers, Vol. X, pp. 21-28, March, Department of Economics, R.B.U., Kolkata.

———, (2007), *Foreign Direct Investment and Trade in India*, Deep and Deep Publications, New Delhi.

Pan, S. and Goswami, R. (2010), "Problem of Water Scarcity and Integrated Water Resource Management in Indian Perspective: An Overview", *Artha Beekshan (Journal of Bengal Economic Association)*, Vol. 19, No. 3, Kolkata.

Paramasivan, G. and Saceratees, J. (2009), "Water Scarcity—Issues and Challenges", *Kurukshetra*, Vol. 57, No. 5, pp. 7-11.

Rajasekaram, V., Nandalal, K.D.W. (2005), Decision Support System for Reservoir Water Management Conflict Resolution, *Journal of Water Resources Planning and Management*, Vol. 131, No. 6, pp. 410-19.

Sharma, S.K. and Chauhan, R. (2011), "Climate Change Research Initiative: Indian Network for Climate Change Assessment", *Current Science*, Vol. 101, No. 3, August.

United Nation (2009), *Human Development Report*.

UNESCO (1994), *Multicriteria Decision Analysis in Water Resources Management*, Paris.

WCED (1987), *Our Common Future*, Oxford University Press, London.

WHO (1992), *Guidelines for Drinking Water*, Geneva.

WMO (1981), *Guide to Hydrological Practices*, WMO No. 168, Geneva.

Chapter 13

Water Resources and Sustainable Development in India

Some Emerging Issues

GIRIBABU, M.

INTRODUCTION

Water is fundamental to the development of Economy. It is an essential for sustaining all forms of life, food production and quality environment for population, animals, plants, and microbes worldwide for their well-being. It is also impossible to substitute for most of its uses, difficult to de-pollute and it is truly a unique gift to mankind from nature. Water is one of the most manageable of the natural resources as it is capable of diversion, transport, storage, and recycling. All these properties impart to water its great utility for human beings. As human populations and economies grow, demand for water increases which addition to threatening the human food supply; water shortages and reduce biodiversity both in aquatic and terrestrial ecosystems. Water pollution facilitates the spread of serious human diseases and diminishes water quality. In recent years the sustainable development and efficient water management is become complex challenge in Indian States (Mehta and Bandyopadhyay, 2002).

Increasing population, growing urbanisation[1] and rapid industrialisation combined with the need for raising agricultural production generates competing claims of water. Per capita food supplies have been decreasing for nearly 20 years in India, in part because of shortages of freshwater, cropland, and the concurrent increase in population. Shortages in food supplies have in part contributed to more than 47 percent of children's exhibit a degree of malnutrition. Major malnourished people in India both iron and protein/calorie deficiencies which results in about 5.6 million deaths each year. Consider that the Indian population currently numbers 1.21 billion with over a 20 million people added each year and it was estimates that approximately 1.56 billion people will be present by 2050. In addition, freshwater demand has been increasing exponentially as population and economies grow. Population growth, accompanied by increased water use, will not only severely reduce water availability per person, but stress all biodiversity in the entire global ecosystem (Patel, C.C., 2009). These conflicts are escalating among new industrial, agricultural, and urban sectors. Government of Indian and its 11th Five Year Plan (2007-12) lays down provisions for efficient management of water resources in the country to provide additional irrigation potential of 299.16 thousand hectare and focus on water harvesting and improving water use efficiency through better maintenance of irrigation system and promoting efficient in judicious, equitable and economic manner of water distribution among the sectors across the states. From the above background the present study made an attempt to examine some emerging issues on water resources and its utilisation by the individuals and agriculture sector in India. The paper is divided into four sections. Section one describes the water resources and its utilisation in India. Section two discusses the issues related to water, agriculture and its sustainability, section three analyses the challenges for water sustainability and strategies for sustainable water management and concluding remarks given in the final section.[2]

WATER RESOURCES AND UTILISATION

Water is part of a larger ecological system. Both the surface water and groundwater resources of the country play a major role in agriculture, hydropower generation, livestock production, industrial activities, forestry, fisheries, navigation, recreational activities, etc. Water resources of a country constitute one of its vital assets. A national water resource in India is shown in Table 1. The table indicates that the India receives annual precipitation of about 4000

TABLE 1

National Water Resources of India at a Glance

Resource	*Quantity*
Geographical Area	329 Million Ha
Annual precipitation (including snowfall)	4000 km^3
Evaporation + groundwater	2131 km^3
Average annual potential flow in rivers	1869 km^3
Per capita water availability	1869 m^3
Estimated utilizable water resources	1123 km^3
Estimated utilizable Surface water (EUSW)	690 km^3
Replenishable groundwater (RGW)	433 km^{3}*
Available groundwater resource for irrigation	362 km^3
Net utilizable ground water resource for irrigation	325 km^3

Source : Website of Ministry of Water Resources (MOWR), 2009-10, GOI.

billion cubic kilometres.[2] The total average annual flow per year for the Indian rivers is estimated at 1953 km^3. The total annual replenishable groundwater resources are assessed as 432 km^3. The annual utilizable surface water and groundwater resources of India are estimated at 690 km^3 and 396 km^3 per year, respectively. With rapid growing population and improving living standards the pressure on our water resources is increasing and per capita availability of water resources is reducing day by day. India's per capita availability of fresh water has fallen 64%, from 5177 to 1869 cubic meters from 1951 to 2009-10, which is perilously close to the 1700 cubic meters mark that would make India a "water-stressed" nation by the UN's definition (World Bank, 2006). Due to spatial and temporal variability in precipitation the country faces the problem of flood and drought syndrome across the States. Over-exploitation of groundwater is leading to reduction of low flows in the rivers, declining of the groundwater resources, and salt water intrusion in aquifers of the coastal areas. The quality of surface and groundwater resources[3] is also deteriorating because of increasing pollutant loads from point and non-point sources. The climate change is expected to affect precipitation and water availability. The efforts initiated under the Hydrology Projects are expected to bridge some of the gaps between the developed advanced technologies of water resources planning, designing and management and their field applications.

Growth process and the expansion of economic activities inevitably lead to increasing demands for water for diverse purposes: domestic, industrial, agricultural, hydro-power, thermal-power, navigation, recreation, etc. One sixth of the world population, i.e. 16 per cent resides in India but the land area of India is only one-fortieth of the world, i.e. only 2.40 per cent. Water resources of India are only 4 percent to that of the World. So far, the major consumptive use of water has been for irrigation. Agriculture is the greatest user of water, accounting for about 70% of all consumption. About 60 per cent of irrigation water is wasted in run-off or inefficient irrigation systems. It is estimated that after considering all these constraints, the utilizable water in terms of diversions would be around 690 billion cubic metres per year from surface sources and about 432 billion cubic metres per year from the ground sources. Unfortunately, much of the water abstracted from surface and groundwater sources for human activities is used very inefficiently. In irrigation, for example, more than 60 per cent of the water seeps from the channels of the distribution systems and is lost by evaporation. Expansion of Irrigation facilities, along with consolidation of the existing systems, has been the main part of the strategy for increasing production of food grains. With sustained and systematic development of irrigation, the irrigation potential through major, medium and minor irrigation projects has increased from 22.6 million hectares in 1951, when the process of planning began in India, to about 102.77 m. ha. at the end of the year 2006-07. Plan-wise irrigation potential created and utilised through major, medium and minor irrigation projects in the country is shown in Tables A.2, and A.3.

In India, the total utilizable water resource is assessed as 1123 billion cubic meters. Out of total 433 billion cubic meters of groundwater, 362 billion cubic meters of the resources is estimated to be available for irrigation. Table 2 indicates that the water utilisation on various purposes indicates that irrigation requirement is going to increase drastically in future in India and presently our total water requirement is about 800 billion cubic meters. This would grow to 1093 billion cubic meters by 2025, and 1447 billion cubic meters by 2050. It is almost at par with exploitable water resources including both surface and ground water thereafter additional supply will be necessary or else scarcity conditions would prevail in Indian States. The estimates by Ministry of Water Resources (MoWR) indicates that, by year 2050, India needs to increase by 5 times more water supplies to industries, and 16 times more for energy production, while its drinking water demand will double, and irrigation demand will raise by 50 percent.

TABLE 2

Water Utilisation and Future Requirements for Various Purposes

Use	*2000*	*2010*	*2025*	*2050*
Irrigation	501	688	913	1072
Domestic	30	56	75	102
Industry	20	12	23	62
Energy	20	05	15	130
Others	34	52	72	80
Total	605	813	1093	1447

Source : Ministry of Water Resources, Government of India, Various Issues.

Similarly, the distribution of population and per capital availability of water and food grains is shown in Table 3. The table shows that population has been increasing continuously at substantial rate in one side and the other side, the per capital availability of water resources and food grains have been decreasing considerably during last decades and it seems to be an acute stress in future demand. The per capita availability of water at national level has been reduced from about 5177 cubic meters in 1951 to the estimated level of 1,625 cubic meters in 2011 with variation in water availability in different river basins. Given the projected increase in population by the year 2025, the per capita availability is likely to drop about 1,000 cubic metres, which could be labelled as a situation of water scarcity (GOI, 2006). A total storage capacity of 212.78 billion cubic meters has been created in the country through major and medium projects. The projects under construction will contribute to an additional 76.26 billion cubic meters, while the contribution expected from projects under consideration is 107.54 billion cubic meters. The irrigation potential of the country has been estimated at around 175 m.ha. with inter-basin sharing. Similarly, the per capital availability of food grains has been reducing at significant rate during the same period. In 1991 the per capital availability of food grains is about 510 grams per day and it has reduced 416 grams in 2001 and it has slightly, increased to 444 grams in 2011.

TABLE 3

Per Capita Water Availability in India

Year	*Population (Millions)*	*Per capita availability of water (Cubic metre)*	*Per capita surface water availability (Cubic metre)*	*Per capita utilizable surface water (Cubic metre)*	*Per capita availability of foodgain (per Day in Grams)*
1951	361	5177	5410	1911	394.9
1991	846	2209	2309	816	510.1
2001	1027	1820	1902	672	416.2
2011	1210	1625	NA	NA	444.0
2025*	1396	1341	1519	495	250.7
2050*	1656	1140	1451	421	275.6

Note : *Projected Figures.
Source : Economic Survey, Ministry of Agriculture/Ministry of Water Resources, GOI.

AGRICULTURE AND WATER

Water and agriculture are considered in terms of water availability and grain productivity, water allocation/reallocation in the economy. Water used by plants is non-recoverable, because some water becomes a part of the plant chemically and remainder is released into the atmosphere. The processes of carbon dioxide fixation and temperature control require plants to transpire enormous amounts of water. Various crops transpire water at rates between 600 to 2000 liters of water per kilogram of dry matter of crops produced. Agriculture plays a fundamental role in food security and socio-economic development. Strategically, its multifunctional role has been to ensure food security, protect and restore agro-ecosystem, health, and reduce rural poverty as well as promote urbanization and modernization. Agriculture has provided food, nutrition, employment and environmental securities to the ever increasing population of human being and livestock. The distribution of agricultural production, productivity, and other agricultural components are sown in Table 4. The Table indicates that in a span of six decades, food grain production, which was barely 50.83 m.tons in 1950-51, crossed 241.56 m.tons during 2010-11. India is not only self-sufficient in meeting the food needs of the vastly increased population but also has built a buffer stock of over 55.5 m.tons of food grains to

TABLE 4

Distribution of Agricultural Production, Per capita Availability and Net Sown and Irrigated Area in India

(in Million Tonnes)

Year	*Rice*	*Wheat*	*Coarse Cereals*	*Pulses*	*Total Foodgrain*	*Per Capita Availability Food grains (grams)*	*Net Sown Area*	*Net Irrigated Area*
(1)	*(2)*	*(3)*	*(4)*	*(5)*	*(6)*	*(7)*	*(8)*	*(9)*
1950-51	20.58	6.46	15.38	8.41	50.83	394.9	118.75	20.85
1960-61	34.58	11.00	23.74	12.70	82.02	468.7	133.20	24.66
1970-71	42.22	23.83	30.55	11.82	108.42	468.8	140.27	31.10
1980-81	53.63	36.31	29.02	10.63	129.59	454.8	140.00	38.72
1990-91	74.29	55.14	32.70	14.26	176.39	510.1	143.00	48.02
2000-01	84.98	69.68	31.08	11.07	196.80	416.2	141.36	55.13
2007-08	96.69	78.57	40.76	14.76	230.78	436.0	140.86	62.69
2008-09	99.18	80.68	40.03	14.57	234.47	444.0	N.A	N.A
2009-10	89.13	80.71	33.77	14.59	218.20	N.A	N.A	N.A

Source : Ministry of Agriculture, Government of India.

tide over any shortages which may arise due to bad weather conditions.

The country's population, which is over 1210 million (2011) at present, is expected to reach a level of around 1396 million by 2025 and 1656 million by 2050. Consequently, the food grain production will, however, have to be raised to around 350 million tons by the year 2025 and 430 million tons by 2050. Similarly, the per capital availability of foodgrains has increased slightly from 394.9 grams per day in 1950-51 to 444 gram in 2008-09. Whereas, the net sown and irrigated area is increased at slower rate during the six decades from 118.75 m.ha. to 140.86 m.ha. 20.85 m. ha. to 62.65 m.ha. respectively. India has become the second largest producer of wheat, rice and sorghum, sugarcane, and the third largest producer of Cotton. In fruits and vegetable production, India shares first position with China. In the Animal Husbandry and Dairy Sector too, the progress has been very impressive with milk production increasing from 17 m.tons in 1950-51 to over 121.5 m.tons 2010-11. As a consequence of water resource development works, apart from the major objectives, India has witnessed developments in inland fish production too. India has now the distinction of being the seventh largest producer of fish in the World and second largest producer of inland fish after China. The compound annual growth rate of various agricultural components is shown in Table 5. The table indicates that the growth rates of major components are at decreasing rate except net and gross irrigated land during 1960's and 1970s. It is an interested to note that the compound growth rate of per capital availability of food grains is in negative growth during 1960s, 1970s and 1990s with increasing population.

Water, Agriculture and Environment: Estimates of water resources and their future availability can only be based on environmental and climatic patterns. The continued loss of forests and other vegetation plus the accumulation of carbon dioxide, methane gas, and nitrous oxides in the atmosphere are projected to lead to environmental degradation and climate change. Over time, such changes may alter precipitation and temperature patterns throughout the society. Current climatic changes are predicting global warming of about 1.4 to 5.8 degrees centigrade during 21st Century, which will create many challenges to agriculture in terms of economic growth, poverty eradication, land degradation, access to water and food security. Climate change does not in itself stimulate development of new adaptive strategies, but it encourages a more

TABLE 5

Compound Growth Rates in Production, Yield and Other Components in Indian Agriculture

	1951-52 to 1960-61	*1961-62 to 1970-71*	*1971-72 to 1980-81*	*1981-82 to 1990-91*	*1991-92 to 2000-01*	*2001-02 to 2007-08*
(1)	*(2)*	*(3)*	*(4)*	*(5)*	*(6)*	*(7)*
Foodgrains	4.91	2.75	2.09	3.13	1.58	1.41
Area Under Cultivation	1.62	0.58	0.34	-1.16	-0.69	-0.14
Yield Per Hectare	2.21	2.12	1.79	2.92	1.64	0.39
Net Sown Area	1.1	0.35	0.02	0.07	-0.02	0.03
Gross Sown Area	1.39	0.60	0.46	0.51	0.18	0.56
Net Irrigated Area	1.60	2.26	2.07	1.72	0.99	1.29
Gross Irrigated Area	1.91	2.99	2.61	0.69	1.51	1.55
Per capital net Availability of Foodgrains (per day in grams)	1.46	-0.29	-1.34	0.46	-1.18	0.72

Source : Ministry of Agriculture, Government of India.

adaptive, incremental, risk-based approach to water management. More precisely, it provides further encouragement for a trend that already is gathering pace. Available Research studies provide directional evidences that climate change would influence the biophysical vulnerability of Indian farmers.

CHALLENGES FOR WATER SUSTAINABILITY

India may have to ready itself for perennial freshwater shortages. The country is among the wettest in the world, with an average annual rainfall of 1170 millimetres. Against the annual precipitation of 4000 billion cubic metres occurring over the Indian landmass, the available run-off is estimated at 2131 billion cubic metres. The balance is lost to atmosphere by immediate evaporation and also to the ground as soil moisture. Out of 2131 billion cubic metres, the utilisable flow is only 1123 billion cubic metres comprising 690 billion cubic metres of surface run-off and 433 billion cubic metres of replenishable ground water. While the ground water is being over-exploited, it is possible to harness only about 250 BCM of river flows through major, medium and minor storages, allowing the balance flow of more than 400 BCM to be wasted to the sea every year. Such an enormous waste of this precious natural resource is going to have a telling effect on the lifestyle of the Indian people. With India's high rate of population growth and intensifying water consumption, per capita availability of water, one of many indicators of an oncoming crisis, has declined steadily over the years. Water scarcity is now common in many parts of India, and scarcity is increasing at alarming rates. As water demand has more than tripled over the last half-century, signs of water scarcity have become commonplace. Some of the water scarce constraints as follow that.

Rainfall shortages and inadequate storages: The rainfall shows great variations, unequal seasonal distribution in Indian States. The rainfalls in India, where 50 percent of precipitation falls in just 15 days and 90 percent of river flows occur in just four months. India can still store only relatively small quantities of its fickle rainfall with 200 cubic meter per capita. Whereas, arid rich countries such as the US and Australia have built over 5,000 cubic meters of water storage per capita, and China can store about 1,000 cubic meters per capita. Moreover, India can store only about 30 days of rainfall, compared to 900 days in major river basins in arid areas of developed countries. Even with the full development of the estimated ultimate irrigation potential of 139.89 million hectares by 2050 and only 65 per cent of net sown area will receive irrigation and remain 35% will still depend on vagaries of the monsoon.

Ground water constraints: Ground water being a dynamic and replenishable resource in India and it is generally estimated on the basis of annual recharge, which could be subjected to development by means of suitable ground water structures. Heavy dependence on ground water for domestic, as well as irrigation coupled with inadequate recharging efforts, ineffective conjunctive use and the neglect of traditional practice of rainwater harvesting have resulted in the depletion of ground water levels, which have fallen by more than 4 metres during 1981-2000.

Agricultural Confronts: Agriculture makes its biggest environmental impact on water. Agriculture is the single largest user and largest polluter of water on the planet. The most important challenge in India is water demand for future irrigation and that of exploding population. Despite the increasing agriculture dependent population, the net sown area (NSA) has remained more or less constant since last decade. The per capital net sown area was decreased from 0.26 ha. in 2000 to 0.16 ha. in 2007-08.

Environment Constraints: Indiscriminate withdrawal from rivers and underground aquifers, without adequate thought to recharge and regeneration, India could become water-stressed country within this decade, dipping below the common indicator of 1700 cubic meters per person per year. Over-extraction and abuse of water has had a devastating impact on the environment. Lack of drainage components caused water logging and concentrated large quantities of salts that have severely damaged irrigated land in Indian Agriculture.

Water Quality and Health Hazards: Indian States have generally paid too little attention to water quality and pollution control and water supplies are of poor quality and are often unsafe for human consumption. Many States do not have standards to control on water pollution adequately or the capacity to enforce. Using polluted waters for human consumption is the principal cause of many health problems such as diarrhoeal diseases which kills more children's and render sick more people. In addition to human suffering, water pollution causes devastating economic and environmental damage.

Soil erosion and water runoff: Soil Erosion adversely affects crop productivity by reducing the availability of water, diminishing soil nutrients, soil biota, and soil organic matter, and also decreasing soil depth. The reduction in the amount of water available to the growing plants is considered the most harmful effect of erosion, because eroded soil absorbs 80% less water by infiltration than un-eroded soils. Thus, deforestation increases water runoff and reduces water availability. A high water runoff causes significant water shortages for growing crops, and ultimately lowering crop yields in Indian agriculture. In addition, water runoff, which carries sediments, nutrients, and pesticides from agricultural fields, into surface and ground waters, is the leading cause of non-point source pollution.

Fresh and Safe Water Crisis: Fresh water crisis is gradually unfolding in India. India's rapidly rising population and changing lifestyles also increases the need for fresh and safe water. Low availability of fresh water causes immense stress on the health and nutrition of women and nearly one million children in India die of diarrhoeal diseases each year directly as a result of drinking unsafe water and living in unhygienic conditions. In rural areas, women and girls still have to walk long distances and spend up to four hours every single day to provide the household with water.

Population explosion, Food security and its future demand: The food requirement of the growing population will be about 450 million tons in 2050 as against the present highest food grain production of around 241 million tons. Two-third of this is obtained from irrigated food grain production areas. Thus irrigation requirements of the country are likely to share a major chunk even in the future. The existing food security has been achieved through increase in irrigated agriculture and introduction of HYV of crops.

STRATEGIES FOR EFFICIENT WATER RESOURCE MANAGEMENT

Water is rapidly becoming a scarce resource in India yet continues to be used inefficiently. If India's aspirations for continued economic growth and improved social and environmental conditions are to be met, then fundamental changes in how water is captured, allocated, planned and managed must occur. We need a plan of action for water accounting and budgeting at national, regional, sub-regional and grassroots level (i.e. village or block level) so as to protect, allocate and manage our available water most judiciously to ensure water security, food security, livelihood security, health security and ecological security for the People. This calls for an institutional set-up for participatory Water Resource Management utilising the facilities available at all possibilities. The future lies with increasing the efficiency and environmental sustainability of water use in irrigation, and improving the existing irrigation, drainage and water supply investments. Action strategies are needed in various aspects.

Watershed Management: For an equitable and sustainable management of water resources, flexible and holistic approach of Integrated Water Resources Management (IWRM) is required, which can cater to hydrological variations in time and space and changes in socio-economic needs along with societal values (Malla Reddy, Y.V., 2000). In view of the existing status of water resources and increasing demands of water for meeting the requirements of the rapidly growing population of the country as well as the problems that are likely to arise in future, a holistic, well planned long-term strategy is needed for sustainable water resources management in India.

Agriculture and water conservation practices: Agriculture consumes more than 70 per cent of the total water resources for irrigation. Farmers should be the primary target for incentives to conserve water and need to follow the priorities for using water wisely such as, (a) Farmers should implement water-conserving irrigation practices, such as drip irrigation, cover crops and crop rotations, to minimize rapid water runoff and soil erosion. (b) Monitoring soil water content and adjusting water application needs to specific crops; (c) Applying organic mulches to prevent water loss and improve water percolation.

Water Harvesting: Since bulk of rainfall occurs during a few days during monsoon season, it is necessary to harness the water flow in the river by construction of large storage reservoirs. Water harvesting is the most conservative method to restore the depleting quantity and quality of ground water. This would involve acquisition of lakhs of hectares of land, mostly from small landholders, displacing millions of poor farmers

Education and Community Awareness: It is necessary to undertake a vigorous mass campaign of education so as to continuously hammer into the minds of the public that water is a precious asset which is becoming increasingly scarce and it is the sacred duty of every citizen to use it most economically and efficiently. Community awareness and management of fresh water resources should be enhanced and water should be treated as an economic resource and water quality should be a central consideration in designing and implementing programmes.

Research and Technology: There is a growing need for new technology for water resource development and management. Present water technology and knowledge would not permit prudent management of existing resources or effective development of future water supplies. In the case of irrigation, increased use of sprinkler and drip irrigation will enable considerable reduction in the use of water. Similarly, in the cas s of urban water supply, change over to new water fittings and better distribution systems will also reduce considerable wastage.

Institutional Support: Water agencies should adopt a comprehensive framework which would help guide decisions about developing water resources, especially those related to managing scarcity of water, the efficiency of service, the allocation of water or environmental damage. Public irrigation systems in many states need substantial investments for rehabilitation, modernization and operation and maintenance. Strengthen the institutions for effective basin-level management, creating and implementing innovative mechanisms for sharing economic, social and environmental benefits of water.

Co-operation for the Sustainability of Shared Water Resources: At the micro-level new water operations require political and social agreements for sharing and managing surface and groundwater resources among beneficiaries within a water basin. We need to redesign the role of the public sector in the delivery of water services to allow for increasing participation of the private sector and the informal sector. Water agencies should empower users to become responsible for the operations of local water networks through the establishment of water users' associations which could manage local allocation and protect water rights at the community level.

CONCLUSION

Water is one of the most essential natural resources for sustaining life and it is likely to become critically scarce in the coming decades, due to continuous increase in its demands, rapid increase in population and expanding economy of the country. Variations in climatic characteristics are responsible for uneven distribution of precipitation in India. This uneven distribution of the precipitation results in highly uneven distribution among the sectors across the States. No matter who we are, where we are, and what we do, we are all dependent on water. We need it every day, in so many ways. We need it to stay healthy, for growing food, vegetation, transportation, irrigation, industry, energy and its sheer life giving properties. For increasing the availability of water resources, there is a need for better management of existing water resources. The vast majority of sicknesses and deaths of people caused by waterborne illness and it can be eliminated by improved water quality, hygiene, and sanitation. Research and new technology should form the foundation for new strategies designed to address the challenges for increasing food production, improving water supply, and ensuring efficient environmental protection. If initiatives are not pushed forward, water will become more constraining factor in the quest for inclusive and sustainable growth. To meet the sustainable development, an efficient management on land, water and vegetation resources are needed through community participation, institutional support in all the ways. So that...

> *"Every drop extracted must be justified. Every drop must be counted. Every drop used must be recycled and reused whenever possible".*

Notes

1. By 2025, about 56% of the population in developing country residents will live in urban areas. This represents a dramatic change from the present situation and will result in a relatively static level of rural population in many developing countries. A Vision of water for food and rural development, 17 March 2000, the Hague. World Commission on Water for 21st century.
2. Cubic Kilometres also referred to as Billion Cubic Meters or BCM. 1 BCM = 1 km^3 or 1 km^3 = 109 m^3 = 1 billion cubic metre (BCM) = 0.10 million ha. m.
3. The annual groundwater extraction exceeds the annual replenishable resource. The stage of groundwater development is above 90 per cent and within 100 per cent of annual replenishable resources in Indian States (Ministry of Water resources, 2007).

References

Annual Report (2007-08), Government of India, Ministry of Water Resources, New Delhi.

Annual Report (2007-08), Central Ground Water Board, Ministry of Water Resources, New Delhi.

Annual Report (2009-10), Government of India, Ministry of Water Resources, New Delhi.

Annual Report (2010-11), Directorate of Water Management, Indian Council of Agricultural Research, Bhubaneswar, Odisha, India.

Bandyopadhyay, Jayant (1987), "Political Ecology of Drought and Water Scarcity: Need for an Ecological Water Resources Policy", *Economic and Political Weekly*, Vol. 50, pp. 2159-69.

Economic Survey (2010-11), Website: Government of India.

Government of India (2006), "Towards Faster and More Inclusive Growth: An Approach to the 11th Five Year Plan (2007-12)", Planning Commission, GOI.

Government of India (2006), *Report of the Working Group on Water Resources For the XI Five Year Plan* (2007-12), Ministry of Water Resources.

James, A.C. (2003), "Institutional Challenges for Water Resources Management: India and South Africa" Project Report .

Malla Reddy, Y.V. (2000), "A Participatory Approach to Watershed Development Programmes: Understanding Constraints and Exploring Solutions", *Waterlines*, 19(2), 13-15.

Patel, C.C. (2009), Water Resources Management, Development and Emerging Issues, *Journal of Applied Hydrology*, Vol. 22, No. 1, pp. 1-17.

Saleth, R. Maria (1994), "Water Markets in India: A Legal and Institutional Perspective", *Indian Economic Review*, 29 (July-December): 157-76.

Shah, Tushaar (1993), *Groundwater Markets and Irrigation Development: Political Economy and Practical Policy*, Bombay, India: Oxford University Press.

World Bank (2005), "India's Water Economy: Bracing for a Turbulent Future", *World Bank Report*, Washington DC, available at *http://go.worldbank.org/QPUTPV5530.*

Appendix

TABLE A-1A

State-wise Ground Water Rresources Available

States	*Annual Replenishable Groundwater resource*				*Total*	*Natural discharge during non-monsoon season*	*Net Annual Ground water Availability*
	Monsoon season		*Non Monsoon season*				
	Research from Rainfall	*Recharge from other sources*	*Research from Rainfall*	*Recharge from other sources*			
(1)	*(2)*	*(3)*	*(4)*	*(5)*	*(6)*	*(7)*	*(8)*
Andhra Pradesh	16.04	8.93	4.20	7.33	36.50	3.55	32.95
Assam	23.65	1.99	1.05	0.54	27.23	2.34	24.89
Bihar	19.45	3.96	3.42	2.36	29.19	1.77	27.42
Gujarat	10.59	2.08	0.00	3.15	15.81	0.79	15.02
Karnataka	8.17	4.01	1.50	2.25	15.93	0.63	15.30
Kerala	3.79	0.01	1.93	1.11	6.84	0.61	6.23
Madhya Pradesh	30.59	0.96	0.05	5.59	37.19	1.86	35.33
Maharashtra	20.15	2.51	1.94	8.36	32.96	1.75	31.21
Orissa	12.81	3.56	3.58	3.14	23.09	2.08	21.01
Punjab	5.98	10.91	1.36	5.54	23.78	2.33	21.44
Rajasthan	8.76	0.62	0.26	1.92	11.56	1.18	10.38
Tamil Nadu	4.91	11.96	4.53	1.67	23.07	2.31	20.76
Uttar Pradesh	38.63	11.95	5.64	20.14	76.35	6.17	70.18
West Bengal	17.87	2.19	5.44	4.86	30.36	2.90	27.46
India Total	248.01	69.59	41.85	73.18	433.02	33.77	399.25

Source : Central Ground Water Board, Ministry of Water Resources, GOI.

TABLE A-1B

State-wise Ground Water Resources Utilisation and Stage of Development

State	*Annual Groundwater Draft*			*Ground water availability for Future Irrigation*	*Projected Demand for domestic and industrial uses*	*Stage of Ground water Development (%)*
	Irrigation	*Domestic and Industrial Uses*	*Total*			
(1)	*(2)*	*(3)*	*(4)*	*(5)*	*(6)*	*(7)*
Andhra Pradesh	13.88	1.02	14.90	2.67	17.65	45
Assam	4.85	0.59	5.44	0.98	19.06	22
Bihar	9.39	1.37	10.77	2.14	16.01	39
Gujarat	10.49	0.99	11.49	1.48	3.05	76
Karnataka	9.75	0.97	10.71	1.41	6.48	70
Kerala	1.82	1.10	2.92	1.40	3.07	47
Madhya Pradesh	16.08	1.04	17.12	1.74	17.51	48
Maharashtra	14.24	0.85	15.09	1.51	15.10	48
Orissa	3.01	0.84	3.85	1.22	16.78	18
Punjab	30.34	0.83	31.16	1.00	-9.89	145
Rajasthan	11.60	1.39	12.99	2.72	-3.94	125
Tamil Nadu	16.77	0.88	17.65	0.91	3.08	85
Uttar Pradesh	45.36	3.42	48.78	5.30	19.52	70
West Bengal	10.83	0.81	11.65	1.24	15.33	42
India	212.50	18.10	230.59	29.14	161.43	58

Source : Central Ground Water Board, Ministry of Water Resources, GOI.

Table A2

Irrigation Potential Created and Utilized during Plan Periods in India

Period	*Major and Medium Projects*		*Minor irrigational Projects*	
	Potential (cumulative) created (m. ha.)	*Potential (cumulative) utilized (m. ha.)*	*Potential created (m. ha.)*	*Potential utilized (m. ha.)*
Pre-Plan period	22.60	22.60	12.90	12.90
First Plan (1951-56)	26.26	25.04	14.06	14.06
Second Plan (1956-61)	29.08	27.80	14.75	14.75
Third Plan (1961-66)	33.57	32.17	17.00	17.00
Annual Plans (1966-69)	37.10	35.75	19.00	19.00
Fourth Plan (1969-74)	44.20	42.19	23.50	23.50
Fifth Plan (1974-78)	52.02	48.46	27.30	27.30
Annual Plans (1978-80)	56.61	52.64	30.00	30.00
Sixth Plan (1980-85)	65.22	58.82	37.52	37.25
Seventh Plan (1985-90)	76.53	68.59	46.61	43.12
Annual Plans (1990-92)	81.09	72.86	50.35	46.54
Eighth Plan (1992-97)	86.26	77.24	53.31	48.77
Ninth Plan (1997-02)	93.95	80.06	56.90	49.05
Tenth Plan (2002-07)	102.77	87.23	63.71	54.49

Source : National Portal Content Management Team.

TABLE A-3

Major and Medium Irrigation Projects (Expenditure Incurred and Potential Created)

Period	*Outlay/ expenditure (Rs. crore)*	*Potential created (m. ha.)*	*Cumulative (m. ha.)*
Pre-Plan period	NA	9.70	9.70
First Plan (1951-56)	376	2.50	12.20
Second Plan (1956-61)	380	2.13	14.33
Third Plan (1961-66)	576	2.24	16.57
Annual Plans (1966-69)	430	1.53	18.10
Fourth Plan (1969-74)	1,242	2.60	20.70
Fifth Plan (1974-78)	2,516	4.02	24.72
Annual Plans (1978-80)	2,079	1.89	26.61
Sixth Plan (1980-85)	7,369	1.09	27.70
Seventh Plan (1985-90)	11,107	2.22	29.92
Annual Plans (1990-92)	5,459	0.82	30.74
Eighth Plan (1992-97)	21,669	2.22	32.96
Ninth Plan (1997-2002)	42,968	4.10	37.06
Tenth Plan (2002-07)	71,213	6.50	43.56
2007-08	NA	5.43	NA
2008-09	NA	5.38	NA

Source : National Portal Content Management Team.

Chapter 14

Water Resources and Sustainable Development in New Millennium

U.P. SINHA

The purpose of this study is to highlight the inequitable access to resources, like water, cause poverty and environmental degradation that results in human conflict. And with conflict comes regional and national disputes that can best be alleviated by the sustainable use of these resources.

Sustainable development is the centerpiece and key to water resource quantity and quality, as well as national security, economic health, and societal well-being. The word sustainability implies the ability to support life, to comfort, and to nourish. For all of human history, the earth has sustained human beings by providing food, water, air, and shelter. Sustainable also means continuing without lessening (Flint *et al.*, 2002). Development means improving or bringing to a more advanced state, such as in our economy.

Thus, sustainable development can mean working to improve human's productive power without damaging or undermining society or the environment—that is, progressive socio-economic betterment without growing beyond ecological carrying capacity: achieving human well-being without exceeding the earth's twin capacities for natural resource regeneration and waste absorption (Flint, 2003). By acting under the principles of sustainable development, our economic desires/demands become accountable both to an ecological imperative to protect the ecosphere and to a social equity imperative to create equal access to resources and minimize human suffering. These requirements are the foundation of sustainable development as represented by the three circle model (principle elements) of sustainability in Model 1.1. These three elements interact with each other so continuously that we cannot make decisions, make policy, manufacture, consume, essentially do anything without considering the effects and costs upon all three simultaneously. Each circle (sustainability principle) is defined in Figure 1 (Flint, 2003).

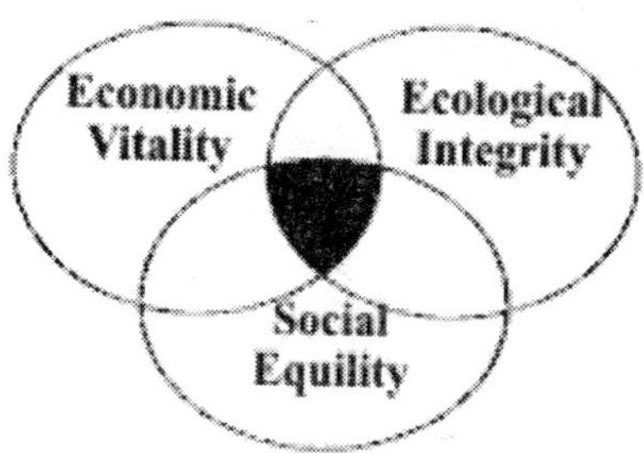

Figure 1 : Sustainability Model

Model 1.1

This conceptual model of sustainable development illustrates the relationship among economic, ecologic, and social issues of concern in decision-making. The black overlap of the three circles represents the nexus of connection among issues.

Economic Vitality (Compatible with Nature) is development that protects and/or enhances natural resource quantities through improvements in management practices/policies, technology, efficiency, and changes in life-style.

Ecologic Integrity (Natural Ecosystem Capacity) is understanding natural system processes of landscapes and watersheds to guide design of sound economic development strategies that preserve these natural systems.

Social Equity (Balancing the Playing Field) is guaranteeing equal access to jobs (income), education, natural resources, and services for all people: total societal welfare.

Carrying out activities that are sustainable requires simultaneous, multi-dimensional thinking about the consequences of

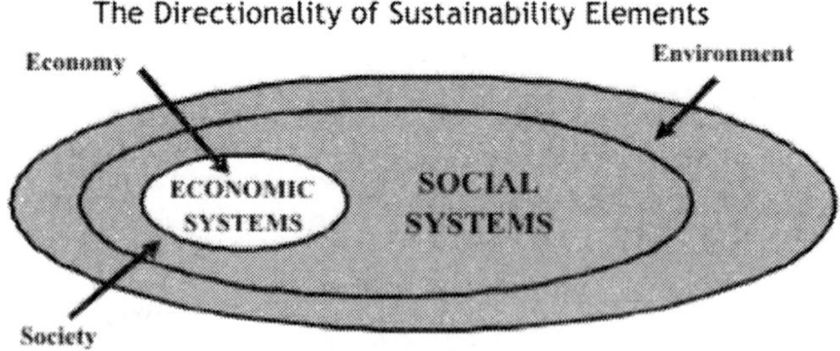

Figure 2

present actions in a cause and effect pattern on future public and environmental health through examination of the connections among environmental, economic, and social concerns when we make choices for action.

In understanding the three overlapping circles, it is also critical to recognize there is "directionality" to each circle's dependence on the others (Model 1.2).

Model 1.2

The directionality of each sector element's dependence upon the other elements of the sustainability model, where financially viable and cultural activities are integrated into natural processes in a cyclic fashion so as not to degade the environment upon which economic prosperity and social stability rest.

It is true that all life depends on natural resources (Wackernagel and Rees, 1996). However, economy and society are no less important to humanity than ecology. Rather, there is a "directionality" of dependence. Sustainable development does not try merely to attain a "balance" between economics and environment as if they were two distinct entities. Rather, it considers directionality, where economic and cultural activities are integrated into natural processes in a cyclic fashion so as not to degrade the environment upon which economic prosperity and social stability rest.

For example, consider the production of electricity. To have a prosperous economy, society demands the continued and added production of electricity. For electricity to be produced to power our economies, society must both develop the appropriate technologies and regulate its demand for this electricity so that the supply of water (environmental issues) used for electrical production is consumed in a sustainable way. Electricity requires both sources of cooling water in traditional fossil-fuel power-production plants and the continuous supply of flowing water in hydropower production facilities. Thus, the directionality of this scenario (Model 2) is that our economic ventures cannot be driven by electricity if society does not provide the human capital resources and there are not adequate supplies of freshwater. In a feedback process, the use of water as a natural resource for making electricity must not impair other users of the water by the activities of power production releasing polluted or in other ways degraded water as an output. In sum, the existence of economies is based solely on the existence of societies and their capacity to add value to natural resources. Furthermore, society cannot exist without an acceptable environment and the resources that the environment provides for basic human needs. This is the directionality of water resources sustainability (Model 1.2). In terms of a three-stage rocket : natural capital (environment) is built or enhanced to power human capital (society) propelling financial capital (economy) through the engines of society and the resources to which society adds value.

EVALUATION STRATEGY TO DETERMINE WATER RESOURCE SUSTAINABILITY

Current piecemeal and consumption-oriented approaches to water policy cannot solve the problems confronting our increasingly complex world.

Traditionally, we apply a sectorial approach to the evaluation of water (e.g., the present conflict over the water resources of the Missouri River among navigation, power generation, and environmental concerns) (Quaid, 2003). The only equitable solution to these problems, however, is a systemic approach that considers ecological integrity and the ecosystem services that natural resources can provide. By considering the ecosystem services that water resources offer, our deliberations become able to more fully integrate the social and economic issues.

Thus, *sustainable development* can mean working to improve human's productive power without damaging or undermining society or the environment—that is, *progressive socio-economic betterment without growing beyond ecological carrying capacity: achieving human well-being without exceeding the Earth's twin capacities for natural resource regeneration and waste absorption* (Flint, 2003). By acting under the principles of sustainable development, our economic desires/demands become accountable both to an ecological imperative to protect the ecosphere and to a social equity imperative to create equal access to resources and minimize human suffering. These requirements are the foundation of sustainable development as represented by the three circle model (principle elements) of sustainability in Model 1. These three elements interact with each other so continuously that we cannot make decisions, make policy, manufacture, consume, essentially do anything without considering the effects and costs upon all three simultaneously. Each circle (sustainability principle) is defined as follows (Flint, 2003): *Economic Vitality* (Compatible with Nature) is development that protects and/or enhances natural resource quantities through improvements in management practices/policies, technology, efficiency, and changes in life-style.

Ecologic Integrity (Natural Ecosystem Capacity) is understanding natural system processes of landscapes and watersheds to guide design of sound economic development strategies that preserve these natural systems that would elude us if our only concern was the environmental aspects of water.

A conceptual framework of a system's perspective to evaluating water resources through development of criteria and indicators could be represented by the theoretical model in Model 1.3. A systems

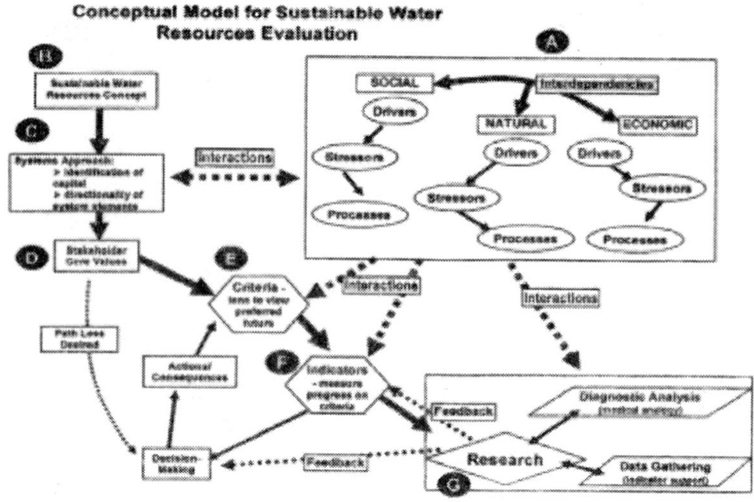

perspective should be used to understand the interactions among the various forms of environmental, social, and economic capital and the processes that most directly affect them in order to guide better decision-making for the sustainable development of water resources (Model 1.3A).

Model 1.3

Systemic framework for evaluating water resources through the development of criteria and indicators: (A) illustrates the systems approach, (B) shows the development of a conceptual view of sustainable water resources, (C) defines water resources "capital" and assesses directionality of issues, (D) elaborates the sustainability goals of stakeholders, (E) develops criteria to judge water resource sustainability, (F) identifies indicators to measure sustainability. (G) demonstrates the research support required by this evaluation strategy.

Using the principles of sustainable development outlined above, the following illustrates the steps one might take in pursuing the guidance of this conceptual framework.

Develop a Conceptual View of Sustainable Water Resources (Model 1.3B)

Because there is fear that too many different perspectives will interfere with the overall goal of developing a strategy, groups of people often avoid the discussion of sustainability in their dialogue about how best to manage resources. Others contend that this discussion is necessary to provide everyone with the perspective of others and to honor the ideas of all who are participating in the discussion. Having this discussion can produce a point of reference that is absolutely necessary for there not to be a constant "moving target" to the focus of discussions. For example, an agreeable statement might include the following: "The sustainable development of water resources is a multi-dimensional way of thinking about the connections or interdependencies among natural, social, and economic systems in the use of water." This view suggests that attempts to achieve economic vitality are done in the context of the enhancement and preservation of ecological integrity, social well-being, and security for all (Conceptual Model group of the Sustainable Water Resources Roundtable, 2003). The sustainable development of water resources:

- involves policies, plans, and activities that improve equality of access and quality of life for all;
- recognizes the limits and boundaries beyond which ecosystem behavior might change in unanticipated ways;
- advocates consideration of spatial scales, recognizing that interactions occur among different geographical ranges—globally, nationally, regionally, and locally; and
- challenges us to look to the future, and to fully assess and understand the implications of the decisions made today on the lives and livelihoods of future generations and the natural ecosystems upon which they will rely.

Categorize the key forms of natural, social, and economic capital that need to be sustained to identify stakeholder core values with regard to water (Model 1.3 C).

Capital refers to the condition and capacity of any stock, inventory, or accumulation of materials or resources found in economic, environmental, or social systems yielding a flow of goods and services that possess a value directly, or may be devoted to the production of other goods (Daly and Cobb, 1994; Wackernagel and Rees, 1996b). For example, natural capital refers to any stock or inventory of natural resources found in our environment that yields a flow of valuable goods and services into the future (e.g., an underground water aquifer or fish stock that can provide a harvest or flow).

Natural capital might include the following: surface/ground water quantity and quality; precipitation/climate trends; biodiversity; fisheries production; wildlife habitat; energy production; atershed/ecosystem services; watershed functional integrity; ecological infrastructure; land-use conversion; or environmental aesthetics (tourism quality). Social capital could include: subsistence rights; drinking water supply; community capacity; fiscal spending ability; regulatory framework (governance capability/resource policies); resource policies; institutional infrastructure; access to knowledge; quality of life; equal resource access; beauty and play; or security. Likewise, economic capital might include: commercial/recreational fisheries; forestry production; energy supply; agricultural production (irrigation); industrial use; resource ownership; true-cost pricing; waste as resource; value-added production; transportation support; waste treatment; flood control; or tourism/recreation.

Develop achievable goals for water resource sustainability that reflect the various stakeholder core values (Model 1.3 D).

Goals can be used to begin the in-depth, integrated assessment of watershed resources that lead to sustainability. These goals, which will represent stakeholder core values, should be formulated to address a number of fundamental principles that underlay the conservation, protection, remediation, and longevity of water resources. Such goals might include:

- Provide safe and equal access to water supplies needed for domestic, municipal, industrial, agricultural, and hydropower uses.
- Provide sufficient water quality/quantity to support ecological function.
- Measure and protect against biological and ecological degradation in aquatic ecosystems and restore integrity of degraded ecosystems.
- Reduce discharges of pollutants into surface waters and eliminate contamination and over-consumption of groundwater.
- Prevent human health risks due to the spread of waterborne diseases, water contamination, and hostile actions.
- Prevent physical modifications from land use/cover changes or hydrologic disturbances within watersheds that cause risks to humans, natural systems, and property.
- Encourage a holistic, watershed-based approach to evaluating all water resource issues that is participatory, democratic, equitable, and socio-economically sensitive.
- Develop.

Define criteria that establish the conditions to protect and maintain all the perceived beneficial uses of water assets (Model 1.3 E).

Following the development of goals all stakeholders can agree to concerning their efforts at sustaining water resources, criteria should be identified that establish the conditions deemed necessary to protect and maintain all the perceived beneficial uses of water assets. In essence, criteria provide a "lens" through which to evaluate the preferred future status of water (i.e., characteristics that best define water sustainability) (Flint *et al.*, 2002).

The definition of criteria is extremely important in this conceptual framework because, by choosing to develop criteria, stakeholders and managers are deciding to pursue a specific path. This path differs from making decisions based upon expressed stakeholder values (Model 1.3). The choice of appropriate criteria can guide communities toward their anticipated outcomes, as defined by their goals, and introduce a process for establishing expected outcomes as well as a means of measuring progress toward those outcomes. Such criteria for water resources might include:

(i) The quantity of groundwater is monitored, and these reserves are rotected from pollution and depletion.
(ii) The water resource in question meets the quality and quantity for designated uses.
(iii) Fish taken from recreational and commercial fisheries are not contaminated.
(iv) Fish populations and other wildlife that rely on aquatic habitats and on the assemblages of species that inhabit aquatic ecosystems are healthy according to standards established by science.
(v) In-stream flows are enhanced and protected for environmental benefits.
(vi) No actions are taken that will harm or threaten endangered species.
(vii) Industrial and municipal point sources of pollution are less than the Total Maximum Daily Load (TMDL) standards for the water resource in question.
(viii) Non-point sources of polluted runoff and erosion from intensive land uses are monitored and sources eliminated through the use of best management practices.
(ix) Watershed-wide assessment programs exist to identify the full range of pollution sources within the watershed, and they use the TMDL approach or its equivalent to integrate a watershed approach.
(x) Decisions on water quantity and quality are considered concurrently because they pose potentially contradictory challenges for water resource management and protection when evaluated separately.
(xi) Water conservation strategies are regularly relied upon for reducing waste of water, using water more efficiently, and meeting new demands upon existing water supplies

(xii) Holistic, integrated assessment strategies with regards to water allocation and transfers are adapted to limit impact on the economic stability of rural communities.

Define Indicators to Measure Sustainability Progress (Figure 3F).

Communities need a believable means of setting sustainability goals and then determining the degree to which these are reached. Policy-makers also need "early warning signals" of poor performance that can enable appropriate adjustments. After a consensus is developed with regard to criteria that describe the future longevity of healthy water resources, indicators to measure sustainability can be defined. The role of an *indicator* is to make complex systems understandable and perceptible (tangible). It clarifies a problem or condition by showing how well a system is working. Indicators point the way and mark progress toward a community vision of sustainable development. An indicator creates a *snapshot* of a resource's economic, social, and environmental system conditions and provides the opportunity to better understand past trends so that the decision-makers can influence future directions of development. A good indicator alerts one to a problem before it gets too bad, and it helps you recognize what needs to be done to fix the problem.

An effective indicator or set of indicators helps a community determine where it is, where it is going, and how far it is from chosen sustainability criteria that reflect established water resource criteria.

"*Where Do We Want To Be*" will reveal the goals or issues that are important. Indicators of sustainability examine a resource's long-term viability based on the degree to which its economic, environmental, and social systems are efficient and integrated in striving to reach community goals. Before time is spent gathering and reporting data for an indicator, it should be compared to the community's perception of sustainability to make sure that the chosen indicator is measuring the right thing. If data do not exist for some chosen indicators, try to define the best indicators and only settle for less as an interim step while developing data sources for better indicators.

Indicators of sustainability are not the traditional indicators of economic success or environmental quality. Because the achievement of sustainability requires a more integrated view of the world, indicators of sustainability should link economy, environment and society as well as point to where these links are weak. For example, an economic indicator that does not include environmental and social effects will not help move water resource protection in a sustainable direction (*e.g.*, the Missouri River conflict). Likewise, an environmental indicator that does not take into account economic and social impacts will not provide adequate insight into the best way to improve water resource health and vitality. A perfect example of what is being said here is the following: when the Exxon Valdez ran aground, the spilled oil killed millions of animals and cost millions of dollars to clean-up. The jobs created from clean-up activities made the U.S. Gross National Product (GNP), a much-relied upon national indicator, go up (Flint and Houser, 2001). In this case, using the GNP as an indicator suggests that we should get more oil tankers to run into rocks more often.

Indicators will tell decision-makers and society in general, how we are doing toward the achievement of sustainable use with regards to water resources. Indicators represent standards for measuring characteristic criteria (conditions) of sustainability, and they are as varied as the types of systems they monitor. However, there are certain characteristics that effective indicators have in common:

- Relevant to sustainability and link economy, society, and environment
- Developed and accepted by the people in the community
- Understandable to the community at large and reflect stakeholder's concerns: important to the lives of the audience
- Attractive to the media and can be used to monitor, analyze, and communicate local trends.
- Accurately measure the issue or goal in a scientifically defensible way
- Focus on long-range view: reliable up to two decades or more
- Flexible enough to incorporate new scientific information and changing public perceptions
- Can be compared to existing and past measures to define trends and identify stresses
- Advance local sustainability, but not at the expense of other regions
- Measure an appropriate geographic area and/or an appropriate time interval
- Provide early warning of changes

- Can measure movement towards or away from a specified target/goal
- Based on reliable and timely information that is easy to gather at modest cost ,
- Outcome (results) oriented: focus on measuring achievements instead of efforts or expenditures

After identifying key indicators and corresponding databases, we must conduct the exercise of setting benchmarks or targets for each indicator. A target is the threshold used to define sustainability from unsustainable practices. These targets will help identify water resource criteria that are sustainable. Unsustainable criteria are long-term problems for the region of concern.

From this conceptual framework evolves the need for added research activities (Model 1.3G). Such activities are an important form of feedback for social learning and adaptive management. In following the criteria/indicator model, there will probably be a need for system diagnosis to explain undesirable trends that may be shown by indicator measures. Such diagnosis, as characterized by the medical analogy example (Heintz, 2003), is a key element in adaptive management processes that should be designed to direct the use of water resources within a sustainable framework and to better help us understand what the system conditions are alerting us to when indicators tell us something is wrong (e.g. high body temperature in humans). With time and continued application of this strategy, a dialogue will also evolve on research needs to address recognized data gaps for identified indicators and to build our understanding of ecosystem processes.

CONCLUSION

More than one-sixth of the world's population does not have access to safe water supplies. The potential conflicts from this disparity are frightening. The escalation of a water crisis in the world is due essentially to the unsustainable use and management of water resources and to the destruction of ecosystems such as forests, wetlands, and soil that capture, filter, store, and release water, through our evaluation of water resource sustainability, we must not only increase public awareness about the challenges the world is facing in relation to water, but we must also change the way the water issue is perceived: from being a driver of conflict to being a catalyst for collaboration. In doing so, we must not only view sustainability as a problem of science, engineering, or economics; it is also founded on values, ethics, and the equal contributions of different cultures. Additionally, all members of a community have a shared future; they are dependent on each other in ways that are both complex and profound. Thus, ideals of preservation and protection, on the one hand, and of economic vitality and opportunity, on the other, are not in conflict. Rather, in a sustainable future, they are linked together. Moreover, we recognize our limited ability to see needs of the future; therefore, any attempt to define sustainability should remain as open and flexible as possible through the use of adaptive management.

We need only about 1.5 to 2.0 quarts of water per person per day to stay alive, the total human population needs the balance of the water resources in the atmosphere, oceans, ice, wetlands, and other aquatic systems to buffer emergencies (Adler, 2002). These masses of water provide crucial functions by absorbing and redistributing energy and waste products from life forms. They shield us from the atmosphere's fluctuations in gaseous content, and they offer transportation and provision of conversion sites for nutrients in food chains. If such resources are spoiled, conditions for human life will inevitably deteriorate. A person's 1.5 to 2.0 quarts of water alone will not save them because we do not know specific quantities that constitute a sufficient buffer. Policies must reflect and be built on the conservative natural distribution and use of the world's total water resources.

References

Dutta, Sujit Kumar (1973), 'Geohydrological Report on Thermal Springs-Munger', Rural Electrification Corporation of India, Undertaking, pp. 2-3.

Dewett, K.K. Singh, Gurucharan and Verma, J.D. (1971), 'Irrigation and Power', Indian Economics, S. Chand and Company Limited, New Delhi, p. 157.

Flint, R.W. (2001), "The Sustainable Development of Water Resources : Water Security in the 21st Century", Five E's Unlimited, 28 Randolph Place, NW, Washington, DC (202) 232-4591.

——, (2004), The Sustainable Development of Water Resources", Universities Council on Water Resources, Update, Issue 127, pp. 41-51, February, Five E's Unlimited, Washington, DC.

Gadgil, D.R. (1945), 'Economic Effects of Irrigation', p. 173.

Knowles, "Economic Development of British Empire Overseas", Vol. I, pp. 367-68.

Mithal, R.S. (1979), "Geotectonic Evaluation for Development of Water Resources in India", Presidential Address at the 66th Session; Indian Science Congress Association, Calcutta, pp. 1-2.

Mamoria, C.B. (1973), 'Irrigation and Floods', Agricultural Problems of India, Kitab Mahal, Allahabad, p. 161.

———, *op. cit.*, p. 162.

Murthy, Y.K. (1970), 'Irrigation Research'. Irrigation and Power in the Fourth Plan, Publication Division Ministry, Patiala House, New Delhi, p. 13

Punmia, B.A. and Bansilal, Brij Pande, *Irrigation and Water Power Engineering*, Standard Publishers & Distributors, Delhi.

———, (1975), The United States Army Corps of Engineers in Oregon, 'Water Resources Development', North Pacific Division, Custom House, Portland, p. 37.

Vohra, B.B. (1971), 'Hand Book on Irrigation Water Management', Water Management Division, Ministry of Agriculture, New Delhi, pp. 5-8.

Chapter 15

Regional Water Policy

An Outline for South India

K. Pazhani

"None of these is as important as the availability of irrigation which alone is the key pre-requisite for determining, the domain of the new technology or of its applicability".

—Amartya Sen

Water is indispensable for the existence and survival of human beings on earth. The requirement of water has increased manifolds with advancement of civilization and rapid increase in population. Especially for uplifting the socio-economic conditions of the rural masses and supply of drinking, water supply plays an important role. Adequate supply of water is a prerequisite for the accelerated development of both farm and non-farm sectors in the rural as well as urban areas of our country. Thus, water is the life blood of development both in the rural and urban areas of any country.

Linking of River Ganga and Cauvery has been a topic of discussion for decades to reduce damages and losses due to flood in the Northern States and to provide water for drinking and irrigation in the Southern States. India has only 4 per cent of world water resources for 16 per cent of the population and lack of water is a serious issue, which affects not only the farming community but people at large. The list of problems confronting Indian agriculture today is rather long, and is well documented by the Ministry of Agriculture (Govt. of

India, 2006). Each problem deserves an in depth analysis, and specific policy intervention to bring the economy in the right track to accelerate economic development. Water Policy is pertinent among them as it is considered as the foundation for an agricultural economy like India.

The agricultural technology would be effective only when the farming community has access to crucial inputs like irrigation. Irrigation plays a vital role in agricultural development as it leads to desirable cropping pattern, registers an increase in yield rate and better labour utilization. Also, the success and efficiency of other farm inputs largely depend on quantity, quality and timing of water supply, the methods of its use and adequacy of control over it. Some economists give top priority to irrigation among all the agricultural inputs. The irrigation factor alone accounts for half the inter-state variation in crop intensity (*Khattar*, 1976).

THE PROBLEM

Water is an important input not only in the production process of farm products and non-farm products but for the preparation and consumption of many products. Rain water is the major water source, which is the base for tank, open-well and tube-well irrigation systems. Even after five decades of planned development we have failed to frame and implement a suitable water policy to solve problems related water resource management and utilisation. The problems related to water is area and time specific. In the case of Northern States, there is the problem of flood and destruction of life and property of the people. In Southern States, there are inter-State variations in rainfall which causes untold misery to farmers because of frequent drought conditions. In both cases, the much affected people are the farmers and agricultural labourers. This situation may be attributed to absence of proper water policy, inadequate irrigation infrastructures to harvest rain water and preserve it for sustainable use. It has resulted in crop failures and farmers' suicide in southern States. There are inter-village inter-district and inter-village conflicts regarding the utilization of this nature's gift.

Since there was sufficient rainfall in the 60's and 70's tanks and well irrigation systems helped farmers to a greater extent and nobody bothered about wastage of water in the South. But due to increase in population, increase in area under cultivation and the demand for water from non-form sectors, time has come to review the existing situation to find fitting solution to the problem. At this juncture, a study of this nature is pertinent to analyse the existing water policies and their deficiencies and to find possible solutions to this basic issue to achieves accelerated development in agriculture and rural development

REVIEW OF RELATED STUDIES

A careful review of some of the available literatures (Sivanappan, 2006; Timmiah, 1997; Jeyakumar, 2001; Khan, 2001; Ali, 2005; Rudrappan, 2006; Sharma, 2006) reveals the following facts:

1. Fluctuations in rainfall, lack of water for drinking and irrigation, lack of maintenance system, uneven distribution of water, traditional method of application/ use of water, wastage in conveyance and excess use by farmers causing drainage and environmental problems is the reasons for the present state of affair.
2. Irrigation is a key variable for sustainable agricultural development
3. Interlinking of rivers would prove to be a boon to water starved areas and a relief to water surplus regions in preventing flood.
4. Inter-basin transfer of river water conveying water to the drought ravaged regions otherwise going waste to the sea.
5. There is the need for rainwater management to maximize water availability to face the increasing demand for domestic consumption and biomass production on sustainable basis.
6. People's participation in watershed development and management is crucial for their successful and cost effective implementation.
7. Panchayatiraj institutions and Gram Sabha are crucial and significant in the development and management of water resources.
8. In the long-run fresh water resources will become scarce if population rises beyond limits.

NEW WATER POLICY

New Water Policy, 2002 (NWP-2002) is a revised version of the National Water Policy-1987. The Ministry of Water Resources has released NWP-2002 at the fifth meeting of the National Water

Resource Council, New Delhi, on April, 2002. According to Fouzdar (2003), the NWP-2002 document is acting against a pro-people agenda:

- Its subtle inclination towards centralization;
- Almost a drag towards engineering aspects of water resources development, at times side tracking essential social and environmental linkages;
- Visible indifference towards micro-level water management options; and
- Overall weak linkage with traditional water use, climatic limitations, drinking water supply, water for environmental (physical and biological) sustenance and the natural system of water resources.

Region-wise separate water policy has to be framed and implemented for the efficient use of rain, river and ground water. It is because the problems confronted by these two regions are different. While water policy of the North aims at flood control, conservation and purposeful utilization of water, South aims at drought management, rain water harvesting, partial diversion of rivers and settlement of river water disputes to get water in times of need. Therefore, a separate water policy should be framed with the following components: (i) Information System, (ii) Infrastructures, (iii) Flood and Drought Management, (iv) Allocation of funds, (v) Resettlement and Rehabilitation, (vi) Diversion of rivers, and (vii) Participatory Management

SWOT ANALYSIS

To have a clear knowledge about the issues related to ILRs, it is pertinent to know the problems and prospects of the project. The weaknesses and threats are the problems and the strengths and opportunities are the prospects of the project.

Strengths

1. The ultimate aim of the ILR project is to ensure that India produces about 450 million tones of food grains by 2050 when the population of India stabilizes at 160 crores.
2. ILR will help for the optimal use of water and reduction in inequalities in the availability of water supply.
3. ILR is a sort of flood control. Flood damages have increased from Rs. 52 crores in 1953 to 5,846 crores in 1998 with an annual average of Rs. 1343 crore affecting Assam.

Bihar, Uttar Pradesh and West Bengal. Excess water could be diverted towards other States like Rajasthan, Gujarat, Madhya Pradesh, Andhra Pradesh, Karnataka and Tamil Nadu

4. The total hydro power potential of the ILR system is estimated to be 34,000 MW. Now we are in a position to generate power worth 22,000 MW capacity only.
5. ILR will help to provide regular water supply to mega cities like Delhi, Mumbai and Chennai.
6. There are 16 peninsular river components and 14 Himalaya River components.

Weaknesses

1. Apart from an estimated cost of Rs. 5,60,000 crores required for ILR, recurring expenditure would be incurred on maintenance of dams, de-silting of reservoirs, relining of canals and creating artificial drainages.
2. ILR will have a disastrous effect on the ecology and the environment of the area.
3. An immediate dialogue with Pakistan and Bangladesh to seek their approval for the net working needed.

Opportunities

1. The construction of ILR will generate very considerable amount of employment and income and will have a huge multiplier effect.
2. It will provide irrigation of about 35 million hectares and construction of hydroelectric plants with installed capacity of 35 MW.
3. The rainy days may be five in desert areas and about 150 days in the North-East. The ILRs will create an opportunity for the proper utilization of surplus water in the North to the water scarce Southern states.

Threats

1. Massive resources are needed for the ILR project, i.e., the estimated cost of Rs. 5,60,000 crores. The ILR can only be completed by taking massive foreign loans, which may push our country into debt trap.
2. ILR requires a lot of land across the country and would

need access rights from millions of land owners. Land acquisition cases need to be settled quickly.

3. Resettlement and rehabilitation for those displaced or otherwise affected.
4. Water is a State subject. Agreement between the concerned states to arrive at a consensus regarding availability of surplus and deficit waters is necessary. Thus, formidable political problems are to be solved before the commencement of the project.
5. Objections on account of submergence of vast agricultural and other useful land, habitats, heritage, flora and fauna, Soil salination and water logging and legitimate problems to be solved.
6. At present the total budgetary deficit is to the tune of Rs. 90,000 crores and there are 400 major, medium and minor ongoing irrigation projects in the country, which require an investment of Rs. 80,000 crores and there is another investment of Rs. 24,000 crores needed for ground water recharge, which remain pending.
7. State Government's failure to utilize the loans and grants issued by the Central Government for the construction of Small and Medium dams and tanks under the Accelerated Irrigation Benefit Programme (AIBP). (See Appnedix I).

NEED FOR REGIONAL WATER POLICY

Andhra Pradesh, Karnataka, Kerala, Tamil Nadu and Pondicherry are the constituent States of South India. The Peninsular Rivers component again involves a number of links, of which the most important would be those connecting Mahanadi, Godavari, Krishna, Pennar and Cauvery. The idea is to transfer the surpluses estimated to exist in the Mahanadi and the Godavari to the deficit southern basins (Cauvery, Vaigai). Other links in the Peninsular component would include Ken-Betwa, Parbati-Kalisindh-Chambal, Par-Tapi-Narmada, Damanganga-Pinjal, etc. There are also perennial rivers like Thamiraparani, which supply water for Tirunelveli, Thoothukudi and Kanyakumari Districts. Another idea is the partial diversion of certain rivers flowing into the Arabian Sea eastwards to link with rivers flowing into the Bay of Bengal (Bedti-Varda, Netravati-Hemavati, Pamba-Achankovil-Vaippar). In addition to this, the State Governments should come forward to construct check dams across rivers and divert excess water to tank during the rainy season.

- Water is an important natural resource, a basic human need and a precious national asset necessary to accelerate economic development in agricultural economy like India. If it is available in excess of demand then it will not be a problem at all. But it is scarce in relation to demand. It necessitates the need for a water policy for the proper and sustainable use of the scarce resource.
- Demand for food grains will grow by more than 2 per cent per year till 2020 AD. It requires adequate and timely supply of water from different water sources.
- Globalisation has created opportunities to export tropical fruits and flowers, processed agricultural and livestock and marine products to the world market.
- Due to availability of larger area of unutilized agricultural land water for irrigation will come under strain.
- Absence of adequate infrastructures—dams, lakes and tanks, to conserve rain and river water leads to conflict of interest in using water in the off season, (e.g.) Gauvery water dispute between Karnataka and Tamil Nadu, Mullaiperiyar river water dispute between Tamil Nadu and Kerala.
- The demand for water for hydro and thermal power generation and for other industries also adds to the existing water problem. Lack confidence on the availability of water is one of the main causes for going for wind and atomic power generation.
- Water is in general considered as a common property. Common property is nobody's property. Therefore, it is being wasted without considering its scarcity and value.
- Above all, improper use of water, continuous drought in some part of our country leads to water scarcity and water salinity problems.

POLICY IMPLICATIONS

The following policy implications emerge out of the present study:

- Rapidly growing population put pressure on all the natural resources especially water. It should be controlled by properly implementing various family planning programmes without further delay.

- The State Government should make budgetary provisions regularly for improving irrigation facilities and also make use of grants and loans available under the AIBP for the construction of additional dams and tanks.
- Tapping uncommitted outflows:
    1. Improve management of existing facilities. A number of policy, design, management and institutional interventions like water pricing, improved distribution practices may allow for an expansion of irrigated areas, increased cropping intensity or increased yields within the service areas.
    2. Reuse return flows through gravity and pump diversions to increase irrigated area.
    3. Add storage facilities of different forms like reservoirs, small tanks, groundwater aquifers, etc. to allow release of more water during drier periods.
- District level authorities should frame water policies to suit the prevailing situations in the area under consideration by including:
    1. removal of encroachments in dams, tanks and canals;
    2. construction of numerous recharge pits;
    3. roof water harvesting; and
    4. treatment and reuse of sewage water for irrigation to adjust the shortage.

CONCLUSION

Former UN Secretary General *Kofi Annan* has aptly forecasted and mentioned: "Fierce national competition over water resources has promoted fears that water issue contains the seeds of violent conflicts". As blood is to the body, water is to the livelihood of human, animal and plant kingdoms. Water is a necessary input for the development of both farm and non-farm sectors. Its supply should be made permanent in order to induce the farmers and producers involved in value addition of agricultural products, to involve in productive activities. It will help to generate much needed employment in both rural and urban areas directly and also indirectly. To achieve this, a region-wise water policy is of prime importance not only to divert the surplus water to the water scarce areas but also prevent majority of the people in the Northern States from damages due to flood.

References

Ali, N. (2005), "An Institutional Approach for Sustainable Rural Development", *Journal of Rural Development*", Vol. 24, No. 2, April-June, pp. 173-92.

Fouzdar, Dilip (2003), "National Water Policy-2002: System of Water at the Receiving End", *Social Action*, Vol. 53, No. 3, July-September, pp. 256-69.

India, 2006, Publication Division, Ministry of Information and Broadcasting, GOI, p. 64.

Irrigation Profile of Tamil Nadu, 2004-05, Special Commissioner & Director, Department of Economics, Chennai.

Jeyakumar, R. (2001), "New Vistas on Irrigation Management", *Kisan World*, Vol. 28, No. 6, June, 2001.

Prasad, Kamta (2003), "Irrigation and Poverty Alleviation", *The Indian Economic Journal*, Vol. 50, No. 2, October-December 2002-03, p. 76.

Yadav, Krishna Nand (2004), "Interlinking of Rivers: Need of the Hour", 87th IEA Conference Volume, pp. 400-401.

Pillai, Karunakaran G. (2004), 'Interlinking of Rivers in India: Objectives and Plans', 87th IEA Conference Volume, p. 379.

Dutt, Ruddar and Sundaram, K.P.M. (2006), "*Indian Economy*", S.Chand & Company Ltd., New Delhi.

Rudrappan (2006), "*Water Resource Planning through Non-conventional Methods: A Study on Inter-Basin Transfers in Peninsular India*", in Foundation Day Seminar on "Democratisation of Water" on 10 and 11 November, NIRD, Hyderabad.

Sharma, S.S.P. (2006), "*Rising Population, Water Scarcity and Conflicts in Rural India*", in Foundation Day Seminar on "Democratisation of Water" on 10 and 11 November, NIRD, Hyderabad.

Sivanappan, R.K. (2006), "Conservation and Utilisation of Monsoon Flood Water", *Kisan World*, Vol. 33, No. 8, August 2006, pp. 34 and 35

Tamil Nadu—An Economic Appraisal, 2003-04 and 2004-05, Evaluation and Applied Research Department, Government of Tamil Nadu, Chennai, p. 39.

Thimmiah, G. (1994), "Tank Rehabilitation and Integrated Rural Development", *Southern Economist*, October 15, pp. 11-14.

APPENDIX I
State-wise Details of Cla/Grant Released under Accelerated Irrigation Benefit Programme (AIBP)

(Rs. in Crores)

Year	*Andhra Pradesh*	*Karnataka*	*Kerala*	*Tamil Nadu*	*Other States*	*All India*
1996-97	35.2500	61.2500	3.7500	20.0000	379.7510	500.0010
1997-98	74.0000	90.5000	15.0000	0.0000	772.6900	952.1900
1998-99	79.6700	94.5000	0.0000	0.0000	947.0100	1119.1800
1999-2000	65.0200	154.1400	0.0000	0.0000	1231.3168	1450.4768
2000-01	95.0200	171.0000	22.4000	0.0000	1567.7800	1856.2000
2001-02	281.6600	492.5000	11.2750	0.0000	1816.5460	2601.9810
2002-03	33.1860	620.8500	5.6650	0.0000	2942.0016	3601.7026
2003-04	205.5300	266.4780	31.0000	0.0000	2625.4929	3128.5009
2004-05	*61.2829	314.7921	34.6080	0.0000	1676.5285	2087.2115
	**26.2641	81.5031	14.8320	0.0000	657.5264	780.1257
2005-06	**17.8890	100.6848	—	0.0000	500.8416	619.4146
Grand Total	974.7670 (5.37)	2451.1980 (13.50)	138.5300 (0.76)	20.0000 (0.001)	14571.4890 (80.25)	18156.9841 (100.00)

Note : *Loans, **Grants.

Source : Annual Report, 2005-06, Government of India, Ministry of Water Resources, New Delhi.

Chapter 16

Drinking Water Management through Community Participation

An Insight into the SWAJAL Project in Uttarakhand

ROLI MISRA

INTRODUCTION

In India with the introduction of 'economic reforms' in 1991, the concept of the role of the government has changed and now the government is limiting its role to build up basic infrastructural facilities. For operation and maintenance of services emphasis is being laid for privatization and decentralization of functions, particularly to local bodies. In addition, there is more and more of the emphasis on community participation. Now it has been fully realized that in the past many of the schemes related to safe drinking water and sanitation have failed due to lack of sustainability and community participation.

It is an accepted theory that the community managed services fosters the sense of ownership and willingness to pay for maintenance and over-all development. Externally imposed solutions can do little to build capacity and provide sustainability. Therefore, the right approach may be to facilitate the community to evolve a system of its own for the purpose, with sustainability aspect in focus. This is more applicable in case of drinking water supply and sanitation sector which is the greatest felt need of the community and many studies have shown that lack of community's involvement has been the main reason for the failure of water supply schemes constructed by the state authorities like Jal Nigam and Jal Sansthan. In fact, these observations were made by Dr. Sudershan Committee, appointed by Government of India in 1989. The Committee had expressed that a large number of water sources were in bad shape in many States requiring heavy repairs. The Committee had also remarked that the water supply sources were not properly maintained by the concerned departments or by the local communities or the panchayats who were the beneficiaries. The Committee laid greater and greater emphasis on community participation making the arrangement more effective towards sustainability.

BACKGROUND

Recent studies convey that there is a paucity of documented evidence on what works for success in rural water and sanitation sector (Mukherjee, 2001). Therefore, there is a need to carefully understand the nature of demand for sanitation services to address the hindrances to full coverage in the water and sanitation sector in developing countries. In U.P. prior to Swajal a programme known as Indo-Dutch Cooperation (IDC) programme was undertaken in 1987 under the auspices of Jal Nigam. A non-Technical structure was created in the form of Project Support Unit (PSU) Foundation. The PSU focused on institution building by creating effective organizations at the grass-root and intermediate levels to reach the beneficiaries. The significant feature of the project was the appointment of social scientists in each district covered under IDC programme for implementing community Participation (CP) component of the project. They were supported by a net work of Cluster Level Workers (CLW), each looking after a cluster of 5-6 villages. According to programme Status and Progress Review Mission Report, the CP approach was found to be very successful and the project had produced good results. However, the programme could not last long for shortage of funds and lack of interest taken by the State Government. Moreover, the Jal Nigam which was the parent body assured the government to continue the programme without any external support. In order to perform the above functions effectively, a cell known as Human Resource Development (HRD) Cell was created by the Jal Nigam in 1996, at the initiative of

Government of India. Under the Jal Nigam approach (GOI sponsored), at the grass-root level Self-employed mechanics (SEMs) were trained to help the Gram Panchayats in operation and maintenance of the sources created at the habitation level. However, this arrangement also did not work well and the main reason for the failure of the scheme was lack of community participation. According to Ministry of Rural Development report of 2004. In the new format, Central Rural Sanitation Programme (CRSP) moves towards a "demand driven" approach. The revised approach in the Programme titled "Total Sanitation Campaign (TSC)" emphasizes more on Information, Education and Communication (IEC), Human Resource Development, Capacity Development activities to increase awareness among the rural people and generation of demand for sanitary facilities. This will also enhance people's capacity to choose appropriate options through alternate delivery mechanisms as per their economic condition. The Programme is being implemented with focus on community-led and people-centered initiatives.

THE SWAJAL PROJECT

The Swajal project was launched in 1996 in undivided Uttar Pradesh after necessary preparations during 1994-96 under the guidance and financial support of the World Bank. The project had all the favourable conditions which a pilot project can have and should have. The staff engaged in the project went to the field only after receiving proper training and with adequate knowledge of the subject. Before the formation of the Village Water and Sanitation Committees (VWSCs) the staff of the District Project Management Unit (DPMU) and the SO paid a number of visits to the project villages and the VWSCs were constituted only when the community was fully satisfied and arrived at a consensus on the issue. The transparency in the working of the project was of the highest order and salient features of the project and progress made in the village was displayed through wall paintings. It was ensured that in future the community and the VWSCs will operate and maintain the water supply schemes without any external support. This project has been unique in the sense that it has changed the whole philosophy and approach of water supply in UP covering 1214 villages in total. This project has been implemented by Project Management unit since 1994 but after the bifurcation of the state in November 2000, the PMU got split up in two parts—one in Lucknow and another was formed in Dehradun to cover the state of Uttaranchal (now Uttarakhand).

PURPOSE OF THE STUDY

In fact, through this paper efforts have been made to look into the important subject of sustainability. Presently there is no document prepared on scientific lines which can throw some light on the present status of sustainability of the Swajal project. Therefore, the need and importance of the present study is obvious. The Sustainability Evaluation Exercise SEE (7th SEE) carried out by the Swajal authorities in 2003 is also over 7 years old now. Therefore, the current situation of the water supply schemes is not known. Under the circumstances the findings of the present study will be a contribution to the knowledge in the field of drinking water supply in Uttarakhand in general and Swajal project in particular. However, to focus on the important issues of the subject, the following objectives need to be addressed:

OBJECTIVES OF THE STUDY

(i) To find out the level of awareness and community participation in general and members of Village Water and Sanitation Committee (VWSC) in particular.

(ii) To examine the level of transparency maintained in the working of the Swajal Project at various levels.

(iii) To study the role of the Project in the field of women empowerment.

(iv) To study the position of sustainability of the Project.

(v) To discuss the factors and reasons for the success and failures of the project.

(vi) To offer suggestions for making the Swajal Project more sustainable.

RESEARCH DESIGN AND METHODOLOGY

The study has made use of both the sources of data collection. The primary sources included in-depth discussions with the beneficiaries (community) and members of VWSC. In order to have discussions with the members of VWSC and the community six DPMUs in Uttarakhand (i.e. Dehradun, Srinagar and Chamoli in Garhwal region and Bhimtal, Almora and Bageshwar in Kumaon) region were visited. In each DPMU 3 villages were visited to have discussions with the office-bearers and members of VWSC and the community. Similarly, some of the NGOs which were associated with the first phase of the Swajal project were contacted and detailed discussions were held with some of such staff members.

COMMUNITY PARTICIPATION

Community participation was the basic approach and philosophy of the Swajal Project. The basis for community participation was through a legal representative and responsive VWSC elected by the beneficiaries. The project focused on providing the means for users to take the lead in decision-making at critical stages, in carrying out their decisions and in collective sharing of benefits. In the first phase of the Swajal project the revenue village was the unit for planning and implementation of the project and in every project village, a legally recognized and representative Village Water Sanitation Committee (VWSC), comprising of 30 percent women and 20 percent SC/ST members was constituted. Before the implementation phase was started the VWSC and the SO had to give an assurance through a signed document that there will be complete coverage within the revenue village including surrounding hamlets that wish to participate. Moreover, community willingness for all the sustainability indicators were appraised before the start of the planning phase and the necessary cash contribution was deposited in the bank.

The activities undertaken could be categorized broadly under two heads: (a) Community Development Activities, and (b) Construction Activities. The community development activities included capacity building of the community to encourage users, particularly women, to participate in decision-making to increase ownership, for long-term sustainability. The programme of Hygiene and Environmental Sanitation Awareness (HESA) and Women's Development Initiatives (WDI) was also part of the community development activities. However, a great emphasis had been on training activities which included environmental sanitation education, health, hygiene, latrine construction and watershed management.

DESIGN CRITERIA FOR WATER SCHEMES

Under the Swajal Project all water supply schemes were designed for a period of 20 year life. The World Bank supported only those schemes which met the eligibility criteria as mentioned earlier. Since ground water in the hills is stored at shallow depths under prelatic conditions (no protective impermeable layer), it is especially vulnerable to pollution from surface. Therefore, under the project adequate attention was paid for the protection of the upstream micro-catchment area for the supply of safe drinking water. It was emphasized that there should be no open pit latrines, no pesticide or fertilizer use in the catchment area, no grazing, no open air human defecation and no small scale industrial activities. The communities with the help of NGOs were required to monitor and evaluate the impacts of project activities on vegetation cover, species composition, water availability and water quality from springs and ground water, fodder and fuel ability and erosion control.

SANITATION

In hills, sanitation facilities are almost non-existent. Therefore, the Project envisaged a large scale sanitation intervention. Appropriate sanitation technology and construction supervision was applied to avoid ground water pollution in areas where it was used as drinking water source. It was kept in mind that in hills ground water velocities might be faster than anticipated because of shallow soils. Therefore, the Project took great care to incorporate suitable environmental improvement programmes including sanitation, environmental management and catchment protection as part of the long-term strategy. It was also taken into account that erosion and water logging due to improper drainage of over-flow from water supply systems and leakage water from leading pipes might occur. It was also considered that improper drainage design and maintenance undermine the construction components such as concrete tanks and pipes and erosion around these concrete structures destabilizes the foundation and exposes pipes and tanks to increased weathering or possible decomposition by Ultra Violet light in the case of PVC pipes, which decreases the structural integrity and diminishes the life of the water supply system. Accordingly under the Swajal project the quality of design had been of good standard. In addition the project had developed a set of technical manuals for construction and training modules.

ROLE OF WOMEN

It was envisaged that the project will increase the access of women and their young children (who at present are engaged in fetching water from a long distance) to improve adequate and safe water and sanitation facilities which in turn will have a positive and direct effect on their health, better education and productivity. In addition to time and energy savings, direct impact on women would include: (a) productivity gains due to improvements in health; (b) more privacy would be brought out by improved sanitation facilities; (c) enhanced women's role and capacity in management of water supply and sanitation (WSS) schemes as well as their health, social and economic welfare; (d) increased literacy through the non-formal education activities; and (e) increased participation of women works who could serve as role models and in turn raise women's aspirations.

As the direct involvement of women, the project has promoted the role of women in five important areas: (a) at least 30 percent representation in VWSCs; (b) focus on women under HESA; (c) separate activities in the name of Women Development Initiatives (WDI) for providing specific skill and management training to increase the scope of income generating activities and access to formal credit system; (d) formation of female tap stand groups to maintain tap stands and collect monthly Operation and Maintenance (O&M) charges; and (e) preference for women to work as scheme maintenance works. It was expected that the project activities designed for the participation of women will create a sense of confidence through increased mobility and interaction around the community and increased access to more productive activities. This will also result in institutional and social benefits, such as well functioning of water user group and enhanced status of women. In short, the most significant benefits of women include development of skills for use in income generating activities and increased participation in community organized activities such as managing the water supply system, made possible by the freeing up of time once spent in fetching water.

It is notable that under Swajal project women friendly technologies were developed. For example, mounting of pulley on the water well require lesser efforts and time in pulling out the bucket full of water. Similarly, setting up of India mark-III hand pumps, placement of flushing cisterns at low heights for easy operation and repairs and sanitary latrines with door and roof needed for privacy to the women are other measures. The knowledge of water quality monitoring for applying corrective measures were imparted to women who are the main collectors and users of water. In short, under the Swajal project women were encouraged to make best use of water and its conservation. In fact, under the Swajal project it was realized that women are agents of change, and very effective vehicle for disseminating information across. A representative body of all the cluster women groups were formed at the village level and known as 'Swajal Saheli Samooh' (SSS). The members of the cluster groups were free to prefix or suffix any name to the SSS and SHG. The cluster groups played a leading role in determining, planning and implementation of the various activities.

The formation of SHGs was another activity under Swajal project for women empowerment. The facility of Private Rural Initiatives Programme (PRIP) grant was admissible to any number of SHGs in a village who fulfilled the conditions as laid down in the guidelines. It is notable that under Swajal Project of Phase-I, in 857 Swajal villages of Uttarakhand, 1095 SHGs were formed. These SHGs had collected over Rs. One crore and Rs. 1.5 crores had been transacted in the form of inter-loaning. In fact, SHG is one area where Swajal project has made remarkable progress. As a background over the past 2-3 decades many social organisations throughout the country have focused on Mahila Mangal Dals (Women groups) and encouraged savings schemes for self-reliance. But, in most cases the programme of Mahila Mangal Dal has not received much success inspite of some success stories. Therefore, under the Swajal project, to provide as an alternative, the programme of Self-Help Group (SHG) was evolved and developed. It is true that under the Swajal project the SHGs were constituted in almost every village.

MEASURES ADOPTED FOR SUSTAINABILITY

Under the Swajal project the transparency criteria in the selection of the scheme was never ignored. The demand and need of the scheme in the village was confirmed from all possible sources. Only those villages were selected where the time saving was considerable and the scheme was the felt need of the people. Similarly, for due to supply of drinking water through stand posts at suitable locations in the village ensuring economic viability only such schemes were undertaken where the per capita investment was below a certain limit. As regards to the technical feasibility of the schemes, it was ensured that the source of water was perennial and in adequate quantity. It was also ascertained that the quality of water at the tap was of the standard quality meeting the prescribed norms. In addition, suitable mitigation measures were taken for any adverse environmental impacts and appropriate arrangements were also made for protecting or enhancing the source of water.

Above all the community ownership of the schemes proved to be the most important factor for ensuring sustainability. The community took all care to protect the sources and the pipelines and the stand posts. For providing the ownership the beneficiaries were required to contribute towards capital cost of the scheme and the operation and maintenance of the scheme were fully borne by the community. The VWSC managed the finances and the full transparency was observed in the maintenance of the accounts. There was no discrimination between households and the entire revenue village was covered under the project. Even the surrounding hamlets were included in the scheme. Therefore, the entire community was satisfied with the project, ensuring sustainability. Moreover in those villages where there were community conflicts and there was a high degree of discord on the scheme, were dropped from the eligibility list. As regards on the availability of land for the water supply schemes where private land was required, an agreement had to be made between the owner and the VWSC agreeing to the use of the land. In fact, all public land acquired was free of cost and in case of private land it was purchased at market rates by the villages and the cost of the land was counted as part of the villages cash contribution. However, land acquired for single schemes was on voluntary basis.

For ensuring financial sustainability, villages were carefully scrutinized through the selection process, and only those villages where the community had made the firm commitment to pay O&M fully, were included under the project. As mentioned above the concept of ownership bestowed the responsibility, resulting sustainability of the scheme. In addition to above measures, Sustainability Evaluation Exercises (SEE) was carried out regularly by the Swajal authorities so as to keep the scheme on track and take corrective measures timely.

Sustainability index (SI) on scale of 100 can be defined as :

Less than 50 percent : Least Sustainability (LSV)
50-75 percent : Moderately Sustainable (MSV)
More than 75 percent : Highly Sustainable (HSV)

In fact, SEE was used as a tool to assess the impact of the project on community and facilitate to plan, develop and implement interventions to redress the problematic areas. In fact, special emphasis was on finding the weaknesses of the system so that remedial measures may be taken accordingly. The tools developed for the evaluation were also discussed with the members of Mission of the World Bank. As per the study conducted by Murugesan, Dayal and Chugh (2011) for 1530 households across 13 districts of Uttarakhand Water available inside the household has been lower in Swajal villages (36%) when compared to non-Swajal villages (43%) in their sample. This could be explained by the fact that villages with the poorest coverage were adopted as Swajal villages (and because Swajal puts hand pumps and taps for common use by many households instead of within the household). But latrine availability was higher in Swajal villages (68%) in the sample as against non-Swajal (44%). This may be due to the importance given to the IEC (Information, Education and Communication) component in Swajal villages for adopting safe sanitation practices and eradication of open-defecation.

The monitoring and evaluation for the assessment of sustainability during the post implementation phase had undergone three major transformational changes. To begin with, Sustainability Monitoring Evaluation (SME) was initiated which was undertaken along with a process termed as Village Immersion Programme (VIP). Based on the SME experience, Rapid Sustainability Appraisal (RSA) was designed. The RSA approach did help to identify problems and issues, especially in the context of functionality and non-functionality of the schemes. Further improvement was made from one exercise to another based on the past experience and the sustainability tool was developed. Earlier the RSA format had provisions only for village level data base. But in the next exercise the functionality and non-functionality of schemes were also taken into consideration. The definition of functionality and non-functionality of the schemes was also redefined. Earlier, if all the stand posts received adequate water, the scheme was considered fully functional. Under SEE, the functionality of scheme was defined as if all the stand posts received adequate water and all filtration units were functional. Similarly, the scheme was considered partially functional if some of the stand posts received inadequate water and some filtration units were non-functional. If all the stand posts had dried up and all the filtration units were non-functional, the scheme was considered to be non-functional.

In all seven exercises were carried out by the PMU for evaluating the position of sustainability. Out of these 3 exercises were carried out under the name of RSA (Rapid Sustainability Appraisal) and the remaining four name of under the SEE (Sustainability Evaluation Exercise). The time for conducting the various exercises was as under:

A: **Under RSA**

1. First Rapid Sustainability Appraisal	October 2000
2. Second Rapid Sustainability Appraisal	April 2001
3. Third Rapid Sustainability Appraisal	October 2001

B: **Under SEE**

4. Fourth as Sustainability Evaluation Exercise	April 2002
5. Fifth as Sustainability Evaluation Exercise	October 2002
6. Sixth as Sustainability Evaluation Exercise	April 2003
7. Seventh as Sustainability Evaluation Exercise	June 2004

The following observations may be made:

- The prospects of sustainability in most of the schemes are positive. Thus the emphasis of the Swajal project on sustainability has produced good results.
- However, the post-implementation support to all the villages covered under the Swajal project of Phase-I, is not only desirable but essential. In fact, some institutional arrangements should be made to take care of the villages covered under Phase-I of the Swajal Project.
- To be more specific, the Swajal project Phase-2 currently going on in the name of SWAp in the State has to find ways of sustaining the interest and the enthusiasm of the communities, especially in those villages where the VWSCs have become effective.
- In short, in the interest of the reputation of the Swajal project and also the projects/schemes designed on the similar pattern, it is necessary to ensure the sustainability of the villages is covered under phase-I of the Swajal project.

CONCLUSION

The Swajal project was not developed in vacuum. The World Bank had the past experienced of carrying out similar projects in some other states of India like Karnataka, Kerala and Maharastra. The First

Phase of the Swajal Project was launched and implemented during 1996-2003 in U.P. and soon it became a sector model in India. The Swajal project was favourably received by the participating communities and earned praise of government officials and sector specialists from other parts of the country. It also received satisfactory performance rating in the Implementation Completion Report (ICR) of the World Bank. The Sector Reforms Project of the GOI was designed on the similar lines and it was implemented in 1999 in the country. The programme later on took the shape of Swajaldhra.

Similarly, the Government of Uttarakhand decided to scale it up for improved coverage in the State, adopting a Sector Wide Approach (SWAp) designed on the Swajal Project pattern. Demonstrated success of SWAp in Utarakhand would contribute to replication of such models in other States of the country.

It is notable that encouraged with the success of the Swajal project, since 1999, the GOI has embarked on a significant programme in the rural water supply and sanitation (RWSS) sector in recognition of the need to move away from a target-based to demand-based approach where users get the service they want and are willing to pay for it. The GOI has developed the Swajaldhara guidelines, which spell out the basic principles for reform in the RWSS sector, which include community participation in the planning, implementation, operation and maintenance (O&M) for the schemes of its choice and the changing role of the government from that of a service provider to a facilitator. The decentralized service delivery approach is also consistent with the 73rd Constitutional Amendment of 1992, which introduced devolution of financial and decision making powers to the three-tier local governments, called the Panchayati Raj Institutions (PRIs).

The Swajal project has aptly demonstrated that rural communities can plan, implement and maintain their systems if they are empowered to take their decisions. Voice and choice of the community are cardinal principles for success of Swajal. The Rural Water Supply and Environmental Sanitation Project of U.P. (inclusive of Uttarakhand) namely the Swajal Project, is pioneer in the field of community empowerment, involvement of women in the process and community contracting. The Planning Commission, GOI in its one of the publications titled "Successful Governance Initiatives and Best Practices: Experiences from Indian States" has included a comprehensive write-up on the Swajal Project. The

Planning Commission has remarked that "By introducing several innovations in a hither to stagnant situation, the project has proved to be not only applicable but also replicable". In short, the Swajal Project can be called as the "Mother of WATSAN Sector Reforms and the path set by Swajal will work as a guide for the central and State Governments to introduce the community participation concept in other development projects.

The World Bank Mission had visited the Swajal project regularly (normally after every six months). After the visit the Mission remarked "results on the ground confirm the viability of the project's approach in which communities make decisions, procure materials, carryout construction, manage funds, share in the capital cost and operate the system in partnership with the support from the SO. PMU is successfully playing the role of facilitator. The project's SO and village selection processes and cost recovery policies have been further improved from Batch-3 onwards and have strengthened the project's demand responsive approach. Overall the project objective of developing and testing an alternative delivery mechanism is being fully achieved." The Planning Commission, Govt. of India in its publication titled "Successful Governance Initiatives and Best Practices : Experiences from Indian States" has included a comprehensive write up on the SWAJAL project. It has remarked by introducing several innovations in a hitherto stagnant situation.

References

A Study on "Role of NGOs in Developing Skills of Grass Root Level Workers for self-Employment in Rural Drinking Water Supply Systems in U.P" (2001), Government of Uttar Pradesh.

A Study on "Working of the Jal Nigam and Jal Sansthans in Uttar Pradesh" (1998). Government of Uttar Pradesh.

Government of India: Guidelines on Central Rural and Sanitation Programme, Department of Drinking Water Supply, Ministry of Rural Development, January 2004.

Misra, Roli (2009), Swajal Project in the State of Uttarakhand: A Success Story, *UPUEA Economic Journal*, Vol. 2, Nos. 2 and 3 April and October.

Murugesan, Dayal and Chugh (2011), An Empirical Study of Sanitation and Health in Rural Uttarakhand, *India available on http://findarticles.com/p/articles/mi_6925/is_10/ai_n28516627/*

Report on "Concurrent Monitoring of Implementation Phase of PRI Villages under Swajal Project in Uttaranchal and Uttar Pradesh" (2002), Government of Uttaranchal.

Report on "The Process of Change: PMU Swajal Project", Government of Uttarakhand (2006).

Seventh Sustainability Evaluation Exercise Report, PMU, Swajal Project, Government of Uttarakhand, (2004).

Staff Appraisal Report (SAR) on Swajal Project in Uttar Pradesh, Government of Uttar Pradesh (1996).

World Bank Project Appraisal Document for the Uttaranchal Rural Water Supply and Sanitation Project (2006), available on *http://swajal.uk.gov.in/files/Documents/UARWSS%20PAD.pdf.*

Chapter 17

Management of Water Resources

A Strategy for Inclusive Growth

BABILATA SHROFF AND PURUSHOTTAM SAHU

MANAGEMENT OF WATER RESOURCES: A STRATEGY FOR INCLUSIVE GROWTH

Water is the most important requirement for sustaining life. But this life-saving natural resource is not available to all the people and all the areas; timely, properly and adequately. It is when we asses water in the framework of our large and fast rising population, the resource is scarce in its supply.

Rural Orissa which is dominated by agriculture suffers from the gambles of monsoon in the absence of adequate irrigation facilities. Gambles of monsoon, flood, drought, heat wave, cold wave, etc. cause frequent crop failure and add fire to make agriculture still unpopular. On the other hand scanty availability of safe drinking water invites epidemics like cholera, diarrhoea and many other diseases and every year take away a toll of human life. The worst affected are the poor. During the last few years *Rayagada* district has drawn the attention of the whole Nation for its epidemic diarrhoea during the rainy days followed by the other districts of undivided *Koraput, Kalahandi and Bolangir* and some other villages of the State. Except a few rainy months water scarcity becomes clearly visible. While coming to urban areas, dominated by the so called educated and sophisticated people of the secondary and tertiary sector, there is a growing demand for water. Its water requirement is almost double the water requirement of the rural people. Moreover, India is rapidly urbanising and urban population has grown almost five times in the last five decades.

Neither India nor Orissa are scarce in water resources but an overwhelming part of it is *untapped*. Our poor live in a rich country of unutilised resources. Hence, there is a need for optimum utilisation of this scarce liquid keeping in view our current and future needs as well as individual and social need.

OBJECTIVES

This paper aims at finding some ways to manage the water resources of the Titilagarh Agriculture District of the Bolangir district of Orissa; which may be considered as a strategy for inclusive growth. The main objectives are: (1) *Check the monsoon water run-off* in the ephemeral channel, which also automatically *control floods in the downstream areas as well as of the perennial rivers;* (2) There will be less contribution of *surface runoff along with sediments* to the downstream water bodies and finally to the ocean; (3) *Economic utilisation of the surplus water keeping in view its sustainable use;* and (4) The ultimate objective is development of all the sectors of the economy.

WATER RESOURCES IN THE DISTRICT

Orissa is quite rich in respect of water resources and is considered as one of the *wettest states*. While the average annual rainfall in India is 1100 mm, it is 1489 mm in Orissa. The whole State becomes flooded with water during the rainy days as Orissa gets a good quantity of rain. The annual normal rainfall of Bolangir district as recorded by Board of Revenue, Orissa is 1443.5 mm (based on the observations of 1901-50). However, the annual average rainfall, based on the observations for the period 1987-2002 was observed as 1188.1 mm. This shows that presently this area is receiving nearly 18% less rainfall than its normal amount. During this period only in 1994 the average annual rainfall of the district was higher than its average. The bulk of precipitation occurs during the rainy season (July to September) by the South-West monsoon. Pre-monsoon showers are experienced in the month of June. Occasionally, some showers fall during January to March and sometimes there may be some thunder and rainy storms in April and May. During October and November post-monsoon showers are also very common. Again on an average the district gets showers of rain in each month. Table 1 shows it clearly.

TABLE 1
Month-wise Average (1987-2002) and Normal (1901-50) Rainfall of Bolangir District

Month	*Rainfall (mm)*	
	Average	*Normal*
January	9.0	13.9
February	8.9	18.2
March	9.9	13.9
April	13.4	18.7
May	37.6	29.1
June	196.6	233.7
July	346.0	391.7
August	331.4	407.1
September	165.5	232.0
October	47.5	65.6
November	19.2	15.9
December	3.1	3.7
Annual	1188.1	1443.5

Source : Board of Revenue of Orissa.

The rainfall of TAD is *fluctuating* in nature. During the period 1987 to 2007 the annual rainfall has reached 2000 mm three times (1990, 1994 and 2001), while in years 1987, 1996, 1998, 1999, 2000, 2002, and 2005 it was recorded to be below 1000 mm (Remote Sensing Based Baseline Information on Titilagarh and Bolangir district). The annual rainfall of the area is 1350.72 mm, 1599 mm and 333.7 mm for 2009, 2010 and 2011 (up to July, i.e. for seven months) respectively. It has also a good number of seasonal rivers as well as stream catchments including dendritic micro catchments and ponds of different carrying capacities. The major stream catchments Kokranjor, Yamunajor and Kundajor as well as the dendrites micro-catchments *almost dry up* during the summer. The seasonal small ponds of the region also remain dry up during major parts of the year. Two large water bodies are in extreme north of Tikari Reserve Forest (Dumerbahal) and other in central part near Burnei Reserve Forests (Mathanpala) are situated in Titilagarh Range. Water is also stored in a reservoir on Kankadajor stream. The project finished just four years back. Bolangir district has also some rivers like Tel, Under, Bairi, Udanti and Lanth. Most of them are ephemeral. Out of the three subdivisions of the revenue district, Titilagarh and Patnagarh sub-divisions which come under the Titilagarh Agriculture District (TAD) and it is a *dry area.*

TAD has *a poor irrigation provision* and has *rain fed agricultural practice.* For Kharif (2005) only *13.8% of land has irrigation potential.* TAD has no major IP, 1815 ha medium IP, 250 number of lift IP covering 4438 ha, 11,661 numbers of dug wells covering 9201 ha, 138 minor IP covering 14,565 ha and 5830 ha are irrigated by other sources like WHS, nalas, ponds, etc. For Rabi 2005-06 was only 4.5%, i.e. 1017 ha is under irrigation. Medium irrigation points cover 506 ha, 12 minor IP covering 815 ha, 231 lift IP covering 3101 ha, 12004 dug wells for 3814 ha and 1939 from other sources.

For drinking and other domestic uses the locality has to depend upon tube wells, wells, nalas, streams, ponds, etc. which are not sufficient enough. Water from the Dumerbahal lake is used exclusively by the Ordinance Factory (25 Kms from the Titilagarh town) and its officials. Water shortage was so acute that during each summer that water was distributed through tankers by the local authorities. Water was also brought from outside places like Sambalpur with the help of train and tankers. According to a newspaper report, in 1999 Rs. 45 lakhs were spent in this water transfer. In 2005, problem of water problem to the town came to an end when the project on water supply from Tel River having two overhead tanks of 1.35 million litres and 2.7 million litres was completed. But the condition of the rural areas remains as usual.

NEED FOR WATER MANAGEMENT

Water management has become a necessity not only for the TAD but also for all the areas due to the following reasons.

(1) Climate change and global warming are now widely recognised as the major environmental problem which has put an additional stress on the ecological, social and economic system of our economy which is already facing tremendous pressure due to rapid urbanisation, industrialisation and economic development. In this climate change regime the monsoon onset is becoming late. Uncertainties are found in case of pre-monsoon arrival, post-monsoon and winter rainfall, number of cloudy days, heat spell, day and night temperatures, etc. To meet the

challenge of climate change (agriculture is badly affected) there is a need for management of water resources to support agriculture and other life-supporting activities.

(2) Depletion of the water level is also experienced which is clearly visible from the wells and tube wells, affecting badly the domestic and agriculture sector. Hence, a check on depletion and recharge of ground water is required. The effectiveness of artificial recharge and water harvest depends on *recharge efficiency, aquifer's storage potentia*l and the *dynamics of interaction between surface flow and ground water.*

(3) Growing demand for water to match its demand with growing population, urbanisation, industrialisation, and the most important cultivation, etc.

(4) Increased supply of waste water may create problems immediately and/or in the future. Thus there is a need for recycling of waste water.

(5) To provide more water to agriculture which is rain fed and agriculture is the main occupation here. Irrigation potential of most of the areas in the State is very poor. Agriculture is highly labour intensive and has the capacity to provide employment to the poorest of the poor. Irrigation leads to expansion of area under cultivation, rise in cropping intensity and per hectare yield. It expands the scope of diversified activities and demand for labour increases.

(6) To utilise the rain water and water of the ephemeral streams which would otherwise flow to the downstream causing flood or carry sediments to the downstream river or ocean. There will be blockades in the downstream river beds and ocean resulting into a number of problems.

(7) To have a sustainable supply of water to match the individual and social needs.

WATER MANAGEMENT THROUGH WATER HARVESTING

Broadly rivers are of two types: (i) perennial, and (ii) ephemeral. This area under study has no perennial rivers. These rivers/streams are ephemeral. Ephemeral rivers/streams are those which flow mainly during rainy season and discharge water to the basin. This is the ephemeral river courses which could be utilized scientifically for solving our water requirements. Simultaneously, it could recharge the ground water which is fast depleting due to over exploitation of ground water reserve in unscientific manner. With the *use of science and technology Israel has transferred its desert territory into blooming orchards.* One aspect of this effort is *efficient management of resources.* This calls for *both resources use and knowledge inputs.*

The idea is that on an average this area gets good rainfall during the rainy season. If we could check certain quantity of monsoon water run off in the ephemeral channel, then unnecessary water blockade at places could be avoided. Automatically, floods in the downstream areas and perennial rivers could be controlled (During some rainy months it is found that River Tel has contributed a lot of surplus water to Mahanadi which is already flooded). There will be less contribution of surface run-off along with sediments to the downstream rivers/ocean. For this purpose we have to go through the following steps of water management:

1. Detailed *morph metric analysis of a particular ephemeral channel* should be carried out along with *topographic survey.*
2. The *basin head should be developed as forest and horticulture. Plants* such as Neem, Babul, Amla; etc. (which is suitable) should be planted. Proper agricultural methods having capacity to check soil erosion and increase ground water recharge should be practised.
3. At *suitable intervals masonry or earthen check dams* as per suitability of the area, economy and availability of materials be constructed. Whoever will construct it should remember that the local bodies must be involved. Emphasis should be laid on the easy maintenance of the structure for its optimum use and longevity. In this way the complete channel/course may be sub-divided into alternative water body and land body of suitable area.
4. Area of the water body should be deepened in the central part and the soil thus received may be used to fill the area developed as land body. Here grass land could be developed for the cattle and used for horticulture.
5. Provision must be made for suitable overhead tanks with pumping facility, drip irrigation and sprinkle irrigation.

After this arrangement is made, plantation should be done. Suitable plantation should be done on the sides and surroundings of the check dam, so that soil erosion could be checked. Care should be taken that strong and harmful fertilisers and pesticides should not be applied to these plants rather natural fertilisers could be used to make this water pollution free.

6. Depending upon the area of the course thus created as water reservoir it may be developed for fishery, prawn culture, tortoise, water plants, etc.
7. The water body may also be used for boating, swimming and other purposes such that more of the local people could be employed and a place of recreation could also be developed.
8. Provision must be made for a tube well to supply water to the reservoir during the period of necessity. Provision of water supply for domestic purposes of the locality should be avoided as it may lead to wastage of water. Instead water posts may be created at suitable intervals as per the population density. This water could also be used for irrigation.

This would also check the widening of beds of the streams. Table 1 show that on an average each month experiences some rainfall. Whenever rain occurs, the water should not be allowed to evaporate, percolate into the soil or run away, but should be collected in the reservoirs.

At the *individual level* also water harvesting could be made. People should be encouraged (if required compelled) to *harvest roof water as well as surface water in underground covered reservoirs* (preferably nearer to the water source of the house like well, tube well, etc. or tanks of suitable capacity) or sintex like tanks of suitable capacity. This has also the capacity to raise the water layer and control water level depletion. *Rainwater harvesting* is the accumulating and storing of rainwater which could be used for many purposes starting from drinking and other domestic uses to use for livestock, irrigation and refill aquifers in a process called groundwater recharge. Rainwater collected from the roofs can make an important contribution, i.e. about half the total water requirement of the people. Depending upon the intensity of rainfall and the efficiency of the harvesting system rainwater can be channelled from the roof to a storage system of gutters and pipes. For agriculture purposes it neither needs purification nor require flush out in the initial periods. But it should be covered to reduce evaporation losses and reduce inclusion of solid waste materials which may block the pipes.

The *waste water* (from washing, bathing, cleaning) of the domestic sector should not be allowed to run away, evaporate or percolate into the soil; rather should be collected in a *covered pit*. This could be reused for gardening purposes and it has also the capacity to raise the water table in the long-run and check water level depletion.

Water transfer *from better-endowed to less-endowed regions* should be practised. Water productivity should be increased. Scope for the application of water-saving technologies should be searched out. The major avenues for *increasing water productivity and water-saving* in agriculture are: *improved irrigation reliability, water reallocation and re-ordered crop patterns.* Emphasis should be given to *search new and more things of satisfaction* which could be received from this water management and *reduction of costs* as well as the efficiency with which the resources are used.

Water Literacy Movement should be launched and regulations should be developed for sustainable use of water. If possible *pricing of water* should be introduced to check wastage of water. *Static and dynamic aspects of water management* should also be taken into consideration.

These water management techniques would also have a *cooling effect*. The town Titilagarh is famous for its highest temperature (touches 50 degree Celsius in most summers) and could be cooled to some extent.

Management of water resources should not be treated independent of other natural resources like land, forests, etc. all these natural resources could be managed in an integrated way to get the best result.

Hence, an efficient management of water resources can be used as a strategy for inclusive growth by supporting agriculture, horticulture, animal rearing, pisciculture, etc. and by *creating a set of employment opportunities* in the rural areas. This could also provide *income and livelihood security* to the rural masses.

CONCLUSION

Approach towards water management should be interred disciplinary and *people's participatory*. Water management requires a set of empirical knowledge concerning *hydrological, economical, social, ecological and institutional issues*. To match the requirements of the huge and growing population, water management is essential. It is true for all the areas. Day-by-day exploitation of the ground water sources is increasing due to the scarcity of the surface water flows. As it is a common property, we have no right to over exploit it. Over-exploitation of the ground water in an unscientific manner may create problems in the long-run. Global warming and climate change has already given an open challenge in terms of irregularities in rainfall, increased temperature, irregularities in heat and cold spell, etc. Hence time has already come to adopt some scientific techniques of managing the scarce resource water to go towards *agriculture development, food security, industrial development, healthy living and help inclusive growth*. Save water and save the mankind.

References

Sengupta, Ram Prasad, Ecology and Economics: An Approach to Sustainable Development; Oxford University Press.

Climate Change in and Around Titilagarh, Dist. Bolangir, Orissa; Submitted to Orissa Forest Department, Bhubaneswar by Tropical Forest Management Research Institute, P.O. RFRC, Mandla Road, Jabalpur.

Mahapatra, Subas C., Natural Resource Preservation, Conservation, Regeneration and Management: Key to Success of 2020 Orissa; Orissa Vision, 2020.

Sahu, Naresh Chandra; Sustainable Management of Common Property Resource Potentials: An Alternative Strategy to Improve the State of Economy of Orissa by 2020; Orissa Vision, 2020.

Hedge, Pandurang (2005), Linking Forests and Rivers; p. 25, *Yojana*, June.

Singh, K.P. (1996), Water Harvesting; *Yojana*, November.

Chapter 18

Sea Water Intrusion and Sweet Water Management in Coastal Aquifer of Saurashtra (Gujarat)

DHIREN VANDRA AND ASHA TANK

INTRODUCTION

The combined human interference with the coastal hydrologic system had led to pollution of coastal ground water aquifers sea water. Incident of ground water pollution due to salt water intrusion has increased manifold in the last two decades. Change in ground water level with respect to mean sea elevation along the coast largely influences the extent sea water intrusion in the fresh water aquifers. The smaller the drop in ground water level, the lesser the sea water intrusion in the aquifers.

When ground water is pumped from a coastal aquifer the fresh water level is lowered and the sea intrudes further into the aquifer with excessive pumping the natural hydraulic gradient towards the sea may be reversed and the intrusion can then extend to the pumping borehole which becomes saline. So, salt water intrusion is the movement of saline water into a fresh water aquifer, where the source of saline water is marine water. This process is known as sea water intrusion.

DEFINITION

By Khiaifi et. al. define sea water intrusion is an important environmental problem in the coastal aquifers of many Mediterranean countries, a large increase in number of pumping wells for irrigation purposes, resulted in significant lowering of water table levels and in a consequent deterioration of water quality.

Teatini et. al. defined as sea water intrusion is an important environmental problem for coastal aquifers of the coastal land, there has been a large increase of the prevail pumping wells used for irrigation resulted in significant lowering of water table and deterioration of ground water quality.

India has been blessed with a vast stretch of coast line. Many urban centers of the country are located on the coastal tract apart from thousands of villages and industrial settlements. Water resources in coastal areas assume a special significant. Since any development activity will largely depend upon availability of fresh water resources in these coastal aquifers are likely to experience disastrous and irreversible impacts in the coming times due to over exploitation of ground water resources and sea level rise. Ground water withdrawals in excess of safe yields, reduced recharge the ground water due to rapidly changing land use pattern along the coasts have increased the incidences of sea water intrusions in the coastal aquifers.

National water policy-2002 also stresses that "Over-exploitation of ground water should be avoided, especially near the coast to prevent ingress of sea water into sweet water aquifers." *The management of ground water resources in coastal aquifers requires special attention to minimize the extension of sea water intrusion into aquifers and upcoming of sea water near pumping stations.*

The coastal tract of Saurashtra (Gujarat state) is highly productive agricultural land. The economy of the region is principally dependent on yields from the cash crops namely: Coconut, Mango, Chikoo, Sugarcane and some other food crops. Besides, the monsoon rains the principal source of irrigation water in this region is an unconfined limestone aquifer. During the last two decades it has been reported that the qualify of ground water in the region adjoining the coast is fast deteriorating due to an increase in the salinity resulting in a sharp fall in agricultural production. It has been summarized that this is due to the lateral ingress of sea water in the coastal aquifer, consequent on heavy ground water withdrawal for irrigation uses

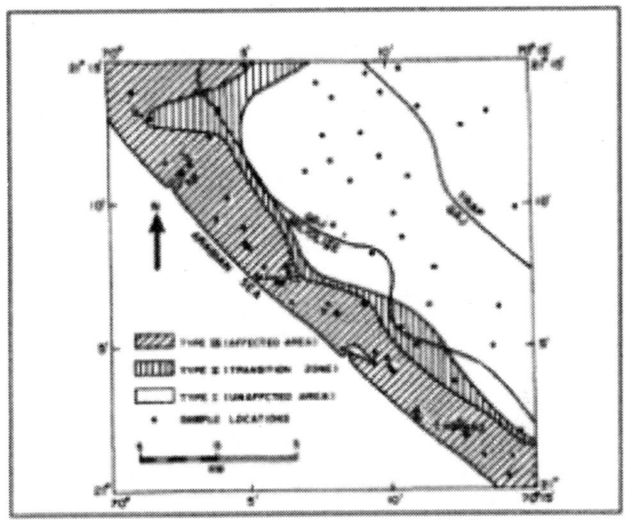

Figure 1 : Location Map of Coastal Region of South Saurashtra Indicating Sea Water Intrusion

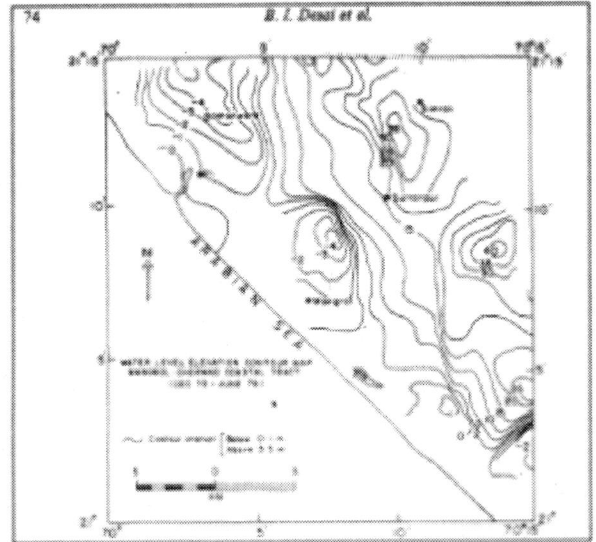

Figure 2 : Contour Map Showing the Elevation of the Groundwater in Coastal Region of South Saurashtra

(PWD, Government of Gujarat, 1975). A study carried out in 1976 by the central ground water board (CGWB) categorically ruled out sea water intrusion as a significant cause of the quality deterioration in this coastal aquifer. It has been suggested that continued use and re-use of the groundwater for irrigation and poor drainage are the principal causes for the increase in seawater intrusion.

OBJECTIVES

There is 500 km sea coast in between Bhavnagar to Dwarka having problem of sea water intrusion up to 10 to 15 km away from sea coast. The present study was carried out with these objectives keeping in mind.

- To know the total area under sea water intrusion or polluted sweet water resources for irrigation purpose
- To know the effects of sea water intrusion on agricultural production
- To evaluate the effect of sweet water trench prepared surface area near coast and fill up with rain water.

REFERENCES

Saline intrusion has occurred in Britain at a limited no. of locations where the chalk and permo-triassic sandstones have been exclusively exploited. The cause is usually industrial abstraction concentrated in coastal areas of large towns. The volume of water pumped is generally limited by the chloride concentration and if the increase in salinity can not be controlled, the boreholes are eventually abandoned. In many sandstones, where the Flore is mainly integranular, saline intrusion moves slowly in land, but in fractured aquifers intrusion can be rapid. To control saline intrusion in seawater hydraulic gradient should be maintained and a proportion of the natural fresh water recharge allowed to flow into the sea. The management of a coastal aquifer is actually concerned with deciding upon an acceptable ultimate land water extent of the saline water and calculating the amount of fresh water discharge necessary to keep it in that position.

To control saline water intrusion the pragmatic and cheapest solution is to reduce or rearrange the pattern of boreholes. This approach has been successfully applied near Brighton. The policy adopted is that in the winter, when fresh water flow to the sea is large, boreholes near the sea are used to provide most of the supply and in land boreholes are rested. This situation is reversed in summer when the flow of fresh water to the sea is much reduced and the potential for intrusion thereby increased (British Geological Survey).

The development and management of fresh groundwater resources in coastal aquifers are seriously constrained by the presence of seawater intrusion. Under utilization of the available groundwater resources means that valuable fresh water discharges naturally to the sea and is wasted, over development on the other hand mines the resources will cause a gradual degradation of water quality due to the encroachment of sea water. Over the years, many models have been developed to represent and study the problem of seawater intrusion. Ernakulam is out of the important ports in west coast of India. Due to increase in population, fast urbanization and land reforms, the region is facing a no. of environmental problems such as flooding, groundwater pollution due to discharge of industrial effluents, *seawater intrusion* etc. There exists an urgent need to study systematically the causes and remedial measures for seawater intrusion. (Dipanjali and Kumar).

Coastal tracts of Goa are rapidly being transformed into settlement areas. The poor water supply facilities have encouraged people to have their own source of water by digging or boring a well . During last decade, there have been large scale withdrawals of groundwater by buildings, hotels and other tourist establishment. Though the seawater intrusion has not yet assumed serious magnitude, but incoming years it may turn to be a major problem if corrective measures are not initiated at this stage. It is necessary to understand how fresh and salt water moves under various realistic pumping and recharge scenarios. Objectives of the present study include simulation of sea water intrusion in a coastal area of Goa. Evaluation of the impact on seawater intrusion, due to various groundwater pumping scenarios and sensitivity analysis to find out the most sensitive parameters affecting the simulation. (Kumar, C.P.)

The most important factors controlling seawater intrusion were found to be the following :

- Groundwater occurrence
- Aquifer Hydraulic Conductivity
- Depth of Groundwater level above the sea
- Distance from the shore
- Impact of existing status of sea water intrusion in the area
- Thickness of the aquifer

These factors in combination from GALDIT are determined to include the basic requirements needed to assess the general seawater intrusion potential of each hydro geologic setting. GALDIT factors represent measurable parameters for which data are generally available from a variety of sources without detailed examination. (Ferreira *et. al.* 2005)

The rapid increase in the salinity of ground water in the Mangrol-Chorwad area of coastal Saurashtra has been reported during the last decade. The hydrological and chemical data of the principal aquifers in the region have been examined with a view to ascertaining the cause of the increasing salinity in the ground water of the region. (Desai *et. al.*, 2009)

MATERIAL AND METHOD

The present study was carried out in the area between Bhavnagar to Dwarka a distance of about 500 km. of coastal line. The area of south Saurashtra in Gujarat state located on Arabian Sea. Gujarat has total 1600 kms. long sea coast line having problem of seawater intrusion. The cities like Bhavnagar, Talaja, Mahuva, Rajula, Kodinar, Somnath, Veraval, Mangrol, Madhavpur, Porbandar and Dwarka are major places on Arabian sea coast.

The students of college of rural studies shardagram, Mangrol collected primary data about proportion of sea water intrusion, its effects on Agricultural production and the effect of sweet water trench prepared and fill up with rain water during rainy days.

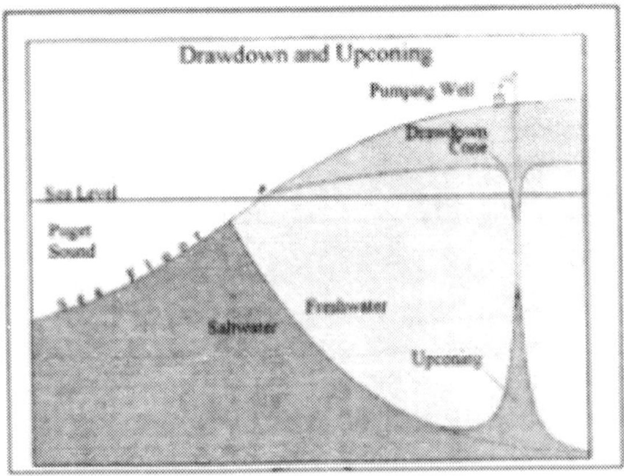

Figure 3 : Process of Seawater Intrusion

Secondary information regarding seawater intrusion was collected from hydrological research station—Mangrol (Dist. Junagadh) by Research articles and reports published. These data and information are summarized as under.

RESULT AND DISCUSSION

(1) The 500 km. Sea Coast area having same problem of seawater intrusion in agricultural land of south Saurashtra. On an average 10 to 15 km. penetration of seawater had been noticed during last 10 years.

The sea coast of south Saurashtra made up from limestone having depth approximately 20 to 25 meters. It works as a natural filter between Seawater and sweet water reservoir. But for last 20 to 30 years the mining business removed this natural filter of limestone, it resulted fast seawater intrusion in agricultural land and irrigation water sources.

Farmers of this area cultivates fruit crops like coconut, mango, chickoo, banana, pomegranate, cash crops like sugarcane and cotton and field crops like wheat, groundnut, etc., which requires more irrigation water. Farmers are using open wells and tube wells for irrigation. They are taking irrigation water up to depth of 30 to 100 meters. So the amount of sweet water is going to reduce and the seawater enters in this. So the total problematic area goes to be 16000 sq. km. in Gujarat and 5000 sq. km. in South Saurashtra sea coast.

(2) The seawater intrusion resulted to pollute the agricultural land, caused salinity. Due to salinity in the soil and saline water of irrigation reduces the crop yield. 30 to 50 percent yield losses noticed by the farmers. Salinity restricts propagation of grapes, mango, chickoo, coconut, battle leaves and other field crops. This is first major effect of seawater intrusion.

Secondly, as the groundwater became salty, the problem of sweet water for human consumption had been arises. People have to use salty water for drinking and bath. It causes skin disease and stones.

As the sweet water trench prepared 500 to 1000 meter away from sea coast and fill up by rain water the pressure of rain water increase in sub-surface aquifer, two mixing processes (diffusion and dispersion) continuously move salt water into fresh water zone. Flow in the fresh water zone sweeps this mixed brackish water towards the shoreline where it discharges a submarine seeps.

The process of the recharge by open sweet water channel changes the position of the interface. By these recharging practices the

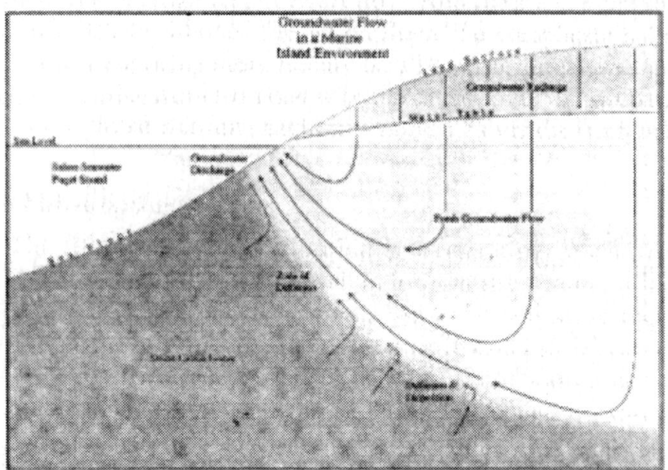

Figure 4 : Groundwater Flow in Marine Environment

groundwater became sweet for a session of cropping or more. Due to this 70 km. long sweet water channel between porbandar to Mangrol the price of agricultural land goes up for 4 to 5 times. Naturally it influence on agricultural production of various field crops and horticultural crops.

CONCLUSION

Various water recharging practices are necessary to reduce seawater intrusion in coaster aquifer, open water channel filled up by rain water reduces the penetration of seawater in coaster aquifer and increased sweet groundwater. It promotes agricultural yield and market price of agricultural land. There must be anyone water recharging technique to restore sweet water resources to sustain agricultural production to prevent seawater intrusion in all the coastal areas of Gujarat as well as in India.

REFERENECS

Anon, (1975), *Hydrogeology of Mangrol*—Chorwad Block, Dist. Junagadh (Gujarat).

———, Seawater Intrusion, British Geological Survey, NERC.

———, (2011), Saltwater Intrusion, Wikipedia—Free Encyclopedia, *http://wikipedia.org/wiki/saltwater_intrusion*, Unpublished report no. GW2/Tech-2.

Desai, B.I. *et. al.* (2009), Hydro Chemical Evidence of Seawater Intrusion, along the Mangrol-Chorwad Coast of Saurashtra, Gujarat, *Hydrological Sciences Bulletin*, 24, 1-3 (1979).

Dipanjali *et. al.*, *Simulation of Seawater Intrusion in Ernakulam Coast*, National Institutional of Hydrology, Roorkee (UC).

Ferreira, J.L.P. *et. al.* (2005), *Assessing Aquifer Vulnerability to Seawater*, Intrusion using GALDIT method. The 4th Inter-Celtic Colloquium on Hydrology and Management of Water Resource, Guimaraes, Portugal, July 11, 14-2005.

Johonson, T. (2007), Battling Seawater Intrusion in the Central and West Coast Basins. *WRD Technical Bulletin*, Vol. 13.

Kelly, D. (2005), Seawater Intrusion, Topic Paper. Approved by WRAC, (3 Feb.), Appróved by BOCC (16 Mar.), Island Country, Washington, State Department of Health.

Kumar, C.P., Modeling of seawater intrusion in coastal area of North Goa. *http://academic.edu*, National Institute of Hydrology—Roorkee and Belgium.

Chapter 19

Watershed Management

A Step Towards Sustainable Growth in Himachal Pradesh

RAMNA

INTRODUCTION

Climate change is one of the most important global environmental challenges, with implications for food production, water supply, health, energy, etc. Addressing climate change requires a good scientific understanding as well as coordinated action at national and global level. The projected climate change under various scenarios is likely to have implications on food production, water supply, coastal settlements, forest ecosystems, health, energy security, etc. The adaptive capacity of communities likely to be impacted by climate change is low in developing countries. The efforts made by the UNFCCC and the Kyoto Protocol provisions are clearly inadequate to address the climate change challenge. The most effective way to address climate change is to adopt a sustainable development pathway by shifting to environmentally sustainable technologies and promotion of energy efficiency, renewable energy, forest conservation, reforestation, water conservation, etc. In this direction, sustainable development in India encompasses a variety of development schemes in social, cleantech. (clean energy, clean water and sustainable agriculture) and human resources segments, having caught the attention of both Central and State governments and also public and private sectors. In fact, India is expected to begin the greening of its national income accounting, making depletion in natural resources wealth a key component in its measurement of gross domestic product (GDP). Land degradation has created a serious ecological and socio economic crisis in many parts of India. To improve the living conditions in rural people Government of India has initiated several schemes to improve the degradation of lands. The problem of droughts, fuel wood, fodder production and environment conservation has become common feature in many parts of the country. To address these problems as well as to provide support to cleantech, watershed approach has been adopted and Watershed Development Projects have been undertaken under different programmes.

In 1994, a Technical Committee under the Chairmanship of Prof. C.H. Hanumantha Rao, was appointed to assess the Drought Prone Area Programme (DPAP) and the Desert Development Programme (DDP) with the purpose of identifying weaknesses and suggesting improvements. This Committee made a number of recommendations and formulated a set of guidelines that brought the DDP, the DPAP and the Integrated Wastelands Development Programme (IWDP) under a single umbrella. The watershed projects taken up by the Ministry of Rural Development (MoRD) from 1994 to 2001 followed these guidelines. In 2000, the Ministry of Agriculture revised its guidelines for its programme, the National Watershed Development Project for Rainfed Areas (NWDPRA). These guidelines were intended to be common guidelines to make the programme more participatory, sustainable and equitable. However, the MoRD revised the 1994 Hanumantha Rao Committee guidelines in 2001 and yet again in 2003 under the nomenclature "Hariyali Guidelines". An insight into the rainfed regions reveals a grim picture of poverty, water scarcity, rapid depletion of ground water table and fragile ecosystems. Land degradation due to soil erosion by wind and water, low rainwater use efficiency, high population pressure, acute fodder shortage, poor livestock productivity, under investment in water use efficiency, lack of assured and remunerative marketing opportunities and poor infrastructure are important concerns of enabling policies. The challenge in rainfed areas, therefore, is to improve rural livelihoods through participatory watershed development with focus on integrated farming systems for enhancing income, productivity and livelihood security in a sustainable manner. The National Rainfed Area Authority (NRAA) has been set-up in November 2006, keeping in mind the need to give a special thrust to these regions. A close analysis of various types of rainfed situations would reveal that soil and water conservation, watershed development and efficient water management are the key to sustainable development of rainfed areas. The watershed approach has been accepted as a major theme for development of rainfed areas with a view to conserving natural resources of water, soil and vegetation by mobilizing social capital.

OBJECTIVES AND METHODOLOGY

Himachal Pradesh, the mountainous state known for its natural wealth, and is endowed with rich cultural and religious heritage. It is situated between 300 22' 40" to 330 12' 20" north latitudes and 750 45' 45" to 790 04' 20" east longitudes in western Himalayas. The altitudes range from 350 metres to 6975 metres above mean sea level. The total geographical area of the state is 55,673 Sq. km with a population of about 6 millions (census 2001). The state has 12 districts namely Bilaspur, Chamba, Hamirpur, Kangra, Kinnaur, Kullu, Lahul Spiti, Mandi, Sirmaur, Shimla, Solan, and Una. The state is divided into four agro-climatic zones : (i) Shiwalik Hills (upto an elevation of about 800 metres above the mean sea level), (ii) Mid Hills (from 800 metres to 1600 metres), (iii) High Hills (above 1,600 metres), and (iv) Cold Dry Zone (above 2,700 metres above mean sea level). Himachal Pradesh has 16997 villages and over 90 per centof State's population lives in rural areas. Agriculture, being the main occupation of the people of Himachal Pradesh, has an important role in the economy of the State. It provides direct employment to about 71 per cent of the main working population. Income from the agriculture and allied sector accounts for nearly 22.5 per cent of the total State Domestic Product. The main objective of the study is to investigate that how 'Integrated Watershed Management Development Programme' is working in the state. Nearly 70 per cent to 75 per cent of the rainfall is received during monsoon season from June to September. During this period the rain water causes severe soil erosion and damages to the cultivated land due to lack of vegetative covers. The water flowing down from the hills simply drains away as surface runoff and causes floods in the plains. The physiography of the state does not allow construction of medium and major irrigational scheme, therefore, the watershed approach is best way to conserve the rain water and use the same after the monsoon season. The present study is based on secondary data the main source of secondary data, is the reports of Rural Development Department of Himachal Pradesh, Directorate of Land Records, related books, Journals, Research Papers, Reports, etc.

RESULTS AND DISCUSSION

Demographic Indicators

Himachal Pradesh having lowest proportion of Urban Population with 9.3 per cent urban population ranks first among all the states of India. Other important demographic features of India and Himachal Pradesh according to 2001 census are as under:

TABLE 1
Demographic Indicators

Sl. No.	*Item*	*Unit*	*Himachal Pradesh*	*India*
1.	Total Area	Square kilometers	55,673	32,87,263
2.	Total Population	Million persons	6.08	1028.61
	Males	Lakh persons	30.88	5321.57
	Females	Lakh persons	29.90	4964.53
3.	Density	Persons	109	313
4.	Sex Ratio	Per 1000 Males	968	933
5.	Rural Population	%	90.20	72.2
6.	Population Below Poverty Line (2002-07)	%	23.87	27.5
7.	Per Capita Income	INR	31198	22946
8.	Literacy Percentage	%	76.5	64.8
	Males	%	85.30	75.3
	Females	%	67.40	53.7

Sources : 1. Statistical Outline, 2007-08, Economics & Statistics Department Himachal Pradesh.
2. Statistical Pocket Book India, 2005, Central Statistical Organization, Government of India.

IRRIGATION FACILITIES IN HIMACHAL PRADESH

As is clear from Table 2 that gross irrigated area is only 18.58 percent of the total sown area in Himachal Pradesh while it is 38.65

TABLE 2
Area Sown, Cropping Intensity, Irrigated Area and Average Size of Operational Holdings in India and Himachal Pradesh

Sl. No.	Particulars	Unit	Himachal	India
1.	Net Area sown	'000 Hect.	5.58	1428.19
2.	Area sown more than once	'000 Hect.	3.59	467.24
3.	Gross cropped area	'000 Hect.	9.47	1895.43
4.	Cropping intensity	%	176	133
5.	Net irrigated area	'000 Hect.	1.05	551.43
6.	Gross irrigated area	'000 Hect.	1.76	732.75
7.	Gross irrigated area	%	18.58	38.65
8.	Average size of operational holdings	'000 Hect.	1.21	1.55

Source : Statistical Outline, 2007-08, Economics & Statistics Department, Himachal Pradesh.

percent for India as a whole. Average size of operational holdings is only 1.21 hectare in Himachal Pradesh.

NATURAL RESOURCES

Natural resources of Himachal Pradesh have a direct relationship with its physiographic conditions including relief, climate, drainage and geology. These in turn influences the type of soils and the kind of vegetation cover. The total area of Himachal Pradesh is 55.673 sq. km. Hardly 10 percent of the total area is cultivated and the actual forest cover extends to 22.5 percent of the total area. Permanent pastures and other grasslands account for about 24 percent of the total area. Barren and unculturable land covers about 14 percent of the area of the state. The state is richly endowed with a hilly terrain having a catchment area of river Satluj, Beas, Ravi and Chenab. As such the State has enormous potential of water resources in the form of glaciers and rivers but ground water resource is limited. In-spite of the fact that a large volume of water is available in the State, only 20 per cent of its cultivated area is irrigated because of its physiographic constraints. The normal monsoon rainfall (June to September) in the State varies from 17 to 120 cm.

GROUND WATER RESOURCES

The ground water resource occurs mainly in unconsolidated sediments of inter-mountain valleys and in the sub-mountain tract. Kangra, Una, Hamirpur, Bilaspur, Mandi, Solan and Sirmour districts, particularly their valley area, depend upon groundwater. The exploitation is done through open wells, tube wells, infiltration galleries and wells. The status of development of ground water resources in the State.

WATERSHED DEVELOPMENT PROGRAMME IN HIMACHAL PRADESH

In Himachal, at most of the places, lift water supply schemes have been constructed lifting the water from rivulets, to the higher reaches. However, the maintenance cost of these schemes is prohibitive due to heavy electrical charges. Thus, in past first the rain which falls on the hilly terrain was allowed to flow into the rivers/ rivulets as runoff and then some parts of it is brought back. All that a dry land farmer has his assets is his soil and the rain water that falls on his land. If one could try to manage them efficiently, the productivity in dry land could be increased, the profitability enhanced, stabilized and sustained. Unlike the irrigated farming, the dry land agriculture has many constrain starting with climate, soil, crops and socio-economic conditions. Rainfall is the critical factor among the climatic parameters, having great influence on the crops to be grown. The rain- fall is not only low but erratic, unpredictable and distributed in short period in rainfalls areas. Well prepared "Micro Watershed Projects" based on the study of climate water and plant resources on the one hand and man and animal resources on the other, offers great scope for bringing about sustained natural resource development. The soil in hills shows great diversity in texture, structure depth, etc. Besides soil and climate, the crop being cultivated in the dry lands are found to be of long duration, which do not synchronize to the actual cropping seasons. These are low yielders and do not respond to improved package of practices. In addition to this, the present cultivators are not tolerant to drought nutrient status, pests diseases and other soil-related constraints hampering crop cultivation.

Therefore, to solve these problems watershed approach has been adopted in Himachal Pradesh since 1995-96. A watershed is geo-hydrological unit, which drains into common point. The aim is to stop and conserve water where it falls, so it can be used for a longer period of time. The watershed development in Himachal Pradesh tries to reduce the volume and velocity of runoff through a series of interventions. The aim is to make the water walk, rather than let it run. The simple methods of stalling rainwater from running off have an enormous impact on the overall health of the watershed. Since rainwater is intervened at regular intervals by watershed structure, it does not flow long distances. Therefore, it cannot gather speed, volume and force.

In Himachal Pradesh, 1837 micro watersheds have been identified with a total outlay of 529.8 Crore INR for treatment of 8,54,386 hectare of land in all 12 districts of the state. The programme was started in 1995-96 and till Jan. 2009, an area of 4,57,609 hectare has been treated with the total expenditure of 286.4 crore INR. There are three programmes which are included in Watershed Development Programme in Himachal Pradesh:

- Drought Prone Area Programme
- Desert Development Programme
- Integrated Wasteland Development Programme

I. Drought Prone Area Programme

This programme is basically an area development programme and aims at integrated development of natural resources like land, water, vegetation, etc. by taking up watershed development projects. The programme is being implemented in 10 blocks of the State. Up to the year 1998-99 the programme was being funded by Central and State Governments on 50:50 sharing basis but from 1-4-1999 the Government of India have changed the funding pattern from 50:50 to 75:25. Under this programme 318 micro-watersheds have been taken up for development in district Bilaspur, Solan and Una for a period of 5 years. During the year 2005-06, 40 new micro-watersheds have been sanctioned by the Government of India under the programme.

2. Desert Development Programme (DDP)

Under DDP, 420 micro-watersheds have been taken up for the development in district of Lahual & Spiti and Pooh Block of district Kinnaur. The Govt. of India has sanctioned 38 new micro-watershed projects under this programme during the current financial year. (23 micro-watershed for Lahual & Spiti and 15 micro-watershed for Kinnaur district.

3. Integrated Wastelands Development Programme

Integrated Wastelands Development Programme is being implemented in all the districts of the state. Prior to 1.4.2000 the watershed projects under this programme were being funded 100 per cent by the Central Government. However, the projects sanctioned after 1.4.2000 are being funded Rs. 5500 per ha. by the GOI and Rs. 500 per ha. by the State Government. During the year 2004-05 the Government of India has sanctioned two new projects with a total project outlay of Rs. 900 lakhs for treatment of 15,000 hectare of land.

Projects Sanctioned Under Integrated Watershed Management Programme in Himachal Pradesh during 2009-10 IN 1st and 2nd Phases.

The first phase three-three blocks of district Bilaspur (Sadar, Jhandutta and Ghumarwin) and Kinnaur (Pooh, Nichar and Kalpa), two-two blocks of district Kangra and Shimla, one-one block of district Chamba, Kullu, Mandi, Sirmaur and Una have been sanctioned projects under Watershed Management Programme in Himachal Pradesh in 2009-10. Total targeted area under this scheme was 91,885 and total project cost was 1,37,82,750.

Intgrated Watershed Management Programme is working in all the districts of Himachal Pradesh. In the second phase total area for treatment under Watershed Management Programme in Himachal Pradesh was 1,11,947 while the poject cost was 16,79,205 in 2009-10. Blocks like Bhijhari, Dehra, Kaza, Keylong, Karsog, Dharampur, Sundernagar, Theog, Theog and Nalagarh of various districts have been sanctioned projects under Watershed Management Programme.

CONCLUDING REMARKS

Government of Himachal Pradesh has launched the Integrated Watershed Development Programmes in the State with the objectives of integrated agriculture and livelihood development in the rural areas of the State. This programme has promoted the overall economic development and improved the socio-economic condition of the rural people. It is trying to mitigate adverse effects of extreme climatic conditions such as drought and desertification on crops, human and livestock population for their overall improvement. It is also encouraging village community for sustained community action for the operation and maintenance of assets created and for further development of the potential of the natural resources in the watershed. Irrigation is one of the important components of agriculture. There is no need to build huge dams, which may have their long-term negative effects. Instead of one big dam, a number of small dams and check dams can be constructed. There should be control over the supply of irrigation water. Farmers should draw water according to their need. In this way, soil salinity can be avoided. Sustainable development largely depends on a correct use of natural resources. Therefore, stewardship of both natural and human resources is of prime importance. Every area has its limitation in the use of its natural resources. If a production system is adopted according to the availability of natural resources, the area can become self-dependent. In the rural areas the efficient and environment-friendly technologies should be given preferences. The technology that can recycle, re-use of waste from agriculture, horticulture, dairying, mining should be promoted. In nutshell, we can say that Integrated Watershed Development Programmes is very much helpful in employment generation, poverty alleviation, community empowerment and development of human and other economic and natural resources in the rural areas. To make this programme more effective, primary responsibility is of the concerning department, to ensure proper planning and implementation of the programme with active participation of communities. At the State level, proposed area for watershed projects should be identified with the help of State Remote Sensing Agency. The provision of funds, capacity building through dedicated institutions, and community mobilization are the important issues for success of watershed management programme.

References

Sathaye, Jayant *et al.* (2006), "Climate change, and sustainable development in India: Global and National Concerns", *Current Science*, Vol. 90, No. 3, 10 Feb, pp. 314-25.

Datye, K.R., "Sustainable Development in India—How and Why?", *Talk and Discussion*, Sunday, September 17, 4:00 PM, Physics Auditorium, Phy. Bldg., Univ. of MD, College Park.

A Research Study of Participatory and Democratic Watershed Management Model Implemented in Himachal Pradesh, Research & Documentation Centre, H.P. State Institute of Rural Development (HIPA), Government of Himachal Pradesh, Fairlawns, Shimla. (Website: http://himachal.gov.in/hipa Email: hipa-hp@nic.in)

Kher, S.K. and Bhagat, G.R. (2003), Sustainability Predictors of Hunger Free India", Surat Singh, S.P. Sinha and Birbal Dass Dhalia (Ed.), *Strategies for*

Sustainable Rural Development, Deep and Deep Publications, New Delhi, pp. 100, 102.

M.V., Joshi (2001), *Theories and Approaches of Environmental Economics*, Atlantic Publishers and Distributors, New Delhi, p. 5.

Sangwan, Satya (2005), *Sustainable Agriculture from Green to an Evergreen Revolution*, Competition, Wizard, June, New Delhi, p. 45.

Statistical Pocket Book India (2005), Central Statistical Organization, Government of India.

Jodha, N.S. (1991), Agricultural Growth and Sustainability: Perspectives and Experiences from the Himalayas, paper presented in, A Contribution of DSE/IFPRI Seminar on *Agricultural and Sustainable Growth and Poverty Alleviations; Issues and Policies* (Feldafing, Federal Republic of Germany) September 23-27, pp. 21-22.

Statistical Outline 2007-08, Economics & Statistics Department, Himachal Pradesh.

Jodha, N.S. (1992), Mountain Perspective and Sustainability: A Framework for Development Strategies, in N.S. Jodha, M. Banskota and T. Partap (Ed.) *Sustainable Mountain Agriculture Perspective and Issues*, Vol. I, Oxford and IBH Publishing Co., New Delhi, p. 30.

Khanna, Sulbha (1995), *Planning for Sustainable Agricultural Development*, Discovery Publishing House, New Delhi, pp. 108-18.

Singh, Surat, Sinha, S.P. and Dahiya, Birbal Dass (2003), Strategies for Sustainable Rural Development, Deep and Deep Publications, New Delhi, p. 91.

Pathania, M.S. and Vashist, G.D. (2001), "Sustainable Development of Small Farms in Hiamachal Pradesh", *Political Economy Journal of India*, Vol. 10, No. 1, Dec., p. 67.

CGWB, Ministry of Water Resources, *H.P. Development Report*

Department of Rural Development, Government of Himachal Pradesh, "Projects Sanctioned Under Integrated Watershed Management Programme", Year 2009-10.

Chapter 20
Water Resources in India

JAYWANT R. BHADANE

INTRODUCTION

India is rich in water resources with network of great rivers and vast alluvial basins to hold ground water. However, conditions may vary widely form region to region. There are some drought-affected areas as well as some other areas, which are frequently subject to damage by floods. On the whole, under the pressure of rapid population growth, the available resources of water are being developed and depleted at a fast rate and situation seriously underlines the need for taking up integrated plans for water conservation and utilization for every agro-ecological area to meet the increasing demands of irrigation, water harvesting, human and livestock's consumption, expanding industry, hydro-electric power generation, recreation, navigation and other uses.

Water is essential for sustaining all forms of life, food production, and economic development and for general well-being. It is impossible to substitute for most of its uses, difficult to de-pollute, expensive to transport and it is truly a unique gift to mankind from nature. Water is also one of the most manageable of the natural resources as it is capable of diversion, transport, storage and recycling. All these properties impart to water its great utility for human being.

WATER RESOURCES IN INDIA

The concept of water resources is multi-dimensional. It is not limited only to its physical measure, i.e. hydrological and hydro-ecological, the flows and stocks but encompasses other more qualitative, environmental and socio-economic dimensions.

India occupies 3.29 million km^2 geographical areas, which forms 2.4 per cent of the world's land area; it supports over 15 per cent of the world's population. The population of India in 2001 stood at 102.7 crore persons. Thus, India supports about 1/6th of the world's population, 1/50th of the world's land and 1/25th of the world's water resources. India also has a livestock population of 500 million, which is about 20 per cent of world's total livestock population. More than 50 per cent of these cattle are forming the backbone of Indian agriculture, and the total utilizable water resources of the country are assessed as 1086 km^3.

TYPES OF WATER RESOURCES

There are two different types of water resources, such as Surface Water Resources and Ground Water Resources. Each of these types is a part of the earth's water circulatory system, called the hydrologic cycle and is derived from precipitation which is rainfall plus snow. They are interdependent and frequently the loss of one is the gain of the other. They are also called as renewable water resources and non-renewable water resources.

SURFACE WATER RESOURCES—CONCEPT AND EXPLANATION

The total run-off in the stream channel includes the snow-melt, the surface run-off, the sub-surface run-off, the ground water run-off and the channel precipitation, i.e. the precipitation falling directly on the water surface of streams, lakes, etc. It constitutes, what is known as the surface water resources.

It may also be defined as the average annual flow of rivers and recharge of aquifers generated from precipitation. It distinguishes between the natural renewable resources, which corresponds to a situation without human influence and the current and actual situation. The computation of the actual surface water resources of a country takes into account of possible reductions in flow resulting from the abstraction of water in upstream countries. So the surface renewable water resources are computed based on the water cycle. Thus, it represents the long-term average annual flow of rivers (surface water) and ground water.

The precipitation that falls upon land and is the ultimate source of both the categories of water resources is dispersed in several ways. A sizable portion is intercepted by the vegetal cover or temporarily detained in surface depressions. Most of it is, later, lost through evaporation. When the available interception or the depression storage is completely exhausted and when the rainfall intensity at the soil surface exceeds, the infiltration capacity of the soils, the overland flow begins. Once the overland flow reaches a stream channel, it is called surface run-off, which together with other components of flow, forms the total run-off.

A part of the water that infiltrates into the surface soil may continue to more laterally at shallow depth as interflow owing to the presence of relatively imperious tenses just below the soil surface and may eventually reach the stream channel when it is called the sub-surface run-off. A part of the sub-surface run-off may enter the stream promptly whereas the remaining part may take a long time before joining the stream flow. A second part of the precipitation which infiltrates is lost through evapo-transpiration, via plant roots and thermal gradients just below the soil surface and third part may remain above the water table in the zone of unsaturated flow.

In the past several organizations and individuals have estimated water availability for the nation. Recently, the National Commission for Integrated Water Resources Development estimated for basin-wise average annual flow in Indian River system as 1953 km^3.

Utilizable water resource is the quantum of withdrawable water from its place of natural occurrence. Within the limitations of physiographic conditions and socio-political environment, legal and constitutional constraints and the technology of development available at present, utilizable quantity of water from the surface flow has been assessed by various authorities differently. The utilizable annual surface water of the country is 690 km^3.

GROUND WATER RESOURCES— CONCEPT AND EXPLANATION

Ground water is the water captured in underground reservoirs. Ground water resources are ground water bodies (deep aquifers) that have a negligible rate of recharge on the human time scale and thus can be considered as non-renewable water resources.

The portion of the precipitation which after infiltration reaches the ground water table together with the contribution made to ground water from a neighboring basin, influent rivers, natural lakes, ponds, artificial storage reservoirs, canals, irrigation etc. constitutes the ground water resources. The quantity of water in the ground water reservoir, which is not annually replenishable is not taken into account as it is a sort of dead storage which cannot be used on continuing basis from year to year. The remaining part of the precipitation percolates deeply in the ground water and this may eventually reach the stream channel and become the base flow of the stream. This portion is termed ground water run-off or the ground water flow.

The annual potential of natural ground water recharge from rainfall in India is about 342.43 km^3, which is 87.56 per cent of total annual rainfall of the country. The annual potential groundwater recharge augmentation form canal irrigation system is about 89.46 km^3. Thus, total replenish able ground water resource of the country is assessed as 431.89 km^3. After allotting 15 per cent of this quantity for drinking and 6 km^3 for the industrial purposes the remaining can be utilized for irrigation purposes. Thus, the available ground water resource for irrigation is 361 km^3, of which utilizable quantity is 325 km^3, i.e. 90 per cent. The estimates of Central Ground Water Board of total replenishable ground water resource; provision for domestic, industrial and irrigation uses and utilizable groundwater resources for future use is described above. The basin-wise per capita water availability varies between 13,393 m^3 per annum for Brahmaputra-Barak basin to about 300 m^3 per annum for Sabarmati basin.

WATER REQUIREMENTS OF INDIA

India is an agricultural-based economy. Therefore, development of irrigation to increase agricultural production for making the country self-sustainable and for poverty alleviation has been of crucial importance for the planners. Accordingly the irrigation sector was assigned a very high priority in the 5 year plans. Giant schemes like the Bhakra Nangal, Hirakud, Domoder Valley, Nagarjunsagar, Sardar Sarover, Rajasthan Cannel Project, etc. were taken up to increase the irrigation potential and maximize agriculture production.

Long-term planning has to account for the growth of population. According to National water policy the production of food grains has increased from around 50 million tons in the 1950 to about 253 million tons in the year 2010. A number of individuals and agencies have estimated the likely population of India by the year

2025 and 2050. According to estimates adopted by National Commission on Integrated Water Resources Development (NCIWRD), by the year 2025, the population is expected to be 150 crores in high growth scenario. Keeping in view the level of consumption, losses in storage and transport, seed requirement and buffer stock the prospected food grain and feed demand for 2025 would be 400 million tons in high demand scenario. For projected population of India for 2025 per capita water availability will be 421 m^3 and utilizable surface water per capita will be 1451 m^3. However, the general situation of availability of per capita is much more alarming.

Irrigation

The irrigated area in the country was only 22.6 million hectares in 1950-51. Since the food production was much below the requirement of the country, due attention paid for expansion of irrigation. The ultimate irrigation potential of India has estimated as 140 million hectares. Out of this, 76 million hectares would come from surface water and 64 million hectares from groundwater sources. The quantum of water used for irrigation by 20-10 was of the order of 300 km^3 of surface water and 128 km^3 of ground water, total 428 km^3. The estimates indicate that by the year 2025 the water requirement for irrigation would be 561 km^3 for low demand and 611 km^3 for high demand scenario.

Industry

It is observed that, the present water use in Industry is about 15 km^3. The use of thermal and nuclear power plants with installed capacities of 40 thousand MW and 1500 MW respectively estimated to be about 19 km^3. In view of shortage of water, the industries are expected to switch over to water efficient technologies. If the present rate of water use continues the water requirement of the industries in 2050 would be 103 km^3, this is likely to be nearly 81 km^3, if water savings technologies are adopted on a large scale.

DRINKING WATER AND OTHER DOMESTIC USES

Community Water Supply is the most important requirement and it is about 5 per cent of the total water use. About 7 km^3 of surface water and 18 km^3 of groundwater are being used for community water supply in urban and rural areas. Alongwith the increase in population another important change from the point of view of water supply to higher rate of urbanization. Accordingly, to the projections, the higher is the economic growth, the higher would be urbanization. It is expected that nearly 61 per cent of the population will be living in urban areas by the year 2050 in high growth scenario as against 48 per cent in low growth scenario.

Different organizations and individuals have given different norms of Water Supply in cities and rural areas. The figure adopted by NCIWRD was 220 liters per capita per day for class I cities. For other cities norms are 165 liters/capita/day for the years 2025 and 220 liters/day/capita for the year 2050. For the rural areas, 70 liters/ capita/day and 150 liter/capita/day have been recommended for the year 2025 and 2050. Based on these norms and projection of population, it is estimated by 2050, water requirement per year for domestic use will be 90 km^3 for low demand scenario and 111 km^3 for high demand scenario. It is expected that surface water resources and the remaining from groundwater will meet about 70 per cent of urban water requirement and 30 per cent of rural water requirement.

Hydropower

The hydropower potential of India has estimated at 84,044 MW @ 60 per cent load factor. At the time of independence, the installed capacity of hydropower projects was 508 MW. By the end of 1998, the installed hydropower capacity was about 22,000 MW. The status of hydropower development is the major baring is highly uneven. According to an estimate, India plans to develop 60,000 MW additional hydropower by the 12th Five Year Plan. 9 includes 14393 MW during the 10th Five Year Plan, i.e. (2002-07), 20,000 MW during 11th FYP (2007-12) and 26,000 MW during 12th (2012-17) FYP. A potential in the order of 10,000 MW is available for development of small hydropower projects in the Himalaya and sub-Himalayan regions of the country. Therefore, it is not only desirable but also a pressing need of time to draw a master plan for development of small, medium and large hydro schemes for power generation.

Frozen Water

Several schemes have been proposed to make use of icebergs as a water source, however to date this has only been done for novelty purposes. Glacier run-off is considered to be surface water.

The Himalayas, which are often called "The Roof of the World", contain some of the most extensive and rough high altitude areas on

Earth as well as the greatest area of glaciers and permafrost outside of the poles. Ten of Asia's largest rivers flow from there and more than a billion people's livelihoods depend on them. To complicate matters, temperatures are rising more rapidly here than the global average. In Nepal, the temperature has risen with 0.6 degree over the last decade, whereas the global warming has been around 0.7 over the last hundred years.

Rapid Urbanization

The trend towards urbanization is accelerating. Small private wells and septic tanks that work well in low-density communities are not feasible within high-density urban areas. Urbanization requires significant investment in water infrastructure in order to deliver water to individuals and to process the concentrations of wastewater both from individuals and from business These polluted and contaminated waters must be treated or they pose unacceptable public health risks. In 60 per cent of European cities with more that 1,00,000 people, groundwater is being used at a faster rate than it can be replenished. Even if some water remains available, it costs more and more to capture it.

FACTOR AFFECTING WATER RESOURCES

The following three major groups of factors influence the water resources of a region, conceived as dynamic phase of the hydrologic cycle.

- (i) Climatic Factors
  - (a) Rainfall: its intensity, duration, distribution
  - (b) Snow
  - (c) Evapo-transpiration
- (ii) Physiographic factors
  - (a) Geometric factors: Drainage area, shape, Slope & Stream density.
  - (b) Physical factors: Land use, surface infiltration conditions, soil type, etc.
  - (c) Carrying capacity and storage capacity-channels.
- (iii) Geological factors
  - (a) Litho logic including composition, texture, sequence of rock types and thickness of rock formation.
  - (b) Structured inducing major faults that interrupt the uniformity of occurrence of types or sequences and rocks types also bode, joints, fissures, cracks, etc.

(c) Hydrologic characterization of the aquifers, permeability, posisity, transmissivity, storability, etc.

The physiographic features not only influence the occurrence and distribution of water resources within a region but these, particularly the orography, play a significant role in influencing rainfall and other climatic factors, such as temperature, humidity and wind. However, within a geographical location and physiographic framework, it is primarily the rainfall (its intensity, duration and distribution) and the climatic factors affecting evapo-transpiration that determine the totality of water resources in the region.

MANAGEMENT OF WATER RESOURCES

In view of the existing status of water resources and increasing demands of water for meeting the requirements of the rapidly growing population of the country, as well as the problems that are likely to arise in future, a holistic, well-planned long-term strategy is needed for sustainable water resources management in India. The water resources management practices may be based on increasing the water supply and managing the water demand under the stressed water availability conditions. Some important aspects are as follows:

MANAGEMENT OF FLOODS

A large fold storage space in reservoirs is required for successful flood management program. It also calls for community participation. Farmers, professional bodies, industries, voluntary organizations have to be aware about flood management. People's participation in preparedness, flood fighting and disaster response is required. The government of India has taken some initiatives in this regards however, the more active participation is required.

MANAGEMENT OF DROUGHT

An integrated basin development approach is required to be developed and implemented for preparing the drought management plan before, during and after the occurrence of drought. There is a need for the development of the decision support system for the monitoring and management of droughts on basin scale utilizing the advanced capabilities of remote sensing geographical steps may taken at political, administrative and technical levels to encourage people participation in the drought management for optimum utilization of the available water supply to meet the demands.

GROUNDWATER MANAGEMENT

To protect the aquifers from over exploitation, an effective groundwater management policy oriented towards promotion of efficiency, equity and sustainability is required. The exploitation of groundwater resources should be regulated. The effects of over-exploitation of groundwater need to be effectively prevented by Central and State Government A joint management approach combining Govt. administration with active people participation is a promising solution. The role of Government will have to switch from that of controller of groundwater development to that of a facilitator of equitable and sustainable development.

RAINWATER HARVESTING

It is the process to capture and store the rainfall for its efficient utilization and conservation to control its run-off evaporation and seepage. Rainwater harvesting increases water availability. It checks the declining water table, it is environmentally friendly, it improves the quality of groundwater thorough dilution, mainly of fluoride, nitrate and salinity and it prevents soil erosion and folding, especially in the urban areas. There is a need to recharge acquirers and conserve rainwater through water harvesting structures.

LEGAL STRATEGIES

One of the active strategies could include provisions of legal restrictions on use of water, mainly during the period of scarcity. In India a National Water Policy has adopted, which includes policy directions for development and management of water resources.

DEMAND MANAGEMENT

Demand management for urban areas and industries is another strategy, which could adopt to reduce the demands in urban water supply or households and industries. Sound water budgeting in industry can reduce the water demand to considerable extent. The water conservation and reuse strategies should be planned at the time of setting of new industry to build in the conservation and reuse requirements from the beginning.

WATER PRICING STRATEGY

Another strategy, which needs consideration, is changes in water pricing structures. Mostly water rates based only on a portion of what it costs to obtain, develop, transport, treat and deliver water to the consumer. The differential pricing system are needed separately for residential, commercial and industrial sectors.

DESALINATION OF WATER

Since last 30 to 40 years, there has been significant commercial development using various desalinations technologies, including distillation, reverse osmosis and electrolysis. This technology is suitable for use in areas where freshwater is scarce but saline water is available and energy is cheap. Compared to water recycling technologies, desalination presents fewer health risks. However, the cost of desalination is much more. It is expected that as the costs come down desalination would become commercially viable.

DATA MONITORING AND INFORMATION SYSTEM

In India, the network of the monitoring of hydro meteorological variables is inadequate. In addition, the data collection, processing, storage and dissemination are not well organized. In this regard, a comprehensive reliable and easily accessible Hydrological Information System is a pre-requisite to achieve these objectives, there is a need to strengthen the existing monitoring network of data and develop the HIS by improving the data processing analysis and dissemination techniques through proper co-ordination among various agencies.

References

Interrated Water Resources Development, Plan for Action, Report of the National Commission for Integrated Water Resources Development, Ministry of Water Resources, New Delhi.

National Water Policy, Ministry of Water Resources, New Delhi.

Shah, T., Groundwater and Human Development, Challenges and Opportunities in Livelihoods Creation and Environment, Lecture delivered during the Workshop on Creating Synergy between Groundwater Research and Management in South Asia.

Lal, M., Climate Change, *Implications for India's water resources.*

Deshpande, R.D. and Gupta, S.K., *Water for India, 2050.*

Archana, Mishra, *Watershed Management.*

Agrawal, Anil and Narayan, Sunita; *Bundo ki Sanskriti*, Center for Science and Environment.

Kumar, Rakesh; Singh, R.D. and Sharma, K.D., *Water Resources of India*, National Institute of Hydrology, Roorkee, India.

International Water Resources Association.

http:ga.water,usgs,gov/edu/waterdistribution.html.

Bose, and Saxena (2001), *Mansoon, Employment News.*
Porous cities, New directions in urban water usage.
www.google.co.in.
World Water Supply and Demand, 1995 to 2025 for the IWMI.
Krishiworld, The pulse of Indian Agriculture.
FAO Corporate Document Repository, Natural Resources Management and Environment Department.
Rao, K.L., *India's Water Wealth*, Orient Longman, New Delhi.

Chapter 21

Economic Instruments for Sustainable Groundwater Management

K. GOVINDARAJALU AND C. MYTHILI

INTRODUCTION

India is now the biggest user of groundwater for agriculture in the world (Shah, 2009). Groundwater irrigation has been expanding at a very rapid pace in India since the 1970s. The data from the Minor Irrigation Census conducted in 2001 shows evidence of the growing number of groundwater irrigation structures (wells and tube wells) in the country. Their number stood at around 18.5 million in 2001, of which tube wells accounted for 50 per cent. There is no reason to believe that the growth in the number of these structures have slowed down since then. In all likelihood, the number of groundwater irrigation structures is now around 27 million with every fourth rural household owning at least one such irrigation structure (Shah, 2009). The share of groundwater in the net irrigated area has also been on the rise. Of the addition to net irrigated area of about 29.75 million hectares between 1970 and 2007, ground water accounted for 24.02 million hectares (80%). On an average, between 2000-01 and 2006-07, about 61 per cent of the irrigation in the country was sourced from groundwater. The share of surface water has declined from 60 per cent in the 1950s to 30 per cent in the first decade of the 21st century.

The most dramatic change in the groundwater scenario in India is that the share of tube wells in irrigated areas rose from a mere 1 per cent in 1960-61 to 40 per cent in 2006-07. By now, tube wells have become the largest single source of irrigation water in India. Data from Minor Irrigation Census (2001) showed that three states (Punjab, Uttar Pradesh and Haryana) accounted for 57 per cent of the tube wells in India. On an average, there were 27 tube wells per square kilometre of net sown area in Punjab, 21.5 in Uttar Pradesh and 14.1 in Haryana in 2001. Interestingly, 68 per cent of the households owning tube wells were of small and marginal farmers, indicating the growing dependence of these households on tube wells as a source of livelihoods. And this, despite the fact that India, along with China and the United States, has far outpaced the world in building large dams (World Commission on Dams, 2000).

As a stern warning, the report of the Expert Group on Groundwater Management and Government states that in 2004 some 28 per cent of India's blocks (nationally recognised administrative units) were showing dangerously high levels of groundwater development as compared to 4 per cent in 1995 (Planning Commission, 2007). A more recent assessment by NASA showed that during 2002 to 2008, three states (Punjab, Haryana and Rajasthan) together lost about 109 km of water leading to a decline in water table to the extent of 0.33 metres per annum (Rodell *et.al.*, 2009). The state-wise status of groundwater resources as on March 2004. We can see that in many states, the net draft of groundwater is either in excess of or close to the net available resource, implying that these states are facing a situation of dangerous over exploitation of their available groundwater resources (Vijay Shankar *et al.*, 2011).

GROUNDWATER VULNERABILITY AT DISTRICT LEVEL IN INDIA

Though groundwater overuse was recognised as a serious problem for quite some time (Dhawan, 1995; Moench, 1992; Macdonald *et al.*, 1995), conventional approaches to groundwater in India until the mid-1990s have involved a clear focus on the "development" of groundwater resources. The mid-1990s saw a slow and reluctant change in thinking, from a development to a management mode. The new thinking, which attempted to look at managing groundwater beyond sinking dug wells and drilling tube wells or bore wells, began to be backed by data from state and central

TABLE 1
State-wise Status of Groundwater Resources

Sl. No.	*State*	*Billion Cubic Metres (BCM)*			*Stage of GW Development (Net Draft/Net Availability* 100)*
		Annual Replenishable Ground Water Resources	*Net Availa-bility*	*Net Draft*	
1.	Andhra Pradesh	36.50	32.95	14.90	45
2.	Assam	27.23	24.89	5.44	22
3.	Bihar	29.19	27.42	10.77	39
4.	Chhattisgarh	14.93	13.68	2.80	20
5.	Gujarat	15.81	15.02	11.49	76
6.	Haryana	9.31	8.63	9.45	109
7.	Jammu and Kashmir	2.70	2.43	0.33	14
8.	Jharkhand	5.68	5.25	1.09	21
9.	Karnataka	15.93	15.30	10.71	70
10.	Kerala	6.84	6.23	2.92	47
11.	Madhya Pradesh	37.19	35.33	17.12	48
12.	Maharashtra	32.96	31.21	15.09	48
13.	Orissa	23.09	21.01	3.85	18
14.	Punjab	23.78	21.44	31.16	145
15.	Rajasthan	11.56	10.38	12.99	125
16.	Tamil Nadu	23.07	20.76	17.65	85
17.	Uttar Pradesh	76.35	70.18	48.78	70
18.	Uttarakhand	2.27	2.10	1.39	66
19.	West Bengal	30.36	27.46	11.65	42
20.	Other states	7.67	7.03	0.86	12
	Total 4	432.42	398.70	230.44	58

Source : Central Groundwater Board (2006).

groundwater agencies. Simultaneously, the methodology of groundwater estimation was also improved (GEC, 1984, 1997). We have district-level data sets on groundwater potential and use from the two recent assessments by the Central Groundwater Board,

Government of India (CGWB, 1995 and 2006) at two time points, 1995 and 2004. The comparability of these data sets is limited by two major factors: (a) changing administrative boundaries of districts; and (b) a slight change in the methodology of assessment in 2006. However, this data can be utilised to track the national scenario on groundwater use, over time. With these data sets, we now build a complete picture of quantitative and qualitative aspects of groundwater vulnerability in India. Vulnerability here implies potential danger to drinking water sources, either in terms of the quantity of water available or the quality of available water or a combination of both. Available data shows that there has been a remarkable change in the groundwater scenario in the country even within a short span of nine years (1995-2004). On the basis of their stage of groundwater development, we classify districts as "safe" and "unsafe" (districts in the "semi-critical", "critical" and "over-exploited" categories).

From Table 1 we can see that the proportion of "unsafe" districts in India has grown from 9 per cent in 1995 to 31 per cent in 2004. The area under "unsafe" districts has risen from 5 per cent to 33 per cent and population affected from 7 per cent to 35 per cent within this short span of nine years.

ECONOMIC CONSIDERATIONS FOR GROUNDWATER MANAGEMENT AND PROTECTION

Economics deals with the allocation and use of scarce resources. As long as a resource is abundant, there is little need to take such decisions. As the resource becomes more scarce (due to quantity or quality constraints) questions about how to utilize and protect it (preferably for the best of society) arise. Economic considerations can help the decision-making process and promote more efficient resource use.

While economic instruments to manage surface water and groundwater are similar, they are not the same as a result of certain peculiarities of the groundwater resource:

- Relatively high cost and complexity of assessing groundwater
- Highly-decentralized resource use, which increases management monitoring costs
- Invisibility of groundwater to the general public, and time-lags with regard to resource impacts

- Varying impacts of contaminant load depending on aquifer vulnerability
- Long time-lags and near irreversibility of most aquifer contamination.

These peculiarities explain why groundwater management tools are generally less developed and applied than those for surface water. However, with increasing water scarcity the economic value of groundwater, and thus the benefit to investment in management, is increasing.

Groundwater tends to be undervalued, especially where its exploitation is uncontrolled. In this situation the exploiter of the resource (in effect) receives all the benefits of groundwater use but (at most) pays only part of the costs—usually the recurrent cost of pumping (providing the energy input is not subsidized) and the capital cost of well construction, but rarely the external and opportunity costs. This undervaluation often leads to economically inefficient resource use.

DETERMINATION OF ECONOMIC VALUE OF GROUNDWATER

The economic value of a resource depends on what one can do with it and on its relative scarcity compared to alternative resources. Thus, the economic value of groundwater in a specific aquifer is derived from the use it can be put to, and from its local availability and quality compared to surface water. For instance, an aquifer in a region with abundant unpolluted surface water will generally have lower economic value than one in a region with polluted surface water or one in an arid region without alternative resources. The economic value of groundwater originates from the benefits that it generates or (in other words) the services that it provides. In many areas of the world, the economic value of groundwater is increasing, due to population growth and economic development (and thus increased water demand), due to pollution of surface water basins and, increasingly, due to climatic variability and the necessity of having a drought-secure resource (Karin Kemperet *et. al.,* 2006).

The economic value of a given groundwater resource is determined by its prospective use. In the absence of a market price for groundwater, economists often measure its value through user ***willingness to pay*** for a given quantity and quality of supply. For instance, an industry that needs water as an input for car production

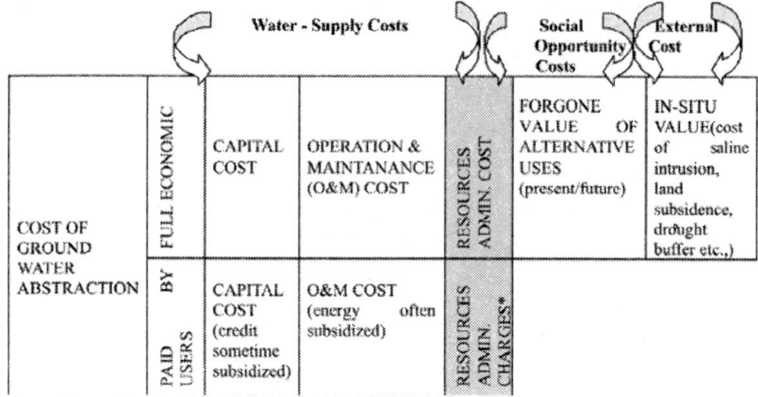

Figure 1 : Measuring the Costs of Groundwater Use

Note : *Frequently not levied or do not cover real costs.

will be willing to pay more per unit volume than a fruit farmer. The economic value of groundwater in the area concerned is thus determined by the willingness of industry to pay-up to the point that their demand is met. The economic value of the next volume used by the fruit farmer will be lower, but still higher than what a subsistence farmer would be willing to pay.

When 'willingness to pay' is not known (usually the case because groundwater markets revealing true price rarely exist), the ***residual value method*** can be used to value groundwater. This method values all inputs for the good produced at market price, except for the groundwater itself. The residual value of the good, after all other inputs are accounted for, is attributed to the water input.

Another method is ***hedonic pricing***, where the behavior of users and markets is observed. For instance, farm prices in an area with good groundwater availability are likely to be higher than in an area with scarce water resources. By comparing differences in farm prices across the region (and assuming other variables are the same), the difference in price would lie in the value of groundwater access.

The above are a selection of methods used by economists to determine the value of public goods such as groundwater, and while none are perfect they do provide guidance to decision-makers on the valuation of groundwater resources and on possible courses of action. An important consideration in this regard is the distinction between short- and long-term benefits expected from groundwater use.

ECONOMIC INSTRUMENTS USED TO IMPROVE GROUNDWATER RESOURCE MANAGEMENT

An economic instrument tries to stimulate an economic actor (groundwater user) to voluntarily adopt a certain behavior. The underlying rationale is that human beings react to price incentives—when prices are high less resource will be consumed. Moreover, while groundwater could be widely used in high-value enterprises and create more income, jobs and wealth, too often it is still put to low-value economic uses and thus is increasingly over abstracted, creating social tension between users.

Economic instruments can provide incentives to allocate and/or use groundwater more efficiently, thus helping to stabilize groundwater levels by reducing over abstraction, diminishing the risk of negative impacts and social conflict, and delaying the need for investment in alternative water resources. There are two categories relevant to groundwater (Table 2), namely those that focus upon:

- *Changing Groundwater Abstraction Costs* by (a) direct pricing through resource abstraction fees, (b) indirect pricing through increasing energy tariffs, and (c) the introduction of water markets

TABLE 2
Values of Groundwater as Determined by Individual Stakeholders

Type of Value	*Groundwater Service*
Use Value	drinking water irrigation supply/industrial use, recreational use
Non-use Value	uncertain use potential existence for future generations
Indirect (Ecosystem) Value	discharge to ecosystems, discharge to rivers and lakes

- *Positive Economic Incentives* for certain activities by (a) modifications to agriculture and food trade policies, and (b) subsidies to encourage the use of more efficient irrigation technologies to achieve real water savings.

DIRECT GROUNDWATER PRICING THROUGH RESOURCE ABSTRACTION FEES

This is the most direct method, since users have to pay an

abstraction fee based on volume—preferably metered (rather than licensed) use to ensure that an incentive exists. Unfortunately, groundwater use by agriculture (usually the largest consumer) is rarely metered and thus controlling irrigation use is not straight forward. Alternative techniques to estimate actual agricultural water use include:

- deriving volume pumped from electrical energy use, and
- assessing actual water consumption by remote sensing techniques.

INDIRECT GROUNDWATER PRICING THROUGH ENERGY TARIFFS

The major cost in groundwater abstraction (once a well is installed) is the energy required to lift water. This cost will depend not only on water table depth, aquifer characteristics and well efficiency, but also on the unit cost of energy for pumping. Thus, energy (electricity or diesel fuel) pricing can be a powerful tool to influence groundwater pumping trends. Paradoxically, in many areas of the world, energy prices are used in the opposite way, with large subsidies in place to decrease farming costs. While it can be legitimate to subsidize poor farmers to improve their livelihood, subsidizing groundwater abstraction in general may not be the best vehicle to do so, because excessive groundwater abstraction can erode the same farmers' resource availability in the longer term. Other measures need to be defined which have a neutral effect on the resource, such as lump-sum payments to poor farmers at the beginning of the year to cover their estimated energy bill. In this way, they would have an incentive to use water more efficiently and consume less, maybe through a shift to higher-value crops. Since they receive lumpsum payments to offset their increased energy bills, they can actually gain twice by being more efficient, and thus improve their livelihoods.

ECONOMIC INSTRUMENTS TO CONTROL GROUNDWATER POLLUTION

The instrument usually prescribed to decrease water pollution is the polluter-pays-principle, by which an industry is charged for the amount of pollution it produces. The less it pollutes, the less it pays. This approach is not directly applicable to aquifer protection because of the special characteristics of groundwater, notably the time-lag of impacts, the persistence of some groundwater contaminants, and the potential cost of some pollution episodes. Instead economic incentives are required for industry and water utilities to invest in adequate wastewater treatment and recycling, especially where aquifer vulnerability assessments suggest high risk of groundwater pollution.

Another important issue is the control of non-point pollution from agricultural cultivation. Crop subsidies tend to lead to monocultures over large land areas, sustained by excessive use of fertilizers and pesticides (themselves sometimes subsidized), regardless of soil and climatic suitability. This can have a major negative impact on groundwater quality due to agro-chemical leaching, the cost of which is not initially taken into consideration. There is a pressing need to re-target such subsidies and thereby provide an incentive to reduce agrochemical leaching. There sometimes may be an argument for going further and putting an 'environmental tax' on fertilizers and/or pesticides to generate funding for water quality monitoring.

CONCLUSION

Groundwater resources play a major role in ensuring livelihood security across the world, especially in economies that depend on agriculture. The socio-economic dependency on groundwater is explained over a range of factors by Burke and Moench (2000). They explain the intricacy in managing groundwater resources. At the same time, groundwater systems have become the "lender of last resort" and depletion of renewable groundwater stocks is taken as the first indicator of water scarcity (Shah and Indu, 2004). Moreover, groundwater is considered to be less vulnerable than surface sources to climate fluctuations and can therefore help to stabilise agricultural populations and reduce the need for farmers to migrate when drought threatens agricultural livelihoods (Moench, 2002). In other words, groundwater resources provide a reliable drought buffer in large regions of the world (Calow *et. al.*, 1997).Groundwater is an open-access, common pool resource. Hence, protection of the resource is not possible unless the users agree to cooperate and manage the resource themselves in a sustainable manner. And also the various economic instruments for Groundwater management must be used to attain sustainability.

REFERENCES

Central Ground Water Board (1995), *Dynamic Groundwater Resources of India*, Ministry of Water Resources, Government of India, New Delhi.

Central Ground Water Board (2006), *Dynamic Groundwater Resources of India(as on March, 2004)*, Ministry of Water Resources, Government of India, New Delhi.

Comman (2005), "Community Management of Groundwater Resources in Rural India" in R. Calow and M. Macdonald (ed.), *Research Report: British Geological Survey Commissioned Report CR/05/36N.*

Dhawan, B.D. (1995), *Groundwater Depletion, Land Degradation and Irrigated Agriculture in India* (New Delhi: Commonwealth Publishers).

Chapter 22

Economic, Institutional and Rights Issues in Groundwater Management at Micro-level

V. MOHANASUNDARAM

WATER: DIFFERENT PERSPECTIVES

From a pure, natural and abundant resource, water now has become a scarce commodity, disproving the established fact that it has only use value and not exchange value. The way in which water (surface water, groundwater) was harvested, utilized, priced and managed, and the assessment of its role have been made from different perspectives. Economists in general, and agricultural economists and resource economists in particular, have propagated the following perspectives regarding water: Economic perspective, Managerial perspective, Sustainability perspective, Institutional perspective and Rights perspective. In this paper the economic perspective with respect to bore well irrigation at a village level has been looked into. A few issues about water institutions that prevailed and the rights that are associated with groundwater in a micro-level are also pointed out.

ECONOMIC PERSPECTIVE

Water has always been treated as a major input in agriculture to maximize the yield. In other words, the economic perspective envisaged yield per unit of water and its optimization. The distribution and pricing of water especially, river and canal water, has always had economic overtones. Irrigation was considered as an enabling factor for the use of its complementary inputs like chemical fertilizers and high yielding variety seeds (HYVs), according to Dhawan (1988). In this context, the development and use of water resources were looked from the perspective of feeding the population with increased food supply, and supporting industries, both as a supplier of the raw materials and a market for industrial products. In brief, the overall process of the economic development itself depended critically on water sector performance. Thus, as pointed out by Saleth and Dinar (2004), the perspective of water as a free good has become outdated and now it has been looked at as an economic good. This type of change in the perspective should necessarily be reflected in the pricing of water, project selection and other related policies.

INSTITUTIONAL PERSPECTIVE

Those who look at water-related issues from an institutional perspective, like Saleth and Dinar (2004), argue that the policies to improve water management should base their instruments in the form of well defined institutions. As countries move from a state of plenty to a state of scarcity, water institutions, which define the rules of water development, allocation, and utilization, have to be concurrently reoriented to reflect the realities of changing supply-demand and quantity-quality balance.

Moose (2003), on the basis of an in-depth analysis of a village located in a hard-rock area in the southern Tamil Nadu, stated that the uncertainty surrounding water availability in this ecology produces its own institutional responses. Water scarcity, short growing seasons, the intensive demand for labor and coping with drought and crop failure were ecologically determined conditions which shape village-level strategies of patronage, alliance, reputation building, or the accumulation of honour.

Institutional reform of the magnitude required at present has been a daunting challenge in most countries with outdated and poorly functioning water institutions. As institutions were a pervasive phenomenon with diverse origins, they affect various dimensions of human relationships and interactions. In this context, Narain (1997) has identified a list of policy and institutional reforms to resolve the impending water crisis in India.

GROUNDWATER EXTRACTION IN INDIA

The present scenario was that the number of over exploited blocks (groundwater extraction more than 100%) continues to grow at a rate of 5.5 per cent per annum and it has been estimated that by 2018 roughly 36 per cent of India's blocks will face serious groundwater problems. Singh (2003) cautions that if and when the balloon bursts, untold misery will be the lot of rural India. Therefore, it needs to be utilized with capacity to increase crop yields.

GROUNDWATER EXTRACTION IN TAMIL NADU

As in many parts of India, rapid expansion of groundwater irrigation has resulted in depletion of groundwater levels in the state of Tamil Nadu. There has been a change in the design and type of wells dug. The conventional large diameter round or square wells were no more used as water levels have fallen due to the adoption of new technologies for both digging wells and pumping the water (Janakarajan, 2006).

From the early 1980s onwards, the depths of the wells have been steadily increasing. It has been reported that wells were dug more than 150 meters deep in several places in India. As far as Tamil Nadu was concerned, in some of the districts, such as Coimbatore, the average depth of bore wells were found to be over 400 meters deep in the over-exploited pockets (Ballukraya, 2005). In such a situation, the plight of the farmers can be expressed, in the words of Black (2005), "villagers in places where the water table has dropped significantly where in a constant state of anxiety, year upon year, at the prospect of wells running dry. As the dry season advances, they may be forced to resort to sources located many miles away, or which were abandoned every year because their yield has become inadequate".

INVESTMENT IN WELL IRRIGATION

Increased depth of wells means higher capital and running costs. Capital costs increase due to the deepening of open wells, the conversion of open wells into in-well bores, and the replacement of open wells with bore wells (Reddy, 2055). As a result, the overdraft of groundwater forced compulsory investment on the part of bore well irrigation and it forced farmers to spend more on bore wells than any other agricultural inputs needed for the cultivation. At the same time, the reaction to the situations like groundwater overdraft, from the farmers, may vary from place to place and also depended on the managerial skills as well as the resource base of the farmers.

RESEARCH ISSUE

With an increasing rate of groundwater exploitation many issues galore—Economic, Ecological, Environmental, Rights, Institutional and Sustainability. Among them economic aspects stands apart. An analysis into the investment in bore wells and the returns are need to be analysed at the micro/village level context to put the rights and institutional perspectives in a proper place.

OBJECTIVES

1. To estimate the capital invested in and appraise the financial feasibility of bore well irrigation at the farm level
2. To examine the groundwater institutions and water rights perspective at the village level

METHODOLOGY

Coimbatore district is one of the hard-rock districts in Tamil Nadu. Out of 19 blocks of the district 11 blocks fall in the category of over exploitation of groundwater (> 100%). Out of this 11, Avinashi block was selected randomly. Among the 33 revenue villages of this block one village, namely, Muriyandampalayam village was selected randomly. It has nine hamlets and 238 farmers. After scrutiny it was found that only 183 (out of 238) are currently engaged in agriculture with bore wells. All of them were selected for an in-depth analysis. The classification of this sample was done on the basis of land size and it came to 41 small farmers, 108 medium farmers and 34 big farmers. Detailed data and information were collected by personal interview method with help of a structured questionnaire. The data relate to the year 2007-08. Financial viability analysis was done by using standard discounting cash flow techniques Pay Back Period (PBP), Internal Rate of Return (IRR), Net Present Worth (NPW) and Benefit Cost Ratio (BCR).

CROPPING PATTERN

Quite unexpectedly the major crops grown in this village was found as water-intensive, namely, Banana, Sugarcane and turmeric. The reason stated were labour availability and marketing problems if they grow other crops. The traditional crops given up were Bajra, Cotton, Tapioca, Vegetables and ground nut.

BOREWELL INVESTMENT

Normally, drilling open well was labour-intensive and time consuming. Once groundwater started decreasing, after 1980s, in the study region, the trend of using modern techniques to drill surface bore well has begun. However, this was a capital-intensive proportions though saves time. This trend, when continued, resulted in the fast depletion of groundwater. Further, bore well failures became more common in the region. A sudden bore well failure with standing crops makes the farmer to run from pillar to post to get money to go in for another bore well, at any cost.

In the present study, the investment per bore well was calculated as Rs. 2,09,500, at current prices (2007-08). The required investment per bore well was common for all type of the farmers in the village. Among the strategies adopted by the selected farmers, the following was the major one: An average farmer was able to mobiles only 22 per cent of the total cost (personal saving + crop income) and another six per cent by the sale of assets. The rest was made by borrowing from friends and relatives (with flexible repayment schedule) and form private money lenders, obviously for higher rates of interest with strict repayment schedule. Yet another way was diversion of crop loans (which means, lower rate of interest). The most significant one was the jewel loan obtained by the farmers. All these revealed the risk and threat involved in such borrowings. Even with the continuous depletion of groundwater in the village, farmers were undertaking such risks reflected their struggle for survival with dignity.

TERMS OF INVESTMENT

The investment on irrigation bore wells comprised of :

1. Cost of drilling a bore well,
2. Cost of submersible pump set, and
3. Other conveyance costs.

The bore well costs considered include mainly the cost of drilling and casing pipes, whereas the investment on submersible pump sets entailed cost of pump, panel board, PVC pipes, deposit to the State Electricity Board and cost of accessories and installation charges.

The estimation of the bore well investment was done with an assumption of depth of 1000 feet (the average depth calculated as 759 feet with the maximum depth of 1150 feet), as it is the order of the day, with a diameter of 6.5" and the use of 10 horse power submersible motor. The investment per well, of 1000 feet, at current prices, has been worked out to Rs. 2,34,500.

FINANCIAL FEASIBILITY OF ANALYSIS

To bring out the differential in the cost component, the financial feasibility of bore wells, in the selected village, two situations were considered.

Situation A : Farm income and expenditure (with paid out cost) and cost of investment in working bore wells.

Situation B : Farm income and expenditure (with paid out plus imputed cost) and cost of investment in working bore wells.

ESTIMATION OF INCOME AND EXPENDITURE

For the estimation of farm expenditure of the selected farmers only the paid out costs were taken into account. Further, the farm income alone was considered. Net farm income was arrived at by deducting all the out of pocket (paid out) expenses from gross crop income. Accordingly, the average net income of small farmers, per year, was Rs. 95,086, for medium and big farmers it came to Rs. 2,22,133 and Rs. 4,37,074 respectively.

INVESTMENT IN BORE WELLS

Estimation of the bore well cost was facilitated the importance in the analysis of income and investment in bore wells by the farmers in the study village. At the first stage, for calculation of investment in working bore wells only were taken into account. The average number of working bore wells was 1.09, 1.41 and 2.63 respectively for small, medium and big farmers and the average estimated investment per bore well was Rs. 2,55,605, Rs. 3,30,645 and Rs. 6,16,735 for the respective category of the farmers.

TABLE 1

Investment of the Selected Farmers in Working Borewells

Sl. No.	*Category of farmers*	*Average number of working borewells*	*Average investment (Rs.)*
1.	Small farmers	1.09	2,55,605
2.	Medium farmers	1.41	3,30,645
3.	Big	2.63	6,16,735

TABLE 2
The Results of Standard Discounting Cash Flow Techniques (Situation A)

Sl. No.	*Particulars*	*Small farmer*	*Medium farmer*	*Big farmer*
1.	Pay back period (years)	2.69	1.49	1.41
2.	Internal rate of return (per cent)	18.04	>50.00	>50.00
3.	Net present worth (Rs.) @ 15% discount rate	15,863	3,03,541	6,31,102
4.	Net present worth (Rs.) @ 20% discount rate	-9,454	2,44,395	5,14,728
5.	Net present worth (Rs.) @ 25% discount rate	-31,050	1,93,944	4,15,459
6.	Benefit cost ratio @ 15% discount rate	1.06	1.92	2.02
7.	Benefit cost ratio @ 20% discount rate	0.96	1.74	1.84
8.	Benefit cost ratio @ 25% discount rate	0.88	1.59	1.67

FINANCIAL FEASIBILITY OF INVESTMENT

The economic feasibility of investment in bore well irrigation was evaluated by using standard discounting cash flow techniques. Accordingly it was found that the payback period (PBP) of small farmers' investment in the bore well was 2.69 years, 1.49 years for medium and 1.41 years for the small farmers. The internal rate of return (IRR) was 18 per cent for the small and it was more than 50 per cent in the case of both medium and big farmers. The net present worth (NPW), at 15 per cent discount rate, was positive for all the three categories of farmers and showed the investment was worthwhile. However, at 20 per cent and 25 per cent the NPW values turned negative for small farmers but positive for medium and big farmers. Similarly, the benefit-cost ratio (BCR) at 15 per cent discount rate was more than one for all the three categories of farmers, and at 20 per cent and 25 per cent discount rates, it turned out to be less than one for small farmers and more than one for the other two categories.

ESTIMATION OF INCOME AND EXPENDITURE

In the second stage, the imputed costs were calculated on the basis of market prices/current wage rates. The item of costs were labour cost (both manual and bullock labour), farm yard manure, and own seeds. Hence, the net farm income arrived with all the above said imputed costs were taken for calculation. Accordingly, the average net income of small farmers came to Rs. 55,166 per year. For medium farmers, it was Rs. 1,28,875 and for big farmers it came to Rs. 2,53,578 per year.

FINANCIAL FEASIBILITY OF INVESTMENT

The arrived net farm income with paid out and imputed costs and the estimated investment of the farmers (only working borewells) were taken for the PBP, IRR, NPW and BCR calculation. It was found that the PBP went beyond the average life of borewells (4 years) in the case of small farmers (4.63 years) and it was 2.5 years in the case of medium and big farmers

The IRR was not applicable for the small (PBP was beyond 4 years) and it was more than 20 per cent in the case of both medium and big farmers. The NPW, at 15 per cent and 20 per cent discount rate, was negative for small farmers and positive for the medium and big farmers. This showed that the investment was feasible for both medium and big farmers. However, at 25 per cent, the NPW turned negative for all the three categories of farmers. Similarly, the BCR, at 15 per cent and 20 per cent discount rate, was less than one for small farmers and more than one for rest of the two categories (medium and big farmers) of the farmers. And, BCR at 25 per cent discount rate, for all three categories of farmers, turned out as less than one.

INSTITUTIONAL DIMENSION

The three major issues with respect to groundwater institutions in the selected village where:

(i) No market existed in the village for groundwater;
(ii) Earlier the Village Panchayat took the initiative in the strengthening of village ponds and tanks on the behest of rich and big farmers and maintenance of such rainwater storage points. Now it has been given up. So the hope of getting groundwater recharged by rainwater harvesting looks bleak; and

TABLE 3
The Results of Standard Discounting Cash Flow Techniques (Situation B)

Sl. No.	*Particulars*	*Small farmer*	*Medium farmer*	*Big farmer*
1.	Pay back period (years)	4.63	2.57	2.43
2.	Internal rate of return (percent)	Not applicable	20.48	23.37
3.	Net present worth (Rs.) @ 15% discount rate	-98,104	37,291	1,07,225
4.	Net present worth (Rs.) @ 20% discount rate	-1,12,796	2,976	39,701
5.	Net present worth (Rs.) @ 25% discount rate	-1,25,325	-26,294	-17,885
6.	Benefit cost ratio @ 15% discount rate	0.62	1.11	1.17
7.	Benefit cost ratio @ 20% discount rate	0.56	1.01	1.06
8.	Benefit cost ratio @ 25% discount rate	0.51	0.92	0.97

(iii) As many farmers given up agriculture, the traditional institutions are found becoming very weak to resolve the village level issues pertaining to storage of rainwater and renovation of percolation ponds.

The current situation is that village tank/ponds renovation works are taken up through MGNREGP without the consultation of Village Panchayat or farmers in the village.

WATER RIGHTS

Theoretically, water rights issues were dealt with rigorously by various authors. Specific to groundwater, however, the focus has been limited unlike canal irrigation, for which many propositions were available and evaluations were done in varying situations. From political economy angle, researchers like Morris (2001) pointed out that the subsidized or free electric power supply is the main cause of over-exploitation of groundwater. Though argument of these lines are questioned by agricultural economists like Narayanamoothy (2001), the observations and discussions held with farmers at selected village's reveal that free electricity supply has been one of the major causes of over exploitation of groundwater. At the same time, the results of the present study show that the electricity supply should be given freely to the small and marginal farmers and not to the big farmers. Otherwise, the question of equity will not find a place in the village economy.

THE WAY OUT

The Tamil Nadu Groundwater Bill (2008) has envisaged a distance of 200 meters between two bore wells. This has been rarely known in the village. Regarding the rights over the groundwater there is no clear cut idea among the farmers. The progressive reduction in the groundwater table is the major concern in the village. And the villagers are expecting, for a long time, that the State will implement a scheme called Avinahsi-Athikkdavu Scheme which aims to bring and divert the excess water flown in River Bhavani to fill the village ponds and tanks, which, the long-run, enhance the groundwater recharge. Speedy implementation of this scheme alone going to save this village from the water crisis.

References

Dhawan, B.D. (1993), 'Groundwater Depletion in Punjab', *Economic and Political Weekly*, Vol. 28, No. 24, pp. 2397-2401.

Janakarajan, S., and Marcus Moench (2006), 'Are Wells a Potential Threat to Farmers' Well-being? : Case of Deteriorating Groundwater Irrigation in Tamil Nadu', *Economic and Political Weekly*, Vol. 41, No. 37, pp. 3977-87.

Moose, David (2003), *The Rule of Water: Statecraft, Ecology and Collective Action in South India*, Oxford University Press, New Delhi.

Narayanamoorthy, A. (2001), "Irrigation and Rural Poverty Nexus: A Statewise Analysis', *Indian Journal of Agricultural Economics*, Vol. 56, No. 1.

Reddy, Ratna V. (2005), 'Cost of Resource Depletion Externalities : A Study of Groundwater Over-exploitation in Andhra Pradesh, India', *Environmental and Development Economics*, Vol. 10, No. 4, pp. 533-56.

Saleth, Maria R. and Dinar, Ariel (2004), *The Institutional Economics of Water : A Cross-Country Analysis of Institutions and Performance*, Edward Elgar Publishing Limited, UK.

Singh, A.K., Adhikari, R.N. and Reddy, K.K. (2003), 'Groundwater Management for Sustainable Livelihood—A Case Study at Chinnahagai Watershed in Semi-Arid Region of Chitradurga District of Karnataka', *Journal of Agricultural Resource Management*, 2 (3&4), pp. 64-67.

Chapter 23

Managing the Water Resources in India

MUN MUN SHARAN AND SUBODH KUMAR SINHA

INTRODUCTION

The UN report, published ahead of the third world water forum in Kyoto, Japan, March 16-23, 2003, says world water reserves are drying up fast and booming populations, pollution and global warming will combine to cut the average person's water supply by a third in the next 20 years.

The report also ranked 122 countries on the quality of their water provision. Belgium was at the bottom of the league, below developing countries including India and Rwanda. By 2050, water scarcity will affect between two billion and seven billion people out of a projected total of 9.3 billion, depending in part on what measures take to tackle the crisis, the report elaborates.

Water is indispensable for the existence and survival of life on earth. With the advancement of civilization, water has found in the large and progressively increasing list of uses. Many nations which have a fair estimate of their oil and mineral resources, hardly know their water resource potential. In a country like India, where the rainfall pattern is highly variable and most of the people depending upon agriculture and allied activities, the appraisal and planning of water resources has became an important components for this development. The Table 1 shows the global distribution of the fresh water.

TABLE 1
Global Distribution of Fresh Water

Sl. No.	*Water Source*	*Quantity of water (in cubic km.)*
1.	Water in ice form	24,000,000
2.	Water in ponds, lakes and reservoirs	2,80,000
3.	Water in streams and rivers	1,200
4.	Water present as soil moisture	85,000
5.	Ground water	60,000,000
	Total	84,366,200

Source : UNO Report (2000).

STATES OF WATER RESOURCES IN INDIA

At recent study by the world bank indicates that per capita availability of water in India, which was in the order of 5000 cubic meter per year at the time of independence, has drastically come down to 2000 cubic meter per year at present. The average annual rainfall of 1100 mm in the country, though fairly high, is marked by wide variations, both spatial and temporal. The total water resources, comprising surface water (1953 bcm) and ground water (423 bcm) are not uniformly distributed, in the sense, roughly 67 percent of the resources are reported to be available in the Indo-Gangetic alluvial basins covering 33 percent of the geographical area of the country as against 33 per cent of the potential in the hard rock regions occupying 67 per cent of the geographical area. Bulk of the utilizable part of surface water resource has more or less been harnessed already by a number of major and medium storage reservoirs. During the last two decades, focus was only on development of groundwater rather than its management. Management aspects like water conservation, recharging, efficiency in water use, water recycling, self-regulation and eco-system sustainability were not paid adequate attention. A 85 percent of rural water supply is sustained by ground water though the rural water supply sector as such uses around 5 percent of the resource. On the other hand, irrigation sector, utilizing nearly 85 percent is the largest consumer of ground water.

The frequent failure of monsoons in some region or other, resulting in drought conditions causing acute drinking water scarcity especially in 1174 blocks in 204 Drought Prone Area Programme (DPAP) and Desert Development Programme (DDP) districts. The ever increasing mismatch between supply demand scenario precipitated by a combination of factors including population explosion, ever increasing desire for higher levels of supply, gross mismanagement of water resources and negligence of the environment have further aggravated the situation in the form of falling water levels, degradation of water quality and concomitant break out of water borne diseases.

IMPORTANCE OF WATER

Water is needed in almost every sphere of human activity. It is required for direct consumption for washing, cleaning, cooling, waste disposal and transportation. Water is essential for the Irrigation, Industries, Livestock management, Thermal power generation, Domestic requirements, Hydro-electric generation and various human activities.

TABLE 2
Sector-wise Consumption of Water in India

Sl. No.	*Sector*	*% of water consumption*
1.	Agriculture	76.0
2.	Power generation	6.2
3.	Industries	5.7
4.	Domestic sector	4.3
5.	Transport and others	7.8

Source : The India Infrastructure Report (1996).

ESTIMATIONS OF FRESH WATER REQUIREMENTS OF VARIOUS SECTORS

The amount of water in the world is finite. A third of the world's population lives in water-stresses countries now. By 2025, this is expected to rise to two-thirds. There is more than enough water available, in total, for everyone's basic needs. The UN recommends that people need a minimum of 50 litres of water a day for drinking, washing, cooking and sanitation. In 1990, over a billion people did not have that. Providing universal access to that basic minimum worldwide by 2015 would like less than 1% of the amount of water we use today. But we're a long way from achieving that.

THREAT TO INDIA'S WATER RESOURCES

Water has become the biggest problem of the 21st century. Global consumption of fresh water increased six-fold from 1900 to 1995, at a rate greater than twice the rate of population growth. If the present trend continued, two out of every three people on earth will have to live in water stressed condition by the year 2005. About 25% of the world's population does not have access to safe drinking water and 40% does not have sufficient water for adequate living and hygiene. More than 2.2 million people die each year from diseases related to contaminated drinking water and poor living conditions, faced with water scarcity. The pre capita availability of fresh water in the country has dropped from an acceptable 5,180 cubic metres in 1951 to 1,820 cubic metres in 2001. It is estimated that it would drop to 1,340 cubic metres by 2025 and 1,140 cubic metres by 2050. The following are all the major threats to India's water resources.

POPULATION EXPLOSION

Population growth is spurring a demographic change, especially as towns become cities and cities become metropolitan cities. Concerns on availability of fresh water have arisen, since India with 16% of world's population has only 2.5% of the world's land resources and 4% of the fresh water resources.

INDUSTRIAL FARMING

Industrial agriculture has emerged as the worst depleter and polluted water, as industrial farming increases water use by a factor of ten, it leads to ground water withdrawals beyond recharge capacity, thus driving the push for large dams and intensive irrigation projects. Pollution by agro-chemicals has contaminated drinking water sources.

WATER EXPLOITATION BY MULTINATIONAL CORPORATIONS

The biggest problem India faces in protecting its water resources is that it does not have effective laws to control water exploitation by multinational companies and large corporate.

WATER PRIVATIZATION

During the Economic Liberalization period in 1990's a set of measures favouring total reduction subsidies, full cost recovery, privatization, etc. has been promoted around the world. This logic has extended to the water sector as well. The world has witnessed increasing privatization of public sector water utilizes in several countries. From the Eightn Plan onwards, water has come to be treated as an economic good like any other commodity in India's official planning commission documents. An expert group on commercialization of infrastructure constituted by Ministry of Finance, Government of India (1996) recommended several measures to operate infrastructure projects, including urban water supply and sanitation, on commercial lines either by private parties or through public-private partnership.

Challenges

1. Ground water depletion
2. Water quality deterioration
3. Low water use efficiency
4. Expensive new water sources
5. Resource degradation
6. Water and health
7. Massive subsidies and distorted incentives
8. Development of new water

Government Initiatives

The National Water Policy has stressed that many of the country's rivers have abundant water and, if properly harnessed, can meet adequately the needs of the people in the basin and still have some water left that can be used elsewhere. Therefore, there is some scope for transferring water from certain river basins to water short areas. This implies that in future water is to be considered as a national resource. People of a particular state or a region cannot be permitted to have claim over the entire water supply in their river basin. The National Water Policy envisages that each State shall formulate its own State Water Policy backed by an Operational Action Plan. The Ministry of Water Resources has formulated an Action Plan for Implementation of the National Water Policy, 2002.

So far, much progress has not been made in basin-wise water resource planning, as only three major river basin plans have been prepared. The Ganga Basin Water Studies Organisation working under the auspices of the Central Water Commission has prepared a perspective plan for the utilization and development of water resources of Ganga. The Sone river Commission has finalised a comprehensive plan for irrigation and power development in the Sone basin. A similar plan has been prepared by the Brahmaputra Board for the development of water resources of Brahmaputra and Barak basins. The National Water Development Agency set-up in 1982 has been examining the possibilities of inter-basin water resource transfer. So far, preliminary studies in respect of 85 river basins have been prepared and circulated among the concerned States for their opinion.

The National Water Policy of 2002 integrates quantity and quality aspects as well as environmental considerations for water through institutional arrangements. The involvement of beneficiaries in the project planning and participatory approach in water resources management have received significant attention in the policy. The policy envisages private sector participation in providing facilities in water resources sector. The policy also emphasis the role of training and research in water resources sector.

STRATEGIES FOR WATER RESOURCES MANAGEMENT

1. Rainwater Harvesting
2. Comprehensive Water Policy Reform and Demand Management
3. Secure Water Rights
4. User Management of Irrigation Systems
5. Reformed Price Incentives
6. Appropriate Technology
7. Environment Protection
8. Tradable Water Rights
9. International Co-operation

RAINWATER HARVESTING

It is well known that rainwater is biologically pure, soft in nature and free from organic matter. Rainwater harvesting has today proved itself to be an effective technique of conserving water by guiding the rainwater that falls on rooftops to storage tanks or underground sumps for future usage. Ground water recharging, in the other hand, is undertaken by guiding water through pipes to wells, bore wells or recharge pits to ensure recharging aquifers, for later use, whenever the need arises.

The principle of collecting and strong precipitation from a catchments surface is referred to as rainwater harvesting. Water harvesting also includes activities aimed at harvesting surface and ground water, prevention of crosses through evaporation and seepage and other techniques aimed to conservation and efficient utilization of limited water endowment. In general, water harvesting is the activity of direct collection of rainwater. The collected water can be stored for direct use of can be used to recharge the ground water.

Rainwater is the primary source of fresh water. Rivers, lakes, and ground water are all secondary sources of fresh water, as they are all stores and channels of rainwater. Water harvesting is aimed at understanding the value of rain and to make optimum use of rain water at the place where it falls we have lot of rain, yet we do not have water. This is because we have rainfall in short spells of high intensity. Due to this intensity and short duration of heavy rain, most of the rain falling on surface tends to flow away rapidly, leaving very little for the recharge of ground water.

QUANTUM OF HARVESTED RAINWATER DEPENDS UPON

(a) Frequency duration and intensity of rainfall
(b) Nature of catchments
(c) Run-off Characteristic

Even if 5 per cent of annual rainfall were harvested properly, that would produce a substantial quantum of water to the tune of 900 million litres.

Rainwater Harvesting Saves Water and ...

1. Improves soil moisture
2. Increases ground water level
3. Improves the quality of water
4. Allows drought-proofing
5. Prevents flooding of storm water drains
6. Saves energy required to lift water
7. Reduces soil erosion
8. An ideal solution of water problem in areas having inadequate water resources

NEED OF RAINWATER HARVESTING

1. To improvc the ground-water quality in aquifers
2. To raise the water in wells and bore wells that are drying up.
3. Surface water is inadequate to meet our demand and we have to depend on ground water.
4. Due to rapid urbanization, infiltration of rainwater into the sub-soil has decreased drastically and recharging of ground water has diminished.
5. Over-exploitation of ground water resource has resulted in decline in water level in most part of the country.
6. To enhance availability of ground water of specific place and time.
7. To arrest seawater ingress.
8. To reduce power consumption.
9. To improve the vegetation cover.
10. To avoid flooding of storm water drains.

RAINWATER HARVESTING PRACTICES

There are two main practices of rainwater harvesting :

1. *Storage of rainwater on surface for future use.* It is a traditional practice and structures used are under ground tanks, ponds, check dams, weirs, etc.
2. *Recharge of ground water* : is a new concept of rain water harvesting and the structures generally used are :
   (a) *Pits*—Recharge pits are constructed for recharging the shallow aquifers.
   (b) *Trenches*—These are constructed when the permeable strata is available at shallow depths.
   (c) *Dug wells*—Drainpipes to a filtration tank, from which it flows in to the dug well divert rainwater that is collected on the rooftop of the building.
   (d) *Hand Pumps*—The existing hand pump may be used for recharging the shallow/deep aquifers, if the availability of water is limited.
   (e) *Recharge wells*—Recharge wells are generally constructed for recharging the deeper aquifer and water is passed through filter media to avoid choking of recharge wells.

(f) *Recharge shafts*—For recharging, the shallow aquifers, which are, located below clayey surface.

(g) *Lateral shafts with bore wells*—For recharging the upper as well as lengths. Deeper aquifers lateral shafts of 1.5 to 2 mt widths and 10 to 30 mt.

(h) *Spreading techniques*—When permeable strata start from top then this technique is used. Water is spread in streams/nalas by making check dams, cement plugs, gabion structures or a percolation pond may be constructed.

INTER-LINKING OF RIVERS

Link Proposals for Peninsular Rivers

The link proposals formulated by NWDA (National Water Development Agency) under Peninsular Component are :

The Mahanadi-Godavari-Krishna-Pennar-Kaveri-Vaigai link running through the eastern region of the peninsular India and inter-connecting all the major east-flowing rivers of the southern India is the main link of the peninsular rivers component. This link system has been divided into several parts as follows :

1. Mahanadi to Godavari
2. Manibhadra-Dowalaiswaram Link
3. Godavari to Krishna
4. Inchampalli-Nagarjunasagar Link
5. Inchampalli-Pulichintala Link
6. Krishna to Pennar
7. Almatti-Pennar Link
8. Srisailam-Pennar Link
9. Nagarjunasagar-Somasila Link
10. Pennarto Cauvery
11. Somasila-Grand Anicut Link
12. Cauvery to Vaigai
13. Kattalai Regulator-Vaigai-Gundar Link
14. Par-Tapi-Narmada and Damanganga-Pinjal links under the component of interlinking of small west-flowing rivers along the west-coast south of Tapi and north of Mumbai.
15. Ken-Betwa and Kalisindh-Chambal links for inter-connecting the southern tributaries of Yamuna.

16. Pamba-Achankovil-Vaippar, Netravati-Hemavati and Bedthi-Varda links for the diversion of surplus water of the west-flowing rivers of Kerala and Karnataka to the east.

LINK PROPOSALS FOR HIMALAYAN RIVERS

The Himalayan Rivers Development Component comprises water balance studies at 19 diversion points, 16 toposheet and storages capacity studies of reservoirs, 19 toposheet studies of links and 14 pre-feasibility studies of links. NWDA has completed all these studies.

Based on NWDA studies, the inter-basin Water Transfer links under Himalayan Component for which feasibility reports are to be prepared by NWDA are as follows :

1. Brahmaputra-Ganga link (Manas-Sankosh-Tista-Ganga)
2. Kosi-Ghagra link
3. Gandak-Ganga link
4. Ghagra-Yamuna link
5. Sarda-Yamuna link
6. Yamuna-Rajasthan link
7. Rajasthan-Sabarmati link
8. Chunar-Sone Barrage link
9. Sone Dam-Southern Tributaries of Ganga link
10. Ganga-Damodar-Subernarekha link
11. Subernarekha-Mahanadi link
12. Kosi-Mechi link
13. Farakka-Sunderbans link
14. Brahmaputra-Ganga link (Jogigopa-Tista-Farakka)

Field surveys and investigations for preparing feasibility reports of links are in progress.

CONCLUDING REMARKS

The water available for use on Earth is finite, and if we are not wise in it's use, clean water will become a globally scarce commodity, as it now is already in so many places. Many solutions are being proposed to solve the problem, but most certainly all these solutions will have trade-offs and costs. No one solution will solve our water scarcity global problem. Soon after independence, the government of India adopted a policy of rapid economic development through extensive and intensive exploitation of natural resources. Unfortunately the Government has allowed private individuals corporate bodies and multinational corporations to encroach upon public lands and literally loot and destroy water resources. The rich and the powerful have gradually but surely appropriated the country's natural resources in their favour. The post-liberalisation period since 1991, with the advent of the multinational capital, has made the hold of these powerful groups on natural resources and the state machinery much stronger. The enthusiasm of the state in executing large water projects through these groups is not matched even remotely by the concern in practice to extend clean water supply to the poor on a sustainable basis. The need for water is continuous and the quantity required per capita per day is several times higher than that of food grains.

Under integrated water mission Dr. A.P.J. Abdul Kalam has rightly said that there is urgent need that 1500 BCM of flood water should be channelised, so that it can be made used for drought affected areas and make sufficient water available to the whole country during non-monsoon months through proper linking, storage and distribution. There is an urgent need to find long-term solution to control flood, store and utilized the surplus water. Water harvesting and recycling of water should be made mandatory. Further, there should be awareness campaign to protect our water resources.

References

Report, 2000.
World Bank Report on Water Crisis.
The India Infrastructure Report.
Govt. of India, Planning Commission, *Eleventh Five Year Plan Proposals on Water Resources Management*.
Indian Economy, Mishra and Puri (29th Revised Edition).
India Year Book, 2010.
Economic Survey, 2010.
Yojana, A Development Monthly, June 2005.
Kurukshetra, A Journal of Rural Development, May 2010.
Govt. of India Report on Policy Issues Related to Water Management.

Chapter 24

Economics of Safe Drinking Water and the Problems of Rural Health

(A Case Study of Bihar)

RABINDRA K. CHOUDHARY, R.P. MAHTO
AND AJAY KUMAR RAO

INTRODUCTION

Existence of life on earth is become possible due to availability of water the most usual chemical. It is the most massive liquid stuff available on earth's surface in one form or another. It is one of the vital resources of life and hence it is something more than what it is something more than what we drink. It is worth to mention the remarks made in international conference on 'water for peace' in regard to relatioship between man and water is long intimate, even mystical and later (water) determined the mode and levels of living of man. No single factor other water could improve the well-being of people of any country. Supply of pure, clean water is essential for the health of people. It offers necessity of life that must be rationed among people.

Being a most important factor for existence of life, water is considered as an important component of development. As it is widely be known that water is the main source of irrigation which infuels the process of cultivation. It is the most important of input in industry and serves as a cooling medium and receptacle of effluents. Swimming, Skling, Floating, etc. are some of the recreational uses of water. In the state of Bihar in particular and in the country as a whole, water has its holy use as famous as holy bath (Ganga Snan, Sangam Snan, etc).

Thus, we may say that water has a multidimensional influence of man's living and man uses water for a variety of purposes : Psychological, Economics, Aesthetic, Scientific and Religious.

COMPOSITION OF WATER SUPPLY AVAILABLE ON EARTH

Composition of water indicates that various sources of water supply available on earth. Various sources of water supply are classified as : (i) oceans, (ii) lakes, (iii) streams, (iv) soil moisture, (v) water vapours in the atmosphere, and (vi) ground water. Respective importance of these water resources can be seen with the aid the data of Table 1.

TABLE 1

Percentage Distribution of the Availablity of Water Resources from Various Sources

Sl. No.	*Item Information*	*Percentage of water available to total water*
1.	Oceans	94.20
2.	Ground Water	4.12
3.	Glaciers	1.65
4.	Lakes	0.02
5.	Soil Moisture	0.01
6.	Atmosphere Pressure	0.00001 Negligible
7.	Rivers	0.0001 Negligible

Source : Economics of Water Supply; K. Nageswar Rao, Himalaya Publishing House, Bombay, 1993. p. 13.

After giving a bird's eye view of the various sources of water, it would become important to throw a flash of light on the demand side of water. Water, the main source of life on earth is in huge demand; due to its uses as mentioned earlier. If all things remains unchanged, demand for water increases with the increase in population the one hand.

On the other hand increased population infuels demand for food, clothes and shelter which in turn expanded in accordance with the process of economic development. Development of all these things along with expansion of industries demand a huge amount of water. At the same time, expansion of industries as well as extensive farming inhance the process of deforestation, the main source of maintaining water supply on earth and hence, supply side of water becomes weaker than the magnitude of demand for water. Inequality, between demand for water and supply of water gives birth of competition for water. Competition for water is primarily consists competition between present uses and future needs, between different uses and between different regions. Such types of competitions for water make water and economic goods—scarce in relation to demand. This is why economic principle and theories are equally applicable to it (water) like other scarce goods in the economy; though; it is a free gift of nature.

With the rise in population, densely populated urban settlement for away from the source of water, demand for safe and clean drinking water. At the same time we know that all water is not fit for human consumption. Therefore, public water supply has become the urgency of the hour for better and smooth functioning of socio-economic and cultural development i.e., public water supply and water management assume great importance in the realm of human as well as economic development.

In this paper, an attempt is made to assess to evaluate the process of safe and clean drinking water supply in rural areas and its impact on the health of rural people. As it has widely been accepted that due to lack of safe and clean drinking water availability in rural areas, the problems of rural health has multiplied. It is worth of UN Conference held in 1975 on water and declared that the society of fresh water is so acute in some areas that women in rural Burma and in some remote villages in India, have to walk 15 km every day to fetch water for their homes. Provisions of adequate water supplies reduces this crushing burden on women and the rural urban migration trends that have economic and social consequences.

The Accelrated Rural Water Supply Programme (ARWSP) aims at providing safe and adequate drinking water facilities to the rural population by supplementing the efforts made by the State Governments/UTs under the State Sector Minimum Needs Programme (MNP). Keeping in view the diefferent kinds of problems arising while providing potable water in the rural areas, 56 Mini-Missions (pilot project) were identified covering all States/UTs. These pilot projects helped to evolve models that arè replicable and can be incorporated in the on-going programmes.

Norms

The provision of drinking water facilities in the problem villages in based on the following norms :

(i) 40 litre of safe drikning water per capita per day (lpcd) for human beings.

(ii) 30 lpcd additionally for cattle in the Desert. Development Programme (DDP) areas.

   (i) One hands pump or stand post for every 250 persons.

   (ii) The water source should exist withing the habitation or within a distance of 1.6 km. in the plains and within 100 metres elevation difference in the hills.

   (iii) Drinking water is defined as safe if it is free from bacteria contamination, chemical contamination viz. fluoride, iron, arsenic, nitrate, brackishness in excess or beyond permissible limits.

Priorities

Viewing the objective of pŕoviding safe drinking water facility in all the villages, there is need for certain order of priority which is as follows :

(i) To cover the "Not Covered" (NC habitants).

(ii) To fully cover the "Partially Covered" (PC) habitations getting less than 10 lpcd.

(iii) To cover all habitations with per capita supply of less than 40 lpcd at the rate of 40 lpcd.

(iv) To provide water supply facilities for the scheduled castes (SC), scheduled tribes (ST) and the landless agricultural labourers.

(v) To provide safe drinking water in every rural primary schools.

Once the task of providing every villages within at least one source of safe drinking water is completed, the enhancement and expansion process may be initiated to provide adequate drinking water. The above mentioned norms can then be liberalised so as to now cover :

(i) Villages that do not have an assured source of safe drinking water within a distance of 0.5 km. (as against 1.6 km).

(ii) To enhance the per capita rate of supply (as against the 40 lpcd rate).

(iii) Adopting the above norms would mean providing one source for every 150 persons (as against one source for every 250 persons).

Hence, this paper is designed to assess and evaluate the provisions and programmes undertaken for insuring safe and clean drinking water in rural areas and its impact on the rural health. The whole paper is divide into four sections. Section 1st given introductory note on the problem. Section 2nd highlights the policy and programmes undertaken for insuring rural water supply section 3rd narrated the programme and policy undertaken during planning era and Section 4th of this paper spells out the summary with appropriate conclusions and suggessions for insuring safe and clean drinking water for accelerating the process of development for solving the problems of rural health.

POLICY AND PROGRAMMES FOR INSURING SAFE AND CLEAN DRINKING WATER IN RURAL AREAS FOR BETTER HEALTH

The WHO initiated a programme for community water supply in 1959 and resolved that priority be given in national programme for provision of safe and adequate water supplies for communities. But it is in 1960 that the benefits provisions of adequate safe water were fully realised.

PUBLIC WATER SUPPLIES AND RAJIV GANDHI NATIONAL DRINKING WATER MISSION

Public water supplies attract the attention of the governement in early fifties. Being a welfare state, government is bound to provide safe drinking water to its people.

Provisions of 'safe' water supply is one of the most important factors that improve health of the population. 'Health' has a high priority in any community and the economic and social development of the society are associated with "Community Health". It has been realised by the governments in the developing countries the inadequate supply of drinking water is one of limiting factors for accelerated development.

The growing concern for the provision of safe water supplies all over the world can be estimated from the creation of special agencies at the international level, declaration of UNDD, financing of water supply schemes by international agencies, the surveys and programmes conducted all over the world, etc. We may briefly review the situation and programmes with regard to water supplies at the global, national and regional levels.

Problems of safe and clean drinking water and the necessity of public water supply can be visualised with the data of Table 2.

As it is evident from the title of this paper, it deals with the problems of Bihar. Hence, it is worth to mention that :

- ❖ Bihar is one of the most populated state of Indian Union in which availability of the per capita land is only 0.22 hectare.
- ❖ Ravages by recurrent flood.
- ❖ 0.4 hospitals per lac of population.
- ❖ Only 3.4 percent population of Bihar has tap water facility.
- ❖ Only 64.6 percent population has tube-well facility for acquiring drinking water. Out of which only 12.87 percent

TABLE 2

Percentage of Population with Reasonable Access to Safe Water

Sl. No.	*Region*	*Population Served (Million)*	*Population with reasonable access (Million)*	*Percentage of Population with reasonable access*		
				1990	*2000*	*2010*
1.	Africa	268	138	30	42	53
2.	America	274	286	68	78	89
3.	Eastern Mediterranean	372	162	48	56	69
4.	Europe	96	42	64	74	88
5.	South East Asia	956	268	32	63	78
6.	Western Pacific	317	64	48	57	69
	Total	2283	960	53	62	71

Source : World Bank, Village Water Supply, 2011.

have deep tube-wells through which they are able to get safe and clean drinking water

- Remaining 30 percent population of rural Bihar are mainly depends upon negihbours' tubewells, wells or public wells. But majority of them are bound to use unhygenic water due to sallow tube-wells.

  - 94.5 per cent population depends upon kerosene oil for domestic light.
  - Only 3.7 per cent population have LPG connection for cooking.
  - 63 per cent families depends upon cow-dung cake for cooking.
  - 39.4 per cent houses are lacking behind separate kitchen.
  - 12.57 per cent households have a cursh to fatch drinking water from.
  - 86.09 per cent family have no latrine in their houses.
  - 46 lacs families are shelterless.
  - 8 districts have more than 70 per cent BPL population.

Without going in detail about the other socio-economic and cultural-academic indicators of Bihar it would be better to throw a flash of light on the comparative picture of figure in regard to percentage of households with selected amenities with a comparison to all major states with the aid of Table 3.

As the data of Table 3 highlights that only 36.34 percent households have the sources of safe drinking water, while national average is 28.71 percent. On the other hand, the report of IHD's study undertaken in the guidance of Dr. Alakh N. Sharma during 1981-82 and 1999-2000, there has been a substantial increase in the number of hand pumps, tube-wells and a drastic reduction in the number of traditional open wells. Approximately 90 percent households in the village now have access to safe drinking water. The report of IHD perhaps indicates the superflous observation of ground reality of rural Bihar in regard to safe drinking water due to following counts :

As per ideals fixed by expert committee in Rajiv Gandhi Drinking Water Programme, at least one hand pump must be made available for five to ten households. In this regard, the availability of hand pumps in rural area in totally mismatched and the report of 90 percent households are found imaginary. Though, in the report itself

TABLE 3

Percentage of Households with Selected Amenities

State	*Drinking Water*		*Electricity Connections*		*Latrine*		*Drainage*	
	Rural	*Urban*	*Rural*	*Urban*	*Rural*	*Urban*	*Rural*	*Urban*
(1)	*(2)*	*(3)*	*(4)*	*(5)*	*(6)*	*(7)*	*(8)*	*(9)*
A.P.	22.75	57.22	59.65	89.66	18.15	78.07	41.43	82.29
Assam	33.61	63.15	16.54	74.29	59.57	94.60	15.00	52.62
Bihar	36.34	70.50	5.13	59.28	13.91	69.69	34.86	68.61
Chhattisgarh	11.90	49.27	46.11	82.85	5.18	52.59	11.31	62.96
Delhi	62.34	75.77	85.50	93.38	62.89	79.03	74.53	91.04
Gujarat	29.30	73.54	72.12	93.39	21.65	80.55	13.65	78.29
H.P.	27.30	73.32	94.48	97.38	27.72	77.22	30.83	86.08
Haryana	30.70	76.01	78.50	92.94	28.66	80.66	71.72	88.41
J & K	17.10	74.65	74.77	97.95	41.80	86.87	26.79	81.84
Jharkhand	9.67	57.15	9.99	75.61	6.57	66.68	17.71	72.36
Karnataka	18.52	56.55	72.16	90.53	17.40	75.23	35.39	80.97
Kerala	69.11	78.93	65.53	84.34	81.33	92.02	15.99	30.89
M.P.	14.03	55.24	62.32	92.26	8.94	67.74	19.84	75.93
Maharashtra	38.86	73.25	65.17	94.28	18.21	58.08	41.14	57.58

(Contd.)

TABLE 3 (*Contd.*)

(1)	*(2)*	*(3)*	*(4)*	*(5)*	*(6)*	*(7)*	*(8)*	*(9)*
Orissa	13.68	52.09	19.35	74.08	7.71	59.69	14.85	57.49
Punjab	81.99	92.05	89.46	96.49	40.91	86.52	78.08	89.77
Rajasthan	19.83	78.79	44.02	89.61	14.61	76.11	23.17	80.19
T.N.	11.95	48.25	71.18	88.00	14.36	64.33	27.36	70.02
U.P.	38.15	77.02	19.84	79.92	19.23	80.01	64.99	92.38
Uttaranchal	32.70	82.06	50.35	90.92	31.60	86.88	34.95	88.24
W.B.	23.41	53.44	20.27	79.56	26.93	84.85	15.91	67.14
All India	28.71	65.38	43.43	87.51	21.92	73.71	34.18	77.87

Source : Census 2001.

narrates that due to lack of proper maintainance, nearly 50 to 60 percent hand pumps are out of order. In this way out of 90 percent hand pumps 60 percent are out of order than the percentage of fit tubewells (hand pumps) is 90 – 54 = 36 per cent. That is still staying at the position of before 1980s.

In our observations in Samastipur and West Champaran districts of Bihar, the picture is quite different. In both the districts, of north Bihar two development blocks from each districts are selected as sample and from each block five villages are taken as sample village, i.e., total no. of sample villages are 1 × 2 × 2 × 5 = 20 villages. From each villages, five households are selected at random for detailed study.

Both the sample districts are of most backward districts of Bihar and characterised as recurrent flood, acute poverty and predominently an agricultural economy. In both the districts, sugar industries are the main source of employment. As far as the proportion of scheduled caste is concerned, this section of society is the main victims of unhygenic drinking water. Majority of these castes are either bound to drink open well's water and compelled to suffer a lot of water prone diseases. On our observation a lot of water problems are found which infuels our thoughts and feelings in regard to drinking water problems in such downtroden families of rural Bihar.

Despite of a lot of investment sources of safe and clean drinking water, still after the six decades of planned development we found that only 39 percent households are become able to have their own sources of water (Tube-wells) while another 35 percent are still depend upon the public sources. While 16 percent are fetching their drinking water from their neighbours tube-wells. And it is a matter of serious concern for the government in general and water resource management department in particular that still 10 percent households depend upon open wells.

The Expenditure Finance Committee (EFC) in its meeting held on 11th of November 1998 has considered approved the proposal to revamp the Accelerated Rural Water Supply Programme. In its meeting EFC has resolved to institutionalize community-based demand driven rural water supply programme with cost sharing by the communities aims at gradually replacing the current programme driven centrally monitored non-people participating Rural Water Supply Programme.

The proposal also envisages and earmarks 20 per cent of the annual outlay to be given to those State Governments who undertake community-based Rural Water Supply Programme by :

(i) Adopting the demand-driven approach based on empowerment of villagers to ensure their full participation in the project, through a decision-making role in the choice of key design and management arrangements.
(ii) 10 per cent of capital cost and 100 per cent of O & M cost to be borne by users.
(iii) The share of States, which do not introduce the reforms, will be given to other states willing to implement the reforms measures.

Since then a lot of programmes are undertaken to ensure rural water supply in India in general and Bihar in particular and to make state responsible for this programme provision is made that 20 percent of total estimated cost of the scheme was contributed by the state. Since then this scheme is implemented, no doubt, a lot of water supply units are established but usefulness of such established units are neither satisfactory nor fruitful. Majority of such units spoke about the misuses as well as mal-practises undertaken in this programme.

After giving the descriptions of rural water supply systems and its position in rural Bihar now we would like to draw your kind attention towards the programmes and provisions launched for insuring safe-drinking water for upgrading rural health by checking water prone disease. The details of such programmes are as follows :

(i) *Control of Brackishness* : Excess brackishness causes the problem of taste and has laxative effects. Control measures include either providing alternate sources free from brackishness or supply of water with total dissolved solids within permissible limit of 1500 ppm (parts per million) by processes like reserve osmosis, electro-dialysis, etc. For treating brackish water, 194 desalination plants were approved by the RGNDWM and 150 plants have been commissioned.
(ii) *Eradication of Guineaworm* : Guineawom is a water-borne disease caused by dracunculiasis medinesis. Efforts to control this disease were started every eighties. It is a good example of how the coordinated efforts of organisations

like National Institute of Communicable Disease (NICD). RGNDWM, International Organisations like WHO, UNICEF, and State Health & PHE departments could attack and eradicate an otherwise difficult problem. India has approached the International Commission for Certification of dracunculiasis eradication.

(iii) *Removal of Excess Iron* : Excess iron in the drinking water is prevent in north-eastern states. Consumption of water within excess iron causes constipating accompanied by other physiological disorders. Control measures include providing alternate sources free from iron or treating iron contaminated water (to within permissible limit 1 ppm) with the help of iron removal plants. For treating iron contaminated water, 16,415 plants were approved and 9355 plants have already been commissioned.

(iv) *Control of Flurosis* : Excess fluoride in drinking water causes dental and skeletal flurosis. The problem is prevalent in 150 districts of 16 states of the country, including Delhi. Control measures include providing alternate sources free from fluoride contaminated water (to within permissible limit 1.5 ppm) with the help of treatment process such as Nalgonda technique or activated alumia process. So far 499 plants (fill and draw type and handpump attached type) have been approved by the Mission of which 427 plants have been installed upto December 1998.

(v) *Control of Arsenic* : Contamination of ground water with arsenic was first noticed in 8 districts of West Bengal in the early 80s. The first attempt to tackle the problem was made by the Government of India in 1988 by sanctioning as investigation project. Thereafter, the Government of India has sanctioned several R & D projects as well as field-oriented projects in the arsenic affected areas. Four water supply projects costing Rs. 349.09 crores have been approved for control of arsenic/providing alternate safe drinking water sources in West Bengal. Rs 3080 lakh have been released during 1998-99.

(vi) *Ensuring Sustainability* : This is an important sub-mission for the success of water supply schemes on a long-term basis. CGW8 and NGRI have been engaged in the programme since the inception of the Mission. With the introduction of scientific methodologies for scientific source finding, the success rate of wells has gone up considerably. Under the water conservation measures, funds worth Rs. 30.75 crores were approved against which Rs. 25.90 crores have been released and the expenditure reported so far is Rs. 20.67 crores.

(vii) *Water quality Surveillance* : For testing of the water quality surveillances, 411 laboratories have been approved and 300 have been established upto December 1998. It is proposed to provide one laboratory in each district of the country. Twenty-two mobile laboratories have also been provided to various states.

On the basis of above said policy and programmes, we have a set a question to know the responses of innocent rural people. In this regard our efforts are mainly concerned with the quality of water used by majority of rural people. Not a single households of the sample area are not aware about such type of water defects and its impact of their health. Besides these disequalities of drinking water, majority of rural households are used shallow tubewells. As it is found in Samastipur district both in Dalsing Sarai and Rousera Ghat Development Blocks, majority of sample households use drinking water, from a tubewells of 40 to 60 deep. A few households reported to have tubewell of 100 to 120 while only 2 to 3 households have 180 deep tubewells. In case of West Champaran district in both the development block named Bettiah Sadar and Nautan we found that majority of sample households use 30 to 50 tubewells. A few of them have 80 to 120 deep tubewells.

It is worth to mention here about the Bharat Nirman : Rural Drinking Water Programme : launched in 2005-06 and its Ist phase is completed in 2008-09 and phase IInd started in 2009-10 and will be completed in 2011-12. Rural Drinking Water is one of the six components of Bharat Nirman.

To enable the rural community to shoulder responsibility in management, operation and maintenance of water supply systems at village level, decentralized, demand-driven, community-managed approach have been adopted. To further strengthen community participation in the drinking water sector the National Rural Drinking Water Quality Monitoring & Survelliance Programme was launched in February 2006 under which 5 persons in each Gram

Panchayat are to be trained to carry out regular survelliance of drinking water sources for which 100 per cent financial assistance including water testing kits, are provided.

Quality-affected habitations : More than 85 per cent of the sources in rural drinking water supply schemes are groundwater-based. Under the NRDWP, chemical contaminants which are sought to be tackled are excess arsenic, fluoride, iron, salinity and nitrate. Except for nitrate, all other occur naturally. Nitrate occurs in drinking water due to leaching of chemical fertilizers and sewerage. The strategy of the Department is to prioritize addressing the problems of arsenic and fluoride in drinking water through alternative surface water sources. The treatment technologies that are available for removal of excess arsenic and fluoride are still not foolproof in respect of reject management and operation and maintenance issues. Though a target of 2.17 lakh quality affected habitations was identified at the begining of Bharat Nirman, the States submitted an action plan for covering only 1,95,813 such habitations. As on 01.04.2006, there were 7,067 habitations reported to be afflicted with arsenic and 29,070 habitations with fluoride contamination. Priority has been given to address the problems in these habitations. It must be admitted however, that due to expansion of testing, more areas are getting identified as having problems of quality.

All these programmes too indicates to be taken or better to say to be completed on paper. In reality, such programmes are not known by any of sample households but the physical achievement as reported by the department during 2010-12 upto 31.3, 2011, 26,807 habitations have been reported as covered as against the outcome budget target of 25,000 in 2010-11.

On the whole, we come to the conclusion, that the availability of safe-drinking water in rural Bihar has mainly depends on the health awareness of rural people and impact of drinking water quality and impact of drinking water quality on their health. It seems that the government agency is only is interested in achieving the physical target fixed for the programme irrespective fixed of its true impact on the real life of the rural people. No doubt they (the machinery of this programme) are contacted with the ward members, mukhiyas and all other public representatives of the rural community and tagged them with the benefits of mal-practices undetaken in such programmes. In this way, the government machinary responsible for the implementation of such programmes, are succeeded to snatch the whole fund and the real effect of the programmes are elucidated and the people of rural areas are left on their own fate.

Perhaps, the formation of Jan-lokpal Bill, will ensure the true implementation of such programmes on ground and people of rural Bihar may be benefited a lot and their health will be improved in near future.

PUBLIC WATER SUPPLY PROGRAMME UNDER FIVE YEAR PLAN

Provisions of water supply and sanitation is mainly the responsibility of the State Government. The Central Government will only be responsible to assits the state in setting up of Public Health Engineering Department in the states. This Department will be the incharge of estimating the requirement designing of the scheme and executing the works relating to water supply. The efforts of five Year Plans can be visualised as follows :

The First Five Year Plan (1956-61)

Though an amount of Rs. 24 crores was originally proposed in this plan, Rs. 12.12 crores for urban water supply, Rs. 11.37 crores for rural water supply schemes and Rs. 50 crores for the training of public health personnels. But the actual expenditure of this plan was only Rs. 11 crores (Rs. 3 crores on urban water supply and Rs. 8 crores on rural water supply schemes).

The Second Five Year Plan (1956-61)

The Second Plan document observed that "Waterborne and other allied diseases are responsible for a large incidence of martality and morbidity in the community which can be brought under control of establishing protected water supplies and sanitary methods of excreta disposal." The benefits of water supply were stressed by many agencies and the state governments expanded their Public Health Engineering Departments.

Taking this view in mind, 208 new schemes for urban areas and 214 schemes for rural areas were undertaken in this plan and an amount of Rs. 27.9 crores were sanctioned for the schemes while actual expenditure was only Rs. 22.50 crores.

The Third Five Year Plan (1961-66)

The 1963-64 National Sample Survey revealed that about 66 percent of India's 540 lakh villages drew their drinking water from wells and almost another 6 per cent from tanks and lakes. In view of this during the Third Plan it was felt that priority be accorded to areas suffering from acute scarcity, areas where water is saline and endemic to waterborne diseases. Further, the Plan called for an intensive effort, effective coordination between various agencies and mobilization of local initiative and contribution.

The plan embarked Rs. 67 crores for rural water supply schemes, of which Rs. 35 crores were to be spent under village water supply programmes to cover the backward areas not covered under the Community Development Schemes. Rs. 10,000 was fixed as the maximum expenditure for each village and half the expenditure to be matched by contributions from the public 1,764 rural water supply schemes were completed during the Plan period.

The Fourth Five Year Plan (1969-74)

From the Fourth Plan onwards, the water supply programme received high priority and the benefits of public, water supplies were stressed in the successive plan.

It was mentioned in the Fourth Five Year Plan designing rural water supply schemes, water available from major and medium irrigation projects would also be integrated for supplying drinking water. Further, "in rural areas water supply schemes would be looked upon as a service which has to be paid for Whenever possible, capital contributions and levies should be collected from the beneficiaries."

During the Fourth Plan, with concerted efforts made to provide water supply, the actual outlay of Rs. 574 crores exceeded the amount originally proposed.

The Fifth Five Year Plan (1974-79)

The plan provided for an expenditure of Rs. 381 crores on rural water supply and sanitation schemes as compared to a total of Rs. 289 crores provided in all the previous plans. In addition to this Rs. 100 crores was made available under the Accelerated Rural Water Supply Programme, a Centrally sponsored scheme, launched in 1972-73.

The Sixth Five Year Plan (1980-85)

The Sixth Five Year Plan witnessed a National Drinking Water Mission (NDWM) launched in 1986; which subsequently was rechristened as Rajiv Gandhi National Drinking Water Mission (RGNDWM) in 1991 with three key objectives.

(i) providing safe drinking water to all villages,
(ii) assisting local communities maintain source of safe drinking water in good condition, and
(iii) giving special attention for water supply to scheduled castes and scheduled tribes.

The Seventh Five Year Plan (1985-90)

In this plan Accelerated Rural Water Supply Programme (ARWSP) was launched achieve the objective of NDWM. In other words, we may say that speedy implementation of NDWM was the main objectives of this plan.

The Eighth Five Year Plan (1992-97)

ARWSP and CRSP was simultaneously implemented with a view to help to break the vicious circle of disease, morbidity and poor health resulting from water borne disease and in sanitary conditions.

The Ninth Five Year Plan (1997-2002)

ARWSP was the main scheme emphasized by the government of India. An amount of Rs. 1299.91 crores was spend during 1997-98 and special attention was given to ensure safe drinking water in rural areas.

The Tenth Five Year Plan (2002-07)

In this plan RGNDWN was given first priority with an objective to extend the coverage of the scheme up to all rural habitations with population of 100 and above, specially the enriched ones ensure sustanability of the system and sources, tackle the problems of water quality and institutionalize water quality monitoring and survelliance through a catchment area approach.

The Eleventh Five Year Plan (2007 to 2012)

In this plan RGNDWM adopts an integrated approach so that conservation and augmentation of water sources is interrelated with water supply scheme to provide sustainable supply of safe drinking water to the rural population. The mission seeks to provide supply of 40 liters of safe drinking water to each family in rural areas.

After giving a brief account of schemes and programmes concerned with safe drinking water in rural areas during planning period; now we would like to summaries the whole discussion in one paragraph for easy understanding of the problems prevails in rural areas in regard to safe drinking water and ground reality.

A lot of efforts have been made right from first plan to eleventh plan with the support of sufficient fund allocation for ensuring safe drinking water in rural areas. No doubt, policy formulation are quite well and adequate funds are also allocated for achieving the aims of all these schemes. But the question arises, how and where these funds are spent, why not hundred per cent households of rural habitations are not made able to safe drinking water after the completion one to eleven five year plans.

The planned expenditure on safe drinking water programmes and ground reality of rural drinking water supply system tell the story of mal-practices undertaken in these schemes in a louder-voice. And their persons concerned with these mal-practices have become so strong, bold and confident that they have not agitated to evaporate the whole funds allocated for commonwealth game in Khel Gram, New Delhi and cause the nation to stand in a shameful situation. But the corruptions prevails in all department of nation and the degree of evaporation of public funds, the process of individualization of public funds have give birth of the Anshan (fasting) of Anna Hazare which not only caused the Central Government but also the whole parliament to think about such chronic disease of nation.

SUGGESSIONS

Water which gives birth of life on earth must be kept safe, clean and sustainable so that life on earth could become long live. To maintain these following steps should be undertaken:

- Anna Hazare should support Megha Patekar in her mission to save earth and should launch Jan-Lok Kranti for safe drinking water instead of Jan-Lokpal Bill.
- Anna Hazare should support Megha Patekar in her mission to save earth and should launch Jan-Lok Kranti for safe drinking water instead of Jan-Lokpal Bill.
- Jan-Lokpal Bill should be chased with Jan-Lokpal Honesty Kranti. So that each and every Indian could become honest and dishonest could become in a condition to commit sauced amongst the honest people.
- No one can be ready to cooperate with dishonest one.
- As the agitation support and cooperation from each and every corner of the nation show a blind support to Anna, in such situation, Anna could motivate the whole nation to become honest and certainly we succeded.

To conclude, we may say that without education in true sense, honesty could not be ensured and without honesty safe and clean drinking water cannot be supplied to one to all houses in rural areas.

References

Economics of Water Supply by K. Nageshwar Rao, Himalaya Publishing House.
Global Meet for a Resurgent Bihar, 19-21 Jan., 2007.
Bharat Nirman, Rural Drinking Water, Department of Drinking Water and Sanitation, Rajiv Gandhi National Drinking Water Mission.
Economics Survey of India, 2007-08.
Various Issues of Yojana, *Kurukshetra.*
The Economic Times, The Times of India.
India, 2012.

Chapter 25

Management of River Water

MANOJ SHANKAR GUPTA AND ASHA SINGH

INTRODUCTION

Water is life. Both the natural and human systems are critically dependent on water. It is the prime requirement for the survival of human beings, as also for the socio-economic development and a healthy ecosystem. In addition, access to water plays a critical role in food security and poverty alleviation, both local and national. Yet there are reports of a looming water crisis arising out of serious demand-supply imbalances especially in developing world. The prevailing trends towards rising population, increasing urbanisation, spread of more water, intensive life styles as well as agricultural technology sweeping round the developing world are going to make water resource even mare scarce unless timely action is taken. How to manage water has thus emerged as one of the great challenges of the 21st century.

The population of India is estimated to reach a figure between 1.5 billion and 1.8 billion by the year 2050. The UN agencies have put the figure at 1.64 billion. It is now generally accepted that the countries with annual per capita water availability of less than 1,700 cubic metre (m^3) are water stressed and less than 1000 m^3 are water scarce. India would, therefore, need 2,788 bcm of water annually by 2050 to be above water stress zone and 1,650 bcm to avoid being a water scarce country.

WATER RESOURCES OF INDIA

The National Commission has assessed the Gross Water Resources of the country for Integrated Development Plan in its "Policy & Issues" paper as 2,384.5 BCM. The country has been divided into twenty river basins comprising of 12 major basins each having drainage area exceeding 20,000 sq. km and remaining medium and small rivers together form eight river basins. The Central Water Commission earlier assessed 1,869.37 BCM in 1993 as the annual mean flow in these river basins. National Commission has reassessed the available water resources as 1,952.87 BCM.

The total utilisable surface water resources by conventional schemes of all the 20 basins have been assessed as 690.3 BCM. The inter-basin transfer proposals by NWDA envisage utilization of additional 200-250 BCM. The replenishable ground water resources have been assessed as 431.9 BCM by the Central Ground Board. The utilisable Gross Water Resources have been assessed as 395.6 BCM. Thus total utilisable water resources by conventional means and by inter-basin transfer proposals are placed at 1,286 to 1,336 BCM. The per capita available and utilizable water resources per year are therefore 2,830 m^3 and 1,288 m^3 respectively.

EMERGING SCENARIO

The scenario that emerges from above projections can be summed up as under:

(i) The expected water requirement by 2050 A.D. may be around 1,422 BCM against gross utilisable water resources of 1,086 BCM through conventional methods. It is expected that the population may stabilise by 2050 A.D. It will be important to augment utilisable water resources to bridge the gap between likely requirement and availability as shortages are bound to create conflicts.

(ii) Even the above quantity of water is not available uniformly over space and time. The drought flood syndrome will continue due to orographic features. Therefore, we have to re-orient our strategies and seectoral requirements to balance requirements with availability, to resort to inter-basin transfer of waters from surplus areas to deficit areas.

(iii) 92 per cent of the country's geographical area is under inter-state rivers, but water is a State subject as per Constitution. Due to shortages/increasing demands of water, there are already some inter-state disputes and delays in execution of projects, which sometimes may lead to increasing law and order problems.

(iv) The per capita availability of water per year has been progressively decreasing and is around 1,250 m^3 at present. This may reduce to around 760 m^3 by the year 2050 A.D.

(v) Shortages in areas with water availability from 1,000 m^3/capita/year to 1,700 m^3/capital/year will be local. Below 1,000 m^3/year, water supply begins to hamper health, economic development and human well-being. According to another definition areas with annual availability between 1,000-2,000 m^3/capita/year are considered water stressed areas and with availabilities below 1,000 m^3/capita/year are considered as water scarce.

PROBLEMS OF DISTRIBUTION OF RIVER WATER IN INDIA

Conflicts of many dimensions (legal, institutional, socio-cultural, ethical and so on) have been observed of different levels and between different sets of parties. Hence, it is vital to study the conflicts of certain kinds in an exploratory manner.

In recent years, there has been much concern over a looming water scarcity (predicted on the basis of projections of future magnitudes of population, pace of urbanization and economic 'growth') and the conflicts that this is likely to generate. That concern is increasingly being expressed in the language of 'security'. Many conferences and seminars are being held all over the world about the

TABLE 1
Irrigation Potential in India

(In million hectares)

	1950-51	*2006-07*
Minor Irrigation	12.9	39.50
Major Irrigation	9.1	62.25
Total	22.0	101.75

Source : Publication Division, Ministry of Information & Broadcasting, Government of India.

security implications and dimensions of scarcities of natural resources, particularly water. Much of the debate takes place under the auspices of institutions and agencies whose primary concern is security in the conventional military sense. A currently fashionable thesis is that future wars will be about water, not oil. In this writer's view water wars are implausible and the analogy with oil is inapt. It is both misleading and dangerous to bring conflicts relating to water under the rubric of 'security'. However, that subject will not be dealt with in detail here: having taken note of it, this paper will put it aside and proceed to discuss water conflicts in certain contexts.

First, let us consider riparian conflicts, whether within a country or between countries. It is interesting to note that conflicts over river waters, whether inter-country or intra-country, seem often to arise in the context of large projects. India-Bangladesh dispute over Ganga water was precipitated by the Farakka Barrage Projects in India. Projects on the Kosi and Gandak were the starting points of a prolonged history of misunderstandings between India and Nepal and that mistrust was further accentuated by the Tanakpur Barrage Project, until it was resolved through the Mahakali Treaty of February 1996; but even after that treaty there are pending issues relating to the Pancheswar Project. Within India, the Cauvery dispute arose because dams and reservoirs built by the State of Karnataka had the effect of reducing the flow into the Mettur Reservoir in Tamil Nadu. Between Karnataka and Andhra Pradesh, there is a dispute over the Alamatti Project of the former on the Krishna river.

Assuming that there is no deliberate intention on the part of any party to cause harm to other, how do conflicts in relation to water or over water-resource development projects arise, whether between countries or between constituent units within a country? They could arise from one or more of the following causes:

- Wrong principles (Harmon Doctrine, prior appropriation, prescriptive rights, etc., asserted in an absolute manner);
- Limited vision (myopic nationalism, blind assertion of local perceptions);
- Lack of sensitivity on the part of the stronger party, excessive touchiness on the part of the weaker;
- Inadequate understanding of implications and consequences; failure to study these fully; ignorance; lack of data/information;

- Unwillingness to share information; failure consult all concerned; failure of imagination about other needs, rights or concerns; and
- Politicisation, i.e., the tendency for differences over water or environmental concerns to become elements in domestic electoral politics.

TABLE 2

Estimates of Water Resources in India

(In billion cubic metre)

Agency	*Estimate in bcm*	*Deviation from 1869 bcm*
First Irrigation Commission (1902-03)	1443	-23%
Dr. A.N. Khosla (1949)	1673	-10%
Central Water and Power Commission (1954-66)	1881	+0.6%
National Commission on Agriculture	1850	-1%
Central Water Commission (1988)	1880	+0.6%
Central Water Commission (1869)	—	

Source : Eleventh Five Year Plan (2007-12), Vol. III, Planning Commission, Government of India, 2008, p. 44.

How can conflicts relating to river waters (and in particular large projects) be avoided or minimized? In this context, we often come across two kinds of 'ideal' recommendations. From a hydrological point of view, the recommendation is that national or political boundaries should be ignored that a hydrological unit such as a basin or sub-basin should be taken as a whole and that there should be integrated water-resource planning for such a unit. From a political/ economic perspective, the recommendation is that regional planning is superior to national planning. There is much force in these propositions but there are also some difficulties that must be taken note of.

The advocacy of regionalism tends to become doctrinaire. There are some problems and issues that are best dealt with on a local basis; some that call for cooperation between two countries or units; and others that demand a regional approach. The circumstances vary from case to case, and in each case the most appropriate route needs to be followed. On the one hand, a rigid bilateralism such as that adopted by the Government of India is unwise and unduly self-limiting; on the other, a dogmatic advocacy of regionalism are inherently superior to a national or bilateral approach would unnecessarily complicate simple issues and render them more difficult to resolve. What is called for is pragmatism rather than doctrine.

The 'basin' approach is theoretically sound but some basins are too large and have to be broken down into sub-basins. Besides, 'basin planning', and the talk of 'integration', carry with them an implicit bias towards gigantism and a technology-driven approach. We need to be conscious of this danger. Further, a 'hydrological' approach that ignores political boundaries may sound right in theory but many not work in practice. In principle it may be possible to argue that benefit-sharing is better than water-sharing and that within a basin or a sub-basin as a whole, food production should be concentrated in one area, power generation in another, and industry in yet another, but this may not be acceptable. Political boundaries, whether between countries or within a country, exist and cannot be forgotten. A theoretically right approach may have to be moderated by a degree of realism. The best need not be the enemy of the good. 'Integration' may be ideal, but it may sometimes be necessary to settle for the second best option of 'coordination'. Similarly, enlightened

TABLE 3

Ultimate Irrigation Potential (UIP), Potential Created and Potential Utilised (In M.H.)

Sector	*Ultimate Irrigation Potential*	*Potential Created*		*Potential Utilized*	
		Till end of Ninth Plan	*Anticipated in Tenth Plan*	*Till end of Ninth Plan*	*Anticipated in Tenth Plan*
MMI	58.47	37.05	5.3	31.01	3.41
MI					
Surface water	17.38	13.6	0.71	11.44	0.56
Ground water	64.05	43.3	2.81	38.55	2.26
Sub-total	81.43	56.9	3.52	49.99	2.82
Total	139.9	93.9	58.82	81.00	6.23

Source : Eleventh Five Year Plan (2007-12) Vol. III, Planning Commission, Government of India, 2008, p. 45.

nationalism or bilateralism may be the first step towards eventual regionalism.

The short point is that if countries falling within a river basin or sub-basin wish to avoid conflict while planning a project, there are enough principles and guidelines to go by. To put it in a nutshell (even if this runs the risk of over-simplification), the upper riparian, in exercising its powers of control over waters, cannot ignore the rights of lower riparian; and the lower riparian, in asserting its rights over the waters, cannot ignore the needs of the upper riparian. Give that kind of understanding, conflicts will either not arise at all or can be resolved without much difficulty when they do.

However, principles are not enough. Knowledge and awareness are important. Large projects are often major interventions in nature and should not be undertaken without the fullest study of the likely consequences and implications of such intervention. This imperative is clear enough in all cases, but becomes even more so when the projects on a terms-boundary river. Environmental Impact Assessments (EIAs) should not stop at boundaries. What happens beyond those boundaries is equally important.

Finally, any such treaty or agreement must of course include suitable provisions—consultations, conciliation, mediation, arbitration, adjudication as may be agreed upon—for the resolution of differences and disputes. As regards institutional mechanisms, there are many models to choose from: bilateral or multilateral commissions; purely governmental bodies or bodies with a large non-official component; advisory or empowered bodies; and so on. What is feasible in given case will be a function of the felt needs and the facts of geography on the one hand, the state of political relations between the countries concerned on the other. It is important that institutional mechanisms appropriate to a given case should be established very early before differences of perception grow sharp and attitudes harden.

At this stage it may be useful to make a brief reference to into-state river water disputes in India and the conflict-resolution mechanism that is available. Article 262 of the Constitution provides for Parliamentary legislation for the adjudication of inter-state river water disputes and in pursuance of those provisions there is a Parliamentary enactment, namely, the Inter-State Water Disputes Act, 1956. These are important features of Indian federalism and provide an essential mechanism for conflict-resolution in relation to river waters. Initially, the machinery seemed to be working well but it has run into serious trouble in recent years, leading to a measure of disenchantment with the constitutional and statutory provisions.

Despite opinions to the contrary (held by many), it is Ramaswamy R. Iyer's view that the existing adjudication system is very necessary as a last-resort mechanism and must be made to work better. This has two aspects. First, the delays to which the process is prone at every stage—the establishment of a tribunal; the proceedings of the tribunal and the giving of an award; the notification of the award in the Gazette and its implementation—need to be drastically reduced. Secondly, it needs to be ensured that the award (declared by the ISWD Act to be final and binding) is in fact, accepted by all parties to the dispute and implemented promptly and unreservedly. On all these matters there are specific recommendations by the Sarkaria Commission which have remained unimplemented for years. These have recently been reiterated and added to by the National Commission on Integrated Water Resources Development Plan in its Report (September 1999). It appears that the present Government has at last taken some decisions on this subject. We have to wait and see what those decisions are and whether they can be acted upon quickly.

From riparian conflicts, let us turn to socio-economic and equity-related conflicts. A large 'water resource development' project creates conflicts of interests between the people of the upper catchments and those downstream; between those who bear the social costs of the project (through the loss of land and habitats to submergence or other construction needs, loss of livelihoods for these or related reasons, severance of ancient links to their natural resource-base, dispersal of integrated communities, and so on) and those who enjoy the benefits such as irrigation or hydro-power; between the head-reach farmers and those at the tail end of the canal system as also between the rich farmers and the power ones in the command area; between those who benefit from the diversion to water through canals and those downstream of the dam who are affected by a reduction in flows; and so on. Such conflicts have been incidental to many projects but have been particularly marked in the case of some.

There are two kinds of theoretical responses to the hardships inflicted by such projects on the affected people, who are often poor, backward and disadvantaged, and in many cases belong to tribal communities. One is to say that while everything must be done to mitigate their hardship, development does involve costs and that some groups may have to accept a measure of hardship ('sacrifice') in the larger interests of the nation. Without entering into a detailed discussion of the fallacies involved in this line of argument, this paper will merely declare that 'sacrifice' is the wrong word to use for an involuntary displacement from land and homestead, and that the imposition of such a 'sacrifice' is morally indefensible. Gandhiji, in whose view the Benthamite doctrine of the maximum good of the greatest number was immoral, would surely have refused to countenance the 'sacrifice for development' argument. Nor is Pareto optimality an adequate answer to this: it is not enough to say that while some are enabled by state action to acquire wealth others must be at least not worse-off. That too is injustice. The project-affected persons (PAPs) must actually benefit from the project.

The leads to the second response referred to above, namely, the recommendation of 'stakeholder consultation/participation' that forms a part of the Dublin/Rio principles and has gained much currency in recent years. Most policy documents and guidelines would now include this as a matter of course. It is also fashionable to refer to PAPs as 'partners in development'. Unfortunately, these sanctimonious formulations bear little resemblance to reality. 'Stakeholders' and 'partners in development' are expressions that have an ironic ring: PAPs are in most cases victims of 'development'. Efforts to involve them in decision-making and to give them their rightful share in the benefits of the projects that impose hardships on them have either not been seriously pursued or been unsuccessful.

These are questions of social justice intertwined with 'political economy' complexities. Answers to such conflicts in the form of principles and institutional arrangements can doubtless be found. For instance, there can be community that is dependent on say, a mountain or a forest or a river; a legal embodiment of the priority given to drinking water by the India National Water Policy of 1978 and the recognition of access to it as a fundamental right; institutionalized consultation with and participation by the people concerned in the planning process, and mandatory public hearings before major projects with significant environment and/or human/ social impacts are formulated or approved; a statutory grievance-redressing mechanism such as an Ombudsman; the statutory conferment on project-affected persons of rights over the benefits to be generated by a project; a machinery for the resolution of conflicts and a legal backing for it; and so on. Unfortunately, making such arrangements work and protecting them from distortion and perversion and from co-option by vested interest is enormously difficult.

There is also the possibility of conflict between the people and the state. It must be noted that in the context of the ISWD Act 'inter-State river-waters disputes' means inter-governmental disputes. Implicit in this is the assumption that rivers are resources of the state to be dealt with be the governments for the people. This fails to recognise that the people could have concerns and interests of their own, and that there could be conflicts between these and the aims and purposes of the government. This point (among many others) came up in the case relating to the Sardar Sarovar Narmada Project but unfortunately the Supreme Court's recent judgment does not countenance this line of thinking; it virtually lays down the doctrine that 'Government knows best'.

Apart from people being affected by governmental decisions, there are also possibilities of conflict between state and civil society institutions and initiatives. In India there was historically a wide range of community-managed systems and practices of local water conservation and management. However, first the colonial state and later the state in independent India assumed control over natural resources, and their management passed into the hands of government officials and engineers. The modern state began to build big, technology-driven, centralized projects, and concomitantly the traditional, community-managed systems and practices went into decline. Now there is a move to revive some of those traditions ('dying wisdom' in the words of the Centre for Science and Environment) as also to promote new community initiatives in local water harvesting and management. These efforts are often hampered by the unhelpful and sometimes hostile attitude of governments towards such initiatives and towards the NGOs inspiring or supporting them.

Turning to groundwater, we need to note the asymmetry in Indian law between flowing surface water and groundwater. In respect of the former, the law does not recognise ownership rights; there are only rights of use. However, in terms of the Indian Easements Act, the ownership of land carries with it the ownership of the groundwater under it, subject to regulation and control by the State. This leads to conflicts and inequities: a rich farmer can install power-driven tubewells or borewells in his land and their operation can make dugwells in the neighbourhood run dry; he can sell water so extracted to his poorer neighbours even though the water may come from a common aquifer and he can deplete the aquifer through excessive exploitation. Water markers doubtless tend to emerge in the context of groundwater extraction through tubewells and borewells and they serve some useful purpose, but it needs to be recognized that there are real dangers of unsustainable extraction as also of inequitable relationships between sellers and buyers. Perhaps the answer lies in regulation but this has so far not been found feasible because of political factors and the legal problem of easement rights. Under the directions of the Supreme Court, the Central Groundwater Authority has been established but it is not yet clear how it will evolve and operate, what kind of regulation it will attempt and with what success.

Above all, conflict can and does arise between 'development' (including and perhaps especially water resources development) and 'sustainability' (which really means the long-term health and even survival of the planet earth and therefore of humanity). That is a vast subject that calls for a separate attention but it must at least be mentioned here. It may be concluded with the following unelaborated proposition: conflicts often arise from the 'greed' (to use Gandhiji's word) that underlies the prevailing notions of the 'development' and that makes unsustainable demands on nature; we cannot learn to live in harmony with our neighbours until we have learnt to live in harmony with nature.

INTER-STATE WATER DISPUTES

Perhaps delay due to inter-state disputes is the most important aspect to be tackled in the present context. So far following methods have been used for resolving water-related conflicts between the States. There are many examples of resolving conflicts of sharing of water by States themselves. Some of the examples are:

- Agreements on Bagh, Pench in Tapi basin between Maharashtra and M.P.
- Bawanthidi, Bhopalapatnam, Kalisarar on the Godavari by standing Bilateral Inter-State Control Boards
- Distribution of flows of Yamuna water between U.P. and Haryana
- Sharing of Mahi river water between Gujarat and Rajasthan

- Parambitkulan-Aliyar between Tamil Nadu and Kerala
- Damodar, Ajay, Mayurakshi and Mahananda between Bihar and West Bengal

LINKING OF RIVERS

The Supreme Court's direction that the rivers of India shall be linked within 10 years is not at all a defuesible instance of judicial activism. That apart, turning to the merits of the direction, one wishes that the learned judges had undertaken a more careful study of the subject before deciding to issue directions. Fortunately these are interim directions and there is still time for a reconsideration of the matter. It is to be hoped that Task Force that is to be set-up as directed by the Supreme Court will consider not merely the 'modalities' of the 'linking of rivers' but also the soundness and wisdom of the idea. It is also urgent need of time to study the 'linking of rivers' in India because some states are having sufficient water while some are facing great challenge and problem of uneven distribution of water by nature and government. Further, with the 'linking of river' project, we may be needed for other unforseen disasters.

One need not labour the point that cooperation across countries, if designed appropriately reflecting each participating country's perspectives on an equitable basis—bilateral and multilateral—is positive-sum win-win for the participating countries. In the case of transboundary rivers, the need for cooperation among the coriparians is particularly beneficial and, hence, important. Studies (e.g. Ahmad *et. al.*, eds., 1994; Adhikari *et. al.*, eds., 2000; Crow, 1995) have shown this to be so. It has also been substantiated by cases of actual water sharing cooperation forged and implemented in this region. The following may be cited in this context.

THE INDUS BASIN TREATY

The Indus Basin Treaty resolved a major conflict between India and Pakistan on water sharing of common rivers. It took nine years and the intervention of the World Bank for India and Pakistan to finally agree and sign the treaty in September 1960. The treaty has provided a unique solution in that it has allocated three rivers Ravi, Beas, and Sutlej to India and three others Indus, Jhelum and Chenab to Pakistan. Each country has unrestricted use of the waters of the rivers allocated to it, with certain exceptions specified in the treaty.

There was a transition period during which Pakistan needed to develop irrigation and other relevant works for properly using the waters of the rivers allocated to it, replacing those hitherto beeen fed from the rivers allocated to India. India made a significant contribution towards the cost of the Indus Basin Development Project undertaken by Pakistan.

The treaty set-up a permanent commission composed of two commissioners, one appointed by each of the governments. The commission oversees the functioning of the treaty arrangements and seeks to reconcile any point of disagreement that may arise. The treaty has worked well ever since it was put into practice, despite two wars in 1965 and 1971 and very tense relations from time to time between the two countries. The lesson: a mutually beneficial cooperative arrangement for transboundry river/water sharing, perhaps also such arrangements in other fields, can transcend whatever other difficulties there may be in the relationship between the participating countries, including even wars.

HYDROPOWER GENERATION IN BHUTAN: BHUTAN-INDIA COOPERATION

The second successful water sector cooperation in the region that one may cite is the 336 MW run-of-the-river Chukha Hydropower Project on the Wangchu in Bhutan, taken up in 1975 under an agreement with India. India undertook to build and fund the project, with 60 percent of the total cost provided as grant and the balance as a loan at 5 percent rate of interest repayable over 15 years from the completion of the project. It was commissioned in 1987. This project initiated a process of transformation of Bhutan's economy. Given Bhutan's limited electricity need and distribution capacity, the bulk of Chukha power is exported to India. Bhutan's economic activity in various sectors has flourished, based on the resource generated through the sale of Chukha power. The per capita income in Bhutan has, largely as a result of this project, increased from about US $ 545 currently. India has also benefited as a result of the access it gained to a much needed additional electricity supply. (Varghese, 1999a, and 1999b).

Encouraged by the successful implementation of the Chukha Project the two countries have entered into similar arrangements for building more hydro projects in Bhutan.

THE GANGES TREATY

The Ganges treaty is about "the sharing between India and Bangladesh of the Ganges waters at Farakka." The treaty provides, on the basis of an agreed formula, that specific amounts of water will be available to each country by 10-day periods from 1 January to 31 May every year. India would make every effort to protect flow of water at Farakka in the 40-year average level for each of the 10-day period, shown in Annexure II of the Treaty. Should the "flow at Farakka fall below 50,000 cusecs in any 10-day period, the two governments will enter into immediate consultations to make adjustment on an emergency basis, in accordance with the principles of equity, fair-play and no-harm to either." A joint committee set-up by the two governments, as provided for in the treaty, is responsible for monitoring the daily flow, during the relevant period, at Farakka below Farakka Barrage, in the feeder canal, at the navigation lock, and the Hardinge Bridge.

The above examples of successful, ongoing cooperation in the water and water-based sectors are all bilateral. Indeed, efforts need to be made to exploit all feasible mutually beneficial bilateral opportunities. But there are areas in which regional/multilateral cooperation would be beneficial to all the participating countries more than otherwise. There are issues which can be addressed only through regional/multilateral cooperation.

COST, PRICE AND VALUE OF WATER IN ALTERNATIVE USES: A CASE STUDY OF SUBERNAREKHA RIVER BASIN

Basic economics require that the price of a service be at least as high as the cost of providing that service. Sustainable and efficient use of water requires the tariff to match not only cost of supply (i.e., O and M and capital costs) but also opportunity costs, economic externality costs, and environmental externality costs. This part presents some results to illustrate that tariffs in irrigation, urban and industrial sectors are far below the full cost. Very often the tariffs do not meet the full supply costs. And sometimes the value of water is lower than the cost of supply. The evidence presented here is from the Subernarekha basin in India.

Costs, Prices and Value of Water

The schematic shown in Figure 1 compare costs and values

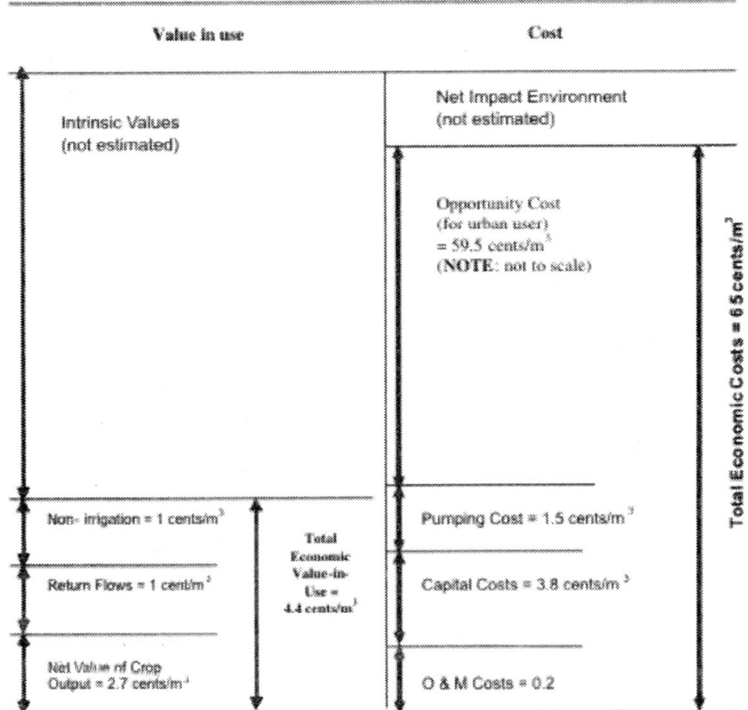

Figure 1 : Estimation of Value-in-Use for Irrigated Agriculture and Costs of Water in Subernarekha River Basin, India

associated with agricultural water use in the Subernarekha River Basin. The total economic value, calculated as the sum of net value of crop output, value of return flow, value of water in non-irrigated uses, and value of other societal objectives, is 9.7 c/m^3. The total economic cost calculated as the sum of O and M costs, capital costs, pumping costs and opportunity cost is 65 c/m^3. Dearth of information and data prevent Rogers *et al.* from calculating the intrinsic value of water and environmental costs of providing irrigation water. Nevertheless, the disparity between value-in-use and cost is very large. Even if the intrinsic value were large it probably would not be large enough to meet this gap plus environmental costs.

The schematic shown in Figure 2 compares costs and values associated with urban and industrial water use in the Subernarekha

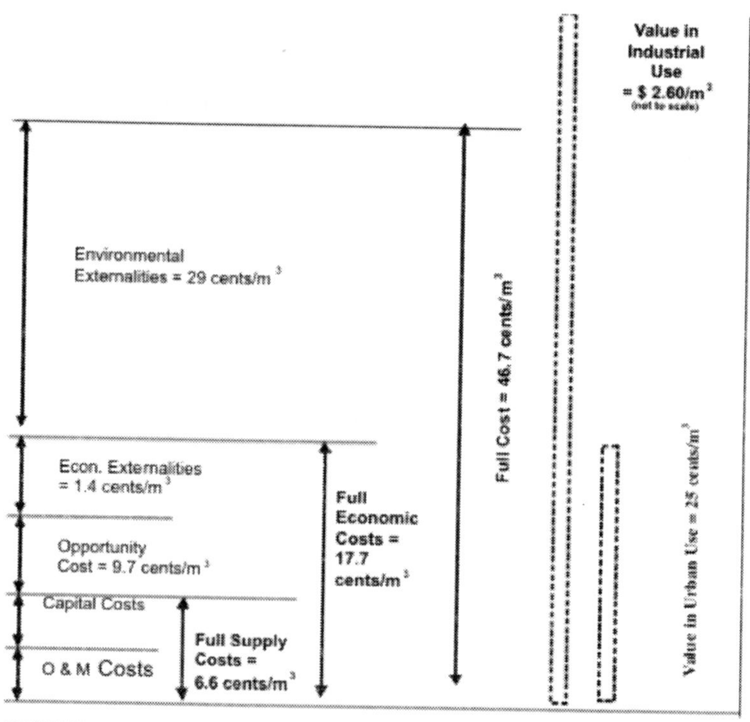

Figure 2 : Estimation of Costs and Values for the Urban and Industrial Sectors in Subernarekha River Basin, India

Source : Rogers *et al.* (1998).

River Basin. Assuming that both sectors use the same source, the same cost structure is used for both. Rogers *et al.* calculate the full cost of water to be 46.7 c/m³. The value in industrial use is $ 2.60/m³, the value in urban use is 25 c/m³.

Why is there such gap in the value of water in the two sectors? Figure 3 shows that the industrial tariff is more than double the urban tariff. So the urbanites over-consume and value the resource less. In this case there is an industrial to domestic to agriculture subsidy. This is true in both Subernarekha and Yamuna River Basins. The agricultural tariffs are much smaller than cost of supply in both basins.

In the above figure, 'cost' includes supply costs and opportunity costs, but not environmental and economic externalities costs. Yet the tariff falls below this cost. In the agricultural sector, costs exceed value of the crop as well. Such low priced water will only encourage wasteful use. Water suppliers must progressively increase tariffs to cover full cost of water.

Opportunity cost is the largest cost component in the irrigation costs given above. When agricultural tariff increases and more water becomes available to the other two sectors, the opportunity cost of agricultural water will decreases. And because of reduced availability in this sector, the value of water in irrigation will increase. The story will be different in the other costs will decrease the 'cost' of industrial and urban water. And because of the more abundant resource, its value will also decrease. So values and costs can be expected to converge across sectors.

Although the above examples were taken from developing countries, water price differentials in differently sectors are not unique to those countries. Such examples are rampant in industrialised countries as well. The Northern Colorado Water Conservancy District in the US, for instance, charges irrigators about \$3.50 per acre-foot (about 0.3 cents/m^3), and about \$7 per acre-foot (about 0.6 cents/m^3) from cities and industries. The capital costs not covered by direct water-related revenues are paid for from real-estate taxes levied against all urban and rural real estates in the District. In effect, industries and households subsidise water for the agriculture sector.

The large variations in values, costs and prices will allow for trading between sectors. Currently agriculture is the largest water user in most countries. On average, 69 per cent of world's water is used in agriculture, and 23 per cent in industry. (In OECD countries though 65 per cent is used in industry, while only 30 per cent is used in agriculture, OECD, 1999b). Trading does not require that all agricultural water be transferred to the urban and industrial sectors. A small transfer of agricultural water can meet all the demands in urban and industrial sectors. On the other hand, since the required transfer is small, increment is also small. At least on the first pass, a small increment in irrigation water prices (where the tariff can still be less than urban or industrial tariff) can help meet the highly valued needs in the other two sectors.

NEED FOR INTEGRATED PRICING

In the example given above, it is shown that water tariffs are generally low and increased water rates can actually help foster efficient use and improve equitable distribution of water. But proper water rates imposed by the public water supplier alone are insufficient to manage the resource. If the supplier charged the full-cost of water and there were no regulations to protect groundwater sources, consumers will gradually exploit the groundwater sources. If there were no proper wastewater charge structure, consumers will pump groundwater and discharge the waste into the public wastewater system with no penalty. "The holistic management of freshwater as a finite and vulnerable resource, and the integration of sectorial water plans and programs within the framework of national economic and social policy, is of paramount importance for actions in the 1990s and beyond...." (Agenda 21, UN, 1992). The holistic management of freshwater requires water-related authorities to work together and formulate complementary pricing schemes that will allow overall efficient use of the resource. In addition, policy-makers must formulate a regulatory backbone that will encourage consumers to adhere to the pricing schemes. This section motivates the need for integrated pricing structures especially in groundwater extraction and wastewater disposal.

Industries' decision to buy from public water suppliers, directly abstract, or treat and reuse depends on many factors. Among these are water qualities required by that industry, if the public supplier charges full-cost from industrial user, and if direct abstraction licenses whose charges reflect the full economic cost of water are available. If one or more water source components are weakly regulated, industries will exploit that weakness to minimize their production disposal services, firms are likely to ignore social costs unless reflected in effluent taxes or extraction taxes.

Integrated water resource pricing requires that the region or utility or the group of water-related service provides integrate water prices, sewerage prices, additional charges for extra-strength effluents, direct industrial abstraction charges, and for direct discharge to water courses. Unfortunately, in both developing and industrial countries there is a huge gap between the concept of integrated water resources planning and how water resources planning and policy-making are actually done. In practice, most water resources planning is done incrementally and is driven by the need to find solutions to relatively immediate, specific problems, and not grand issues of river basin or regional development.

POLICY ON WATER MANAGEMENT

Lack of an agreed policy framework is the main stumbling block in interstate negotiations for the development of the water resources of trans-boundary basins. According to the India Constitution, water is a state subject with limited role for the Centre. As a result, there are different perceptions among the states on policies on water resources development. While the lower riparian advocate development with basin as the planning unit, the upper riparian oppose it on, *inter alia*, grounds of their established riparian rights. These and other related conflicts have prevented adoption of a National Water Policy and development of an appropriate institutional framework under it. As a result, integrated development of water resources has not been possible in most parts of the country. In some cases, efforts to protect the rights of lower riparian has resulted in widespread apprehension and dissatisfaction among the upper riparian. Under the present system of governance even the water from surplus areas cannot be transferred to deficit areas. There is, therefore, a need for evolving suitable policies, through close interaction with all stakeholders so that the interests of all concerned in sharing of water and allied benefits are protected.

The existing institutional arrangement for a dialogue with the states is mainly at the political level. The interactions at the administrative and technical level are rare and far between. There is an urgent need to strengthen these mechanisms to accelerate the process of dialogue with states. Media and civil society could take up advocacy campaign to facilitate the process.

It is often seen that some international funding agencies try to impose their norms for water resources development on developing countries without regard to their requirements of accelerated development and constraints. The resultant conflicts are then blown up out of proportion, which adversely affects development.

INDIAN WATER LAWS

Indian water laws concerning the Centre are mainly under the River Boards Act, 1956. The Act provides for constitutions of river basin organization for integrated development of the basins. Apart from the Damodar Valley Corporation and Narmada Control Authority, Brahmputra Board, Ganga Flood Control Commission, etc., which have some features of an ideal River Basin Organization, only a few river boards have been constituted to address issues relating to operation specific projects. The main difficulty in setting up river basin organisations is differing perceptions about adoption of a National Water Policy. The underlying reasons are political and need to be addressed through advocacy by non-governmental institutions, civil society, media, etc.

The Inter-State Water Disputes Act, 1956 enacted by the Centre needs amendment to empower independent institutions to oversee implementation of awards by the Tribunals. At the state level, the main laws are in the form of Irrigation Acts. These vary greatly from state to state and are very old, some being over 150 years old. In order to address conflicts in the irrigation sector, it is necessary to revise these Acts taking into consideration the present requirements. This should be an interdisciplinary exercise involving institutions dealing with Water Resources, Land and Revenue, Civil Administration, Rural Development, National/International Law, etc. while revising these Acts and the related rules, the overall context and objective would need to be kept in mind. The important frame of reference is that last 50 years the country has developed about 50 per cent of its exploitable water resources and in accordance with the India Water Vision-2025, the pace of development would need to be considerably accelerated to develop the remaining 50 per cent during the next 25 years. Another aspect that needs to be kept in mind is that the existing laws which are very old, were enacted taking into consideration the acute socio-economic diversity of rural India at that time. The new laws should, therefore, be in accordance with the present and the projected future scenarios.

In India, a multidisciplinary Environmental Monitoring Committee (EMC) has been constituted by the Ministry of Water Resources for overseeing the implementation of environmental safeguards in water resources development projects stipulated by the Union Ministry of Environment and Forests. The committee comprises of the representatives of the ministries of Water Resources, Environment and Forest, Agriculture, Welfare and the Planning Commission. State Level Monitoring Committees and Project Level Environmental Management Committees assist the EMC.

RURAL WATER SUPPLY

In India, rural water supply is mostly from groundwater. However, rural water supply programme in many areas is severely by contamination of groundwater by certain harmful chemicals like Arsenic, Fluorides, Iron, etc. Treatment of contaminated water at many remote/isolated locations to desired levels is not always feasible for various techno-economic, social and logistic reasons. In cases of high concentrations of contaminants, high doses of treatment chemicals spoil the taste of water, which is unacceptable to the people. In many water scarce regions like western Rajasthan and the Kutch area of Gujarat, this is a source of bitter conflict between the people and the government. In such cases the solution would probably lie in identifying alternate sources of surface water. It is necessary, therefore, that strong institutional linkages are established between the concerned departments of water resources and those of rural development and public health engineering. Non-governmental institutions like voluntary organisations, village committees, etc. need to be developed to take up mass awareness and educational programmes and advocacy campaigns to sensitize the political leadership.

LARGE DAMS *VERSUS* SMALL DAMS

Many environmentalists and social activists are highly critical of large dams and advocate other methods of water resources development like water harvesting and watershed management and run-of-the-river diversions as viable alternatives. They are of the view that where storages are unavoidable, it would be better to build a number of small dams rather than one single large dam. It is necessary that an appropriate institutional arrangement is to bridge the communication gap between the proponents and of large dams.

MAJOR-MEDIUM IRIGATION *VERSUS* MINOR IRRIGATION

There are no conflicts in irrigation development, as long as there is a realization that Major-Medium and Minor irrigation are mutually complementary and are intended for optimal and sustainable development of surface and ground water in cost effective manner. However, this is not always the case. There is a general perception especially among the critics of major projects that minor irrigation, which is mostly from groundwater is more cost effective than major and medium irrigation. Such a view does not take into consideration huge private investments in wells/tubewells and heavy subsidies on electricity. Reliability of minor irrigation sources under drought conditions is also not duly considered. However, such a perception often influences the strategy for water resources planning, which in turn results in over exploitation of groundwater with adverse environmental impacts. Such conflicts can be avoided through dispassionate economic analysis and technical viability of the two modes of irrigation under diverse conditions. It is therefore, necessary that strong institutional linkages are established between the water resources/irrigation departments and agricultural economists. Appropriate mechanism would also need to be developed within the water resources/irrigation departments for collection of accurate field data to facilitate such studies.

FLOOD MANAGEMENT

The contentious issues in the area of flood management are flood plain zoning and bringing about legislation to regulate human activity in the flood plains. While on one hand, there is a general recognition of the efficacy of these measures in reducing losses due to flood, on the other hand there are differing perceptions about the modalities of applying these measures without depriving the people of the economic benefits from the flood plains. There is need for a dialogue between the water resources planners and the flood plain dwellers together with advocacy campaign to sensitise the political leadership.

There are also serious differences of opinion among the people in the flood prone areas about the benefits of flood embankments. While most people are in favour of embankments, some strongly oppose these on the grounds that these deprive the agricultural fields of the annual replenishment of fertilising silt during flood. They also complain that stagnation of floodwater behind the embankments causing waterlogging that persists even after the floods recede. The existing technical organisations and agriculture scientists under the concerned organisations need to take up detailed studies on this issue and to educate the people about the overall benefits of flood embankments.

CONCLUSION

To cope with shortage of water and for integrated development of water resources, it is necessary to have an agreed policy framework with appropriate regulatory mechanism to deal with various issues and to resolve conflicts at various levels. People participation at various levels is a basic step to resolve the conflicts. Mass awareness and educational programmes need to be taken up in collaboration with NGOs to apprise the people of the various economic and social benefits of their participation in water management and resolution of conflicts. This would participation in water management and resolution of conflicts. This would require development/ strengthening of technical, administrative, social, economic and political institutions with appropriate linkages. In this context, the following actions or measures should be taken before disputes and water conflicts:

1. To amend the Constitution of India so as to transfer development and management of water resources from the State List to the Union List.

   Or

   To include the subject of Water Resources Development in the Concurrent List through constitutional amendment.

   Or

2. To enact suitable legislation in the ambit of existing provisions as regards water resources development under Entry 56. There is already precedence of including 'Forests' under concurrent list and environmental laws to make them more effective. The existing mechanism of discussions and agreements between the 'State and State' and 'States and Centre' has proved very tardy and time consuming. There is need to introduce effective centre-state consultation mechanism for expediting decisions on matters relating to water.
3. Institutional arrangement should be backed by legal backing for making the states to come together for holding serious discussions on sharing of waters.
4. River basins organisations/authorities should be formed for each major inter-state river urgently with constitutional powers for development of water resources.
5. Guidelines for water sharing, technical standards for development of basin for optimum benefits, etc. should be issued by the Centre.
6. In case of continued disagreement, there should be a Standing Water Disputes Tribunal to which the issue could

be referred. The tribunal may give the award within 3-5 years depending upon complexities may give the award may be binding on all. The tribunal may be headed by a serving or retired Supreme Court judge or in very contentious issue, a Bench of 3 judges may give the judgment. The majority judgment may be binding on all concerned.

7. There are many other issues relating to cost sharing of inter-state water transfer proposals which will prove contentious even after water sharing agreements are reached between states, e.g. unit water basis or unit benefit to respective states. These, issues should be taken up and guidelines finalised.
8. There are no rules/regulations/provisions for sharing of water by non-cobasin states at present. Any such sharing arrangements evolved by the Centre may be challenged in courts of law if adequate constitutional safeguards are not provided. This is a serious issue, which needs to be deliberated and discussed by legal experts, and adequate provisions made expedite execution of inter-basin water transfer proposals without loosing time.

REFERENCES

Prasad, R.S. and Khanna, R.K. (2003), "Indian Experience in Development and Management of Water Resources", pp. 121-36 in *Water Resources and Sustainable Development* (Kamta Prasad, ed.), Shipra Publications, Delhi.

Ghosh, R. and Bathija, T.S. (2003), "Review of Constitutional Provisions Governing Water Resources of India", pp. 257-65 in *Water Resources and Sustainable Development* (Kamta Prasad, ed.), Shipra Publications, Delhi.

Iyer, R.R. (2003), "Water Conflicts: A Note", pp. 299-307 in *Water Resources and Sustainable Development* (Kamta Prasad, ed.), Shipra Publications, Delhi.

Iyer, R.R. (2002), "Inter-State Water Disputes Act, 1956—Difficulties and Solutions", *Economic and Political Weekly*, Vol. XXXVII, No. 28, July 13-19, pp. 2907-10.

Ahmad, Q.K. (2003), "Regional Cooperation in Water Management: Achievements and Prospects", pp. 352-56 in *Water Resources and Sustainable Development* (Kamta Prasad, ed.), Shipra Publications, Delhi.

Ahmad, *et. al.* (1994), Q.K. Ahmad, Ramaswamy R. Iyer, S.K. Malla, B.B. Pradhan, B.G. Verghese (eds.), *Converting Water into Wealth: Regional Cooperation in Harnessing the Eastern Himalayan Rivers*, BUP/Academic Publishers, Dhaka.

Adhikari, *et. al.* (2000), K.D. Adhikari, Q.K. Ahmad, S.K. Malla, B.B. Pradhan, Khalilur Rahman, R. Rangachari, K.B. Sajjadur Rasheed and B.G. Verghese (eds.), Cooperation on Eastern Himalayan Rivers: Opportunities and Challenges, (Bangladesh Unnayan Parishad/Centre for Policy Research/ Institute for Integrated Development Studies), Konnark Publishers Pvt. Ltd., New Delhi.

Crow (1995), Ben Crow, *Sharing the Ganges*, University Press Limited, Dhaka.

Verghese, B.G. (1999a), *Waters of Hope*, Oxford & IBH Publishing Co. Pvt. Ltd., New Delhi/Calcutta.

Verghese, B.G. (1999b), "An Emerging Tiger", *The Hindustan Times*, 24 July, 1999.

Iyer, R.R. (2002), "Linking of Rivers: Judicial Activism or Error?", *Economic and Political Weekly*, Vol. XXXVII, No. 46, November 16-22, pp. 4595-96.

Bhatia, Ramesh (2003), "Cost, Price and Value of Water in Alternative Uses: A Case Study of Subernarekha River Basin", pp. 357-61 in *Water Resources and Sustainable Development* (Kamta Prasad, ed.), Shipra Publications, Delhi.

Diwan, P.L. (2003), "Conflict Resolution in Water Sector through Institutional Development", pp. 341-51 in *Water Resources and Sustainable Development* (Kamta Prasad, ed.), Shipra Publications, Delhi.

Index